THE LIBRARY OF CHRISTIAN CLASSICS

GENERAL EDITORS

JOHN BAILLIE
Principal, New College,
Edinburgh

JOHN T. McNEILL
Auburn Professor of Church History,
Union Theological Seminary,
New York

HENRY P. VAN DUSEN
President, Union Theological Seminary,
New York

THE LIBRARY OF CHRISTIAN CLASSICS

VOLUME XXII

CALVIN: THEOLOGICAL
TREATISES

Volume XXII

CALVIN:
THEOLOGICAL
TREATISES

Translated
with Introductions and Notes by

THE REV. J. K. S. REID, M.A., B.D.

Professor of Theology
The University of Leeds

Philadelphia
THE WESTMINSTER PRESS

Published simultaneously in Great Britain and the United States of America
by the S.C.M. Press, Ltd., London, and The Westminster Press, Philadelphia.

First published MCMLIV

GENERAL EDITORS' PREFACE

The Christian Church possesses in its literature an abundant and incomparable treasure. But it is an inheritance that must be reclaimed by each generation. THE LIBRARY OF CHRISTIAN CLASSICS is designed to present in the English language, and in twenty-six volumes of convenient size, a selection of the most indispensable Christian treatises written prior to the end of the sixteenth century.

The practice of giving circulation to writings selected for superior worth or special interest was adopted at the beginning of Christian history. The canonical Scriptures were themselves a selection from a much wider literature. In the Patristic era there began to appear a class of works of compilation (often designed for ready reference in controversy) of the opinions of well-reputed predecessors, and in the Middle Ages many such works were produced. These medieval anthologies actually preserve some noteworthy materials from works otherwise lost.

In modern times, with the increasing inability even of those trained in universities and theological colleges to read Latin and Greek texts with ease and familiarity, the translation of selected portions of earlier Christian literature into modern languages has become more necessary than ever; while the wide range of distinguished books written in vernaculars such as English makes selection there also needful. The efforts that have been made to meet this need are too numerous to be noted here, but none of these collections serves the purpose of the reader who desires a library of representative treatises spanning the Christian centuries as a whole. Most of them embrace only the age of the Church Fathers, and some of them have long been out of print. A fresh translation of a work already

translated may shed much new light upon its meaning. This
is true even of Bible translations despite the work of many
experts through the centuries. In some instances old translations
have been adopted in this series, but wherever necessary or
desirable, new ones have been made. Notes have been supplied
where these were needed to explain the author's meaning. The
introductions provided for the several treatises and extracts
will, we believe, furnish welcome guidance.

JOHN BAILLIE
JOHN T. MCNEILL
HENRY P. VAN DUSEN

CONTENTS

PART II: APOLOGETIC

PART III: CONTROVERSIAL

General Introduction

I T IS NO DOUBT BY THE "INSTITUTES" THAT THE reputation of Calvin as a theologian stands or falls. The work is said to contain all Calvin and the whole of Calvinism, and its writer is commonly regarded as a man of one book. Pressed far enough, this judgment would leave little justification for a volume devoted to the Treatises. Doumergue, judicious as usual, redresses a balance when he writes [1]: "To know Calvin truly and completely, his thought, character and personality, one must consult not one source but three: his Institutes, his Sermons and his Letters." But even when this has been said, one is as far as ever from an assessment of the place of Calvin's Treatises.

There is a massive homogeneity in the thought of Calvin which must be reckoned with here. It has been given to few men to write more than Calvin: "Like Augustine, he wrote more than another can well read" [2]; and fewer still have written so much with such immense consistency. But his is a consistency based not on poverty of ideas but on remarkable systematization of thought. The pieces fit together in a close and articulate manner, and it therefore happens that whatever piece is picked up has recognizable features. This is true not only of works written contemporaneously, but even of those belonging to different periods. As Beza early affirmed of his notable associate, Calvin's views over the period during which twenty-five impressions of his *Institutes* appeared remained substantially unaltered. There is continual amplification, but little change. It is therefore not surprising to discover that the homogeneity

[1] *Jean Calvin*, Vol. IV, p. 1.
[2] A. Mitchell Hunter, *The Teaching of Calvin*, p. 3.

13

that pervades the parts and the periods of his work manifests itself also in the types of writing to which he turned his hand. But if this is so, we shall not look for a variation of content as the differentia of the Treatises, but for something else.

The fact is that the Treatises introduce to the reader not a change of matter but a diversity of application. Calvin the thinker is, of course, always present in all the works which he composed. But there is a diversity of function discharged by them. Even the increased range mentioned by Doumergue must be further extended. Calvin is, of course, letter-writer and preacher, and the theologian is continually apparent in both letters and sermons. But he is more also: he is all that is loosely comprised in the word administrator. Into all the parts which as administrator he was called upon to play, he brought not only the massive powers which are evident in the major theological works, but also the same theological principles. "The conclusion is," Doumergue ends his volume on the theological thought of Calvin,[3] "that Calvin was the great systematic thinker of the Reformation, and that in no system has practice been so closely and intimately united with theory"; and he quotes with approval: "We believe that his theological thought predetermined his views in civil as well as ecclesiastical government."

This man, to whom friend and foe alike by admiration or hostility paid tribute, applied himself and his talents to the edification of the reformed Church with the same magisterial ease and ability as to more theoretical affairs. The situation of his time offered abounding opportunity to industry and wisdom. Alongside Calvin the theologian there must be placed the Calvin of other roles. There is the teacher, first and preeminently. It is as teacher that the first edition of the *Institutes* represented their author. Only as the succeeding editions of this work grew and expanded to express the capacious thought of their author and to meet the need for solid theological foundation for all the purposes of the reformed Church, did the function of teaching the ordinary lay Christian and his children separate itself off from that of the more profound and systematic theologian. To this teaching aspect of Calvin's work, the Confessions and Catechisms that came from his pen or sprang from his influence are witness. But further, there is the administrator, from whom the politician, the social reformer, the moralist and the apologist are not easily separated. Of this kind

[3] *Op. cit.,* p. 476.

of activity copious evidence is available in the famous Ecclesiastical Ordinances and the whole family of writings similar to or dependent on them; while if any further memorial of the ecclesiastical administrator be required, one has only, according to the phrase, to look around, and this not of course only in the country where he for the most part worked, but in several others where the Church still wears a Calvinist pattern. Besides these varied functions, there is that of the controversialist. This is a part played less than any other to the exclusion of the theologian. But here the theologian, instead of choosing his own subject and his own procedure, has both thrust upon him: he rises to meet the challenge offered by criticism or misunderstanding, and he must confront it on territory of its own choice.

The Treatises then cover the work of Calvin in his more variegated role. And as the situation evoking the response differs, so the form in which the response is cast differs also. Indeed it differs more widely than the narrow compass of this volume can adequately show. All that can be hoped at this point is that something of the astounding versatility of Calvin may be presented.

Two cardinal considerations have suggested if not determined the selection of the works here translated. The first is that just mentioned—the varied function which Calvin discharges, as the theologian becomes occupied, though never preoccupied, with the diverse work of the administrator. This first consideration has really imposed upon the present volume its general pattern. Part I has been given the title Statement. In treatise after treatise, varying in both length and form, Calvin's theology finds reiterated expression. His thought will not be found to differ much from what he sets forth in systematic form in the *Institutes*; but for the varying purpose he has in mind, it is thrown into different moulds. Part II is devoted to Apologetic. Affirmation required to be supplemented by commendation. It was not enough to declare the doctrine; the case for the Reformed faith had also to be stated. The cantonal Churches of Switzerland and the Churches of Germany and elsewhere had to be induced to understand the need for reformation and the effectiveness of the reforms proposed. Part III is occupied with the controversial side of Calvin's work. That controversy would break out with the champions of the hitherto undivided and unreformed Western Church could have been expected. Unhappily it was not confined to this sphere alone. History records the sharp and often violent differences of opinion that

were early manifested among the Reformers themselves. So long
as the differences were capable of being composed, Calvin
shows an admirably eirenical spirit. Once hope of concord was
abandoned, he relapses with some suddenness into the prevailing acrimony of tone with which disputes were commonly
conducted, as though, to use words recently made sadly notorious, his patience were exhausted. Doumergue's list of abusive
terms employed by Calvin when this occurred makes sad
reading.

So much for the general architectonic of what is here presented. Choice of the particular works included has been
influenced by a second consideration. Certain characteristic
doctrines have commonly and certainly not unjustly been attributed to Calvin—the sovereignty of God, the pre-eminence and
authority of Holy Scripture and the Word of God, Predestination, a certain view of the Eucharist. It seemed right to include
here treatises that expounded the positions which he occupied
in such cardinal matters, and the selection made is based on
this judgment.

A word concerning authenticity. The question is difficult
enough to resolve when single authorship is an established or
at least accepted fact. It becomes much more complex, however, in the case of documents designed to serve some public
use, whose survival depends on the approval of official bodies,
and whose employment or application is possible only on the
basis of more or less popular assent. No one seriously challenges
the origin of (for example) the brief but pungent reply in
refutation of the calumnies of a "certain worthless person." But
a different range of problems opens up when the question of
the authorship of the *Genevan Confession* is raised, or of the
Ecclesiastical Ordinances. In such cases, there is little point in
enquiring for, let alone demanding, single unaided authorship.
Others besides the person chiefly responsible will be implicated,
who with him must champion documents through "committee
stages" of investigation, or put them into effect in the parishes
and congregations of Churches newly awakened to vigour and
self-consciousness. A wider canon of authenticity must therefore
be applied. The rubric that the *Corpus Reformatorum*[4] adopts

---

[4] *Corpus Reformatorum* (hereafter referred to as *C.R.*), Vols. XXIX–LXXXVII
(Brunswick 1860–1900), from which the translation has been made; the
numbers quoted in the text refer to the volumes in the collection of *Joannis
Calvini opera quae supersunt omnia* within the larger *Corpus*, and numbered
in a series of their own.

here has a certain generous breadth. Referring[5] to the *Confessions*, it is pointed out that, besides those that without doubt may be attributed to Calvin, there are others of more dubious origin, and others whose omission would go undisputed. "Since, however," *C.R.* continues, "these also belong to the elucidation of Calvinist affairs, and have an even closer connection with Calvinist studies, we were unwilling to remove them out of our camp." The limits of our camp here are certainly much more restricted. Yet the force of this contention applies, and the rule has been adopted that, granted reasonable grounds for Calvin's authorship or complicity, and its inclusion in *C.R.*, the interest inherent in a document outweighs suspected dubiety of exact authorship.

Some introductory notes precede each of the Treatises, indicating with extreme brevity the place they occupy in the literary and historical context. This Introduction may conclude by referring to the contents of the Treatises selected, where comment seems requisite. But it is clear that for the most part they must speak for themselves, as they are very well qualified and entitled to do.

Little need be said about the *Genevan Confession 1536*. Written in the same year as the first edition of the *Institutes*, it follows the same general pattern as the longer work, a pattern which was to recur in the expanded later editions. It is noteworthy that the first article explicitly indicates the source from which the further contents proceed—the Word of God: the rule of faith and religion is Scripture alone. Thus an eminently characteristic and recurrent feature of Calvin's thought and writing early receives prominent expression.

The chief interest of the *Lausanne Articles* lies in the occasion they offer for Calvin's interpolation in the debate. The subject of both interventions is the same; in the first case the article under discussion directly gives rise to it, in the second only indirectly. But thus early an indication is given of what becomes a burning issue for Calvin personally and for the whole reformed Church.

In the *Ecclesiastical Ordinances*, Calvin turns his attention to practical affairs, and the ordering of the Church and of the city of Geneva in accordance with his theological presuppositions. *C.R.* comments thus: "When a new ecclesiastical order was to be constituted, the course of events in the free states was almost everywhere as follows. When once the errors and abuses of the

[5] Vol. IX, li.

papacy in any town began to be contested by private men, either with the co-operation of the magistracy or against its vain opposition, disputations were held at the demand of the citizens concerning points at issue, either between the leaders of the parties or in public. The defenders of the Roman faith being defeated and hissed off the stage, their altars and buildings were deserted. Then, at the proposal of the senate, with the people solemnly gathered to consider it in groups, the matter was determined by majority vote, or most frequently by the unanimous consent of all. Then at last, by public edict, the mass and the other rites of the Roman Church were abrogated, preaching of the evangelical doctrine instituted, and the reformation which they prescribed was made part of the law of the republic. Of course these things were not effected without consultation with those who had been the first exponents of the Reformed faith. But the civil magistracy, exercising its customary rights, was able to bring a moderating and restraining influence to bear upon theologians in burning questions and thorny matters less pertinent to salvation or disputed among evangelicals themselves, which less concerned laymen or were quite petty grievances to them." [6]

In these circumstances, it was not to be expected, nor did it so turn out, that Calvin should have his own way unopposed. Yet, as *C.R.* puts it, all the documents as successively they came before the official councils bear the impress of his opinion and his hand, and in their final and definitive form this decisive influence is never obliterated. Calvin was both a strict observer of laws and an inexorable judge. It is perhaps not on the whole surprising that contemporaries should be heard to declare that they would rather be in hell with Beza than in heaven with Calvin. *C.R.* adds the mollifying comment that it is only right to take into account the variety, complexity and strangeness of the secular matters that necessarily occupied the attention of Calvin the legislator. [7]

The *Genevan Catechism* ranks with the most notable statements of the Christian faith ever to be produced, and, if in the first place constructed for children, it has nevertheless deservedly remained a permanent source of spiritual and theological edification.

A great deal of Calvin's attention was devoted to the right statement of what ought to be believed concerning the nature of the Holy Communion or Holy Supper. Many of his state-

[6] *C.R.* IX, li.   [7] *C.R.* X/I, ix.

ments are included in documents of (it must be admitted) tedious and repetitious length. There therefore seemed good reason to include the quite admirable *Short Treatise on the Lord's Supper*, and to supplement it with the very brief *Confession of Faith concerning the Eucharist* which, in summary form, says much that is elsewhere said at prodigious length.

There are added to this part two further documents, whose inclusion is determined by the subjects with which they respectively deal. No collection of Calvin's Treatises could very well omit reference to the notorious doctrine of Predestination, which is briefly set forth in the *Concerning Predestination*. Similar considerations seemed to justify the inclusion of the short *Summary of Doctrine concerning the Ministry of the Word and Sacraments*. The title itself commends the document, but its special interest may be held to lie in its account of the function of the "internal minister," the internal testimony of the Holy Spirit.

Part II, Apologetic, is devoted to one document, and even this is not given in complete form. Of the treatises included in this volume, this is the only one that has been abbreviated. The nature of the document, inseparable as it is from the occasion of its composition, is good enough ground for its inclusion. For the excision that has been made two other reasons may be supplied. The original *Exhortation* is a very long work—much longer than any other here presented. Purely formal reasons made it inadvisable to include in these pages a work which unshortened must have occupied nearly one third of the total space available. There is, however, another reason. The original in its introductory part runs at one point as follows: "To accomplish (my end), I must take up together the three following points. First, I must briefly enumerate the evils which compelled us to seek for remedies. Then I must show that the particular remedies which our Reformers employed were apt and salutary. Last, I must make it plain that we were not at liberty any longer to delay putting forth our hand, in as much as the matter demanded immediate amendment." And further: "The first point, as I merely advert to it for the purpose of clearing the way to the other two, I shall endeavour to dispose of in a few words." In fact, to call them few hardly fits the facts, but to have *wished* them few may be taken as evidence of the lesser importance of at least this first point to be made. There is no indication of inferior importance in the case of the third of the points; but there is this further to be said about all three. In his exposition of them all, Calvin follows the same carefully constructed order. This is best outlined in his own words, in which he sets before his readers, not only the programme to be followed for part one, but that which is in fact followed in all three parts. "If it be enquired by what things chiefly the Christian religion exists among us and maintains its truth, it will be found that the two that follow, not only occupy the principal place, but comprehend under them all the other parts and thus also the whole substance of Christianity:—knowledge of the way in which God is rightly worshipped; and of the source from which salvation is to be sought. These neglected, for all we may glory in the name of Christ, our profession is empty and vain. After these come the sacraments, and then the government of the Church, which, as they were instituted for the preservation of these two branches of doctrine named above, ought to be applied to no other purpose; nor is there any other way of ascertaining whether they are administered purely and duly or otherwise, than to exercise them to this end. If you will have a clearer and homelier illustration: rule in the Church, the pastoral office, and all other matters of order including the sacraments, resemble the body; whereas the doctrine, which prescribes the rule for the right worship of God and points out the ground on which the conscience of men must base their confidence in salvation, is the soul which animates the body and renders it lively and active, and in short makes it other than a dead and useless corpse."

This order, then, doctrinal including the rule for the right worship of God and the source from which men have hope of salvation, followed by the sacraments, and then by ecclesiastical government, is faithfully followed in each of the three parts. It is evident that no very wide distinction separates any of the three heads from the others: the remedies are fitted to existent evils, and the speed and time of their application is determined by the stage which the evils have reached. There is in fact one theme here, regarded from three different angles. The wonder perhaps is rather that Calvin found so much to say without exact repetition. But repetition there is, and this may be held to be sufficient reason for excising from this translation of the *Necessity* the first and third points with which Calvin proposed to deal.

The field of Calvin's controversial writings is a wide one, and some of the documents in which this part is played are very long and repetitious. Calvin's is not a mind that continually finds new arguments with which to present the truth of what he holds, and this largely because from the first he penetrates to the

logical foundations of his beliefs, because from these foundations it is not possible to move him, and because on them he
bases both the exposition and the commendation of his views.
The vast quantity he wrote requires us to take samples only, and
the remarkable homogeneity of his writing which has its source
in what has just been mentioned makes this necessary sampling
less misleading than it might well have been.

Few will contest the claims of Calvin's epistolary retort to
Sadolet to represent his controversial engagements with the
unreformed Church and churchmen of his day.

There are more competitors and a wider selection for representing Calvin's controversies with other Reformers. Here again
sampling must be the rule in view of the amount of material
available. More typical of this aspect of Calvin's work than any
other would be something concerning the sacraments and
especially, of course, concerning the Eucharist. Of the possibili-
ties of this kind that offer themselves, the controversies with
Westphal and with Heshusius are the most considerable, both
in length and interest. Which of these, since both cannot be
included, is to be chosen?—the controversy with the pastor of
Hamburg, or that with the teacher of Heidelberg? Perhaps not
very much really hangs upon the decision. In the *Clear
Explanation*, Calvin on several occasions declares that the
erroneous doctrine of Heshusius is similar to that of Westphal
already confronted and confuted. The issues at stake are not
widely different, and both controversies give occasion to the
student of Calvin to learn the detail of his thought concerning
this all-important and controversial subject. Where the balance
swings so evenly, considerations of lesser importance may be
allowed to determine on which side it is finally to fall. Calvin's
part in the controversy with Heshusius is briefer and more self-
contained, compared with the three treatises (a *First* and a
Second Defence, and a *Last Exhortation*) in which he combats
Westphal. The Heshusius controversy is later, and Calvin's
argument may be supposed to have gained something from the
earlier engagement. Further Calvin's eirenical intention comes
to splendid expression in the *Best Method of Obtaining Concord if
the Truth be sought without Contention*, the "little tract" which
supplements and concludes Calvin's response to Heshusius. It
may be added that the moving apostrophe to Melanchthon
with which this expression of his views *Concerning the True
Partaking of the Body and Blood of Christ* begins has its own human
interest and value. It is accordingly this *Clear Explanation* upon

which choice has fallen to represent this aspect of Calvin's work.

Finally, there comes the brief *Reply to a Certain Worthless Person*. Here again, if representation of Calvin's thought concerning predestination is to find place at all, the choice in theory is wide but in practice limited. The tracts against Pighius *Concerning the eternal Predestination of God* and *Concerning Free Will*, would have been likely candidates for inclusion here, if their sheer length had not quite precluded them. The way thus opens for the admission of the *Brief Reply*. The title continues: to calumnies by which he tried to defile the doctrine of the eternal predestination of God. In fact, the occasion being offered and prepared by his opponent rather than himself, Calvin presents here only certain aspects of the doctrine of predestination. Of special value is the vindication of human free will under and within the wider and overarching conception of the omnipotence of God. Some of the notable features that distinguish the longer treatise on predestination directed against Pighius do not receive expression. Especially noteworthy is the omission of all mention that predestination is "in Christ" and from this fact borrows all its confident assurance for the Christian soul. At the same time, this shorter writing sheds much of the prolixity which characterizes the argument of the other, where too the doctrine assumes a forbidding form. What here comes to clear expression is the exculpation of God, the vindication of his justice and his righteousness, the overruling might of God, and the inadequacy of the conception of "permission." For the sake of these elements, the reader is asked to overlook the offensive bitterness of tone which characterizes the treatise, or, without being offended himself, to regard with interest Calvin conducting controversy in one of his less eirenical moods.

As to the translation itself: all but three of the treatises have been translated directly from the texts as given in *C.R.*; several of them (it is believed) are here for the first time rendered into English. In the case of the remaining three treatises, the *Necessity*, the *Reply to Sadolet*, and the *Clear Explanation*, the earlier translation by Henry Beveridge (Edinburgh: Calvin Translation Society, 1844 ff.) has been before the writer along with the original; but it has been so substantially altered that a virtually new translation has been made. The attempt has been made to render Calvin's own words into readable modern English, without entirely sacrificing archaisms where the meaning and manner of the original require their use.

PART I

STATEMENT

The Genevan Confession

INTRODUCTION

BEZA REGARDS CALVIN AS AUTHOR OF THIS DOCUMENT when, speaking of the year 1536, he simply says that Calvin drew it up, as a formula of Christian doctrine suited to the Church of Geneva, when it had scarcely emerged from the infamies of Romanism. Colladanus in his *Vie de Calvin* concurs in this opinion. More recent writers have unanimously credited Farel with the authorship. It is, however, hardly possible that Calvin, as Farel's friend, was not involved in compiling or improving it, and this is confirmed by the theological ability which the document displays. Moreover the records of the Senate establish that on November 10, 1536, the *Confession* was presented by Farel and Calvin to the magistracy, and by it received and set aside for more detailed examination. The complicity of Calvin, if not his sole authorship, may then be admitted.

Both the Latin and the French editions find place in *C.R.*, of whose introduction the above note is a summary. The translations are virtually identical, and the English here given is made from the French. (See *C.R.* X/I, 5.)

Confession of Faith
which all the citizens and inhabitants of Geneva and the subjects of the country must promise to keep and hold
(1536)

1. THE WORD OF GOD

First we affirm that we desire to follow Scripture alone as rule of faith and religion, without mixing with it any other thing which might be devised by the opinion of men apart from the Word of God, and without wishing to accept for our spiritual government any other doctrine than what is conveyed to us by the same Word without addition or diminution, according to the command of our Lord.

2. ONE ONLY GOD

Following, then, the lines laid down in the Holy Scriptures, we acknowledge that there is one only God, whom we are both to worship and serve, and in whom we are to put all our confidence and hope: having this assurance, that in him alone is contained all wisdom, power, justice, goodness and pity. And since he is spirit, he is to be served in spirit and in truth. Therefore we think it an abomination to put our confidence or hope in any created thing, to worship anything else than him, whether angels or any other creatures, and to recognize any other Saviour of our souls than him alone, whether saints or men living upon earth; and likewise to offer the service, which ought to be rendered to him, in external ceremonies or carnal observances, as if he took pleasure in such things, or to make an image to represent his divinity or any other image for adoration.

3. THE LAW OF GOD ALIKE FOR ALL

Because there is one only Lord and Master who has dominion over our consciences, and because his will is the only principle of all justice, we confess all our life ought to be ruled in accordance with the commandments of his holy law in which is contained all perfection of justice, and that we ought to have no other rule of good and just living, nor invent other good works to supplement it than whose which are there contained, as follows: Exodus 20: "I am the Lord thy God, who brought thee," and so on.

4. NATURAL MAN

We acknowledge man by nature to be blind, darkened in understanding, and full of corruption and perversity of heart, so that of himself he has no power to be able to comprehend the true knowledge of God as is proper, nor to apply himself to good works. But on the contrary, if he is left by God to what he is by nature, he is only able to live in ignorance and to be abandoned to all iniquity. Hence he has need to be illumined by God, so that he come to the right knowledge of his salvation, and thus to be redirected in his affections and reformed to the obedience of the righteousness of God.

5. MAN BY HIMSELF LOST

Since man is naturally (as has been said) deprived and destitute in himself of all the light of God, and of all righteousness, we acknowledge that by himself he can only expect the wrath and malediction of God, and hence that he must look outside himself for the means of his salvation.

6. SALVATION IN JESUS

We confess then that it is Jesus Christ who is given to us by the Father, in order that in him we should recover all of which in ourselves we are deficient. Now all that Jesus Christ has done and suffered for our redemption, we veritably hold without any doubt, as it is contained in the Creed, which is recited in the Church, that is to say: I believe in God the Father Almighty, and so on.

7. RIGHTEOUSNESS IN JESUS

Therefore we acknowledge the things which are consequently given to us by God in Jesus Christ: first, that being in our own nature enemies of God and subjects of his wrath and judgment, we are reconciled with him and received again in grace through the intercession of Jesus Christ, so that by his righteousness and guiltlessness we have remission of our sins, and by the shedding of his blood we are cleansed and purified from all our stains.

8. REGENERATION IN JESUS

Second, we acknowledge that by his Spirit we are regenerated into a new spiritual nature. That is to say that the evil desires of our flesh are mortified by grace, so that they rule us no longer. On the contrary, our will is rendered conformable to God's will, to follow in his way and to seek what is pleasing to him. Therefore we are by him delivered from the servitude of sin, under whose power we were of ourselves held captive, and by this deliverance we are made capable and able to do good works and not otherwise.

9. REMISSION OF SINS ALWAYS NECESSARY FOR THE FAITHFUL

Finally, we acknowledge that this regeneration is so effected in us that, until we slough off this mortal body, there remains always in us much imperfection and infirmity, so that we always remain poor and wretched sinners in the presence of God. And, however much we ought day by day to increase and grow in God's righteousness, there will never be plenitude or perfection while we live here. Thus we always have need of the mercy of God to obtain the remission of our faults and offences. And so we ought always to look for our righteousness in Jesus Christ and not at all in ourselves, and in him be confident and assured, putting no faith in our works.

10. ALL OUR GOOD IN THE GRACE OF GOD

In order that all glory and praise be rendered to God (as is his due), and that we be able to have true peace and rest of conscience, we understand and confess that we receive all benefits from God, as said above, by his clemency and pity, without any consideration of our worthiness or the merit of our works, to which is due no other retribution than eternal confusion. None the less our Saviour in his goodness, having received us into the communion of his son Jesus, regards the works that we have done in faith as pleasing and agreeable; not that they merit it at all, but because, not imputing any of the imperfection that is there, he acknowledges in them nothing but what proceeds from his Spirit.

11. FAITH

We confess that the entrance which we have to the great treasures and riches of the goodness of God that is vouchsafed to us is by faith; inasmuch as, in certain confidence and assurance of heart, we believe in the promises of the Gospel, and receive Jesus Christ as he is offered to us by the Father and described to us by the Word of God.

12. INVOCATION OF GOD ONLY AND INTERCESSION OF CHRIST

As we have declared that we have confidence and hope for salvation and all good only in God through Jesus Christ, so we confess that we ought to invoke him in all necessities in the name of Jesus Christ, who is our Mediator and Advocate with him and has access to him. Likewise we ought to acknowledge that all good things come from him alone, and to give thanks to him for them. On the other hand, we reject the intercession of the saints as a superstition invented by men contrary to Scripture, for the reason that it proceeds from mistrust of the sufficiency of the intercession of Jesus Christ.

13. PRAYER INTELLIGIBLE

Moreover since prayer is nothing but hypocrisy and fantasy unless it proceed from the interior affections of the heart, we believe that all prayers ought to be made with clear understanding. And for this reason, we hold the prayer of our Lord to show fittingly what we ought to ask of him: Our Father which art in heaven, . . . but deliver us from evil. Amen.

14. SACRAMENTS

We believe that the sacraments which our Lord has ordained in his Church are to be regarded as exercises of faith for us, both for fortifying and confirming it in the promises of God and for witnessing before men. Of them there are in the Christian Church only two which are instituted by the authority of our Saviour: Baptism and the Supper of our Lord; for what is held within the realm of the pope concerning seven sacraments, we condemn as fable and lie.

15. BAPTISM

Baptism is an external sign by which our Lord testifies that he desires to receive us for his children, as members of his Son Jesus. Hence in it there is represented to us the cleansing from sin which we have in the blood of Jesus Christ, the mortification of our flesh which we have by his death that we may live in him by his Spirit. Now since our children belong to such an alliance with our Lord, we are certain that the external sign is rightly applied to them.

16. THE HOLY SUPPER

The Supper of our Lord is a sign by which under bread and wine he represents the true spiritual communion which we have in his body and blood. And we acknowledge that according to his ordinance it ought to be distributed in the company of the faithful, in order that all those who wish to have Jesus for their life be partakers of it. In as much as the mass of the pope was a reprobate and diabolical ordinance subverting the mystery of the Holy Supper, we declare that it is execrable to us, an idolatry condemned by God; for so much is it itself regarded as a sacrifice for the redemption of souls that the bread is in it taken and adored as God. Besides there are other execrable blasphemies and superstitions implied here, and the abuse of the Word of God which is taken in vain without profit or edification.

17. HUMAN TRADITIONS

The ordinances that are necessary for the internal discipline of the Church, and belong solely to the maintenance of peace, honesty and good order in the assembly of Christians, we do not hold to be human traditions at all, in as much as they are comprised under the general command of Paul, where he desires that all be done among them decently and in order. But all laws

The Lausanne Articles
and Two Discourses on the Articles

INTRODUCTION

IN THE MONTH OF OCTOBER 1536, THE SENATE OF Berne initiated at Lausanne, with much ceremony, a colloquy or disputation between Roman and Reformed churchmen, for the purpose of facilitating the entrance of the canton of Vaud into the evangelical alliance. The Ten Articles were proposed in a sermon by Farel to both sides, and thus defined both the matter and the order of discussion.

It can hardly be held that Calvin is their author. But it is the case that in the course of the Colloquy he did on two occasions speak. Hence the justification, not only for the inclusion of the Discourses which present what he there said, but also for the Articles themselves as matter to which he lent his support and advocacy.

Ruchat, *Histoire de la Réformation de Suisse*, Vol. IV, p. 284 f., is cited by the editors of *C.R.* to give the orientation of the Discourses. The first was delivered on October 5, 1536, when "the debate concerned the third of the Ten Articles proposed, and discussion centred on the question of the real presence of the glorified Christ." The second discourse (Ruchat, *op. cit.* Vol. IV, p. 327) is offered when, two days later, the "disputation considers Article 8, and Calvin breaks his silence to attack the dogma of transubstantiation through the person of Pope Gregory VII." (See *C.R.* IX, liii.)

and regulations made binding on conscience which oblige the faithful to things not commanded by God, or establish another service of God than that which he demands, thus tending to destroy Christian liberty, we condemn as perverse doctrines of Satan, in view of our Lord's declaration that he is honoured in vain by doctrines that are the commandment of men. It is in this estimation that we hold pilgrimages, monasteries, distinctions of foods, prohibition of marriage, confessions and other like things.

18. THE CHURCH

While there is one only Church of Jesus Christ, we always acknowledge that necessity requires companies of the faithful to be distributed in different places. Of these assemblies each one is called Church. But in as much as all companies do not assemble in the name of our Lord, but rather to blaspheme and pollute him by their sacrilegious deeds, we believe that the proper mark by which rightly to discern the Church of Jesus Christ is that his holy gospel be purely and faithfully preached, proclaimed, heard, and kept, that his sacraments be properly administered, even if there be some imperfections and faults, as there always will be among men. On the other hand, where the Gospel is not declared, heard, and received, there we do not acknowledge the form of the Church. Hence the churches governed by the ordinances of the pope are rather synagogues of the devil than Christian churches.

19. EXCOMMUNICATION

Because there are always some who hold God and his Word in contempt, who take account of neither injunction, exhortation nor remonstrance, thus requiring greater chastisement, we hold the discipline of excommunication to be a thing holy and salutary among the faithful, since truly it was instituted by our Lord with good reason. This is in order that the wicked should not by their damnable conduct corrupt the good and dishonour our Lord, and that though proud they may turn to penitence. Therefore we believe that it is expedient according to the ordinance of God that all manifest idolaters, blasphemers, murderers, thieves, lewd persons, false witnesses, sedition-mongers, quarrellers, those guilty of defamation or assault, drunkards, dissolute livers, when they have been duly admonished and if they do not make amendment, be separated from the communion of the faithful until their repentance is known.

20. MINISTERS OF THE WORD

We recognize no other pastors in the Church than faithful pastors of the Word of God, feeding the sheep of Jesus Christ on the one hand with instruction, admonition, consolation, exhortation, deprecation; and on the other resisting all false doctrines and deceptions of the devil, without mixing with the pure doctrine of the Scriptures their dreams or their foolish imaginings. To these we accord no other power or authority but to conduct, rule, and govern the people of God committed to them by the same Word, in which they have power to command, defend, promise, and warn, and without which they neither can nor ought to attempt anything. As we receive the true ministers of the Word of God as messengers and ambassadors of God, it is necessary to listen to them as to him himself, and we hold their ministry to be a commission from God necessary in the Church. On the other hand we hold that all seductive and false prophets, who abandon the purity of the Gospel and deviate to their own inventions, ought not at all to be suffered or maintained, who are not the pastors they pretend, but rather, like ravening wolves, ought to be hunted and ejected from the people of God.

21. MAGISTRATES

We hold the supremacy and dominion of kings and princes as also of other magistrates and officers, to be a holy thing and a good ordinance of God. And since in performing their office they serve God and follow a Christian vocation, whether in defending the afflicted and innocent, or in correcting and punishing the malice of the perverse, we on our part also ought to accord them honour and reverence, to render respect and subservience, to execute their commands, to bear the charges they impose on us, so far as we are able without offence to God. In sum, we ought to regard them as vicars and lieutenants of God, whom one cannot resist without resisting God himself; and their office as a sacred commission from God which has been given them so that they may rule and govern us. Hence we hold that all Christians are bound to pray God for the

prosperity of the superiors and lords of the country whe[re they] live, to obey the statutes and ordinances which do not c[ontra]vene the commandments of God, to promote welfare, pea[ce and] public good, endeavouring to sustain the honour of thos[e over] them and the peace of the people, without contriving or at[tempt]ing anything to inspire trouble or dissension. On the othe[r hand] we declare that all those who conduct themselves unfai[thfully] towards their superiors, and have not a right concern f[or the] public good of the country where they live, demonstrate t[hereby] their infidelity towards God.

The Lausanne Articles

Issues to be discussed at Lausanne in the new province of Berne on the first day of October 1536

I

Holy Scripture teaches only one way of justification, which is by faith in Jesus Christ once for all offered, and holds as nothing but a destroyer of all the virtue of Christ anyone who makes another satisfaction, oblation, or cleansing for the remission of sins.

II

This Scripture acknowledges Jesus Christ, who is risen from the dead and sits in heaven at the right hand of the Father, as the only chief and true priest, sovereign mediator and true advocate of his Church.

III

Holy Scripture names the Church of God all who believe that they are received by the blood of Jesus Christ alone and who constantly and without vacillation believe and wholly establish and support themselves on the Word, which, having withdrawn from us in corporeal presence, nevertheless by the virtue of his Holy Spirit fills, sustains, governs and vivifies all things.

IV

The said Church contains certain who are known to the eyes of God alone. It possesses always ceremonies ordained by Christ, by which it is seen and known, that is to say Baptism and the Supper of our Lord, which are called sacraments, since they are symbols and signs of secret things, that is to say of divine grace.

V

The said Church acknowledges no ministry except that which preaches the Word of God and administers the sacraments.

VI

Further this Church itself receives no other confession than that which is made to God, no other absolution than that which is given by God for the remission of sins and which alone pardons and remits their sins who to this end confess their fault.

VII

Further this same Church denies all other ways and means of serving God beyond that which is spiritually ordained by the Word of God, which consists in the love of himself and of one's neighbour. Hence it rejects entirely the innumerable mockeries of all ceremonies which pervert religion, such as images and like things.

VIII

Also it acknowledges the civil magistrate ordained by God only as necessary to preserve the peace and tranquillity of the state. To which end, it desires and ordains that all be obedient in so far as nothing contrary to God is commanded.

IX

Next it affirms that marriage, instituted by God for all persons as fit and proper for them, violates the sanctity of no one whatever.

X

Finally as to things that are indifferent, such as foods, drinks and the observation of days, it allows as many as the man of faith can use at all times freely, but not otherwise than wisdom and charity should do.

Two Discourses on the Articles

1. *Session of October 5, 1536*

I held myself absolved from speaking up to now, and would have deliberately abstained until the end, seeing that my word is not very necessary for adding anything to the adequate replies which my brothers Farel and Viret give. But the reproach which you have made concerning the holy doctors of antiquity constrains me to say one word to remonstrate briefly how wrongly and groundlessly you accuse us in this connection. You charge us with condemning and wholly rejecting them, adding the reason that it is because we feel them to be contrary and hostile to our cause. As for condemning, we should not at all refuse to be judged by the whole world as not only audacious but beyond measure arrogant, if we held such servants of God in so great contempt, as you allege, as to deem them fools. If it be so, we should not at all take the trouble to read them and to use the help of their teaching when it serves and as occasion offers. So that those who make parade of according them great reverence often do not hold them in such great honour as we; nor do they deign to occupy their time reading their writings as we willingly do. This could be proved, not to you, but to anyone willing to take a little more trouble. But we have always held them to belong to the number of those to whom such obedience is not due, and whose authority we will not so exalt, as in any way to debase the dignity of the Word of our Lord, to which alone is due complete obedience in the Church of Jesus Christ.

For this there is more than sufficient reason. It is the fear of being found rebels under the sentence which our Lord pronounced so expressly by his prophet in Isa. ch. 8. Now I demand whether his people ought not to be satisfied with his voice, without listening to the living or the dead. Hence the

38

command that one apply himself to the law and the prophets. In order therefore not to be children of the devil but veritably the people of God, we rest ourselves upon the divine Word, fixing there our hearts, our thoughts, our eyes, and our ears, without turning away from it. Further since our Lord commands repeatedly by his apostle Peter, that those who speak in his Church speak his Word and not their own doctrine, we, who have to teach the people of Jesus according to his will and ordinance, do not wish to instruct it in human doctrines, but in celestial wisdom which has been committed to us for faithful transmission. It comes from a certain ignorance in you of us that you object that it would by any means be necessary to do away with all the power of human laws. For we are dealing here not with temporal policy for this present life; the question rather concerns the spiritual realm of God for life eternal, of which he must be acknowledged as sole king and legislator: as is said in Isa. ch. 33, exercising his power and administering his government by the Word in which consists alone his sceptre and dominion. And in order that you be not ignorant of the consequences this prerogative and pre-eminence implies for the subjection of the Church of God to his laws, James makes it plain, when he declares that there is only one legislator who is able to save or destroy. You see how he demonstrates and argues, that anyone who can impose law upon the Church has the power to save or damn; and hence that there can be no other legislator than God alone, who is the Lord of life and death. It is true that the pope by his intolerable impudence and devilish pride has tried to arrogate this power to himself, thus accomplishing what is attributed to Antichrist, who elevates himself far above all majesty and all honour which is given to God.

But we do not wish to measure these blessed persons by the standard of Antichrist, thus making them the adversaries and enemies of Jesus, whose good servants they were. In fact, we do them such honour as may according to God be accorded to them, while we attend to them and to their ministry, to search the Word of God, in order that, having found it, we should with them listen to and observe it with all humility and reverence, reserving this honour for the Lord alone, who has opened his mouth in the Church only to speak with authority, and in order that every ear be ready to listen to it and every soul to obey it. Even Cyprian speaking of the present matter that now occupies us in Bk. 2 of the Letters, Letter 3, does not wish us to have any regard to what was said or what is done by those before us, but only that we should consider what Christ our Lord says, who is before us all.

As to the reason which you have adduced, that we fear to be convinced by their authority since they all contradict us, it would be very easy to cite all the matters that today are controversial between you and us, and to show that this reason is as true as the reproach you make against us. But because there is no present opportunity to denounce this proposition, I restrict myself in the present matter and content myself with showing you how at this point, where you allege facts so adverse to us, we are able in reality to take them as defenders of our opinion. To do this I shall not adduce all that might be said, but briefly present certain passages by which I shall prove my intention so evidently that you will be unable to make a contradictory reply.

First, Tertullian very close to the time of the apostles, refuting the error of Marcion, who affirmed the body of Jesus Christ to have been only a phantasm and vain appearance, such as you contrive for us, deprived and spoiled of all the reality and properties of a human body, proves by this argument that Christ had a true body, because he left the form of it by representation in the Holy Supper. If it be, as he says, that there can be no image or representation except of real things, he implies that Christ took a real body when he descended to us, since in the Supper he left us a figure of this body. Note further the conclusion of the argument, that again, when naming this sacrament, which you maintain to be the material body of Christ, he calls it a figure of the body.

Whoever be the author of the unfinished commentaries on Matthew which are attributed to John Chrysostom and are included with his works in the 11th Homily about the middle, wishing to remonstrate that it is a much greater offence in us to contaminate and pollute ourselves than to profane the vessels in which are administered the elements of the Supper, he adds this reason: while we are the true vessels which God inhabits, those contain not the true body of Jesus Christ, but only the mystery of his body. He speaks word for word thus. Observe how, reversing all your doctrine, he simply establishes ours, saying openly that we must not look for the natural body of Jesus Christ, but a mystery of the communion which we have in his body.

Augustine, whom you have made your advocate, in Epistle

23 very near the end, after having spoken of the faith which little children bring to Baptism, and having said that it is improper to speak of infants believing, completes his purpose by these similes. We make use, he says, of these forms of speech when we say that the Lord is risen on the day when we celebrate Easter, and also was crucified on the day we celebrate his Passion, and he who would speak thus is not to be at all repressed. Similarly the bread and the wine, which are sacramental of the body and of the blood of Christ, we call in some sense the body and the blood: *quodammodo vocamus sacramenta*. Observe first for what reason he holds that the symbols of bread and of wine can be called the body and the blood of our Saviour: it is evidently because they are representative of them. More, he expressly takes this particular *quodammodo*, in some sense, to demonstrate more clearly and expressly the inexactness of speaking of it in this way.

In the Book against Adimantus the Manichee, about the middle, refuting the calumny which Adimantus alleges on the passage of Gen. ch. 9, that the blood of an animal is its soul, he declares that he is easily able to show that this is said to point out that the blood is not substance but sign. So our Lord has no hesitation in saying: "This is my body," when he gives them the sign of his body. It is not possible to declare more clearly all that we hold than what is said of it in these words. So that if we should speak thus of it and in the same words, you would be able to hold nothing against us.

Under Ps. 98, interpreting the passage *Adorate scabellum pedum eius quoniam sanctum est*, he confesses that the Jews ate the body of Jesus Christ in the same way as we eat it.

At the beginning of a Homily on the Gospel of John, about the 8th or 9th section (I cannot exactly recall which), beginning to exhort the people to listen to the voice of Jesus, by way of objection, he asks how they are able to listen to what does not speak personally with them; and then he replies: While this age endures, it is necessary that the Saviour be on high; but he has left his Word on earth by which he speaks to us. For it had to be that his body which ascended into heaven be in one place; but his truth is spread over all. How will you then reconcile the view that the body appears on all the altars, is enclosed in all the little boxes, is every day and at the same time in a hundred places, with what you affirm about his blessed person?

Further, in the book *De fide ad Petrum Diaconum* (though it is uncertain whether it belongs to him or to some other Father),

ch. 19, he says that the patriarchs and prophets under the Old
Testament have offered to our Lord Jesus Christ the best
animals, and that now the Church universal continually offers
him the sacrifice of bread and wine in the charity of faith. And
just as in these carnal sacrifices there is the representation of
the body of Christ which it is right to offer, so in the sacrifice of
the New Testament is effected an act of thanksgiving and
commemoration for the flesh of Christ which he offered, and
for the blood which he poured out for the remission of our sins.
Weigh all these words and syllables (if it appear good to you),
to see whether in the least they favour your error.

Finally, in the Epistle *ad Dardanum*, which is full and long, he
testifies clearly what he thinks. For in the first part he treats of
how Jesus Christ according to his divinity fills all, dwells in all,
and is spread through heaven and earth. In the second, he
shows how according to his humanity he is in heaven, not on
earth. For in transferring (as he says) and exalting his body on
high, he gave it glory and immortality, but withdrew from it
neither its reality nor its substance.

And here I address myself to you, Doctor Blancherose,[1]
asking you to try to speak more soberly. First, of how the presence of God pervades all; second, of what assistance we have
from Christ in his humanity. For what you adduce from the
Psalmist to show that God is below, does not, when the passage
is carefully examined, do much to prove your contention, since
he says no more than that, being stricken and afflicted by the
hand of the Lord, he does not know how to avoid his anger or
to hide from his power, whether he mounts up to heaven, or
descends to the centre of the earth, or flees to the ends of the
sea.

Nevertheless Scripture equally testifies that God is over all
when it declares that he is contained in no place, as Solomon
says: the heavens are not able to contain him. But again what
is said of the divine essence ought not to be understood to apply
to the humanity of Christ, which has properties distinct from
the divinity. If you object to me that all that is said of God
pertains to Jesus Christ in whom humanity and divinity are not
separated, the answer is easy: that Jesus Christ in taking human
flesh joined his divine nature to our humanity in the union of his
person, so that (as John says) the Word was made flesh, and
one and the same Jesus Christ is God and man. Yet this union

---

[1] Claude Blancherose, a medical doctor at Lausanne, and of French origin,
was one of the most zealous orators on the Roman side at the Colloquy.

is without confusion, as the Athanasian Creed teaches. Thus it does not follow that, if the divinity of Christ is infinite, hence his body must also be so. In speaking thus, we do not divide Jesus Christ, but only distinguish the properties of his two natures which are entire in him, as without dividing a man one may point to difference between soul and body.

The whole world is easily able to understand with what audacity you reproach us with being contrary to the ancient doctors. Certainly if you had seen some of their pages, you would not have been so foolhardy as to pass such judgment as you have done, not having even seen the evidence, as the above witnesses present it. And one could cite others besides. But I content myself with those that can be reached readily without using great subtlety in citing them.

Now I give you to know that it is not without reason or for our own pleasure that we do not concur with that foolish opinion which has been introduced to the world by the instigation of Satan, but that being constrained by the great absurdities which follow from it, we teach this doctrine which you find so strange. I will try to answer from Scripture the grounds which you give. For when Paul says that we await our salvation from heaven, which will transform our vile and mortal body into his glorious body, he evidently affirms that the glorious body of Christ is not other or of another nature than the bodies of the faithful will be after the Resurrection. I ask you if on your conscience you believe that the bodies of the children of God, when glorified, will be in all places without being limited or circumscribed and having none of the properties of their nature. Your judgment must convince you that this is an absurdity which you cannot concede. No more then ought it to be accorded to the body of Christ, which (according to the apostle) they will resemble.

I ask you further whether we do not eat the same body and in the same form as did the apostles at the Last Supper? This you cannot deny. But now you have to confess that the apostles ate either the glorified body or the mortal body. If it be the mortal, the consequence is that Jesus Christ will be again for ever mortal and passible, contrary to the Scriptures, which declare that it is divested of all infirmity. If it be immortal and glorious, it involves your view in another dilemma, that, when he distributed it at the Last Supper, he must be in one part mortal and passible, and in another immortal and glorified. For Jesus Christ being seated at the Table with his apostles had a body mortal and passible, both in approaching death and passion, and in the very hour of his greatest weakness. And yet by your confession he distributed his glorious and immortal body. From this there follow all the absurdities one can imagine, so that the dreams of Marcion would never be so fantastic as the consequences which could be drawn from what you wish to believe.

Since you pretend to have a great reverence for the words of the Saviour, emphasizing so strictly the words: *Hoc est corpus meum*, I shall force you by the same logic to separate and divide, as the words suggest, the body from the blood. Thus I shall precipitate you into the awkward position of granting that the body of Christ, being exalted into the glory of celestial kingship can be divided from his blood, which is an abominable thought. For our Lord saying: This is my body, when indicating the bread, and in indicating the wine: This is my blood, indicates the body and the blood separately. And it is a mockery to allege this concomitance by which you are accustomed to escape.[2] For if the body were in the chalice, it would be falsely spoken by the Lord of truth to say: This is my blood, especially after having pointed out his body separately. Yet if we confine ourselves to the words as you wish, there is nothing left to do but confess that under the bread is the body, under the wine the blood, and to separate them in this way. I leave you to consider how great the absurdity of this would be. For these reasons which are of great importance as any one can see, we say that it is not the natural body of our Lord Jesus nor his natural blood which is given to us in his Holy Supper. We affirm that it is a spiritual communication, by which in virtue and in power he makes us participant of all that we are able to receive of grace in his body and blood; or again, to declare better the dignity of this mystery, it is a spiritual communication by which he makes us truly participant of his body and his blood, but wholly spiritually, that is by the bond of his Spirit. In order that you may understand that this interpretation is no gloss invented or dreamt on our own testimony, I shall show you how it is manifestly delivered to us by the words of two apostles themselves. For where Matthew and Mark declare that our Lord in delivering the chalice says: This is my blood, Luke and Paul say: This is the new testament in my blood; that is to say, the new alliance which the Father has made with us, forgetting and effacing our sins in his compassion, receiving us in grace and mercy as his

2 *Evader* is a conjecture—word half illegible in original.

children and heirs of his Kingdom, and writing his law in our hearts by his Spirit. This alliance has been confirmed and ratified by the blood of Jesus. Now if what our Lord said was: This cup is my blood, on the interpretation of Luke and Paul he wished to say nothing else than that it is the testament in his blood; and similarly what is said of the bread, that it is the body, has no other significance than that it is the testament in his body; for you make no difficulty about taking what is said as much of the bread as of the wine in the same sense.

If I have satisfied you about the falseness of your objections, and in my view you ought to be manifestly content, I advise and beseech you to charge us no longer with contradicting the ancient doctors in this matter with whom we are in fact in such accord; nor with corrupting Scripture at our pleasure, when constrained by such vital reasons we interpret it on the true analogy of faith; nor with glossing it on our own testimony, when we suggest no gloss which is not itself expressed in it.

2. *Session of October 7*

Recollection accords to Hildebrand the first definition of this monstrous doctrine of transubstantiation. It is therefore good to note what the sanctity of this person was, and in what reverence he himself held the sacrament, which he determined and defined to be the true body of Christ, in order that the advocates of transubstantiation may consider what assurance they have for their doctrine, realizing who its author was and from what source it has arisen. I leave aside the corruptions, perjuries, superstitions, homicides, thefts, simonies, deceptions, violences, which would be horrible to hear, as Cardinal Beno recounts them in a tract inserted into the commentaries of the Council of Basle made by Pius II. But among other things, he reproaches him with desiring at his Council of Versailles to conclude that the bread changes and transforms into the body of Christ. But being uncertain and ill assured of his thesis, he commanded that they fast in order to attain some revelation which might declare how the case stands and who had the better of it, he or Berengarius. And not at all deterred by the fact that no revelation came, he did not hesitate to draw a quite deliberate conclusion. I do not know how you dare to hold a thing resolved in this way, which was so ill-founded in the mind of him who transmits it to you. Second, he accuses him, when wishing once to practise his enchantments and sorceries, of

46 CALVIN: THEOLOGICAL TREATISES

taking this bread which he said was God, and throwing it down
into the fire. On which one of his cardinals cried out in public
in the hearing of many that Hildebrand and he had done
something which if the world knew it would burn them alive.
Come now, and say that the bread is your God, on the assurance
of one who burns it to perform his magical conjurations.

Articles concerning
the Organization of the Church and of Worship
at Geneva 1537

INTRODUCTION

THE ARTICLES WHEN PRESENTED BY CALVIN IN January 1537 to the Council of Ministers, had a rough passage, and were accepted neither in their entirety nor in the form proposed. The demand for a monthly celebration of the Holy Supper was refused, in favour of a continuation of the customary quarterly observance. Nor were the introduction of discipline, and excommunication or the setting up of a disciplinary council agreed upon. Though the *Confession of Faith* had been accepted in the previous year, the Council did not implement the recommendation that magistrates, followed by the citizens, should attest their adherence to it. Nor was the Commission set up, which was to regulate matrimonial questions (*C.R.* X/I 5).

But it is the principle of theocratic government embodied in the document which is of first class importance, not the limited success which in the early stages it achieved.

Articles concerning
the Organization of the Church and of Worship at Geneva proposed by the Ministers at the Council
January 16, 1537

Right Honourable Gentlemen: it is certain that a Church cannot be said to be well ordered and regulated unless in it the Holy Supper of our Lord is always being celebrated and frequented, and this under such good supervision that no one dare presume to present him self unless devoutly, and with genuine reverence for it. For this reason, in order to maintain the Church in its integrity, the discipline of excommunication is necessary, by which it is possible to correct those that do not wish to submit courteously and with all obedience to the Word of God. Further, it is a thing very expedient for the edification of the Church, to sing some psalms in the form of public devotions by which one may pray to God, or to sing his praise so that the hearts of all be roused and incited to make like[1] prayers and render like praises and thanks to God with one accord. Third, it is strictly required and quite necessary for maintaining the people in purity of doctrine, that infants of tender age be so instructed that they are able to give reason for the faith, so that evangelical doctrine is not left to decay, and also that its substance be diligently maintained and transmitted from hand to hand and from father to son. Finally out of the tyranny which the   ![2] exercised in the matter of marriage and the iniquitous laws which he imposed, many controversies persist. To settle them, it would be advisable to make certain ordinances by which they may be controlled, and, if any difference of opinion arise, to take appropriate steps for composing them.

[1] Original has *parolles*, manifestly a copyist's error for *pareilles*.
[2] The original leaves a blank space; *the pope*, of course, is meant, but, as *C.R.* remarks, the author is unwilling to write the abhorrent name, and allows an exclamation mark to express his feelings.

As for the trouble and confusion which existed in this city at the beginning, before the gospel was with one accord received and recognized, it is not possible to reduce everything to good order in a moment, if only because the ignorance of the people would not allow it. But now that it has pleased the Lord a little better to establish his reign here, it seemed to us good and salutary to confer together concerning these things; and, after having taken counsel of the Word of the Lord, and having invoked his Name and besought the assistance of his Spirit, whose guidance it would be good to follow hereafter, we have concluded by presenting to you in the form of articles what we have deliberated concerning the knowledge which the Lord has vouchsafed to us, praying you in the Name of God that it be your pleasure not to spare yourselves from playing the part that pertains to your office. If, that is, you see that our advice is from the holy Word of the gospel, take good care that these observations be received and obeyed in your city, since the Lord in his goodness has given you this knowledge; for the ordinances by which his Church is preserved are that it be truly and as nearly as possible conformed to his Word, which is the certain rule of all government and administration, but especially of ecclesiastical government.

It would be well to require that the Communion of the Holy Supper of Jesus Christ be held every Sunday at least as a rule. When the Church assembles together for the great consolation which the faithful receive and the profit which proceeds from it, in every respect according to the promises which are there presented to our faith, then we are really made participants of the body and the blood of Jesus, of his death, of his life, of his Spirit and of all his benefits. As for the exhortations made there, we are to recognize and magnify by professing his praise the marvellous things graciously vouchsafed by God to us; and finally we are to live as Christians, being joined together in one peace and brotherly unity as members of one and the same body. In fact, it was not instituted by Jesus for making a commemoration two or three times a year, but for a frequent exercise of our faith and charity, of which the congregation of Christians should make use as often as they be assembled, as we find written in Acts ch. 2, that the disciples of our Lord continued in the breaking of bread, which is the ordinance of the Supper. Such also was always the practice of the ancient Church, until the abomination of the mass was introduced, in which, in place of this communion of all the faithful, there was set up the horrible sacrilege that one man sacrifices for all. In this the Supper has been wholly destroyed and abolished. But because the frailty of the people is still so great, there is danger that this sacred and so excellent mystery be misunderstood if it be celebrated so often. In view of this, it seemed good to us, while hoping that the people who are still so infirm will be the more strengthened, that use be made of this sacred Supper once a month in one of three places where now preaching takes place, viz., St. Pierre, Riue or St. Gervais, in such a way that once a month it take place at St. Pierre, once at Riue, and once at St. Gervais, and then return in this order, having gone the round. It will be always not for one quarter of the city alone, but for all the Church; and for it a convenient hour will be chosen and announced everywhere on the previous Sunday. So that there be no cause for contempt, but this high mystery be treated with the greatest dignity possible, it has seemed to us the more advisable course, that the ministers of the Word, on whom the office of administering all that pertains to the mysteries of God properly belongs, distribute the bread and the wine, the form and sacrament of the body and blood of our Lord. And so that this take place with fitness and without confusion or impropriety, we have proposed to make it our duty to show and indicate such order as the people ought to observe; to advocate one that avoids confusion, and will supply you with means that will be found expedient, that things be well conducted and we come with such particular reverence as Paul commands us.

But the principal rule that is required, and for which it is necessary to have the greatest care, is that this Holy Supper, ordained and instituted for joining the members of our Lord Jesus Christ with their Head and with one another in one body and one spirit, be not soiled and contaminated by those coming to it and communicating, who declare and manifest by their misconduct and evil life that they do not at all belong to Jesus. For in this profanation of his sacrament our Lord is gravely dishonoured. Hence it behoves us to be on our guard that this pollution, which abounds with such dishonour to God, be not brought amongst us by our negligence, in view of the so great vengeance, mentioned by Paul, on those who treat this sacrament unworthily. It is then necessary that those who have the power to frame regulations make it a rule that they who come to this Communion be approved members of Jesus Christ.

For this reason, our Saviour set up in his Church the correction and discipline of excommunication, by which he desired that those who were disorderly in their life and unworthy of the name of Christian, and who, after being admonished, despise coming to amendment and returning to the right way, should be expelled from the body of the Church, and, like decayed members, should be cut off, until they come to repentance and recognize their fault and error. This manner of correction was commanded by our Lord for his Church in Matt. ch. 18. We ought then to use it, lest we despise the commandment which he has given us. We have an example of it in Paul, I Tim. ch. 1 and I Cor. ch. 5, with grave warning that we keep no kind of company with those who call themselves Christians and yet are notoriously lewd, avaricious, idolatrous, slanderous, or drunken and given to robbery. Hence if there is in us any fear of God, this ordinance must have place in our Church. Again, the same reasons on which it is founded and the profit which it yields, ought to move us to make use of it, were there no such express command. First, that Jesus Christ be not blasphemed and dishonoured as if his Church were a confederation of evil persons, dissolute in all vices. Second, that those who receive such correction, being ashamed and disturbed by their sin, should come to know and amend themselves. Third, that others be not corrupted and perverted in their way of life, but rather by their example be turned from manifesting like faults.

This use and practice persisted in the ancient Church for some time with particular usefulness and profit for Christianity, until some wicked bishops, or rather robbers taking the place of bishops, turned it into a tyranny and abused it for their evil cupidity. So that nothing today is more pernicious and evil in the dominion of the pope than excommunication, though it is in fact one of the most profitable and salutary things which the Saviour vouchsafed to his Church.

Now this fault appeared because the false bishops took from the assembly of the faithful and attracted to themselves the right and power of excommunication. This in fact according to the Word does not belong to them. And after having usurped this domination, they converted it into all kinds of perversity.

Having then considered that a Church cannot retain its true condition without observing this ordinance,[3] and that it is greatly to be feared that contempt of it may be punished by the mighty vengeance of God, the expedient thing seemed to us to be

[3] In the original, *ordonnance* is followed by *du* and a blank space. Gaberel, *Histoire de L'Eglise de Genève* (Geneva, 1858) prints the whole document, and here supplies *pape*. But the emendation does not fit easily into the context.

what was committed to the Church and exercised according to the rule which we have in Scripture. And yet on the other hand, one is to take good care not to fall into any impropriety which depraves and corrupts it by ill usage.

To do this, we have deliberately required of you to be pleased to ordain and elect certain persons of good life and witness from among the faithful, persevering and not easily corrupted, who should be dispersed and distributed in all the quarters of the city, having oversight of the life and government of each of them; and if they see any vice worthy of note to find fault with in any person, that they communicate about it with some of the ministers, to admonish whoever it is that is at fault and to exhort him in brotherly fashion to amendment. If it be found that such remonstrances have no result, he must be advised that his obstinacy will be reported to the Church. And then if he recognize his error, how great is the profit of this discipline! If he do not attend to it, the time has come when the minister appointed by those who are in charge of the case should announce publicly in the assembly what has been done to bring him to amendment and all without result. By then it will be realized whether he will persevere in hardness of heart, and this is the time for excommunication. That is to say, he is to be held as expelled from the company of Christians and left in the power of the devil for his temporal confusion, until he give good evidence of his penitence and amendment; and as sign of this he is to be barred from the communion of the Supper, and denounced to other believers that they have no intimate dealings with him. But he is never to omit coming to sermon to receive teaching, in order to prove whether it will please the Saviour to touch his heart and turn him into the right path.

The vices which are to be corrected in this way are those which you have had already named by Paul and others similar. When others, such as neighbours or parents, have knowledge of the vices before the said disputes are perceived, they themselves would be able to make the remonstrance; and when they realize that they have no effect, they should turn the matter over to those deputed to proceed according to their office.

This, it seems to us, is a good way of reducing excommunication in our Church and yet of maintaining it in its entirety; and without this correction the Church is quite unable to proceed. But if there be anyone so insolent and abandoned to all perversity that he only laughs at being excommunicated and does not mind living and dying in such rejection, it will be your duty to consider if you must for long tolerate and leave unpunished such contempt and mockery of God and his gospel.

Further, because there are grave suspicions and even obvious evidences that there are again several inhabitants in this city who have not at all fallen in with the gospel, but deny it, so that in their heart are harboured all the superstitions conflicting with the Word of God, it will be expedient to make a beginning with this first, to get to know who desire to acknowledge the Church of Jesus Christ and who do not. For if there is need to expel by excommunication from our assembly those who truly with good reason would have been taken as members of it, how much more necessary to discern those who ought to be received as members from those who should not be accepted.

Second, it is certain that there is no greater distinction than that of faith, and hence if those who join with us in the faith are for their vices alone to be excommunicated, there is stronger reason why those should not be tolerated within the Church who are in everything contrary to us in religion. The remedy for this which we have thought of is to suggest to you that all the inhabitants of your city have to make confession of and give reason for their faith, in order to recognize those in harmony with the gospel, and those loving rather to be of the kingdom of the pope than of the kingdom of Jesus Christ. It would be then the act of Christian magistrates if you, Gentlemen of the Council, each for himself, would make in your council a profession, by which it would be shown that the doctrine of your faith is really that by which all the faithful are united in one Church. For by your example you would show what each following you would have to do; and after, you would ordain some of your company, who, joining with some minister, would require each to do the same. Let this be done for this once only, though it has not at all been settled yet what doctrine each holds to be proper for setting up a Church.

On the other hand there are the psalms which we desire to be sung in the Church, as we have it exemplified in the ancient Church and in the evidence of Paul himself, who says it is good to sing in the congregation with mouth and heart. We are unable to compute the profit and edification which will arise from this, except after having experimented. Certainly as things are, the prayers of the faithful are so cold, that we ought to be ashamed and dismayed. The psalms can incite us to lift up our hearts to God and move us to an ardour in invoking and exalting with praises the glory of his Name. Moreover it will be thus appreciated of what benefit and consolation the pope and those that belong to him have deprived the Church; for he has reduced the psalms, which ought to be true spiritual songs, to a murmuring among themselves without any understanding.

This manner of proceeding seemed specially good to us, that children, who beforehand have practised some modest church song, sing in a loud distinct voice, the people listening with all attention and following heartily what is sung with the mouth, till all become accustomed to sing communally. But in order to avoid all confusion, you must not allow that anyone by his insolence, and to put the congregation to derision, should come to disturb the order you have adopted.

The third article concerns the instruction of children, who without doubt ought to make a confession of their faith to the Church. For this purpose, in ancient days, a definite catechism was used for initiating each one in the fundamentals of the Christian religion; and this might be a formula of witness, which each could use to declare his Christianity. The children were individually taught from this catechism, and had to come to testify their faith to the Church, to which they were unable at their Baptism to render witness. For we see that Scripture has always joined confession with faith; and it has told us that, if we truly believe with the heart, it is right that we ought also to confess with the mouth to that salvation which we believe. Now if this ordinance has ever been proper and appropriate, it is more than ever necessary now, in view of the neglect of the Word of God which we see in most people, and the contempt of parents in instructing their children in the way of God, from which one sees a remarkable rudeness and great ignorance which is quite intolerable in the Church of God.

The order which we advise being set up is that there be a brief and simple summary of the Christian faith, to be taught to all children, and that at certain seasons of the year they come before the ministers to be interrogated and examined, and to receive more ample explanation, according as there is need to the capacity of each one of them, until they have been proved sufficiently instructed. But may it be your pleasure to command parents to exercise pains and diligence that their children learn this summary and that they present themselves before the ministers at the times appointed.

Finally, inasmuch as the   [4] has so confused matrimonial

---

[4] Once again, a blank space is held to be more expressive than the name of the pope.

cases, by making degrees at his pleasure, determining differences iniquitously and against all reason, it is required and necessary to review the controversies that often ensue from this in the light of the Word of God. So we seriously suggest to you, to make the matter more certain, that you give charge and commission to certain persons of your company to judge and decide all cases which may come before them, joining with them some ministers the better to secure that what is done is in accordance with the Word of God. These commissioners with the council of ministers aforesaid will first make ordinances from the cases commonly occurring, and they will have these to judge by. But these are afterwards to be presented to you for approval before proceeding further.

Now, right honourable gentlemen, we beseech you affectionately with one accord, asking in the name of God, if you regard these intimations and exhortations as being truly from the Word of God, and take them not at all as from us, but as from him from whom they do proceed, that you similarly consider of what importance and consequence they are for the maintenance of the honour of God in this State and the conservation of the Church in its integrity. These considerations will forbid you to spare yourselves from putting into diligent execution what you see not only to belong to your office, but also to be so necessary for the maintenance of your people in good order. Nor ought you to be moved by the difficulty which some will allege to be inherent in these matters. For we ought to have this hope, since we attempt to follow what is ordained by God, that of his goodness he will make it prosper and conduct our enterprise to a successful end, as you yourselves have hitherto sufficiently experienced in all the affairs where the Lord has given you grace to seek his glory. May he assist you by his power to bring everything to a successful issue.

Draft Ecclesiastical Ordinances

INTRODUCTION

THE COMMENT OF *C.R.* IS AS FOLLOWS: "WE POSSESS IN this document without any doubt the original minute of the draft ordinances, which was drawn up in conformity with the decision of the Council, taken at the session of September 13, 1541, by Calvin and his ministerial colleagues with a commission of six councillors nominated for the purpose. . . . Calvin records that the revision was finished in twenty days. But by decision of September 16, the Articles had also to be submitted for examination by the Little Council, the Two Hundred, and the General Council. This work does not seem to have been accomplished without difficulty. From the beginning, opposition showed itself very lively. Some of the members of the Council were even summoned 'under oath,' so as not to embarrass the work by their abstention; and the Council had to decide that, despite the rejection of certain articles, it was desirable to persist in order to succeed in establishing a rule and to come to an agreement on each point." There were deliberations in both the Little Council and the Two Hundred, and alterations were made. "The latter in their session of November 9, made again some modifications. The revised draft having been thus definitively passed, it was on Sunday, November 20, submitted to the assembly of the General Council; and the minute for the day records: 'The Ordinances of the Church were passed without contradiction.' "

This revision, definitive and become official by formal vote of the General Council, exists no longer, as it appears, in the Archives of the State; but it has been conserved in a text in the Reports of the Venerable Company (Vol. A, pp. 1–15). This appears from the introduction which precedes the text, and is confirmed by the following express mention contained in the Reports of the Little Council, November 25, 1541: "The Ministers having been heard,—*Resolved* to send both to them and to the Deputies of the Consistory the text of the Ordinances passed by the Little, Great and General Council for the Ordering of the Christian Religion."

In notes under the text are given the alterations (as contained in *C.R.*) effected on the Draft in its passage through the Councils and which the definitive and official version contains. *C.R.* supplies another list of amendments "by another hand." About half of these are wholly or substantially incorporated into the official version; the other half it has not been thought worthwhile to give here. (See *C.R.* X/1, 15.)

Draft Ecclesiastical Ordinances
September & October 1541

There [2] are four orders of office instituted by our Lord for the government of his Church.

First, [3] pastors; then doctors; next elders; and fourth deacons.

Hence if we will have a Church [4] well ordered and maintained we ought to observe this form of government.

As to the pastors, whom Scripture also sometimes calls [5] elders and ministers, their office is to proclaim the Word of God, to instruct, admonish, exhort and censure, both in public and private, to administer the sacraments and to enjoin brotherly corrections along with the elders and colleagues.

Now in order that nothing happen confusedly in the Church, no one is to enter upon this office without a calling. In this it is necessary to consider three things, namely: the principal thing is the examination; then [6] what belongs to the institution of the ministers; third, what ceremony or method of procedure it is good to observe in introducing them to office.

[1] Instead of the title, the following: In the Name of Almighty God, we, the Syndics of the Small and the Great Council with our people assembled at the sound of trumpet and great bell, according to our ancient customs, having considered that it is a thing worthy of commendation above all others, that the doctrine of the Holy Church of our Lord be well preserved in purity and the Christian Church be duly maintained, that the youth be in the future faithfully instructed, the hospital kept in good condition for sustaining the poor, all of which cannot be done unless there be a certain rule and manner of life by which each estate attends to the duties of its office: For this reason it appeared good to us that the spiritual government such as our Lord showed and instituted by his Word should be reduced to good order and have place and be observed among us. Hence we have commanded and established to be followed and observed in our city and territory the Ecclesiastical Constitution which follows, seeing that it is taken from the gospel of Jesus Christ.

[2] First there are   [3] namely   [4] the Church

[5] superintendents, elders, etc.   [6] then to whom it belongs

The examination contains two parts, of which the first concerns doctrine—to ascertain whether the candidate for ordination has a good and holy [7] knowledge of Scripture; and also whether he be a fit and proper person to communicate it edifyingly to the people.

Further to avoid all danger of the candidate[8] holding some false opinion, it will be good that he profess his acceptance and maintenance of the doctrine approved by the Church.

To know whether he is fit to instruct, it would be necessary to proceed by interrogation and by hearing him discuss in private the doctrine of the Lord.

The second part concerns life, to ascertain whether he is of good habits and conducts himself always without reproach. The rule of procedure in this matter which it is needful to follow is very well indicated by Paul.

There follows, to whom it belongs to institute Pastors

It will be good in this connection to follow the order of the ancient Church, for it is the only practice which is shown us in Scripture. The order is that ministers first elect such as ought to hold office[9]; afterwards that he be presented to the Council; and if he is found worthy the Council receive and accept him [10], giving him certification to produce finally to the people when he preaches, in order that he be received by the common consent of the company of the faithful. If he be found unworthy, and show this after due probation, it is necessary to proceed to a new election for the choosing of another.

As to the manner of introducing him, it is good to use the imposition of hands, which ceremony was observed by the apostles and then in the ancient Church, providing that it take place without superstition and without offence. But because there has been much superstition in the past and scandal might result, it is better to abstain from it because of the infirmity of the times.[11]

---

[7] sound

[8] *retenir* of the Draft is replaced by *recepvoir*, but the phrase with "candidate" equally translates both.

[9] Add: having made it known to the Seigneury

[10] Add: as he will see to be expedient

[11] The article runs: As to the manner of introduction, since the ceremonies of time past have been perverted into much superstition, because of the weakness of the times, it will suffice that a declaration be made by one of the ministers denoting the office to which ordination is being made;

When he is elected, he has to swear in front of the Seigneury. Of this oath there will be a prescribed form, suitable to what is required of a minister.[12]

Now as it is necessary to examine the ministers well when they are to be elected, so also it is necessary to have good supervision to maintain them in their duty.

First it will be expedient that all the ministers, for conserving purity and concord of doctrine among themselves, meet together one certain day each week, for discussion of the Scriptures; and none are to be exempt from this without legitimate excuse. If anyone be negligent, let him be admonished.

As for those who preach in the villages, throughout the Seigneury, they are to be exhorted to come as often as they are able. For the rest, if they default an entire month, it is to be held to be very great negligence, unless it is a case of illness or other legitimate hindrance.

If there appear difference of doctrine, let the ministers come together to discuss the matter. Afterwards, if need be, let them call the elders[13] to assist in composing the contention. Finally, if they are unable to come to friendly agreement because of the obstinacy of one of the parties, let the case be referred to the magistrate to be put in order.

To obviate all scandals of living, it will be proper that there be a form of correction[14] to which all submit themselves. It will also be the means by which the ministry may retain respect, and the Word of God be neither dishonoured nor scorned because of the ill reputation of the ministers. For as one is to correct those who merit it, so it will be proper to reprove[15] calumnies and false reports which are made unjustly against innocent people.

But first it should be noted that there are crimes which are quite intolerable in a minister, and there are faults which may on the other hand be endured while direct fraternal admonitions are offered.

Of the first sort are:

heresy, schism, rebellion against ecclesiastical order, blasphemy open and meriting civil punishment, simony and all

then that prayers and petitions be made, in order that the Lord give him grace to discharge it.

[12] Add: as follows—(then is to be inserted the form to be used).

[13] and the clerk at the Seigneury

[14] correction of ministers, as will be later set forth

[15] repress

corruption in presentations, intrigue to occupy another's place, leaving one's Church without lawful leave[16] or just calling, duplicity, perjury, lewdness, larceny, drunkenness, assault meriting punishment by law, usury, games forbidden by the law and scandalous, dances and similar dissoluteness, crimes carrying with them loss of civil rights, crime giving rise to another separation from the Church.

Of the second sort are:

strange methods of treating Scripture which turn to scandal, curiosity in[17] investigating idle questions, advancing some doctrine or kind of practice not received in the Church, negligence in studying and[18] reading the Scriptures, negligence in rebuking vice amounting to flattery, negligence in doing everything required by his office, scurrility, lying, slander, dissolute words, injurious words, foolhardiness and evil devices, avarice and too great parsimony, undisciplined anger, quarrels and contentions, laxity either of manner or of gesture and like conduct improper to a minister.[19]

In the case of the crimes which cannot at all be tolerated, if some accusation and complaint arise, let the assembly of ministers and elders investigate it, in order to proceed reasonably and according to whatever is discovered in judging the case, and then report judgment to the magistrate in order that if required the delinquent be deposed.[20]

In the case of the lesser vices which may be corrected by simple admonition, one is to proceed according to the command of our Lord, so that as a last step it come for ecclesiastical judgment.

To keep this discipline in operation, let the ministers every three months take special notice whether there be anything to discuss among themselves, to remedy it as is reasonable.

[16] licit holiday

[17] *de chercher* instead of *à chercher*

[18] and principally in reading

[19] The rest of the article reads: If there are civil crimes, that is crimes which should be punished by the laws, should any ministers fall into them, the Seigneury is to take them in hand, and beyond the ordinary penalty they are accustomed to impose on others, deposition from office will be the punishment.

[20] As to the other crimes of which the first investigation belongs to the ecclesiastical Consistory, the clerks or elders with the ministers are to be watchful for them. And if anyone is convicted of them, they are to make a report to the Council with their advice and judgment; thus the final sentence of punishment is to be reserved to the Seigneury.

Of the number, place and time of preachings

Each Sunday, there is to be sermon at St. Peter [21] and St. Gervais at break of day, and at the usual hour at the said St. Peter and St. Gervais.

At midday, there is to be catechism, that is, instruction of little children in all the three churches, the Magdalene,[22] St. Peter and St. Gervais.

At three o'clock second sermon in [23] St. Peter and St. Gervais.

For bringing children to catechism, and for receiving the sacraments, the boundaries of the parishes should as far as possible be observed; that is, St. Gervais embracing what it had in the past, the Magdalene similarly, St. Peter what belonged formerly to St. Germain, St. Cross, Our Lady the New, and St. Legier.

Besides the two preachings which take place, on working days there will be a sermon at St. Peter three times a week, on Monday, Tuesday [24] and Friday [25] one hour before beginning is made at the other places.

To maintain these charges and others pertaining to the ministry, it will be necessary to have five ministers and three coadjutors who will also be ministers, to aid and assist as necessity requires.

Concerning the second order, which we have called Doctors

The office proper to doctors is the instruction of the faithful in true doctrine, in order that the purity of the Gospel be not corrupted either by ignorance or by evil opinions. As things are disposed today, we always include under this title aids and instructions for maintaining the doctrine of God and defending the Church from injury by the fault of pastors and ministers. So to use a more intelligible word, we will call [26] this the order of the schools.

The degree nearest to the minister and most closely joined [27] to the government of the Church is the lecturer in theology, of

21 Add: at the Magdalene   22 St. Peter, the Magdalene and St. Gervais
23 At three o'clock also in all the three parishes   24 Wednesday
25 For the end of the article: These sermons are to be heard one after another at such an hour that they can be finished before beginning elsewhere. If some extraordinary prayer for the necessity of the time is to be made, the order for Sunday will be observed.
26 *lapellerons* substituted for *apellerons*   27 conjoined

As for the hospital for plague, it should [53] be wholly separate and apart, and especially if it happen [54] that the city be visited by this scourge of God.

For the rest, to discourage mendicancy which is contrary to good order, it would be well, [55] and we have so ordered it, that there be one of our officials at the entrance of the churches to remove from the place those who loiter [56]; and if there be any who give offence or offer insolence to bring them to one of the Lords Syndic. Similarly for the rest of the time, let the Overseers of Tens take care that the total prohibition of begging be well observed.

Of the Sacraments [57]

Baptism is to take place at the time of Sermon, and should be administered only by ministers or coadjutors. The names of children with those of their parents are to be registered, that, if any be found a bastard, the magistrate may be informed.

The stone or baptismal font is to be near the pulpit, in order that there be better hearing for the recitation of this mystery and practice of baptism.

Only such strangers as are men of faith and of our communion are to be accepted as godparents, since others are not capable of making the promise to the Church of instructing the children as is proper.

Of the Supper

Since the Supper was instituted for us by our Lord to be frequently used, and also was so observed in the ancient Church until the devil turned everything upside down, erecting the mass in its place, it is a fault in need of correction, to celebrate it so seldom. [58]

Hence it will be proper that it be always administered in the city once a month, in such a way that every three months it take place in each parish. Besides, it should take place three times a year generally, that is to say at Easter, Pentecost and

[53] let there be   [54] if it come
[55] The Seigneury should appoint some of its officers, and so we have ordained
[56] resist   [57] Add sub-title: Of Baptism
[58] Add: For the present, let it be advised and ordained that it always be administered four times in the year.

which it will be good to have one in Old Testament and one in New Testament.

But because it is only possible to profit from such lectures if first one is instructed in the languages and humanities, and also because it is necessary to raise offspring for time to come, in order not to leave the Church deserted to our children, a college should be instituted for instructing children [28] to prepare them for the ministry as well as for civil government.

For the first, a proper place ought to be assigned for both doing lessons and accommodating the children and others who would profit. There must be a man learned and expert in arranging both the house and the instruction, who is able also to lecture. He is to be chosen and remunerated on condition that he have under his charge lecturers both in languages and in dialectic, if it can be done. Likewise there should be some matriculated persons to teach the little children; and [29] these we hope shortly to appoint to assist the master.

All who are there will be subject like ministers to ecclesiastical discipline.

There need be no other school in the city for the little children, but let the girls have their school apart, as has hitherto been the case.

Let no one be received if he is not approved by the ministers [30] on their testimony, for fear of impropriety.

Concerning the third order which is that of Elders [31]

Their office is to have oversight of the life of everyone, to admonish amicably those whom they see to be erring or [32] to be living a disordered life, and, where it is required, to enjoin fraternal corrections themselves and [33] along with others.

In the present condition of the Church, it would be good to elect two of the Little Council, four of the Council of Sixty, and six of the Council of Two Hundred, men of good and honest life, without reproach and beyond suspicion, and above all fearing God and possessing spiritual prudence. These should be

[28] to instruct them   [29] this we wish and order to be done
[30] by the ministers having first informed the Seigneury; and then let him again be presented to the Council along with their testimony, for fear of impropriety. The examination ought always to be conducted in the presence of two gentlemen of the Little Council.
[31] who are to be sent or deputed by the Seigneury to the Consistory.
[32] and
[33] and then to make them along with others

so elected that there be some in every quarter of the city, to keep an eye on everybody.[34]

The best way of electing them seems to be this, that[35] the Little Council suggest the nomination of the best that can be found and the most suitable; and to do this, summon the ministers to confer with them; after this they should present those whom they would commend to the Council of Two Hundred, which will approve them. If it find them worthy,[36] let them take the special oath, whose form will be readily drawn up.[37] And at the end of the year, let them present themselves to the Seigneury for consideration whether they[38] ought to be continued or changed. It is inexpedient that they be changed often without cause, so long as they discharge their duty faithfully.

The fourth order of ecclesiastical government, that is, the Deacons

There were always two kinds in the ancient Church, the one deputed to receive, dispense and hold goods for the poor, not only daily alms, but also possessions, rents and pensions; the other to tend and care for the sick and administer allowances to the poor. This custom we follow again now[39] for we have procurators and hospitallers.[40]

The[41] number of procurators appointed for this hospital seems to us to be proper; but we wish that there be also a separate reception office, so that not only provisions be in time made better, but that those who wish to do some charity may be more certain that the gift will not be employed otherwise than they intend. And if the revenue assigned by their Lordships be insufficient, or should extraordinary necessity arise, the Seigneury will advise about adjustment, according to the need they see.

The election of both procurators and hospitallers is to take

---

[34] Add: what we wish to be done.

[35] Similarly, we have determined that the method of electing them will be such that

[36] Add: after being approved   [37] will be drawn up as for ministers.

[38] that it be considered whether they ought to be continued or changed.

[39] *de* is replaced by *a*

[40] And in order to avoid confusion, for we have procurators and hospitallers, one of the four procurators is to be receptionist at the said hospital for all its goods, and is to have a suitable wage, in order that he discharge his office properly.

[41] The number of four procurators is to remain as it is, of whom one will have charge of reception, as has been said, so that the

---

place like that of the elders; and in electing them the rule proposed by Paul for deacons is to be followed.[42]

With regard to the office[43] of procurator, we think the rules which have already been imposed on them by us are good, by means of which, in urgent affairs, and where there is danger in deferment, and chiefly when there is no grave difficulty or question of great expense, they are not obliged always to be meeting, but one or two can do what is reasonable in the absence of the others.

It will be their duty to watch[44] diligently that the public hospital is well maintained, and that this be so both for the sick and the old people unable to work,[45] widowed women, orphaned children and other poor creatures. The sick are always to be lodged[46] in a set of rooms separate from the other people who are unable to work, old men, widowed women, orphaned children and the other poor.

Moreover, care for the poor dispersed through the city should be revived, as the procurators may arrange it.

Moreover, besides the hospital for those passing through which must be maintained, there should be some attention given to any recognized as worthy of special charity. For this purpose, a special room should be set aside to receive those who ought to be assisted by the procurators, which is to be reserved for this business.

It should above all be demanded that the families of the hospitallers be honourably ruled in accordance with the will of God, since they have to govern houses[47] dedicated to God.

The ministers[48] must on their side enquire whether there be any lack or want of anything, in order to ask and desire the Seigneury to put it in order. To do this, some[49] of their company with the procurators should visit the hospital every three months, to ascertain if all is in order.

It would be good,[50] not only for the poor of the hospital, but also for those of the city who cannot help themselves, that[51] they have a doctor and a surgeon of their own[52] who should still practise in the city, but meanwhile be required to have care of the hospital and to visit the other poor.

---

[42] I Tim. 3; Tit. 1.   [43] and authority of the procurators, we affirm

[44] *beiller* of the original is corrected to *veiller*.

[45] moreover widowed women   [46] They are always to be lodged

[47] a house dedicated

[48] and the assistants or elders with one of the Lords Syndic

[49] certain   [50] It should also be   [51] that there be

[52] at the expense of the city

Christmas, in such a way that it be not repeated in the parish in the month when it should take place by turn.

The ministers are to distribute the bread in proper order and with reverence; and none are to give the chalice except the colleagues or deacons with the ministers. Hence there should not be a large number of vessels.

The tables should be beside the pulpit in order that the mystery be more [59] conveniently set forth beside the tables.

It should be celebrated in the church at the most fitting time.

The Sunday before the celebration, intimation is to be made, in order that no child come before it has made profession[60] of its faith as proved by examination by the Catechism, and also that all strangers and new-comers may be exhorted first to come and present themselves at the church, so that they be instructed and thus none approach to his own condemnation.

Of Marriage

After the announcement of the customary banns, the marriage ceremony is to take place as the parties require, whether Sunday or working day, provided it be at the beginning of Service. It is proper that one abstain from this on the day when the Supper is to be celebrated, in honour of the sacrament.

It will be good to introduce ecclesiastical songs, the better to incite the people to prayer and to praise God.

To begin with, little children are to be instructed; then in time all the Church will be able to follow.

With regard to differences in matrimonial cases, because it is not a spiritual matter but involved with civil affairs,[61] we remit these to their Lordships, desiring them nevertheless to be willing to set up a Consistory without delay to judge in such matters, to which, if it seem good to them, there could be joined some ministers as counsellors. Above all may it please them to appoint men to make ordinances which may be followed forthwith.

[59] better and more conveniently
[60] the profession
[61] it will remain the business of the Seigneury. Nevertheless we have advised leaving to the Consistory the duty of hearing the parties, in order to report their advice to the Council. For assessing judgment, proper ordinances are to be set up, which will be followed henceforward.

Of Burial

The dead are to be buried decently in the place appointed. The attendance and company are left to each man's discretion.

It will be good[62] that the carriers be warned by us[63] to discourage all superstitions contrary to the Word of God, not to do duty at too late an hour, and to make a report in the case of sudden death, in order to obviate all inconvenience that might thereby arise.

Moreover they are to do duty not earlier than twelve hours after death, and not later than twenty-four.

Of the Visitation of the Sick

There are many people negligent in comforting themselves in God by his Word when they are afflicted with sickness, and so many die without the admonition or teaching which is more salutary for a man then than at any other time. It will be good [64] therefore that their Lordships ordain and make public that no one is to be totally confined to bed for three days without informing the minister, and that each be advised to call the ministers when they desire it in good time, in order that they be not diverted from the office which they publicly discharge in the Church.[65] Above all it is to be commanded that parents, friends and attendants do not wait until the patient is about to die, for in this extremity consolation is in most cases hardly useful.

Of the Visitation of Prisoners

It will be good that their Lordships ordain[66] a certain day each week on which admonition be given to prisoners, to reprove and exhort them; and if it seem good to them, [67] let them depute someone of their company in order that no fraud be committed. If they have anyone [68] in irons, whom it is not desir-

---

[62] we have further advised and ordained   [63] before the Seigneury
[64] For this cause we have advised and ordained that none but
[65] Add: And to avoid all excuses, we have resolved that it be so.
[66] Further we have ordained
[67] And two of the Gentlemen of the Council are to be deputed to assist, in order that there be committed
[68] And if there be anyone in irons

able to take out, if it seems good to them,[69] they could give entry to some minister to console him in their presence as above. For if one waits until they are about to die, they are often so preoccupied with fear of death, that they can neither receive nor listen. The day for doing this, it is decided, will be Saturday after dinner.

The Order to be observed in the case of little Children

All citizens and inhabitants are to bring or convey their children on Sundays at midday to Catechism, of which something has been said.

A definite formulary is to be composed by which they will be instructed, and on this, with the teaching given them, they are to be interrogated about what has been said, to see if they have listened and remembered well.

When a child has been well enough instructed to pass the Catechism, he is to recite solemnly the sum of what it contains, and also[70] to make profession of his Christianity in the presence of the Church.

Before this is done, no child is to be admitted to receive the Supper; and parents are to be informed not to bring them before this time. For it is a very perilous thing, for children as for parents, to introduce them without good and adequate instruction; for which purpose this order is to be used.

In order that there be no mistake, let it be ordained that children who come to school assemble there before twelve o'clock, and that the masters conduct them in good order in each parish.

The fathers are to bring the others or have them conducted. In order that there be the less confusion, the distinction of parishes in this connection is to be observed as far as possible, as has been said above concerning the sacraments.

Those who contravene these regulations are to be called before the company of the elders,[71] and, if they will not yield to good advice, they must be reported to their Lordships.[72]

To advise who do their duty and who do not, elders[73] are to keep an eye over all to give warning.

[69] when it seem good to the Council, it could   [70] and so
[71] or assistants if they do not wish
[72] let report be made to the Seigneury.
[73] the assistants above mentioned

Of the Order which is to be observed in the case of those in authority, for the maintenance of supervision in the Church

The elders,[74] as already said, are to assemble once a week with the ministers, that is to say on Thursday morning, to see that there be no disorder in [75] the Church and to discuss together remedies as they are required.

Because they have no compulsive authority or jurisdiction, may it please their Lordships,[76] to give them one of their [77] officials to summon those whom they wish to admonish.

If anyone refuse with contempt to comply, their office will be to inform their Lordships,[78] in order that remedy be applied.

There follows the list of persons whom the elders ought to admonish, and how one is to proceed.

If there be anyone who dogmatizes against the received doctrine, conference is to be held with him. If he listen to reason, he is to be dismissed without scandal or dishonour. If he be opinionative, he is to be admonished several times, until it is seen that measures of greater severity are needed. Then he is to be interdicted from the communion of the Supper and reported to the magistrate.

If anyone is negligent in coming to church, so that a noticeable contempt of the communion of the faithful is evident, or if any show himself contemptuous of the ecclesiastical order, he is to be admonished, and if he prove obedient dismissed in friendliness. If he persevere in his evil way, after being three times admonished, he is to be separated from the Church and reported.[79]

As for each man's conduct, for the correction of faults, proceedings should be in accordance with the order which our Lord commands.

Secret vices are to be secretly admonished; no one is to bring his neighbour before the Church to accuse him of faults that are not in the least notorious or scandalous, unless after having found him contumacious.

For the rest, those who despise particular admonitions by their neighbour are to be admonished anew by the Church; and if they will not at all come to reason or acknowledge their fault

[74] the assistants above mentioned
[76] we have advised
[78] the Council

[75] to the Church
[77] our officers
[79] to the Seigneury.

when convicted of it, they will be informed that they must [80] abstain from the Supper until such time as they return in [81] a better frame of mind.

As for vices notorious and public which the Church cannot dissimulate, if they are faults that merit admonition only, the duty of the elders [82] will be to summon those who are implicated to make friendly remonstrance to them in order that they make correction, and, if amendment is evident, to do them no harm. If they persevere in doing wrong, they are to be admonished repeatedly; and if even then there is no result, they are to be informed that, as despisers of God, they must abstain from the Supper until a change of life is seen in them.

As for crimes which merit not merely remonstrance in words but correction by chastisement, should any fall into them, according to the needs of the case, he must be warned that he abstain for some time from the Supper, to humble himself before God and to acknowledge [83] his fault the better.

If any in contumacy or rebellion wish to intrude against the prohibition, the duty of the minister is to turn him back, since it is not permissible for him to be received at the Communion.

Yet all this should be done with such moderation, that there be no rigour by which anyone may be injured; for even the corrections are only medicines for bringing back sinners to our Lord. [84]

These regulations are to be not only for the city but also for the villages dependent upon the Seigneury.

Form of Oath prescribed for Ministers, July 17, 1542[85]

The form and fashion of oath and promise which ministers of the gospel, admitted and received in the city of Geneva, are

[80] that they because of it must
[81] to
[82] of the assistants of the elders
[83] know
[84] additional article: All this is to take place in such a way that the ministers have no civil jurisdiction, nor use anything but the spiritual sword of the Word of God, as Paul commands them; nor is the Consistory to derogate from the authority of the Seigneury or ordinary justice. The civil power is to remain unimpaired. Even where there will be need to impose punishment or to constrain parties, the ministers with the Consistory having heard the parties and used such remonstrances and admonitions as are good, are to report the whole matter to the Council, which in their turn will advise sentence and judgment according to the needs of the case.
[85] C.R. comments as follows: "The draft proposed by the ministers in September 1541, in demanding that the pastor elected and accepted should take oath before the Seigneury, contented itself with saying that

to make before the Lord Syndic and Council of the said city runs as follows:

I promise and swear that in the ministry to which I am called I will serve faithfully before God, setting forth purely his Word for the edification of this Church to which he has bound me; that I will in no way abuse his doctrine to serve my carnal affections nor to please any living man; but that I will employ it with pure conscience in the service of his glory and for the profit of his people to which I am debtor.

I promise also and swear to defend the Ecclesiastical Ordinances as they are approved by the Little, the Great and the General Councils of this City, and, in the measure in which I am given charge of administering those that have come short, to acquit myself loyally, without giving place to hatred, or favour, or vengeance, or any other carnal feeling, and in general to do what is proper to a good and faithful minister.

Thirdly, I swear and promise to guard and maintain the honour and welfare of the Seigneury and the City, to take pains, so far as is possible for me, that the people continue in beneficial peace and unity under the government of the Seigneury, and to consent in no wise to those who would violate it.

Finally, I promise and swear to be subject to the polity and constitution of this City, to show a good example of obedience to all others, being for my part subject to the laws and the magistracy, so far as my office allows; that is to say without prejudice to the liberty which we must have to teach according to what God commands us and to do the things which pertain to our office. And in conclusion, I promise to serve the Seigneury and the people in such wise, so long as I be not at all hindered from rendering to God the service which in my vocation I owe him.

'there would be a written form, suitable to what is required of a minister.' But the Ordinances as published on November 20 of the same year did not even give this reference: they only spoke as before of it being inserted at the place indicated. Apparently the revision continued to be cautious, as is expressly said of the oath to be exacted from members of the Consistory, whose imposition was decreed. 'They are to take a specific oath whose form will be readily drawn up,' says the draft; 'whose form will be drawn up as for the ministers' says the official text'' (X/1, 31).

The document here, by the change it suffered on revision, is proved to be the Draft presented by Calvin to the Little Council.

Draft Order of Visitation of the Country Churches

INTRODUCTION

THE ORDINANCES OF 1541 ALREADY CONTAIN CERtain articles intended to guarantee unity and discipline among the ministers of the city and territory of the republic, by means of periodical reunions, of which one object among others would be the exercise of mutual censure. But the organization of the parishes in the country appears to have been inadequately based at first. This is evident from the Registers of the Council of May 1544.

The conversations of this date, however, appear to have led to no happy results. The document given here bears the date January 11, 1546 and shows that at this time the reformer realized the need for drawing up a new draft for organizing a regular inspection of the country churches, in order to ensure the maintenance of good order and the supervision of ministers in the exercise of their functions, as well as of the congregations in the discharge of their religious duties. Calvin presented his draft to the meeting of the Council on January 25, 1546 when it was adopted. The Register of the Venerable Company reports the introduction of these visitations in these terms: "In the month of (? January) 1546, it was resolved by the brethren met in general assembly, that henceforth visitations be made of all the parishes of the Church of Geneva. It was also agreed by those present, and ordained, that two counsellors should also go with the ministers to visit the local lords, so that the minister on his side might make enquiry concerning the doctrine and life of the pastor of the place and the counsellors of the life of the squire." This rule later found a place in the Ordinances of 1561. (From *C.R.* X/1, 45 f.)

Draft Order of Visitation of the
Country Churches
January 11, 1546

First, in order to maintain proper uniformity of doctrine in the whole body of the Church of Geneva, that is to say in the city and also in the parishes dependent on the Seigneury, the Magistracy is to elect two of their Lordships of the Council and similarly the Ministers two of their Congregation, who will be charged with going once a year to visit each parish, to enquire whether the Ministry of the place have accepted any doctrine in any sense new and repugnant to the purity of the gospel.

Second, this Visitation is to enquire whether the Minister preaches edifyingly, or whether there be anything at all scandalous, or unfitting to the instruction of the people because it is obscure, or treats of superfluous questions, or exercises too great rigour, or some similar fault.

Third, to exhort the people to attendance at Service, to have a liking for it, and to find profit in it for Christian living; and to expound what is the office of the Ministry, in order that they understand how they ought to discharge it.

Fourth, to know whether the Minister is diligent not only in preaching but also in visiting the sick, and particularly in admonishing those that need it, and to prevent anything that might be for the dishonour of God.

Fifth, to discover whether he lead an honest life, and show a good example, or if he commit any dissoluteness or frivolity which renders him contemptible, or if he get on well with his people and likewise with all his family.

The Method of Visitation

The Minister deputed for this office, after preaching and admonishing the people as said above, is to enquire of the

74

Guardians and the Procurators of the Parish concerning both the doctrine and the life of their Minister; and likewise concerning his diligence and method of instruction, praying them in the name of God to allow nothing to be concealed that impedes the honour of God, the advancement of his Word, and the welfare of all.

According to what he discovers, he is publicly to inform the congregation of it, so that, if there be any fault in a brother, of which there is no question that it merit greater correction than by the Word, he be admonished according to custom. If there be any graver offence, which cannot at all be tolerated, procedure is to be in accordance with the articles which are approved; that is, the four deputies to report the business to us, in order that things proceed fittingly.

This Visitation is not to take hearing of any case nor to dispense any jurisdiction. It is to be only a remedy for obviating any scandals, and especially for seeing that the Ministers become neither degenerate nor corrupt.

Nor is it to impede at all the course of justice, nor is it to exempt Ministers from common subjection to justice, so that they be not answerable in civil causes as individuals before ordinary justice; or not personally interrogated about crimes, or not punished when they have offended. In short, their status is to remain for the future what it is at present.

Such has always been the order in the ancient Church from the time of the apostles; and today is observed in the Churches reformed according to the pure doctrine of the gospel.

We Syndics and Council of Geneva, etc., having seen and heard the Ordinances above written: they are now by us ordered and ordained to be observed and to come into effect. Made and approved in our ordinary Council, the 11th of January, the year of our Lord one thousand five hundred and forty six.

The aforesaid Lords Syndic and Council.

The Ordinances for the Supervision of Churches in the Country

INTRODUCTION

THE LAST PARAGRAPH OF THE ARTICLES OF 1541 stated that the regulations were to be applied to the villages dependent on the Seigneury. But the introduction and exercise of the rules encountered difficulties in the parishes outside the city, and need was felt to ensure good order and the application of the principles of the Reformation by a code specially designed for the state of mind and custom among the people of the country. Calvin, in collaboration with the other Ministers his colleagues, provided for this towards the end of 1546, as is explained in the preamble found at the top of the copy of the draft Ordinances inserted in the Registers of the Venerable Company in the following terms:

"On Friday the 17th day of December 1546, it was represented to us by the Ministers of the Church of Geneva, being met in general assembly, that it would be a useful thing forthwith to set down the deliberations, intimations, ordinances and other matters worth remembering concerning the state and condition of the Church, to give it timely local help. And it was resolved that to do it one of the Ministers should record this. The same day certain ordinances were proposed concerning the reformation of the village parishes. These were found to be good and useful, and it was agreed that they be presented to their Lordships, as they were drawn up as much at their counsel and demand. These then were passed by them and declared in the Council on the 3rd day of February 1547; and then also passed to the Two Hundred."

It was on May 17, 1547, that the draft was thus publicly adopted. It was not inserted into the 1561 edition of the Ordinances. (From *C.R.* X/1, 51.)

Ordinances for the Supervision of Churches in the Country

February 3, 1547

Ordinances for the Supervision of the Churches dependent on the Seigneury of Geneva, which it is advised be put in force, subject to the complete discretion of their Lordships

SERMONS

1. Everyone in each house is to come on Sundays, unless it be necessary to leave someone behind to take care of children or animals, under penalty of 3 sous.

2. If there be preaching any weekday, arranged with due notice, those that are able to go and have no legitimate excuse are to attend, at least one from each house, under penalty as above.

3. Those who have man or maid servants, are to bring them or have them conveyed when possible, so that they do not live like cattle without instruction.

4. Everyone is to be present at Sermon when the prayer is begun, under penalty as above, unless he absent himself for legitimate reason.

5. Everyone is to pay attention during Sermon, and there is to be no disorder or scandal.

6. No one is to leave or go out from the church until the prayer be made at the end of Sermon, under penalty as above, unless he have legitimate cause.

CATECHISM

1. Because each preacher has two parishes, Catechism is to take place each fortnight. Those who have children are to bring them, with the rest of their household who have not been to Sermon, as above.

2. The same attention, honest and regular, is to be given to Catechism as has been said for Sermon.

PENALTIES

1. Those who fail in their duty of coming are to be admonished by the Guardians, both themselves and their family.

2. If after intimation they continue to default, they are to be fined three groats, for each time. Of this one third will be applied to the Guardians; the other two thirds will be applied to the poor of the parish, and put into the funds of the Church for distribution according to need as it becomes known.

3. If anyone come after Sermon has begun, he is to be admonished, and if after this is done he does not amend, for each fault he is to be fined three sous, which will be applied as above.

4. If during Sermon anyone make any disturbance or scandal, he is to be reported to the Consistory to be cautioned, in order that procedure be in proportion to the fault; that is, if by carelessness he is to be well told off, if it happen by intended malice or rebelliousness he is to be reported to their Lordships to be punished appropriately.

BY WHOM FINES ARE TO BE EXACTED

1. The local lord, in conjunction with the Ministers and the Guardians, is to oblige the delinquents to pay the fines they have incurred, when they will not pay of their own free will. Legitimate excuses are to be admitted, but this is to be done without any formal procedure.

2. If there be any so rebellious that, despite the above fines, they do not at all amend, they are to be reported to the Consistory with advice to the effect that their Lordships punish them according to the seriousness of their obstinacy.

3. Fathers are to be responsible for their children, and, if there be a penalty, it is to be exacted from them.

OF BAPTISM

1. Baptism is to be administered any day, provided that there be Sermon along with it. The Ministers are always to exhort the people to link it up with the Catechism.

2. Children are to be brought at the beginning of Catechism or Sermon.

3. Fathers are to be present, unless they have legitimate excuse of which cognizance will be taken by the Consistory.

4. No godfather is to be admitted for presenting a child, unless he is of an age to make such a promise; that is, he must have passed fifteen years, be of the same confession as ourselves, and be duly instructed.

5. As to names, let their Lordships' ordinances be careful both to avoid all superstition and idolatry and to remove from the Church of God everything foolish and indecent.

6. If midwives usurp the office of Baptism, they are to be reproved or chastised according to the measure of fault found, since no commission is given them in this matter, under penalty of being put on bread and water for three days and fined ten sous; and all who consent to their action or conceal it will be liable to the same penalty.

Of the Supper

1. No one is to be received at the Supper unless he first have made confession of his faith. That is to say, he must declare before the Minister that he desires to live according to the reformation of the gospel, and that he knows the Creed, the Lord's Prayer and the Commandments of God.

2. Those who wish to receive the Supper are to come at the beginning of the Service; those who come at the end are not to be received.

3. Other impediments are to be within the cognizance of the Consistory, to deal with them, in accordance with what has been ordained.

4. All are to remain until the end, unless there be a legitimate excuse which is recognized as above.

Of Times of Meeting at Church

Buildings are to remain shut for the rest of the time, in order that no one outside the hours may enter for superstitious reasons. If anyone be found making any particular devotion inside or nearby, he is to be admonished: if it appear to be a superstition which he will not amend, he is to be chastised.

Faults Contravening the Reformation besides those already Mentioned

First, Superstitions

1. Those found to have any paternosters or idols for adoration are to be brought before the Consistory, and, besides the

punishment imposed on them there, they are to be brought before their Lordships.

2. Those who have been on pilgrimages or voyages the same.

3. Those who observe the papistical feasts or fastings are to be admonished only, unless they are obstinate in their rebellion.

4. Those who have attended mass, besides admonition, are to be brought before their Lordships.

5. In such cases, their Lordships will have the right of chastising by means of prison or otherwise, or of punishing by extraordinary fines, at their discretion.

In the case of fines, they are to apply some small portion of them to the Guardians, if the delict was notified by them.

Blasphemies

1. Those who have blasphemed, swearing by the body or by the blood of our Lord, or suchlike, ought to do reverence[1] for the first time; for the second a penalty of five sous; for the third ten sous; and for the last time put in the pillory for an hour.

2. Anyone who abjures or renounces God or his Baptism is for the first time to be put for ten days on bread and water; for the second and third time he is to be punished with some more rigorous corporal punishment, at the discretion of their Lordships.

Contradiction of the Word

1. If there are any who contradict the Word of God, let them be brought before the Consistory to be admonished, or be remanded to their Lordships to receive chastisement according to the needs of the case.

2. If the contradiction or rebellion amount to scandal which demands prompter remedy, the local lord is to take a hand in the matter for the maintenance of the honour of the Ministry and the Magistracy.

---

[1] The original has *baisser terre*, given alternatively as *donnera baiser terre*. The phrase is rather obscure. Huguet's *Dictionnaire de la Langue Française du Seizième Siècle* (Paris 1925) says that it refers to "une pratique habituelle des soldats qui allaient engager le combat, ou une forme d'hommage à quelqu'un" (following Plattard in *Revue des Études rabelesiennes* VII. 449), which perhaps has Old Testament associations (Sainéau in the same Revue, x. 258).

Drunkenness

1. There is to be no treating of one another to drinks, under penalty of three sous.

2. The taverns are to be closed during Service, under penalty that the taverner pay three sous and anyone entering them the same.

3. If anyone be found drunk, he is to pay for the first time three sous and be brought before the Consistory; the second time he must pay the sum of five sous; and the third ten sous and be put in prison.

4. There are to be no carousals, under penalty of ten sous.

Songs and Dances

If anyone sing songs that are unworthy, dissolute or outrageous, or spin wildly round in the dance, or the like, he is to be imprisoned for three days, and then sent on to the Consistory.

Usury

No one is to lend at interest or for profit greater than five per cent, on pain of confiscation of the capital sum and of being required to make appropriate amends according to the needs of the case.

Brawling

1. No one is to cause noise or dispute on pain of being punished according to the needs of the case.

2. If there be any who causes sedition or assembling to make or support quarrels, he is to be punished with more rigorous penalties according to what he merits.

Complaints

If there be a complaint or dispute between two people, the Minister, summoning the Guardians, will do his duty to bring them to accord; and if he is unable to prevail, he will remand them to the Consistory.

Games

No one is to play at games that are dissolute, or at games played for gold or silver or at excessive expense, on pain of five sous and loss of the sum staked.

Fornication

1. As to those who are caught in fornication, if it be an unmarried man with an unmarried woman, they are to be imprisoned for six days on bread and water, and pay sixty sous amends.

2. If it be adultery, one or the other being married, they are to be imprisoned for nine days on bread and water, and pay amends at the discretion of their Lordships, as the crime is much more grave.

3. Those who are promised in marriage are not to cohabit as man and wife until the marriage be celebrated in church, otherwise they will be punished as for fornication.

OF THE ELECTION OF GUARDIANS

The local lord assembling the more responsible and better part of the parishioners, and duly advising them, election of Guardians is to take place before them. They are to be men of substance and fearing God. He then brings the said Guardians to the Consistory, to be instructed in their office, and from there they will be brought before their Lordships to take the oath.

FOR REMANDING TO THE CONSISTORY

The decision of the Minister and the Guardians or of one of them, the local lord, or in his absence one of the assistants, may remand delinquents to the Consistory.

On May 16, 1547, the above Ordinances were read, and then approved and accepted; and it is further declared that the penalties for offences are to be applied in part to the Guardians of the parishes, in part to the local lord and the municipal council, and in part to the poor of the parish and district.

> By command of their Lordships,
> the Syndics and Council of Geneva.

The Catechism of the Church of Geneva

INTRODUCTION

INTERNAL EVIDENCE CONTAINED IN THE PREFACE yields some information about this famous document. It appears from here that it is a *Catechismus posterior*. The *Catechismus prior* bears no certain date in either its French or its Latin edition. At all events it was not long used in Geneva. On his return to the city from exile, Calvin published another in answer to the expressed desire of many people. After giving the reasons for his publication of this new Catechism in the Latin language, the preface goes on to refer to the earlier one, published seven years previously. Of this it appears there had been only one edition, and Calvin mentions his fear that it might be quite lost to sight, and this he will if possible avoid. This purpose he achieves, not by reissuing this earlier Catechism, but by turning into Latin a later work "which he preferred." It is impossible to think that this later preferred work translated into Latin by Calvin was not his own, and it is therefore to be concluded that he himself is the author of both a French and a Latin edition of the Catechism.

The French edition is then the earlier. The translation given here is based upon the Latin or later edition, upon the ground that, though the differences between the two are inconsiderable, the Latin embodies Calvin's amendments upon the earlier document. *C.R.* incorporates both editions συνοπτικῶς. In the translation here given, the Scripture references are added out of the French edition. Further, from the French is also borrowed, and appended in the note which follows this, the Sunday by Sunday scheme of instruction.

The Catechism is thrown by Calvin into the form of Question and Answer. Luther in his Shorter (though not in his Larger)

83

Catechism had resuscitated this form from the dissuetude into which it had lapsed, and it so proved its usefulness that it was widely adopted and is still employed up to the present day. It can hardly be maintained that Calvin entirely avoided all the disadvantages that such a form imposes. By the time the Westminster Confession of Faith came to be written, for example, the form has acquired crispness and direction, and really does have the character of an interrogation or even examination. In the work before us, there is more of the character of dialogue between Minister and Child. Many of the queries of the Minister are unashamedly "leading questions"; and at many points the Minister supplies as much to the substance of the doctrine as does the pupil under interrogation. Indeed, on occasion it almost appears that the roles of Minister and Child are transposed. For example, on page 109, to the extended comment of the Minister concerning the prohibition upon worshipping God in images, the Child replies: *Verum*, which is not unjustly translated: Quite right!

But no minor blemishes of this order can take away from the excellence and the clarity with which the Catechism expounds the contents of the Christian faith. (See *C.R.* VI, ix.)

To facilitate use of the Catechism and enable it to be more easily committed to memory, the French text carries footnotes which divide the whole into the work assigned to 55 Sundays. The division supplies a useful summary of the contents of the Catechism, and is as follows:

1st Sunday: The end of our life; the sovereign good of men; the manner of rightly honouring God in four heads.

2nd Sunday: The first point in honouring God is to trust in him; ground for having confidence; the Apostles' Creed.

3rd Sunday: Fourfold division; concerning the Trinity; the first part; the Father; the significance of the power of God; the power of God not otiose.

4th Sunday: A mirror for the contemplation of God; of the providence of God; devils; the devil able to do nothing without God.

5th Sunday: Jesus Christ; what the title Christ means; the Kingdom of Christ; the Priesthood of Christ; Christ as Prophet.

6th Sunday: Christ the fountain of all good; how the Kingdom of Christ concerns us; the Priesthood of Christ; the Prophetic function of Christ.

7th Sunday: Christ the only Son of God; anointing of Christ; Christ true man; recovery in Christ of what we lack; Christ conceived by the Spirit.

8th Sunday: Christ our Lord; Jesus Christ condemned to absolve us; Christ condemned for us; Christ our pledge.

9th Sunday: Jesus Christ subjected to curse to deliver us; Christ enduring death which he vanquished; death of the faithful the passage to life.

10th Sunday: Descent of Christ into hell; torment of Christ and of sinners, how they differ.

11th Sunday: The fruit and virtue of the death of Jesus Christ contained in three heads; the first, the benefit of the resurrection.

12th Sunday: Christ ascended to heaven; the benefit of the ascension in two heads; seated on the right hand of God.

13th Sunday: Christ our Judge and Advocate.

14th Sunday: Part 3—concerning the Holy Spirit and his gifts.

15th Sunday: Part 4—the Church; what the Church is; fruit of the death of Christ; meaning of catholic; the communion of the faithful.

16th Sunday: The Church still imperfect; of the remission of sins; remission of sins not without the Church.

17th Sunday: The resurrection.

18th Sunday: What true faith is; the Holy Spirit illumines us; it is faith that justifies us.

19th Sunday: All human works before regeneration to be condemned.

20th Sunday: Of good works done by faith; how to make works acceptable to God; true faith never otiose; meaning of belief in Jesus Christ; faith and repentance.

21st Sunday: What repentance is; the true service of God; the law; the two parts of the law; exposition of the first table.

22nd Sunday: The first commandment; deliverance from Egypt; sum of the first commandment; the honour due to God.

23rd Sunday: The second commandment; images and their adoration; adoration addressed to images; what painting is forbidden.

24th Sunday: Spiritual uncleanness; how God punishes the children for the sake of their fathers; mercy on a thousand generations.

25th Sunday: The third commandment; concerning oaths; the honour of the name of God.

26th Sunday: The fourth commandment; three reasons why rest is instituted; the number seven.

27th Sunday: Meditation on the works of God to be continual; the institution of days.

28th Sunday: The fifth commandment; what is honour to

father and mother; long life; earthly goods conditional; punishment of disobedient children.

29th Sunday: The sixth commandment; the seventh commandment; all uncleanness condemned; nature of the Lawgiver.

30th Sunday: The eighth commandment; theft; internal theft; the ninth commandment; general doctrine concerning swearing.

31st Sunday: The tenth commandment; all temptation is wrong; the sum of the law; to love God with all the heart, etc.

32nd Sunday: What is meant by neighbour; no one without guilt before the law.

33rd Sunday: The office of the law; obedience to the law.

34th Sunday: The third head in the true honouring of God; invocation of the saints; sign of infidelity.

35th Sunday: Prayer to be from the heart.

36th Sunday: Prayer to be made with sure confidence; prayer to be made only in the name of Christ.

37th Sunday: The Christian prayer which our Lord taught us; division of the dominical prayer.

38th Sunday: Meaning of the word *Father* applied to God; of *our*.

39th Sunday: The first petition; how the name of God is hallowed; the second petition; in what consists the Kingdom of Christ; the Kingdom of Christ perfected.

40th Sunday: The third petition; that the will of God be done; renewal; will of God done in heaven.

41st Sunday: The fourth petition: what it means to ask daily bread; God blesses work; daily bread.

42nd Sunday: The fifth petition; there is no one so holy that he does not need God to pardon him; what is remission of sins; fruit of the remission of sins; pardon of faults is gratuitous; disowning as children of God.

43rd Sunday: The sixth petition; temptation.

44th Sunday: The fourth part of the true honouring of God.

45th Sunday: Salvation offered us by the Word of God; pains to be taken to apprehend; of Pastors of the Church.

46th Sunday: Of the sacraments: the sacraments are given for our infirmity.

47th Sunday: The sacraments are necessary; effect of the sacraments; seeking Jesus Christ in the sacraments; increase of faith by the sacraments; imperfection of the children of God.

48th Sunday: Number of the sacraments; Baptism and the Supper; of Baptism; meaning of Baptism.

49th Sunday: The water of Baptism; why the water is poured on the head; the blood of Christ is our laver, not the water; truth joined with symbol; its virtue lies in regeneration; practice of Baptism.

50th Sunday: Of the Baptism of little children; promises of the people of Israel extended to all the world; on what condition infants are to be baptized.

51st Sunday: Of the Supper; Christ by the bread represents his body, and by the wine his blood; in what confidence of our salvation consists; how we receive Jesus Christ.

52nd Sunday: What we have by the sign of bread; what we have by the sign of wine; that the Supper is not sacrifice; Christ the alone eternal sacrificer.

53rd Sunday: The sign double because of our infirmity; the reality accompanies the symbol; what must be done to have the reality of the sacrament; pledge of the resurrection.

54th Sunday: Sign of being member of Christ; why Baptism is received once, and the Supper oftener.

55th Sunday: To whom belongs the administration of Baptism and of the Supper; to whom the Supper is to be barred; why Judas was received at the Supper.

The Catechism of the Church of Geneva
that is
a Plan for Instructing Children
in the Doctrine of Christ

LETTER TO THE READER

It has always been a practice and diligent care of the Church,
that children be rightly brought up in Christian doctrine. To
do this more conveniently, not only were schools formerly
opened and individuals enjoined to teach their families properly, but also it was accepted public custom and practice to
examine children in the Churches concerning the specific
points which should be common and familiar to all Christians.
That this be done in order, a formula was written out, called
Catechism or Institute. After this, the devil, miserably rending
the Church of God and bringing upon it his fearful destruction
(of which the marks are all too evident in most parts of the
world), subverted this sacred policy; nor did he leave surviving
anything more than certain trivialities, which give rise only
to superstitions, without any edifying fruit. Of this kind is that
Confirmation, as they call it, made up of gesticulations which
are more than ridiculous and suited rather to monkeys, and rest
on no foundation. What we now bring forward, therefore, is
nothing else than the use of a practice formerly observed by
Christians and the true worshippers of God, and never neglected
until the Church was wholly corrupted.

JOHN CALVIN TO THE FAITHFUL MINISTERS OF CHRIST WHO
PREACH THE PURE DOCTRINE OF THE GOSPEL IN EAST FRIESLAND[1]

Since it is proper for us by every means to endeavour to make
that unity of faith shine forth among us which is so highly
commended by Paul, the solemn profession of faith which is
joined to our common Baptism ought to be directed chiefly to
this end. It might therefore be wished, not only that there exist

[1] *Sleumer's Kirchenlateinisches Wörterbuch* (Limburg-a-d-Lahn 1926) identifies
this with the modern Prussia or Hanover.

a perpetual consent by all in pious doctrine, but that there be also a single form of Catechism for all Churches. But since for many reasons it will hardly ever be otherwise than that each Church have its own Catechism, we should not too strenuously resist it; provided, however, that the variety in the kind of teaching be such that we are all directed to the one Christ, by whose truth, if we be united in it, we may grow together into one body and one spirit, and with one mouth also proclaim whatever belongs to the sum of the faith. Catechists who do not pursue this end, besides seriously injuring the Church by the dissemination of material of dissension in religion, introduce also an impious profanation of Baptism. For what further use is Baptism, unless this remain its foundation, that we all agree in one faith? Those who publicly bring out Catechisms ought therefore to be all the more diligently careful, lest by producing something rashly they do grave harm to piety and inflict a deadly wound upon the Church, not only for the present but also in posterity.

I wanted to say this by way of preface to testify to my readers that I also, as is right, have made it a first charge on my attention, not to transmit anything in this Catechism of mine that is not agreeable to the doctrine held by all the pious. This declaration of mine will not be found vain by those that bring candour and sound judgment to their reading. I trust I have succeeded so far that, even if it be not entirely satisfying, my work may be acceptable to all good men, so that it be considered useful by them.

I have written it in Latin, and, even if this decision perhaps does not commend itself to some, I had many reasons for it, though it would be unprofitable to refer to them all here. I shall select such as seem to be enough to obviate censure. First, in this confused and divided state of Christendom, I judge it useful to have public testimonies by which Churches, that agree in Christian doctrine though widely separated in space, may mutually recognize each other. For besides the fact that this contributes not a little to mutual confirmation, what is more desirable than that mutual congratulations should pass between them, and that they should devoutly commend each other to the Lord? To this end, while a consensus of faith still existed and flourished among all, bishops used once to send synodal letters across the sea, with which, as by tokens, they might establish sacred communion between the Churches. How much more necessary it is now, in the dreadful devastation of the Christian world, that those Churches, which worship God rightly, few and dispersed and hedged about by the profane synagogues of Antichrist as they are, should give and receive mutually this sign of holy fellowship, and thereby be incited to that fraternal embrace of which I have spoken? And if this be necessary for today, what are we to think of posterity? About it I am more anxious than I almost dare to think. For unless God give miraculous assistance from heaven, I cannot avoid thinking that the world is threatened with extreme barbarism. I could wish that our children do not shortly find this to be a true prophecy and no mere conjecture. All the more, then, must we labour to gather by our writings such remains of the Church as may persist or even emerge after our death. There are other kinds of writing to show what are our views in all matters of religion; but what agreement in doctrine our Churches had among themselves cannot be observed with clearer evidence than from the Catechisms. For in them there appears not only what someone or another once taught, but what were the rudiments with which both the learned and the unlearned among us were from youth constantly instructed, all the faithful holding them as the solemn symbol of Christian communion. This indeed was my chief reason for publishing this Catechism.

A second reason, however, carried not a little weight with me: that I heard that it was desired by a great many, who hoped it might not be unworthy of reading. Whether they were right or wrong is not for me to say; but it was a right thing to do as they wished. It was almost necessity that was laid upon me, and I could not rightly decline. For since, seven years earlier, there was edited by me a brief summary of religion under the name of Catechism, I feared, unless I anticipated by bringing this one forward, the other would be driven into the background; and this I did not wish. Hence consideration of the public good required me to take care that this one which I prefer should occupy the position. Besides I think it belongs to good example to testify to the world that we, who undertake the restitution of the Church, faithfully exert ourselves everywhere for the rightful return of the use of Catechism, abolished some centuries ago under the papacy. For this holy custom cannot be sufficiently commended for its usefulness: nor can the papists be sufficiently condemned for the flagrant corruption, because by turning it into puerile trifles they not only set it aside, but also basely misuse it as the occasion of impure and impious superstition. For they deck out that spurious Confirmation, which they have substituted in its place, like a harlot, with great splendour of ceremonies and splendid pomps without measure. They even, in wanting to adorn it, ornament it with execrable blasphemies, giving out that it is a sacrament of greater dignity than Baptism, and calling only half-Christians those that have not been besmeared with their rank oil. In fact the whole business consists in nothing but theatrical gesticulations, or rather the wanton sporting of monkeys, without even imitative skill.

To you, my very dear brothers in the Lord, I have chosen to dedicate this work, because some of your number, besides showing me that they love me and that the most part of them take pleasure in my writings, also expressly demanded in letters that I undertake it for their sake. For the rest, there was one just and sufficient reason: that I learned long since from the statement of serious and pious men things concerning you that bound me to you with my whole soul. Now I ask of you what I trust you will do of your own accord, that you take in good part this testimony of my good will towards you. Farewell. The Lord daily increase you more and more in the spirit of wisdom, prudence, zeal and fortitude, to the edification of his Church.

Geneva, November 27, 1545.

Concerning the Faith

Minister: What is the chief end of human life?

Child: That men should know God by whom they were created.

M: What reason have you for saying so?

C: Because he created us for this, and placed us in the world, that he might be glorified in us. And it is certainly proper that our life, of which he is the beginning, be directed to his glory.

M: What then is man's supreme good?

C: The very same.

M: Why do you hold this to be the supreme good?

C: Because without it our condition is more unhappy than that of any of the brutes.

M: So then we clearly perceive that nothing worse can happen to man than not to live to God?

C: It is so.

M: What then is true and right knowledge of God?

C: When he is so known, that his own proper honour is done him.

M: What is the right way of honouring him?

C: To put all our trust in him; to study to serve him all our life, by obeying his will; to call upon him, whenever any need impels us, seeking in him salvation and whatever good things can be desired; and lastly, to acknowledge him with both heart and mouth to be the only author of all good things.

M: Now to consider these things in order and explain them more fully—what is the first head in this division of yours?

C: That we place all our trust in God.

M: How is this done?

C: When we know him to be mighty and perfectly good.

M: Is this enough?

C: Far from it.

M: Why?

C: Because we are unworthy that he should exercise his power to help us, or for our salvation show us how good he is.

M: What then is needed further?

C: Just that each of us should affirm with his mind, that he is loved by him, and that he is willing to be his Father and the Author of his salvation.

M: Where will this be apparent to us?

C: In his Word, where he reveals his mercy to us in Christ, and testifies of his love towards us.

M: Then the foundation and beginning of faith in God is to know him in Christ? (John 17:3).

C: Quite so.

M: Now I would hear from you in a few words what the sum of this knowledge is.

C: It is contained in the confession of faith, or rather in the formula of confession, which all Christians hold in common. It is commonly called the Apostles' Creed, because from the beginning of the Church it was always received among all the pious, and because either it came from the lips of the apostles or was faithfully collected from their writings.

M: Repeat it.

C: I believe in God the Father Almighty, Maker of heaven and earth; and in Jesus Christ his only Son our Lord, who was conceived by the Holy Ghost, born of the Virgin Mary, suffered under Pontius Pilate, was crucified, dead and buried: He descended into hell; the third day he rose again from the dead, he ascended into heaven, and sitteth on the right hand of God the Father Almighty; from thence he shall come to judge the quick and the dead. I believe in the Holy Ghost; the Holy Catholic Church; the communion of saints; the resurrection of the body; and the life everlasting. Amen.

M: To understand the several points more thoroughly—into how many parts shall we divide this Confession?

C: Into four principal parts.

M: Name them to me.

C: The first refers to God the Father; the second concerns his Son Jesus Christ, and also includes the entire sum of man's redemption. The third part concerns the Holy Spirit; the fourth the Church and the divine benefits vouchsafed to it.

M: Since there is no God but one, why do you here mention three, Father, Son and Holy Spirit?

C: Because in the one essence of God it is proper to regard God as beginning and origin, the first cause of all things; then the Son, who is his eternal wisdom; and last the Holy Spirit, as his virtue diffused through all things, which yet perpetually resides in himself.

M: You mean that there is no absurdity if in one divinity we affirm these three persons, and that God is not thereby divided?

C: Just so.

M: Repeat the first part.

C: I believe in God the Father Almighty, Maker of heaven and earth.

M: Why do you call him Father?

C: Primarily with regard to Christ, who is his eternal wisdom, begotten of him before all time, and who, being sent into the world, was declared his Son. From this, however, we infer that, since God is the Father of Jesus Christ, he is also our Father.

M: In what sense do you accord him the attribute almighty?

C: That not only he has might he does not exercise; but that he has all things under his power and hand; so that he governs the world by his providence, constitutes all things by his will, and rules all creatures as seems to him good.

M: Then you do not suppose God's power to be inactive, but think it to be such that his hand is always engaged in working, so that nothing is done but through him and by his decree?

C: That is so.

M: Why do you add: Maker of heaven and earth?

C: Because he manifested himself to us through his works, and in them he is to be sought by us (Ps. 104; Rom. 1:20). For our mind is incapable of entertaining his essence. Therefore there is the world itself as a kind of mirror, in which we may observe him, in so far as it concerns us to know him.

M: By heaven and earth you understand, do you not, whatever creatures exist?

C: Yes, certainly: but in these two names are comprised all things, since they are either heavenly or earthly.

M: Why then do you call God merely creator, when it is much more excellent to defend and preserve creatures in their being, than once to have made them?

C: This term does not merely imply that God so created his works once that afterwards he took no care of them. Rather, it is to be held that the world, as it was once made by him, so now is preserved by him, and that similarly both the earth and all other things persist only in so far as they are sustained by his virtue and as it were his hand. Besides, since he has all things under his hand, it also follows from this that he is the supreme ruler and lord of all. Hence from his being Creator of heaven and earth, we are to understand that it is he only who with wisdom, goodness and power rules the whole course and order of nature; who is the author of both rain and drought, hail and other storms, as also of serenity; who fertilizes the earth of his beneficence, or again renders it sterile by withdrawing his hand; from him also both health and disease proceed; to whose power finally all things are subject and at whose nod they obey.

M: Now what shall we say of wicked men and devils? Shall we say that they too are subject to him?

C: Although he does not govern them by his Spirit, yet he checks them by his power, as with a bridle, so that they are unable even to move unless he permits them to do so. Further, he even makes them ministers of his will, so that they are forced, unwilling and against their inclination, to effect what seems good to him.

M: What benefit accrues to you from the knowledge of this?

C: Very much. For it would go ill with us, if anything were permitted wicked men and devils without the will of God; then our minds could never be tranquil, for thinking ourselves exposed to their pleasure. Only then do we safely rest when we know them to be curbed by the will of God and, as it were, held in confinement, so that they cannot do anything but by his permission, especially since God himself undertakes to be our guardian and the captain of our salvation.

M: Now let us come to the second part.

C: It is that we believe in Jesus Christ his only Son our Lord.

M: What is principally contained here?

C: That the Son of God is our Saviour; and at the same time is expounded the means by which he has redeemed us from death, and procured life.

M: What does the name Jesus which you apply to him mean?

C: It means what the Greeks meant by the word σωτήρ. In Latin there is no proper name which rightly expresses its force. Hence the term Saviour was commonly accepted. Moreover, the angel gave this name to the Son of God by the command of God himself (Matt. 1:21).

M: Does this mean more than if men had given it to him?

C: Certainly. For since God wished him to be thus named, it is necessary that he be so forthwith.

M: What force then has the name Christ?

C: By this epithet his office is even better expressed. For it signifies that he is anointed by his Father to be King, Priest and Prophet.

M: How do you know this?

C: Because Scripture applies anointing to these three uses; and also because it often attributes these three offices to Christ.

M: But with what kind of oil was he anointed?

C: Not with visible oil, such as was employed in the ancient anointings of kings, priests and prophets; but more excellently, that is by the grace of the Holy Spirit, which is the essence of that external anointing (Ps. 45).

M: But what kind of kingdom is it you mention?

C: A spiritual kingdom, contained in the Word and Spirit of God, which carry with them righteousness and life.

M: And the priesthood?

C: It is the office and prerogative of presenting oneself before the face of God to obtain grace, and of offering sacrifice, which may be acceptable to him, to appease his wrath.

M: Now in what sense do you call Christ prophet?

C: Because, when he descended into the world, he proclaimed himself an ambassador to men and an interpreter; and to this end, that by fully declaring the Father's will he might put an end to all revelations and prophecies (Isa. 61:1; Heb. 1:2).

M: But do you reap any benefit from this?

C: Indeed all these things have no other purpose than our good. For Christ is vouchsafed these things by the Father, in order that he may share them with us, and out of this fulness of his we all draw (John 1:16).

M: Explain this to me a little more fully.

C: Christ was filled with the Holy Spirit and loaded with a perfect abundance of gifts, that he may impart them to us, according to the measure, of course, which the Father knows to be appropriate (Eph. 4:7). So from him as the only source we draw whatever spiritual blessings we possess.

M: What does his Kingdom confer upon us?

C: Just this, that by its benefit we are accorded freedom of conscience for pious and holy living, are provided with his spiritual riches, and also armed with strength sufficient to overcome the perpetual enemies of our souls, sin, the flesh, the devil and the world.

M: What is the purpose of his priestly office?

C: First, that on this ground he is our mediator, who reconciles us to the Father. Then too, because through him there is opened up for us a way to the Father, so that with boldness we may come into his presence, and ourselves also offer in sacrifice to him ourselves and all we have. And in this way he makes us his colleagues in the priesthood (Heb. 7; 8; 9; 10; 13).

M: There remains prophecy.

C: It is an office of teaching bestowed upon the Son of God for the benefit of his own; and its end is that he illumine them with the true knowledge of the Father, instruct them in truth, and make them household disciples of God.

M: All that you have said, then, comes to this, that Christ's name comprises three offices which the Father conferred on the Son, that he might transfuse their strength and fruit into those who are his.

C: That is so.

M: Why do you apply the term only to the Son of God, when God deems us also worthy of the title?

C: That we are sons of God is something we have not by nature but only by adoption and grace, because God gives us this status. But the Lord Jesus, who is begotten of one substance with the Father, is of one essence with the Father, and with the best of rights is called the only Son of God (Eph. 1:5; John 1:14; Heb. 1:2), since he alone is by nature his Son.

M: You mean, then, that this honour is properly his as due to him by right of nature, whereas it is communicated to us by gratuitous favour, in that we are his members?

C: Precisely. Hence with regard to this communication, he is elsewhere called the first-born among many brethren (Rom. 8:29; Col. 1:15).

M: In what sense do you understand him to be our Lord?

C: In that he was appointed by the Father to have us under his power, to administer the Kingdom of God in heaven and earth, and to be the head of men and angels.

M: What is intended by what follows?

C: It shows the manner in which the Son was anointed by the Father to be our Saviour, namely that, assuming our flesh, he performed all things necessary for our salvation, as are here mentioned.

M: What do you mean by these two phrases, conceived by the Holy Ghost, born of the Virgin Mary?

C: That he was formed in the womb of a virgin, of her substance, to be the true seed of David, as had been foretold by the predictions of the prophets; and that this was effected by the miraculous and secret agency of the Spirit, without male intercourse (Ps. 132:11; Matt. 1:1, 16; Luke 1:32, 55).

M: Was it then of importance that he should assume our flesh?

C: Very much so; because it was necessary that the disobedience committed by man against God be expiated also in human nature (Rom. 5:15). In no other way indeed could he be our mediator to effect reconciliation between God and men (I Tim. 2:5; Heb. 4:14; 5:1).

M: You say, then, that Christ had to be made man, in order, as in our own person, to fulfil the requirements of our salvation?

C: That is what I think. For we must obtain from him whatever is lacking in ourselves; and this can be done in no other way.

M: But why was this effected by the Holy Spirit, and not rather by the common use and form of generation?

C: Because human seed is wholly corrupt, it was necessary and proper that the Holy Spirit should intervene in the generation of the Son of God, that he might not be affected by this contagion but endued with the most perfect purity.

M: Thus then we learn that he who sanctifies others is immune from every blemish and endued with purity from the original womb (as one may say), so that he might be entirely sacred to God and infected with no human failing.

C: I understand the matter so.

M: How is he our Lord? [2]

C: He was appointed by the Father to rule us, and, obtaining empire and divine dominion both in heaven and earth, he is acknowledged head of angels and all pious men (Eph. 5:23; Col. 1:18).

---

[2] This question and this answer subjoined appears to be an insertion by Beza. It adds nothing that has not been said. *C.R.* retains it italicized in the Latin version, on the ground that the note of the themes for the 8th Sunday implies its presence.

M: Why do you make the transition forthwith from birth to death, omitting all the story of his life?

C: Because nothing is dealt with here, except what so pertains to our redemption, as in some degree to contain the substance of it.

M: Why do you not say simply in one word that he died instead of adding also the name of the governor under whom he suffered?

C: This has reference not only to our credence of the story, but that we may know his death to be connected with his condemnation.

M: Explain this more clearly.

C: He died so that the penalty owed by us might be discharged, and he might exempt us from it. But since we all, because we are sinners, were offensive to the judgment of God, in order to stand in our stead, he desired to be arraigned before an earthly judge, and to be condemned by his mouth, so that we might be acquitted before the heavenly tribunal of God.

M: But Pilate pronounces him innocent (Matt. 27:23; Luke 23:14), and hence does not condemn him as malefactor.

C: Both things must be considered. For the judge bears testimony to his innocence, so that there may be evidence that he suffered not for his own misdeeds but for ours. Nevertheless at the same time he is formally condemned by the same judge to make it plain that he suffered as our surety the judgment which we deserved, that thus he might free us from guilt.

M: Well said. For if he were a sinner, he would not be a fit surety to pay the penalty of another's sin. Nevertheless, that his condemnation might secure our acquittal, it was requisite that he be reckoned among the malefactors (Isa. 53:12).

C: So I understand it.

M: Is the fact that he was crucified of greater importance than if he suffered any other kind of death?

C: Certainly, as even Paul reminds us (Gal. 3:10), when he writes that he hung upon the tree to take our curse upon himself; and by this we are absolved from it. For this kind of death was regarded with execration (Deut. 21:23).

M: What? Is it not to offer an affront to the Son of God to say that he was subject to a curse, even before God?

C: Not at all; for by undergoing it he abolished it. Nor does he meanwhile cease to be blessed, in order that he bestow his blessing on us.

M: Go on.

C: Since death was the punishment imposed on man because of sin, the Son of God endured it, and by enduring conquered it. But that it might better appear that he suffered real death, he desired to be laid in the tomb, just like other men.

M: But we seem to gain nothing from this victory, since we still have to die.

C: That is no obstacle. For death for believers is now nothing but the passage to a better life.

M: Hence it follows that death is no longer to be dreaded, as if it were a fearful thing. We are rather to follow Christ our leader with undaunted mind, who, as he did not perish in death, will not suffer us to perish?

C: We should do so.

M: As for what immediately follows, that he descended into hell, what does this mean?

C: That he endured not only common death, which is the separation of the soul from the body; but also the pains of death, as Peter calls them (Acts 2:24). By this word I understand the fearful agonies with which his soul was tormented.

M: Tell me the cause and manner of this.

C: Because, in order to make satisfaction for sinners, he arraigned himself before the tribunal of God, it was requisite that his conscience be tormented by such agony as if he were forsaken by God, even as if he had God hostile to him. He was in this agony, when he cried to the Father: "My God, my God, why hast thou forsaken me?" (Matt. 27:46; Mark 15:34).

M: Was this not an affront to the Father?

C: Not at all, But he exercised this severity against him, that he might fulfil what was prophesied by Isaiah: He was smitten by the hand of God for our sins, wounded for our iniquities (Isa. 53:4; I Pet. 2:24).

M: But since he is God, how could he be seized by fear of this kind, as if he were forsaken of God?

C: We must hold him to have been reduced to this necessity in respect of the feelings of his human nature. That this might happen, his divinity was for a short while concealed, that is, it did not exercise its power.

M: Yet on the other hand, how can it be that Christ who is the salvation of the world should have been subjected to this condemnation?

C: He did not so endure it as to remain under it. For he was so seized by those fears I have mentioned as not to be overwhelmed. Rather, contending with infernal might, he subdued and broke it.

M: Hence we conclude that the torment of conscience he endured differed from that which torments sinners, whom the hand of an angry God pursues. For what was temporary in his case is perpetual in theirs; and what was for him like a prick stinging him is for them a mortal sword wounding, as one may say, the very heart.

C: Just so. For the Son of God, though beset by agonies of this kind, did not cease to hope in the Father. But sinners, condemned by God's judgment, rush into despair, rage against him, and break forth even into open blasphemies.

M: Can we infer from this what benefit the faithful obtain from the death of Christ?

C: Certainly. For a beginning, we see it to be a sacrifice by which he expiates our sins in the sight of God, and so appeases the wrath of God and restores us to grace with him. Then, too, his blood is a laver in which our souls are purged of every stain. Lastly, the memory of our sins is erased, so that they never come before God; and thus the handwriting by which we were declared guilty is cancelled and abolished.

M: Does it not offer us any other advantage besides?

C: Yes, indeed. For by his benefit, if we are true members of Christ, our old nature is crucified, and the body of sin is destroyed, so that the lusts of perverse flesh no longer rule in us.

M: Proceed with the remaining articles.

C: There follows: the third day he rose again from the dead. By this he shows himself to be conqueror over sin and death. For by his resurrection he swallowed up death, broke the fetters of the devil, and reduced all his power to nothing (I Pet. 3:18).

M: What are the manifold benefits that come to us from his resurrection?

C: Three. For by it righteousness is obtained for us (Rom. 4:24); it is a sure pledge of our future immortality (I Cor. 15); and even now by its virtue we are raised to newness of life, that we may obey God's will by pure and holy living (Rom. 6:4).

M: We go on to the rest.

C: He ascended into heaven.

M: But did he so ascend as to be no longer on earth?

C: Just so. For after he had performed all things enjoined him by the Father and pertaining to our salvation, there was no need for him to continue longer on earth.

M: What good do we obtain from the ascension?

C: There is a double benefit. For since Christ is entered into heaven in our name, as he had descended to earth for our sakes, he opens up for us a way there; so that the gate is now open to us which was formerly closed on account of sin (Rom. 8:34). Then, too, he appears before God as intercessor and advocate on our behalf (Heb. 7:25).

M: But did Christ in taking himself to heaven withdraw from us, so that now he has ceased to be with us?

C: Not at all. On the contrary, he has undertaken to be with us even to the end of the world (Matt. 28:20).

M: But when he is said to dwell with us, does this mean that he is bodily present?

C: No. There is on the one hand the body received up into heaven (Luke 24:51; Acts 1:9); and there is on the other his virtue which is diffused everywhere.

M: In what sense do you say that he sits at the right hand of the Father?

C: These words mean that the Father conferred on him the dominion of heaven and earth, so that he rules all things (Matt. 28:18).

M: But what is meant by the right hand, and what by his sitting?

C: It is a metaphor taken from princes, who are wont to place at their right hand those whom they make their vicegerents.

M: You mean, then, nothing but what Paul says, namely, that Christ is constituted head of the Church (Eph. 1:21), and raised above all principalities, and given a name which is above every name.

C: Just as you say (Phil. 2:9).

M: We go on to other things.

C: From thence he will come to judge both the quick and the dead. The meaning of these words is that he will come openly to judge the world, just as he was seen to ascend (Acts 1:11).

M: Since the day of judgment is not before the end of the world, how do you say that there will be some men still alive, when it is appointed to all men once to die? (Heb. 9:27).

C: Paul answers this question when he says that they who survive will pass into a new state by a sudden change, so that, the corruption of the flesh being abolished, they will put on incorruption (I Cor. 15:52; I Thess. 4:17).

M: Then you understand this change to be like death for them, that there will be an abolition of the first nature and the beginning of a new?

C: That is what I mean.

M: Does it give any happiness to our conscience to know that Christ will one day judge the world?

C: Indeed, a quite peculiar happiness. For we know that he will come for our salvation only.

M: Then it is not proper that we should dread this judgment as though it struck terror into us?

C: No indeed, since we shall stand only at the tribunal of a judge who is also our advocate, and who has taken us into his faithful protection.

M: Let us come to the third part.

C: It concerns faith in the Holy Spirit.

M: What does he do for us?

C: The intention is that we should know that God, as he has redeemed and saved us by his Son, makes us by his Spirit heirs of this redemption and salvation.

M: How?

C: As we have purification in the blood of Christ, so our consciences must be sprinkled by it to be washed (I Pet. 1:19; I John 1:7).

M: This needs a rather clearer explanation.

C: I mean that the Spirit of God, while he dwells in our hearts, operates so that we feel the virtue of Christ (Rom. 5:5). For when we conceive the benefits of Christ with the mind, this happens by the illumination of the Holy Spirit; it is by his persuasion that they are sealed in our hearts. In short, he alone gives them a place in us (Eph. 1:13). He regenerates us, and makes of us new creatures (Tit. 3:5). Hence whatever gifts are offered us in Christ, we receive them by virtue of the Spirit.

M: Let us proceed.

C: The fourth part follows, in which we confess our belief in one Holy Catholic Church.

M: What is the Church?

C: The body and society of believers whom God has predestined to eternal life.

M: Is this article also necessary to belief?

C: Yes indeed: if we would not render Christ's death ineffective and reduce to nothing all that has hitherto been said. For the one effect of all this is that there be a Church.

M: You think, then, that up to now the cause of salvation has been treated and its foundation shown, when we explained that by Christ's merits and intercession we were received into the love of God, and this grace was confirmed in us by the virtue of the Holy Spirit. But now the effect of all this is to be explained, that by the very facts our faith may stand the firmer.

C: It is so.

M: In what sense then do you call the Church holy?

C: In this sense, that all whom God chooses he justifies, and remakes in holiness and innocence of life (Rom. 8:29), so that in them his glory may be displayed. This is what Paul intends, when he affirms that Christ sanctifies the Church which he redeemed, that it might be glorious and free from all stain (Eph. 5:25).

M: What is the meaning of the attribute catholic or universal?

C: By it we are taught that, as there is one head of all the faithful, so all ought to unite in one body, so that there may be one Church spread throughout the whole earth, and not a number of Churches (Eph. 4:3; I Cor. 12:12, 27).

M: But what is the force of adding forthwith the Communion of Saints?

C: This is put here to express more clearly that unity which exists between the members of the Church. At the same time it is indicated that whatever benefits God bestows upon the Church serve the common good of all, since all have communion with each other.

M: But is this holiness which you attribute to the Church now perfect?

C: Not yet: that is, so long as it battles in this world. For it always labours under infirmities, nor is it ever wholly purged of the vestiges of vice, until it completely adheres to Christ its Head by whom it is sanctified.

M: But is it possible to know this Church other than by the faith with which it is believed?

C: There is indeed also a visible Church of God, which he has described to us by sure marks and signs. But strictly this question concerns the company of those who, by secret election, he has adopted for salvation; and this is not always visible with the eyes nor discernible by signs.

M: What comes next?

C: I believe in the forgiveness of sins.

M: What do you mean by the word forgiveness?

C: I mean that God by his gratuitous goodness forgives and pardons the faithful their sins, so that they are not summoned to judgment nor is punishment exacted from them.

M: It follows then that in no sense do we by our own satisfaction merit the pardon of sins which we obtain from God?

C: That is true. For Christ alone, by paying the penalty, made satisfaction. As for us, no compensation from our side procures what we have from God: we receive this benefit gratuitously out of his sheer liberality.

M: Why do you subjoin the forgiveness of sins to the Church?

C: Because no one obtains it, unless he has previously been united with the people of God, cultivates this unity with the body of Christ up to the end, and thus testifies that he is a true member of the Church.

M: You conclude from this that outside the Church there is no salvation but only damnation and ruin?

C: Certainly. Those who disrupt from the body of Christ and split its unity into schisms, are quite excluded from the hope of salvation, so long as they remain in dissidence of this kind.

M: Repeat what remains.

C: I believe in the resurrection of the body, and the life everlasting.

M: Why is this article included in the confession of faith?

C: To remind us that our happiness is not located on earth. The advantage and use of this knowledge is double. First we are taught that we are to live in this world as foreigners, thinking continually of departure, and not allowing our hearts to be involved in earthly thoughts. Then too, however deeply the fruit of the grace of Christ bestowed upon us may lie hid and buried, we are not therefore to despond, but patiently wait until the day of its revelation.

M: What, then, will be the order of resurrection?

C: Those who were dead before will receive their bodies, the same as they had before, but endowed with the new quality of being no longer liable to death and corruption. But those who will then be living, God will marvellously raise up by sudden change (I Cor. 15:52).

M: But will it be the same for the pious and the impious?

C: There will be a single resurrection for all; but their states will differ (John 5:29; Matt. 25:46). For some will rise to salvation and bliss; others to death and extreme misery.

M: Why, then, is there mention only of eternal life and not of hell?

C: Since nothing is held by faith except what contributes to the consolation of the souls of the pious. Hence there are here recalled the rewards which the Lord has prepared for his servants. Therefore it is not added what fate may await the impious whom we know to be outcasts from the Kingdom of God.

M: The foundation on which we have found faith to rest ought readily to yield a definition of true faith.

C: It does so. It may be defined thus: as a sure and steadfast knowledge of the fatherly goodness of God towards us, as through the gospel he declares that he will be, for the sake of Christ, our Father and Saviour.

M: Do we conceive faith of ourselves or do we receive it from God?

C: Scripture teaches that it is the special gift of God, and experience confirms this.

M: Tell me what experience you mean.

C: Our mind is too rude to be able to grasp the spiritual wisdom of God which is revealed to us through faith; and our hearts are too prone to distrust or to perverse confidence in ourselves or other creatures to rest of their own accord in God. But the Holy Spirit by his illumination makes us capable of understanding those things which would otherwise far exceed our grasp, and brings us to a sure persuasion by sealing the promises of salvation in our hearts.

M: What advantage accrues to us from faith, when once we have obtained it?

C: It justifies us in the sight of God, and this justification makes us heirs of eternal life.

M: What? Are men not justified by good works, when they study to approve themselves before God by holy and righteous living?

C: If anyone could be found perfect to this degree, he might be reckoned just on merit. But since we are all sinners, guilty in many ways before God, we must seek elsewhere that worthiness which may reconcile us with him.

M: But are all men's works so despicable and worthless that they are unable to obtain favour with God?

C: First, whatever works proceed from us as properly to be called our own are vicious; then further, they can do nothing but displease God and be rejected by him.

M: You say then that, before we are reborn and remade by the Spirit of God, we are able to do nothing but sin, just as the bad tree produces only bad fruit (Matt. 7:17).

C: Precisely so. For whatever appearance they may have in the eyes of men, they are none the less evil so long as the heart, to which God chiefly looks, is depraved.

M: Hence you conclude that we cannot anticipate God by any merits, or evoke his beneficence. Rather, whatever works we proffer or attempt fall under his wrath and condemnation.

C: That is what I think. It is therefore by his sheer mercy and not in respect of works that he graciously embraces us in Christ and holds us acceptable, by attributing to us his accepted righteousness as if it were our own, and by not imputing our sins to us (Tit. 3:5).

M: How then do you say that we are justified by faith?

C: Because in embracing the promises of the gospel with a sure and heartfelt confidence, we in a manner obtain possession of this righteousness of which I speak.

M: You mean that as justice is offered to us by God through the gospel, so it is received by us in faith?

C: That is so.

M: But when God has once embraced us, are not the works which we do at the direction of the Holy Spirit acceptable to him?

C: They please him, but not by reason of their own merit, but as he liberally dignifies them with his favour.

M: But since they proceed from the Holy Spirit, do they not merit favour?

C: Yes; some defilement from the infirmity of the flesh is always mixed in them, by which they are vitiated.

M: How comes it, then, or for what reason is it, that they please God?

C: It is faith alone that procures favour for them; for we rest with certain confidence on this, that they will not be brought to the standard of supreme justice, because God will not examine them according to the rule of his severity, but, their defects being covered and their impurities buried in the purity of Christ, he holds them as though they were absolutely perfect.

M: But are we to draw the conclusion from this that the Christian man is justified by works after he is called by God, or that by merit of works he contrives to be loved by God, whose love is eternal life for us?

C: Not at all. Rather we are to hold what is written: No mortal man can be justified in the sight of God (Ps. 143:2); and therefore we pray that he enter not into judgment with us.

M: But we do not therefore judge the good works of believers to be useless?

C: By no means. For God does not in vain promise them reward both in this life and in the future. But this reward springs from the gratuitous love of God as source. For he first embraces us as sons, and then, burying the memory of the vices which proceed from us, he visits us with favour.

M: But can this righteousness be separated from good works, so that one may have the one and lack the other?

C: That cannot happen. For when we receive Christ by faith, as he offers himself to us, he not only promises us deliverance from death and reconciliation to God, but also the gift of the Holy Spirit, by which we are regenerated into newness of life. It is necessary that these things be held together, lest we should divide Christ from himself.

M: Hence it follows that so far is it from diverting us from the study of them, faith is the root from which are born all good works?

C: Just so. And hence the whole doctrine of the gospel is comprised in two branches: faith and repentance.

M: What is repentance?

C: Dissatisfaction and hatred of sin, and love of righteousness, arising out of the fear of God; for these things lead us to denial of self and mortification of the flesh, so that we yield ourselves to be ruled by the Spirit of God, and bring all the actions of our life into obedience to the divine will.

M: But this second branch was named in the division which you set forth at the beginning, when you showed the method of worshipping God rightly.

C: True; and at the same time it was added that the true and proper rule for worshipping God is to obey his will.

M: Why so?

C: Because the only worship approved by him is not what it pleases us to devise, but what by his own authority he prescribes.

CONCERNING THE LAW

M: What rule of life has he given us?

C: His law.

M: What does it contain?

C: It consists of two parts: the first of these contains four commandments, the other six. So the whole law consists of ten commandments in all (Ex. 24:12; 32:15; 34:29; Deut. 4:13; 10:3).

M: Who is the originator of this division?

C: God himself, who delivered it written on two tablets to Moses and often declared it reducible to ten sentences.

M: What is the subject of the first table?

C: The offices of piety towards God.

M: And of the second?

C: How we are to act towards men and what we owe them.

M: Repeat the first commandment or head.

C: Hear O Israel; I am the Lord thy God, who brought thee up out of the land of Egypt, out of the house of bondage: Thou shalt have no other gods before me (Ex. 20; Deut. 5).

M: Now explain the meaning of the words.

C: At the beginning he makes use of a kind of preface to the whole law. For when he calls himself Lord he claims right and authority to command. Then, that he may win our favour for the law, he adds that he is our God. For these words have the same force as if he called himself our preserver. Now since he confers this blessing on us, it is fitting that we should in return show ourselves an obedient people to him.

M: But does not what he immediately adds about deliverance and breaking the yoke of the Egyptian slavery apply specifically to the people of Israel and to it alone?

C: I admit this as far as the facts themselves go. But there is another kind of deliverance which applies equally to all men. For he has rescued us all from spiritual bondage to sin and from the dominion of the devil.

M: Why does he recall this in prefacing his law?

C: So as to remind us that we shall be guilty of the greatest ingratitude, unless we devote ourselves wholly to his obedience.

M: But what does he require under the first head?

C: That we maintain his honour entirely for himself alone, transferring no portion of it elsewhere.

M: What honour is peculiar to him which it is wrong to ascribe elsewhere?

C: To adore him, to place our trust in him, to call upon him, and, in short, to pay him all the deference appropriate to his majesty.

M: Why is the phrase added: Before my face? [3]

C: As nothing is so hidden as to be concealed from him, and he is the knower and the judge of secret thoughts, it means that he requires not only the respect of external profession, but also the true piety of the heart.

M: Let us pass to the second head.

[3] The Latin version of the commandment here quoted has *coram facie mea,* as has also the French (Segond) *Devant ma face,* where the A.V. has *before me*; the Vulgate on the other hand has simply *coram me.*

C: Thou shalt not make unto thee any graven image, or any likeness of any thing that is in heaven above, or that is in the earth beneath, or that is in the water under the earth: Thou shalt not bow down thyself to them, nor serve them.

M: Does this prohibit us entirely from painting anything or sculpting likenesses?

C: No; but it does forbid these two thing: that we make images either for representing God or for worshipping him.

M: Why is it forbidden to represent God in visible shape?

C: Because there is no resemblance between him, who is Spirit eternal and incomprehensible, and corporeal, corruptible and dead figures (Deut. 4:15; Isa. 41:7; Rom. 1:23).

M: You think then that injury is done his majesty, when he is represented in this way?

C: I think so.

M: What kind of worship is here condemned?

C: When we turn for prayer to a statue or image, and prostrate ourselves before it, or pay honour to it by bending the knee or other gestures, as if God represented himself to us in it.

M: We are not then to understand that these words simply condemn every picture and sculpture whatever. Rather we are forbidden to make images for the purpose of seeking or worshipping God in them, or, what is the same thing, worshipping them in honour of God, or of abusing them at all for superstition and idolatry.

C: Quite right.

M: Now what is the purpose of this head?

C: As under the former head he declared that he only is to be worshipped and adored, so now he shows us what is the correct form of adoration, by which he may recall us from all superstition and other vicious and carnal fictions.

M: Let us go on.

C: He adds the sanction that he the Lord is our God, strong and jealous, visiting the iniquity of the fathers upon the children, unto the third and fourth generation of them that hate him.

M: Why is his strength mentioned?

C: Thereby he indicates that he has power enough to vindicate his own glory.

M: What does the word jealous mean?

C: To be unable to brook an equal or associate. For as he has given himself to us of his infinite goodness, so he desires us to be wholly his. And the purity of our souls consists in being dedicated to him and entirely cleaving to him, as on the other hand they are said to be polluted with adultery who turn aside from him to superstition.

M: In what sense is it said that he avenges the iniquity of the fathers on the children?

C: To strike more fear into us, he threatens not only that he will exact punishment from those who offend, but also that their offspring will be cursed.

M: But is it consistent with the equity of God to punish one man on account of another's wrong?

C: The question is answered by considering what the condition of the human race is. For by nature we are all liable to curse; nor have we anything to complain of in God, if he leaves us in this condition. But now, as he demonstrates his love for the pious by blessing their posterity, so he executes his vengeance against the impious by depriving their children of blessing.

M: Proceed.

C: To attract us with lovable tenderness, he promises to take pity on all who love him and observe his commands.

M: Does he mean that the innocence of the pious will be the saving of all his posterity?

C: Not at all; but that he will pour out his goodwill towards the faithful to such an extent, that for their sakes he will show himself good also to their children, not only by giving them prosperity so far as this life is concerned, but by also sanctifying their souls, and so counting them among his flock.

M: But this is not always apparent.

C: I admit it. For as he retains for himself freedom to show mercy to the children of the impious when he please, so he does not so tie his favour to the children of the faithful as not to reject at his pleasure those of them whom he will (Rom. 9:11, 21). But this he so moderates as not to render vain and false his promise (Rom. 2:6).

M: Why does he here say a thousand generations, whereas in the case of punishment only three or four?

C: To show that he is inclined more to humanity and beneficence than to severity. This also he elsewhere testifies, when he declares that he is ready to pardon but slow to anger (Ex. 34:1, 6; Ps. 103:8; 145:8).

M: Now for the third commandment.

C: Thou shalt not take the name of the Lord thy God in vain.

M: What is the meaning?

C: He forbids us to abuse the name of God, either by perjury or by swearing unnecessarily.

M: Can the name of God be used legitimately in making an oath?

C: Certainly: when it is used in a just cause. First, in affirming the truth; then, too, when the business is of such importance that it is proper to take an oath for the maintenance of mutual charity and concord between men.

M: But does it go no further than to restrict oaths by which the name of God is profaned or his honour threatened?

C: The mention of one kind warns us in general, never to bring forward the name of God except with fear and reverence and for the purpose of making his glory apparent. For since it is sacrosanct, we ought by every means to guard against seeming to hold it in contempt or giving others occasion for contempt.

M: How is this to be done?

C: By never speaking or thinking about God and his works except to honour him.

M: What follows?

C: A sanction, declaring that anyone who takes his name in vain will not be guiltless.

M: As in another place he declares that he will punish the transgressors of his law, what more is contained here?

C: By this he desires to indicate how highly he holds the honour of his name, that we should be the more careful of it, when we see the punishment prepared for any who shall profane it.

M: Let us come to the fourth commandment.

C: Remember the Sabbath day, to keep it holy. Six days shalt thou labour and do all thy work: But the seventh is the Sabbath of the Lord thy God: in it thou shalt not do any work, thou, nor thy son, nor thy daughter, nor thy manservant, nor thy maidservant, nor thy cattle, nor thy stranger that is within thy gates: For in six days the Lord made heaven and earth, the sea, and all that in them is, and rested the seventh day: wherefore the Lord blessed the Sabbath day, and hallowed it.

M: Does he order us to labour six days, in order that we may rest on the seventh?

C: Not exactly: but he permits six days for men's labours, and excludes the seventh, that it may be devoted to rest.

M: From what kind of labour are we barred?

C: This commandment has a distinct and peculiar ground. Since the observation of rest is part of the old ceremonies, it was therefore by the advent of Christ abrogated.

M: Do you mean that this precept properly refers to the Jews, and so was merely temporary?

C: Yes, so far as ceremonial is concerned.

M: What then? Is anything besides ceremonial subsumed under it?

C: It was given for three reasons.

M: Give them to me.

C: To symbolize spiritual rest; for the preservation of the ecclesiastical polity; for the relief of servants.

M: What do you mean by spiritual rest?

C: When we keep holiday from our own works, that God may perform his works in us.

M: How then is this carried out?

C: By crucifying the flesh; that is, we renounce our own inclination, that we may be guided by the Spirit of God.

M: Is it enough that this be done on the seventh day?

C: No: continually. For when we have once begun, we must continue through the whole course of life.

M: Why then is a certain day appointed to symbolize it?

C: There is no need for the reality to agree at all points with the symbol, if only it suit sufficiently for the purpose of symbolizing.

M: Why, then, is the seventh rather than any other day prescribed?

C: This number denotes perfection in Scripture. Therefore it is suitable to indicate perpetuity. At the same time, it suggests that this spiritual rest only begins in this life, and does not reach perfection until we depart this world.

M: But what is the meaning of the Lord exhorting us by his own example to rest?

C: When he finished the creation of the world in six days, he dedicated the seventh to the contemplation of his works. To incite us more strongly to this, he sets before us his own example. For nothing is more to be desired that that we be formed in his image.

M: But our meditation of the works of God ought to be continuous. Is it sufficient that one day out of seven be devoted to it?

C: It is right for us to be employed in it every day. But because of our weakness one special day is appointed. And this is the arrangement that I have mentioned.

M: What then is the order to be observed on this day?

C: The people are to meet for the hearing of Christian doctrine, for the offering of public prayers, and for the profession of their faith.

M: Now explain what you meant by saying that the Lord in this commandment wished to offer relief to servants.

C: That some kind of relaxation might be given to those who are in the power of others. Indeed this also contributes to maintain a common polity. For when one day is assigned for rest, everyone accustoms himself to work the rest of the time.

M: Let us see now how far this command refers to us.

C: As to ceremony, since its reality existed in Christ, I hold it to be abrogated (Col. 2:20).

M: How?

C: Just because our old nature is by virtue of his death crucified, and we are raised up to newness of life.

M: How much of the commandment then remains for us?

C: Not to neglect the sacred ordinances which contribute to the spiritual polity of the Church; especially to attend the sacred assemblies for the hearing of the Word of God, the celebration of the mysteries, and the regular prayers as they will be ordained.

M: But does the symbol lead us no further?

C: Certainly: for it recalls us to the reality behind it, namely, that being grafted into the body of Christ and made members of his, we cease from our own works and so resign ourselves to the government of God.

M: Let us pass to the second table.

C: It begins: Honour thy father and thy mother.

M: What does this word honour mean for you?

C: That children be with modesty and humility compliant and obedient to their parents, that they give them reverence, that they help them in need, and that they devote their labour to them. For in these three branches is contained that honour which is owed to parents.

M: Go on.

C: To the command a promise is added: that thy days may be long upon the land which the Lord thy God giveth thee.

M: What does this mean?

C: That by God's blessing those that offer due honour to their parents will live long.

M: When this life is so full of hardships, why does God promise its long continuance as a blessing?

C: However great the miseries to which it is exposed, yet there is a blessing of God towards believers in his nourishing and preserving them here, if only for this reason, that it is proof of his paternal favour.

M: Does it follow conversely that the man who early and before his due time is snatched away from the world is cursed by God?

C: Not at all. Rather it sometimes happens that the more a man is loved by God the earlier he is removed from this life.

M: But by doing so, how does he fulfil his own promise?

C: Whatever earthly blessings God promises to us are received on this condition: in so far as is expedient for the good and salvation of our soul. For the ordinance would be very preposterous unless the matter of the soul always took precedence.

M: What about those who are contumacious towards parents?

C: They will not only be punished at the last judgment; here also God will inflict punishment on their bodies, either by removing them in the midst of their days, or by bringing them to an ignominious death, or by other means.

M: But does not the promise speak expressly of the land of Canaan?

C: That is so, so far as the Israelites are concerned; but for us the term extends most widely and ought to be expanded. For whatever locality we inhabit, since the whole earth is the Lord's, he assigns it to us for a possession (Ps. 24:1; 89:2; 115:16).

M: Is there nothing more remaining in this commandment?

C: Though the words refer to father and mother only, we must understand all who are over us, since they have the same ground.

M: What is the ground?

C: This, that the Lord has raised them to a degree superior in honour. For there is no authority, either of parents, or princes, or governors of any kind, no empire and no honour, except by God's decree; for so it pleased him to order the world.

M: Repeat the sixth commandment.

C: Thou shalt not kill.

M: Does it forbid nothing but the perpetration of murder?

C: It forbids more. For since God speaks here, he lays down the law not only for external works, but also for the affections of the mind, and indeed chiefly for them.

M: You appear to insinuate some kind of secret murder, from which God here prohibits us.

C: That is so. For anger and hatred, and any kind of injurious desire, by which our neighbour may be harmed, is counted murder in the sight of God.

M: Do we discharge our obligations if we regard no one with hatred?

C: By no means. Since the Lord by condemning hatred and restraining us from any harm by which our neighbour may be injured, shows us at the same time that he requires us to love all men from the heart, and to apply ourselves to their maintenance and care.

M: Now to the seventh.

C: Thou shalt not commit adultery.

M: Explain what the substance of it is.

C: That every kind of fornication is cursed in the sight of God. Hence, unless we wish to provoke the wrath of God against us, we must diligently abstain from it.

M: Is nothing else required?

C: The nature of the legislator is always to be borne in mind. We have said that he observes not only the outward deed, but rather notes the affections of the mind.

M: What more does it therefore include?

C: Since both our bodies and our souls are temples of the Holy Spirit (I Cor. 3:16; 6:15; II Cor. 6:16), we are to maintain a chaste purity in both, and accordingly be chaste not only in abstaining from external licentiousness, but also in heart and speech, bodily gesture and action. In short, the body is to be pure from all lasciviousness, the mind from all lust, and no part of us is to be defiled by the pollution of unchastity.

M: Let us come to the eighth commandment.

C: Thou shalt not steal.

M: Does this prohibit only those thefts punished by human laws, or does it go further?

C: Under the name of theft, it includes all kinds of evil deed, of defrauding and swindling, by which we hunt after other men's goods. We are therefore forbidden here either to raid the goods of our neighbours by violence, or by wiles and cunning to lay hands upon them, or by any other devious means to try to possess them.

M: Is it enough to abstain from the overt deed; or is the desire also condemned?

C: We must always return to this: Since the legislator is spiritual, he does not wish to forbid only external thefts, but all intentions and wishes which incommode others in any way; and in the first place cupidity itself, that we do not long to enrich ourselves at the expense of our brothers.

M: What then is to be done to obey this commandment?

C: We must take care that each man have his own in safety.

M: What is the ninth commandment?

C: Thou shalt not bear false witness against thy neighbour.

M: Does this forbid perjury in the law courts only, or lying in general against our neighbours?

C: A general doctrine is comprised under a single heading, that we do not charge our neighbour falsely, nor by our evil speaking and calumnies damage his reputation, or offer any injury to him in his goods.

M: But why is public perjury expressly mentioned?

C: That it may inspire us with greater aversion to this vice. For it suggests that, if anyone is given to evil speaking and calumny, the degeneration to perjury is rapid, if occasion is given to defame his neighbour.

M: Is the purpose to keep us from evil speaking only, or also from false suspicion and uncharitable and unjust judgment?

C: It here condemns both, for the reason already given. For what it is wrong to do before men, is wrong even to wish in the sight of God.

M: Explain what it means in sum.

C: It forbids us to be inclined to think evil of our neighbours, or to defame them; but commands that rather we be possessed of equity and humanity, so that we think well of them, as far as truth allows, and try to preserve their reputation intact.

M: Repeat the last commandment.

C: Thou shalt not covet thy neighbour's house, thou shalt not covet thy neighbour's wife, nor his manservant, nor his maidservant, nor his ox, nor his ass, nor anything that is thy neighbour's.

M: Since the whole law is spiritual, as you have so often said before, and since these commandments above are laid down not only to curb outward acts, but also to correct the affections of the mind, what further is added here?

C: The Lord desired in these other commandments to rule and moderate desires and affections. But here he imposes a law even on thoughts which carry some cupidity with them, even though they do not reach the status of purpose.

M: Do you call the very least of these cupidities, which come stealthily upon believers, and enter into their minds, sins, even if we resist rather than assent to them?

C: It is quite apparent that all depraved thoughts, even if they do not win consent, proceed from the evil of our nature. But I will only say this: this commandment condemns vicious desires which titillate and solicit the heart of a man, but yet do not drag him to a firm and deliberate volition.

M: Thus then you understand those evil affections, to which men acquiesce and by which they allow themselves to be overcome, to have been prohibited before; but now such a strict integrity is required of us, that our hearts are to admit no perverse desire by which they may be incited to sin.

C: Just so.

M: May we now frame a brief compendium of the whole law?

C: Undoubtedly: for we may reduce it to two heads. The first is that we love God with our whole heart, our whole mind and our whole strength; and the second: that we love our neighbours as ourselves.

M: What is contained under the love of God?

C: To love him as God should be loved. That is that he be acknowledged as at once Lord and Father and Saviour. So to the love of God is joined reverence to him, the will to obey him, and trust placed in him.

M: What do you understand by the whole heart, the whole mind and the whole strength?

C: Such vehemence of zeal, that there be no place in us at all for any thoughts, any desires, any intentions which conflict with this love for him.

M: What is the meaning of the second head?

C: As we are naturally so inclined to love ourselves, that this feeling overcomes all others, so love of our neighbour should so rule in us, that it govern us in every part, and be the principle of all our purposes and all our actions.

M: What do you understand by the word neighbour?

C: Not only kindred and friends or those connected to us by any necessary tie; but also those who are unknown to us, and even enemies.

M: But what connection have these with us?

C: They are certainly joined by that bond by which God gathers the whole human race at once. But it is a tie, sacred and inviolable, which cannot be loosed by depravity.

M: You say then that if any man hate us, this is his own business, but that he nevertheless remains neighbour to us, and is so to be regarded by us, because God's order stands inviolable, and establishes this connection between us.

C: It is so.

M: Since the law demonstrates the form for rightly worshipping God, ought we not to live according to its direction?

C: That is certainly so. But all suffer from infirmity, so that no one fulfils in every respect what he ought.

M: Why then does God require a perfection which is beyond our ability?

C: He exacts nothing which we are not obliged to perform. For the rest, if we strive after the form of living here presented, even though we be wide of the mark, that is of perfection, the Lord forgives us what is lacking.

M: Do you speak of all men in general, or only of the faithful?

C: The man that is not yet regenerated by the Spirit of God will not be fit to start upon the smallest item of the law. Besides, even if anyone were found to comply with the law in some respect, still we shall not judge that he has discharged his duty to God. For he pronounces all those to be accursed who have not fulfilled all the things contained in it (Deut. 27:26; Gal. 3:10).

M: Hence the conclusion is that, as there are two classes of men, so the office of the law is double.

C: Quite so. For its effect on unbelievers is nothing but to exclude them from all excuse before God (Rom. 3:3). This is what Paul means when he calls it the ministry of death and condemnation (II Cor. 3:7). For believers it has a quite different use.

M: What?

C: First, while they learn from it that they are unable to obtain righteousness by works, they are thus instructed in humility; and this is indeed a true preparation for seeking Christ. Second, as it exacts much more of them than they are able to offer, it moves them to seek strength from the Lord, and at the same time reminds them of their perpetual guilt, lest they presume to be proud. Finally, it is a kind of curb upon them, holding them in fear of God (Rom. 3:20; Gal. 2:16; 4:3).

M: Therefore, although we never satisfy the law in this earthly pilgrimage of ours, yet we shall not consider it to be superfluous, because it demands such strict perfection from us. For it shows us the mark at which we ought to aim and the goal to which we must strive; that each of us, according to the measure of grace bestowed upon him, may try to conform his life to the highest rectitude, and by assiduous care make more and more progress.

C: That is my opinion.

M: Have we not in the law a perfect rule of righteousness?

C: Yes indeed, so that God desires nothing more of us than that we follow it, while on the other hand he repudiates and holds void whatever we undertake beyond his prescription. For he holds no other sacrifice than obedience acceptable (I Sam. 15:22; Jer. 7).

M: Why are there then so many admonitions, commandments, exhortations, which both prophets and apostles everywhere employ?

C: They are nothing but mere expositions of the law, which conduct us into obedience to the law, rather than lead us from it.

M: But he lays down nothing concerning the private vocation of the individual?

C: When he commands us to render to each man his due, we immediately gather what things properly belong to each man's private status and kind of life. And there are throughout Scripture, as has been said, scattered expositions of particular commandments. For what the Lord has summarily comprised here is developed elsewhere with more fulness and detail.

Concerning Prayer

M: Now that the second part of Divine Worship, which consists in service and obedience, has been sufficiently discussed, let us proceed to the third part.

C: We said it was invocation, in which we take refuge in him in any necessity.

M: Do you think that he alone is to be invoked?

C: Certainly. For he requires this as the proper worship of his divinity.

M: If this is so, how is it permissible to ask men to lend us their aid?

C: There is indeed a wide distinction between the two things. For when we invoke God, we testify that we look for good from no other quarter, and that we locate our defence nowhere else; but still we ask the help of men, as far as he allows and confers on them the power of helping us.

M: In resorting to faith in men and their help, then, you say there is nothing that stands in the way of our invoking the one God, since our trust is not in the least placed in them. Nor do we implore them on grounds other than that God, in furnishing them with the power of doing good, appoints them to be in a measure ministers of his beneficence to us, and desires to help us by their hands, and summon for us the resources which he deposited with them.

C: I believe so. And thus whatever benefits we receive from them we should regard as received from God, since he alone in truth bestows all these things upon us through their instrumentality.

M: But are we not to show gratitude to men, whenever they do any kind of service for us? This surely natural justice and the law of humanity dictates.

C: Of course we are to do this, if only because God adorns them with the honour of directing to us by their hands, as through channels, the blessings that flow from the inexhaustible spring of his liberality. In this way he puts us under obligation to them, and desires us to acknowledge it. Therefore whoever does not show himself grateful to men thus betrays also his ingratitude to God.

M: May we gather from this that it is wrong to invoke angels and the holy servants of the Lord who have departed this life?

C: This is a right conclusion. For God does not accord to the saints the duty of aiding us. But so far as angels are concerned, though he uses their labour for our salvation, yet he does not wish us to ask them for it.

M: You say, then, that whatever does not square aptly and congruously with the ordinance of God is repugnant to his will.

C: That is so. For it is a certain sign of infidelity not to be content with the things which God gives us. Then, if we throw ourselves on the protection of saints or angels, when God calls us to himself alone, and transfer to them part of that faith which ought to reside entirely in God alone, we fall into idolatry, since we share with them what God claimed for himself alone.

M: Now let us consider the manner of praying. Does it suffice to pray with the tongue, or does prayer demand also the mind and the heart?

C: The tongue indeed is not always necessary, but the intelligence and devoutness true prayer must never lack.

M: How will you prove this to me?

C: Since God is a Spirit, and in other cases always requires of men their heart, so especially in prayer by which they communicate with him. Therefore he promises to be near those only who call upon him in truth; but on the other hand he abominates and curses all who pray to him deceitfully and dishonestly (Ps. 145:18; Isa. 29:13).

M: All prayers conceived by the tongue only will then be vain and worthless?

C: Not only so, but will also be deeply displeasing to God.

M: What kind of feeling does God require in prayer?

C: First, that we feel our want and misery, and that this feeling generate in our minds grief and anxiety. Then that we burn with earnest and vehement desire to obtain grace from God, who also kindles in us the longing to pray.

M: Does this feeling emanate from man's native temper, or does it proceed from the grace of God to them?

C: God must needs help us here. For we are quite incapable on both counts. It is the Spirit of God who arouses in us groanings that cannot be uttered, and shapes our minds to those desires that are required in prayer (Rom. 8:20; Gal. 4:6).

M: Does the doctrine imply by this that we are to sit quiescent, and as it were lazily await the movement of the Spirit, and not that each is to urge himself to pray?

C: Not at all. The meaning rather is that when the faithful feel themselves cold and sluggish or somewhat indisposed to pray, they should forthwith flee to God and demand that they be inflamed with the fiery darts of his Spirit, so as to be rendered fit for prayer.

M: But do you mean that no use is to be made of the tongue in prayer?

C: No indeed. For often it is of assistance for elevating the mind and preventing it from so readily straying from God. Besides, since it more than other members was created to display the glory of God, it is right to employ its full capacity to this purpose. Further, vehemence of desire on occasion impels a man to break out into speech with the tongue unintentionally.

M: If this is so, what is the advantage of people praying in a strange tongue unintelligible to them?

C: This is nothing else than mockery of God. Therefore this hypocrisy should cease among Christians (I Cor. 14).

M: But when we pray, do we do it fortuitously, uncertain of success, or ought we to hold it for sure and certain that God will hear us?

C: This is the constant foundation of prayer, that we shall be heard by God, and that we shall obtain whatever we demand, so far as expedient for us. For this reason, Paul teaches that true invocation arises from faith (Rom. 10:14). For no one will ever rightly call upon him, unless he have a prior and certain trust in his goodness.

M: What happens then to those who pray hesitantly, without deciding in their minds what they are to pray for, who are even uncertain whether their prayers will be heard by God?

C: Their prayers are vain and invalid, for no promise supports them. For we are commanded to pray with a sure faith, and the promise is added that whatever we ask believing, it will be given us (Matt. 21:22; Mark 11:24).

M: It remains to be seen whence such great confidence comes, so that while we are in so many ways unworthy in God's sight, we may yet dare to present ourselves before him.

C: First, we have promises on which we must simply take our stand without reference to our unworthiness (Ps. 50:15; 91:3; 145:18; Isa. 30:15; 65:24; Jer. 29:12; Joel 2:32). Then too, if we are sons of God, his Spirit animates us and incites us, so that we do not hesitate to betake ourselves to him in familiar manner, as to a Father (Matt. 6:9). And as we tremble at his glorious majesty because we are like worms and oppressed by consciousness of our sins, he puts forth Christ as Mediator (I Tim. 2:5; Heb. 4:16; I John 2:1), who opens up a way for us so that we are not at all anxious about obtaining favour.

M: Do you think we are to pray to God only in the name of Christ?

C: I think so. For thus it is laid down in express words, and the promise is added, that by his intercession he will contrive that we obtain what we ask (John 14:13).

M: One is not then to be accused of temerity and arrogance, if, trusting this Advocate, he approaches God intimately and holds Christ before God and himself as the only mediator through whom he will be heard?

C: By no means. For he who prays thus conceives his prayers as from the mouth of Christ himself, since he knows his own prayer to be assisted and recommended by the intercession of Christ (Rom. 8:34).

M: Let us consider now what the prayers of believers ought to contain. Is it permissible to ask anything that comes into the mind, or is there a certain rule to be observed?

C: It would be a very preposterous method of praying to indulge our own desires and the judgment of the flesh. For we are too foolish to be able to judge what is expedient for us, and we labour under this intemperance of desire which has necessarily to be bridled.

M: What then must be done?

C: It only remains that God himself prescribe for us a right form of prayer, that we may follow him as he guides us as by his hand and even sets words for us.

M: What law has he prescribed for us?

C: The doctrine of this matter is amply and copiously delivered throughout the Scriptures. But to provide us with a more certain aim, he framed and as it were dictated a formula, in which he briefly comprised, and under a few heads summarized all that we may ask rightly of God and profitably for ourselves.

M: Repeat it.

C: Our Lord Christ, when asked by his disciples how to pray replied (Matt. 6:9; Luke 11:1): When you would pray, say thus: Our Father, which art in heaven, Hallowed be thy name. Thy kingdom come, thy will be done in earth, as it is in heaven. Give us this day our daily bread. And forgive us our debts, as we forgive our debtors. And lead us not into temptation, but deliver us from evil: For thine is the kingdom, and the power, and the glory, for ever. Amen.

M: Let us divide it into heads to understand better what it contains.

C: It has six parts, of which the first three refer to God's glory as their end without respect to ourselves; the remaining parts refer to ourselves and consider our interest.

M: Are we then to ask from God anything from which we derive no advantage?

C: He indeed of his infinite goodness so orders all things that nothing contributes to his glory without being also salutary to us. Therefore when his name is hallowed, he causes it to turn to our sanctification also; nor does his Kingdom come, without us being in some sense partakers of it. But in asking all these things, it is appropriate to regard only his glory and overlook our own advantage.

M: According to this doctrine, these three requests have a certain connection with our good, but ought to be directed to another end, that the name of God be glorified.

C: That is so; and so in the other three, the glory of God should be considered, though they are directed to ends which belong to our concern and salvation.

M: Now let us proceed to expound the words. To begin with, why is the name Father, rather than any other, given to God?

C: Because a sure and trustful conscience is in the first place necessary for praying rightly, God assumes this name, which suggests nothing but pure kindness. So that, banishing all anxiety from our minds, he may invite us to pray to him intimately.

M: Therefore we may dare to approach him directly, as children are wont to go to their parents?

C: Precisely; and indeed with greater assurance of obtaining what we ask. For, as our Master teaches us, if we who are evil are unable to deny good things to our children and to send them away unanswered, or to give them poison for bread, how much more beneficence is to be expected from the heavenly Father, who is not only the supreme good, but even goodness itself? (Matt. 7:11.)

M: May we not from this name draw the conclusion which was mentioned at the beginning, that all our prayers to be approved must rest on the intercession of Christ?

C: This is a quite certain conclusion. For God holds us for children only in so far as we are members of Christ.

M: Why do you call God in general our Father, and not in particular your Father?

C: Each believer may indeed call him his own Father. But our Lord used the common term to accustom us to exercise charity in prayer, not neglecting others in caring only for ourselves.

M: What is the force of the added phrase, that God is in heaven?

C: It is the same as if I were to call him exalted, powerful and incomprehensible.

M: How is this and why?

C: By this means we are taught to raise our minds upwards, when we pray to him, lest we should think carnally or materially of him, or measure him by the gauge of our own little standard; so that, thinking meanly of him, we should wish to reduce him to obedience to our will, instead of learning rather to look up with fear and reverence to his glorious majesty. This tends also to excite and confirm our faith in him, when he is proclaimed Lord and Governor of heaven, who rules all things by his will.

M: Repeat to me the substance of the first petition.

C: By the name of God, Scripture understands the acknowledgment and fame with which he is honoured among men. We ask therefore that his glory may be promoted everywhere and in all things.

M: But can anything add to or detract from his glory?

C: In itself it neither increases nor diminishes. But we rightly pray that it be displayed among men; so that, whatever God does, all his works may appear glorious as they indeed are, and thus he himself be glorified.

M: What do you understand by the Kingdom of God in the second petition?

C: It consists chiefly of two parts: that he would govern the elect by his Spirit; and that he would prostrate and destroy the reprobate who decline to submit themselves to his obedience; thus making it manifest that there is nothing which has the power to resist his will.

M: In what sense do you pray that this kingdom come?

C: That the Lord may daily increase the number of the faithful, and load them repeatedly with new gifts of his Spirit, till he wholly fill them. And further, that he render conspicuous and apparent his truth for the dispersal more and more of the darkness of Satan, and that he abolish all iniquity by furthering his own righteousness.

M: Are these things not done daily?

C: They are so far done that one can say the Kingdom of God is begun. Therefore we pray that he assiduously increase and advance it, until it reach the summit of its power; which we hope for only at the last day, when God, having reduced all creatures to order, will alone be exalted and pre-eminent, and thus be all in all (I Cor. 15:28).

M: When you ask that God's will be done, what is your meaning?

C: That all creatures be subdued to his obedience, and so dependent on his nod that nothing be done but by his will.

M: Do you think then that anything can be done against his will?

C: We pray not only that what he has in his own counsel decreed come to pass, but also that, all contumacy being overcome and subdued, he may subject the wills of all to his own and direct them to his obedience.

M: Do we not by thus praying yield up our own wills?

C: Certainly. And not only for this end, that he may invalidate whatsoever desires of ours conflict with his will; but also that he may form new minds and new hearts in us, so that of ourselves we may wish nothing, but rather that his Spirit rule our desires, so that they may have complete agreement with God.

M: Why do you pray that this be done in earth as in heaven?

C: As the holy angels who are his celestial creatures have this one intention, that they obey him in all things, always listen to his word, and are prepared voluntarily to do him service, I desire such instant obedience in men, so that each may yield himself in complete voluntary subservience.

M: Now I come to the second part: what do you mean by this daily bread for which you ask?

C: In general, whatever contributes to the preservation of the present life, not only by way of nourishment and clothing, but also all those other helps supplied, by which the needs of external life are met; so that we may peacefully eat our bread, in so far as the Lord knows it is expedient.

M: But why do you ask God to give you what he commands us by our labour to provide?

C: Although we are to work and even sweat to provide food, nevertheless we are not nourished by our labour or industry or diligence, but by God's blessing only, by which the labour of our hands is prospered, which would otherwise be in vain. Besides we should understand, even when abundance of food is supplied to our hand and we eat it, that it is not by its substance that we are nourished, but solely by the virtue of God. For it has no natural inherent power of this kind, but God supplies it from heaven, using it as instrument of his beneficence (Deut. 8:3, 17).

M: But are you right to call it your bread, when you ask God to give it to you?

C: Of course; because it is made ours by his goodness, though it is by no means owed to us. We are also reminded by this word, to restrain ourselves from coveting the bread of others, and to be content with such as has legitimately come to us from the hand of God.

M: Why do you add "daily" and "this day"?

C: By these two terms we are incited to moderation and continence, lest our desires should exceed necessity.

M: As this prayer ought to be common to all, how can the rich, who have abundance at home, and have provision stored up for a long time, ask it to be given to them daily?

C: The rich like the poor should hold this for certain, that nothing they have will profit them, unless in so far as God allows them its use and contrives of his grace that its use be fruitful and efficacious. Therefore in possessing all things we have nothing, except we receive them hour by hour from the hand of God, as is necessary and sufficient for us.

M: What does the fifth petition contain?

C: That the Lord forgive our sins.

M: Will no mortal man be found so righteous as not to need this pardon?

C: No one at all. For when the Lord gave this form of prayer to his disciples, he intended it for the whole Church. Therefore whoever wishes to exempt himself from this need must leave the society of the faithful. We have the clear evidence of Scripture that the man who tries to clear himself in one particular before God will be found guilty in a thousand (Job 9:2, 20). Hence the only refuge left for us all is his mercy.

M: How do you suppose sins to be remitted?

C: As the words of Christ themselves declare: There are debts,[4] namely, which hold us liable to eternal death, until of his sheer liberality God liberate us.

M: Therefore you say we obtain pardon of our sins through the gratuitous mercy of God?

C: Just so. For if the punishment of only one and that the smallest sin had to be expiated we could not at all satisfy it. Hence he must freely pardon and forgive all.

M: What advantage accrues to us from this remission?

C: We are then accepted as if we were just and innocent; and at the same time our conscience is confirmed in trust in his fatherly goodness, in which our salvation is assured.

M: Does the supplying of this condition, that he will forgive us as we forgive our debtors, mean that we merit pardon from God by pardoning men who have sinned against us?

C: Not at all. For thus remission would not be gratuitous nor founded, as is right, solely on the satisfaction of Christ made for us on the Cross. But as, by forgetting the injuries done to us, while we imitate his clemency and goodwill, we in fact show that we are his children, God desires us to confirm it by this pledge; and at the same time to show on the other hand that, unless we manifest ourselves ready and willing to forgive, nothing is to be expected from him but the supreme, inexorable and rigorous severity.

M: Do you say that all who cannot from the heart forgive offences are set aside by God and blotted out from the number of his children, so that they can hope for no place of pardon in heaven?

C: I mean this; so that the Word may be fulfilled: with what measure ye mete, it will be measured to you again.

M: What comes next?

4 The original Latin has *nomina*, which Beza first amended to the more usual *debita*; but the meaning remains the same.

C: Lead us not into temptation, but deliver us from evil.

M: Is all this included in one petition?

C: It is one petition only. For the latter half explains the former.

M: What in substance does it contain?

C: That the Lord do not permit us either to rush or to fall into sin; that he do not allow us to be overcome by the devil, or by desires of the flesh which wage constant war with us (Rom. 7:8; Gal. 5:17); that he would rather supply us with his strength to resist, sustain us with his hand, and defend and cover us with his protection; that we may dwell in safety under his care and guardianship (I Cor. 10:13).

M: How is this done?

C: When governed by his Spirit we are imbued with such love of righteousness and desire for it, that we overcome sin, the flesh and the devil; and on the other hand with such a hatred for sin as may keep us separated from the world in pure holiness. For our victory lies in the virtue of his Spirit.

M: Have all need of this help?

C: Who can dispense with it? For the devil perpetually threatens us, and goes about like a raging lion seeking whom he may devour (I Peter 5:8). But let us steadily consider what our weakness is. Indeed it would be all over with us every moment, unless God equipped us for the battle with his armour, and strengthened us by his hand.

M: What does the term temptation mean to you?

C: The stratagems and deceits of Satan, by which he constantly attacks us, and would easily and quickly overwhelm us, unless we were helped by the assistance of God. For both our mind by its native vanity is susceptible to his frauds, and our will, which is always more inclined to evil, would forthwith surrender to him.

M: But why do you pray that God lead us not into temptation? This seems more appropriate to Satan than to God.

C: As God keeps the faithful by his protection, lest they be either oppressed by Satan's wiles or overcome by sin, so those whom he intends to punish he not only leaves destitute of his grace, but even hands over to the tyranny of Satan, strikes with blindness, and abandons to a reprobate mind, so that they may be entirely enslaved to sin, and exposed to all the assaults of temptation.

M: What does this little added phrase mean: for thine is the kingdom, and the power, and the glory, for ever?

C: Here again we are reminded that our prayers depend more on the power and goodness of God than on any trust of ours. Besides we are taught to conclude all our prayers with praise.

M: Is it right to ask nothing of God but what is included here?

C: Although we are free to pray with other words and in another way, yet we ought to hold that no prayer can please God, which has no reference to this which is the only right standard of prayer.

Concerning the Sacraments [5]

M: The order outlined and adopted by us demands that now we consider the fourth part of divine worship.

C: We have said this consists in acknowledging God as the author of all good, and in honouring his goodness, justice, wisdom, and power with praise and thanks, that the glory of all good may substantially reside entirely in him.

M: Has he prescribed no rule for this part?

C: All the praises in Scripture ought to be a rule for us.

M: Has the Lord's Prayer nothing relevant here?

C: Yes. When we desire the hallowing of his name, we desire that his glory be set forth in all his works; that he be regarded in pardoning sinners as merciful, in exacting punishment as just, or in fulfilling his promises as true; in short, that whatever of his works we may notice should excite us to glorify him. This is indeed to accord to him the praise of all good.

M: What are we to conclude from the matters that have been treated by us?

C: What truth itself teaches and I proposed at the beginning: this is life eternal, to know the one true God as Father and Jesus Christ whom he sent (John 17:3). I say to know him, in order that we may offer to him the honour and worship that is due, so that he be not only Lord to us, but also Father and Saviour (Matt. 1:21), that we on our side be his children and servants, and accordingly dedicate our life to display his glory.

M: By what road does one come to such blessedness?

C: To this end God has left us his sacred Word. For spiritual doctrine is a kind of door, by which we enter into his celestial Kingdom.

---

[5] The older versions read *De Sacramentis*. Beza reads *De Verbo Dei* here, and below (p. 131), before the question: Is there no other medium, etc., inserts the title *De Sacramentis*.

M: Where must we seek this Word?

C: In the Holy Scriptures in which it is contained.

M: How should it be used to obtain profit from it?

C: If we lay hold on it with complete heartfelt conviction as nothing less than certain truth come down from heaven; if we show ourselves docile to it; if we subdue our wills and minds to his obedience; if we love it heartily; if having it once engraved on our hearts and its roots fixed there, so that it bring forth fruit in our life; if finally we be formed to its rule—then it will turn to our salvation, as intended.

M: Are all these things placed within our power?

C: None of them whatever; but all this I have mentioned is of God only, to be effected in us by the gift of his Spirit.

M: But are we not to apply diligence and strive with all zeal to advance in it by reading, hearing and meditating?

C: Certainly; while everyone ought to exercise himself in daily reading, at the same time also all are to attend with special regularity the gatherings where the doctrine of salvation is expounded in the company of the faithful.

M: You deny then that it is enough for each to read privately at home; and affirm that all should meet together to hear the same doctrine?

C: They must meet when they can, that is, when opportunity offers.

M: Can you prove this to me?

C: The will of God alone ought to be abundantly sufficient proof for us. But this order which he commends to his Church (Eph. 4:11) is not what two or three might observe, but what all should obey in common. Further, he declares this to be the only way of either edification or maintenance in the faith. Let this therefore be a sacred and inviolable rule for us; nor is anyone to think it right to be wise beyond his Master.

M: Is it therefore necessary that pastors be set over churches?

C: Indeed it is also necessary to hear them, and to receive their exposition of the doctrine of Christ from their lips with fear and reverence. Therefore whoever holds them in contempt or dissuades from hearing them, holds Christ in contempt and disrupts from the society of the faithful (Matt. 10:40; Luke 10:16).

M: But is it enough for a Christian once to have been instructed by his pastor, or must he hold to this course all his life?

C: It is little to have begun unless you continue. For it behoves us to be disciples of Christ up to the end, or rather without end.

But he has committed this office to the ministers of the Church, that they teach us in his place and name.

M: Is there no other medium, as they call it, than the Word by which God communicates with us?

C: He has joined the sacraments to the preaching of the Word.

M: What is a sacrament?

C: An outward attestation of the divine benevolence towards us, which represents spiritual grace symbolically, to seal the promises of God in our hearts, by which the truth of them is better confirmed.

M: Does there subsist in the visible sign such virtue as to establish our conscience in assurance of salvation?

C: This it has not of itself indeed, but of the will of God, for it was instituted to this end.

M: Since it is the proper function of the Holy Spirit to seal the promises of God in our minds, how do you attribute this to the sacraments?

C: There is a wide difference between the two. For to move and affect the heart, to illumine the mind and to render the conscience sure and tranquil is the business of the Spirit alone, so that it ought to be considered wholly his work and be ascribed to him, lest his praise be transferred to another. But this does not in the least prevent God using the sacraments as secondary instruments, and applying them to any use he deems proper; and this he does without derogating in any way from the virtue of the Spirit.

M: Then you judge the power and efficacy of a sacrament not to lie in the external element, but wholly to emanate from the Spirit of God?

C: I think so: that it pleased God to exercise his virtue through his instruments, for to this end he destined them. And this indeed he does, so as in no way to detract from the virtue of his Spirit.

M: Can you give me a reason why he acts thus?

C: By this means he has consideration upon our weakness. For if we were wholly spiritual like the angels, we should be able to see both him and his gifts. But as we are surrounded by this gross earthly body, we need symbols or mirrors, to exhibit to us the appearance of spiritual and heavenly things in a kind of earthly way. For we could not otherwise attain to them. At the same time it is to our interest that all our senses be exercised in the promises of God, by which they are the better confirmed to us.

M: If it is true that God instituted the sacraments to be an aid to our necessity, should it not be rightly condemned as arrogance, that anyone should judge himself able to do without them as though they were unnecessary?

C: Certainly. Hence if anyone abstain voluntarily from their use, as if he had no need of them, he holds Christ in contempt, rejects his grace, and quenches the Spirit.

M: But what kind of confidence and how certain is the assurance that can be conceived from the sacraments for establishing our conscience, when good and bad indiscriminately use them?

C: Though the impious, as I may say, reduce the gifts of God conferred in the sacraments to nothing so far as they are concerned, yet they do not thereby contrive to remove from the sacraments their power and nature.

M: Then how and when does the effect follow the use of the sacraments?

C: When we receive them by faith, seeking in them Christ alone and his grace.

M: Why do you say Christ is to be sought in them?

C: I mean that we are not to cling to the visible signs and there seek our salvation, or imagine the virtue of conferring grace to be fixed and confined in them. Rather we are to regard the sign in the light of an aid, by which we may be directed straight to Christ, and from him seek salvation and real felicity.

M: If faith is required for their use, how do you say that they are given for the confirmation of faith, to render us more certain about the promises of God?

C: It is not at all enough that there be in us only the beginning of faith, unless it be constantly nourished and increase more and more daily. Hence the Lord instituted the sacraments for this nourishment, strengthening and furtherance. This Paul indicates when he affirms their force to be to seal God's promises.

M: But is it not an indication of unbelief not to have a firm faith in the promises of God unless they are confirmed from another source?

C: Certainly it argues weakness of faith, from which even the children of God suffer while not on this account ceasing to be faithful, though they have been granted hitherto only a small and imperfect faith. For as long as we continue in this world, vestiges of distrust always adhere to our flesh, which we are not able otherwise to shake off than by continually advancing until the end of life. It is necessary, therefore, always to be pressing forward.

M: How many are the sacraments of the Christian Church?

C: There are two only, commonly in use among believers.

M: What are they?

C: Baptism and the Holy Supper.

M: What likeness or difference is there between them?

C: Baptism is for us a kind of entry into the Church. For in it we have a testimony that we, while otherwise strangers and aliens, were received into the family of God, so that we are reckoned among his household. But the Supper testifies that God himself manifests to us as Father by feeding our souls.

M: Let us consider each of them separately, so that the truth of both may be made clearer to us. First, what is the meaning of Baptism?

C: It has two parts. For there is remission of sins; and then spiritual regeneration is symbolized by it (Eph. 5:26; Rom. 6:4).

M: What similarity has water to these things, that it represents them?

C: Forgiveness of sins is a kind of washing, by which our souls are cleansed from all their stains, just as bodily defilements are washed away by water.

M: What about regeneration?

C: Since the mortification of our nature is the beginning, and the end that we be new creatures, the metaphor of death is set before us in the pouring of water upon the head; but of new life in that we do not remain immersed under the water, but only for a moment descend into it as into a sepulchre, in order immediately to emerge.

M: Do you regard the water as the washing of the soul?

C: Not at all. For it is wrong to snatch this honour from the blood of Christ, which was poured out in order that, all our stains being wiped away, he might render us pure and unpolluted before God (I Peter 1:19; I John 1:7). And we perceive the fruit of this cleansing when the Holy Spirit sprinkles our conscience with that sacred blood. The seal of this we have in the sacrament.

M: But do you attribute nothing more to the water than to be a mere symbol of ablution?

C: I think it to be such a symbol that reality is attached to it. For God does not disappoint us when he promises us his gifts. Hence both pardon of sins and newness of life are certainly offered to us and received by us in Baptism.

M: Is this grace bestowed on all indiscriminately?

C: Many by their wickedness preclude its entry, and so render it empty for themselves. Thus its fruit reaches the faithful only. But thereby nothing is lost to the sacrament.

M: But whence comes regeneration?

C: From both the death and the resurrection of Christ. For his death has this power, that by it our old nature is crucified and the wickedness of our being is as it were buried, lest it flourish any longer in us. But it is the benefit of the resurrection that we are remade into a new life of obedience to the righteousness of God.

M: How are these benefits conferred on us through Baptism?

C: Because unless we render the promises unfruitful by re- jecting them, we are fed [6] with Christ and granted his Spirit.

M: But what have we to do to use Baptism rightly?

C: The right use of Baptism lies in faith and repentance. That is, we must first hold with a firm and hearty confidence that we, having been cleansed from all stains by the blood of Christ, are pleasing to God; then we are to feel his Spirit dwelling in us and declare this to others by our deeds, and so practise ourselves unceasingly in meditating on the mortification of the flesh and obedience to the righteousness of God.

M: If these things are requisite to the legitimate use of Baptism, how does it come about that we baptize infants?

C: It is not necessary that faith and repentance always pre- cede Baptism. They are required from those only who by age are already capable of them. It will be sufficient if infants, when they have grown up, exhibit the power of their Baptism.

M: Can you show with reason that there is nothing absurd in this?

C: Certainly: if you concede that the Lord has instituted nothing that is at variance with reason. For while Moses and all the prophets taught that circumcision was the sign of repent- ance (Deut. 10:16; 30:6; Jer. 4:4), and was even the sign of faith, as Paul witnesses (Rom. 4:11), so we see that it does not exclude infants.

M: But are they now admitted to Baptism for the same reason as was valid for circumcision?

C: Exactly the same: for promises which God had given once to the people of Israel are now promulgated through the whole world.

---

[6] Original and *Instit.* 1550 has *vescimur*, which is replaced by *vestimur* in all other editions.

M: But do you conclude from this that the sign is also to be taken over?

C: He who carefully deliberates everything in both cases will come to this conclusion. For Christ did not by this law make us partakers of this grace, which was before conferred on Israel, in order that it should be more obscure to us or in any respect diminished. Rather he pours it forth more clearly and more lavishly on us.

M: Do you think, if infants are denied Baptism, something is thereby subtracted from the grace of God, so that it can be said to have been diminished by the advent of Christ?

C: That is evident. For to take away the sign which tends powerfully to witness to God's mercy and to confirm his promises, would be to deprive us of a splendid consolation which the ancients enjoyed.

M: So you think thus, that since God under the Old Testament, in order to show himself the Father of infants, desired the promise of salvation to be graven on their bodies in a visible sign, it would be unworthy if the faithful had less confirmation since the advent of Christ. For the same promise is intended for today as formerly for the fathers, and God holds out to us a clearer example of his goodness in Christ.

C: I think so. Besides, when it is sufficiently established that the force and substance, as I may say, of Baptism is common to infants, to deny them the sign which is inferior to the substance, would be a manifest injury to them.

M: On what condition are infants to be baptized?

C: To testify that they are heirs of the blessing promised to the seed of the faithful, and that, after they are grown up, they may acknowledge the fact of their Baptism, and receive and produce its fruit.

M: Let us pass to the Supper. And first I should like you to know what its meaning is.

C: It was instituted by Christ that he might teach us by the communion of his body and blood that our souls are being brought up in the hope of eternal life, and that he might make us certain of this.

M: But why is the body symbolized by bread and the blood by wine?

C: By this we are taught that the body of our Lord has the same virtue spiritually to nourish our souls as bread has in nourishing our bodies for the sustenance of this present life. As wine exhilarates the heart of men, refreshes their strength, and fortifies the whole body, so from the blood of our Lord the very same benefits are received by our souls.

M: Do we then eat the body and blood of our Lord?

C: I understand so. For since all our confidence of salvation is placed in him, so that the obedience he offered to the Father may be accepted for us just as if it were our own, it is necessary that he be possessed by us. For he communicates his benefits to us in no other way than in making himself ours.

M: But did he not give himself when he exposed himself to death, in order that he might reconcile us, redeemed from the judgment of death, to the Father?

C: That is quite true. But it is not enough for us, unless we now receive him, so that the efficacy and fruit of his death may reach us.

M: Does not the method of receiving consist in faith?

C: I admit it. But at the same time I add that this is done not only by our believing that he died to liberate us from death and was raised to procure life for us; but also by our acknowledging that he dwells in us and that we are joined in a union of the same kind as that by which members cohere with their head; so that by the virtue of this union we are made partakers of all his benefits.

M: Do we obtain this communion through the Supper only?

C: No indeed; for through the gospel also, according to Paul, Christ is communicated to us (I Cor. 1:21). And Paul rightly teaches this, since there we hear that we are flesh of his flesh and bone of his bone (Eph. 5:30), that he is the living bread which came down from heaven for the nourishment of our souls (John 6:51), and that we are one with him as he is one with the Father (John 17:21), and so on.

M: What more do we obtain from the sacrament, or what benefit besides does it confer on us?

C: This, that the communion of which I have spoken is confirmed and increased in us. For though both in Baptism and in the gospel Christ is exhibited to us, yet we do not receive him wholly but only in part.

M: What then do we have in the symbol of bread?

C: The body of Christ, as it was once sacrificed for us to reconcile us to God, is now thus also given to us, that we may certainly know that reconciliation is ours.

M: What in the symbol of wine?

C: Christ, as he poured out his blood once for satisfaction for sins and as the price of our redemption, so now holds it forth for us to drink, that we may feel the benefit which ought to accrue to us from it.

M: According to those replies of yours, the Holy Supper of our Lord refers us to his death, in order that we may partake of its virtue.

C: Quite so: for then the one and perpetual sacrifice, which suffices for our salvation, was made. There remains nothing further, except to enjoy it.

M: Then the Supper is not instituted with the object that the body of his Son be offered to God?

C: Not at all. For he himself only, since he is the eternal Priest, has this prerogative (Heb. 5:5). And this his words declare, when he says: Take and eat. For there he commands, not that we offer his body, but only that we eat it (Matt. 26:26).

M: Why do we make use of two symbols?

C: Thereby our Lord had consideration for our weakness, teaching us more familiarly that he is not only food for our souls, but also drink, lest we should seek any part of our spiritual life elsewhere than in him only.

M: Should all alike and without exception use both?

C: This is the meaning of the command of Christ; and it is the height of impiety for anyone to derogate from it in any way, by attempting something contrary.

M: Have we in the Supper a mere symbol of those benefits you mention, or is their reality exhibited to us there?

C: Since our Lord Jesus Christ is the truth itself, there can be no doubt but that the promises which he there gives us, he at the same time also implements, adding the reality to the symbol. Therefore I do not doubt but that, as testified by words and signs, he thus also makes us partakers of his substance, by which we are joined in one life with him.

M: But how can this be, when Christ's body is in heaven, and we are still pilgrims on earth?

C: He accomplishes this by the miraculous and secret virtue of his Spirit, for whom it is not difficult to associate things that are otherwise separated by an interval of space.

M: Then you think that the body is not enclosed within the bread, nor the blood within the chalice?

C: By no means. Rather I think that in order to enjoy the reality of the signs our minds must be raised to heaven where Christ is and whence we expect him to come as judge and redeemer. But in these earthly elements it is improper and vain to seek him.

M: To summarize what you have said: You affirm that there

are two things in the Supper, the bread and the wine, which are seen by our eyes, handled by our hands, and perceived by the taste; and second, Christ, by whom our souls are inwardly fed, as by their own proper nourishment.

C: True—so much so that even the resurrection of the body is there confirmed to us, as by a given pledge, since the body itself shares in the symbol of life.

M: What then is the right and legitimate use of this sacrament?

C: It is as Paul defines it: Let a man examine himself, before he come to it (I Cor. 11:28).

M: What does he investigate in this examination?

C: Whether he is a true member of Christ.

M: By what evidence does he come to a knowledge of this?

C: If he is endued with true faith and repentance, if he exercise sincere love to his neighbours, and if he hold his soul free of all hatred and malice.

M: Do you require both perfect faith and perfect charity in a man?

C: It is right that both be entire and free of all deceit. But to demand a perfection complete in all counts and lacking in nothing would be vain; since such will never be found in man.

M: Then the imperfection under which we labour does not prevent us approaching?

C: On the contrary: if we were perfect, the Supper would have no further utility for us. For it ought to be an aid for removing our foolishness and a support for our weakness.

M: Have these two sacraments besides no other end in view?

C: They are also marks and as it were badges of our profession. For by using them, we profess our faith before men, and testify that we are in entire agreement with the Christian religion.

M: If anyone were to affect to despise their use, how would he be regarded?

C: This would indeed be an indirect denial of Christ. Certainly such a person, because he does not deign to confess himself Christian, is unworthy to be reckoned among Christians.

M: Is it sufficient to receive both once in a lifetime?

C: One Baptism suffices, and it may not be repeated. But the case of the Supper is different.

M: What is the difference?

C: By Baptism the Lord adopts us and brings us into his Church, so that we are thereafter held to be of his household. After he has inscribed us in the number of his own, he testifies by the Supper that he takes a perpetual interest in nourishing us.

M: Does the administration of both Baptism and the Supper belong indiscriminately to all?

C: They are the proper function of those to whom the public office of teaching is entrusted. For the two things, feeding the Church with the doctrine of salvation and administering the sacraments, are joined to each other by a lasting tie.

M: Can you prove this to me by Scriptural evidence?

C: Christ gave specific commandment to the disciples to baptize (Matt. 28:19). In the celebration of the Supper he bade us follow his example. But the evangelists relate that in administering it he performed the office of a public minister.

M: But ought pastors, to whom the administration is entrusted, to admit everyone always and without discrimination?

C: So far as Baptism is concerned, because it is now only conferred on infants, there is no room for discretion. In the case of the Supper, the minister ought to be very careful to offer it to none who is manifestly unworthy.

M: Why is this?

C: Because otherwise it cannot be done without affront and profanation of the sacrament.

M: But was not Christ pleased to admit Judas to communion, impious though he was?

C: I admit this; for his impiety was still secret. For though it was not concealed from Christ, yet it had not come to light and to the knowledge of men.

M: What is to be done with hypocrites?

C: The pastor is not able to bar them as unworthy. He must restrain himself, until God reveals their iniquity so that it is apparent to men.

M: What if he knows or has been informed that an individual is unworthy?

C: Even this would not be enough to forbid them communion unless there is added legitimate enquiry and decision of the Church.

M: It is of importance, then, to have a certain order of government established in the Churches?

C: It is: for otherwise they are neither well managed or properly constituted. And this is the method, that elders be chosen to preside as censors of morals, to guard against reprehensible offences, and to bar from communion those whom they do not believe to be capable of receiving the Supper or to be able to be admitted without profaning the sacrament.

Short Treatise on the Holy Supper of our Lord and only Saviour Jesus Christ

INTRODUCTION

LITTLE NEED BE SAID BY WAY OF EXPLANATION OF THE Short Treatise, since it carries within itself its own exposition. In the Editions of the *Institutes* of 1536 and 1539, as well as in the earlier Catechism referred to in the preface to the Catechism published in this volume, Calvin had already set forth his views on the nature of the Holy Supper. But the time was ripe for something more and other. The controversy between Lutherans and Zwinglians raged bitterly, and deeply agitated the minds of ordinary people. There was room, as *C.R.* puts it, for a little book specially written in his native French, to show calmly and clearly a middle way between the contending parties. The *Treatise* was written in 1540, and seems to have been, after some difficulty in finding a printer, published in Geneva the next year.

Calvin's doctrine is expounded with the utmost clarity here, and in its main outline is repeated in other much longer and more controversial works but not with equal lucidity. He puts aside the view that the elements of the Holy Supper are bare signs, figures or symbols; on the other hand, as appears with greater emphasis elsewhere, he turns his face against any view that would so tie the body of Christ to the elements as to subject it to being consumed by unworthy communicants. He affirms a true and real presence of Christ in the elements. Those enjoy this presence and all allied blessings who, complying with the primitive eucharistic injunction, lift up their minds and hearts on high, and so, not stopping at the visible signs, partake of the gifts Christ crucified procured and Christ exalted dispenses.

Almost as notable as the firm precision of the contents of the *Treatise*, is the dispassionate and conciliatory tone in which refer-

ence is made to the parties contending within the Reformed
Church. It is a tone, one must concede, that is not maintained
in all his later controversial writings. Here, however, his express
aim is to explain if not to justify the sharpness of the debate to
those pained by the appearance of controversy, and this apologetic purpose is admirably advanced by the eirenic tone in
which the whole is couched.

Textual variations in this *Treatise* are inconsiderable, in the
sense that the meaning is never once in doubt. Nor has it often
seemed worthwhile to draw attention to them.

Here, as elsewhere, shorter paragraphs have been introduced,
and for ease in following the course of the argument the
divisions referred to by Calvin in the text have been marked as
separate sections. (See *C.R.* V, xlix.)

Short Treatise on the Holy Supper of our Lord and only Saviour Jesus Christ

Because the holy sacrament of the Supper of our Lord Jesus Christ has been for long entangled in several major errors, and during these past years involved anew in diverse opinions and contentious disputes, it is no wonder if weak consciences are unable rightly to resolve what view they ought to hold, but remain in doubt and perplexity, waiting until, all contentions being laid aside, the servants of God come to some agreement in the matter. However, since it is a very perilous matter not to have any certainty concerning this ordinance, knowledge of which is so needful for our salvation, I have thought that it would be a very useful labour to try briefly and yet clearly to extract the chief substance of what it is necessary to know of the matter. It should be added that I have been asked to do this by certain worthy persons, who realized the need for it, and whom I could not refuse without violating my duty.

But in order to be rid of all difficulty, it is expedient to note the order which I propose to follow. First, then, we shall expound to what end and for what reason the Lord instituted this holy sacrament for us. Second, what fruit and benefit we obtain from it, when it will likewise be shown how the body of Jesus Christ is given to us. After this, what is its legitimate use. Fourth, we shall detail with what errors and superstitions it has been contaminated, where, too, it will be shown how different should be the servants of God from the papists. And last, we shall mention what has been the source of the dispute, which has been so sharply conducted, even among those who in our time have brought back the gospel into the light, and employed themselves in rightly edifying the Church in sound doctrine.

I

REASON FOR THE INSTITUTION OF THE HOLY SUPPER

As to the first article: Since it pleased our loving God to receive us by Baptism into his Church, which is his house, and which he will maintain and govern, and since he has received us not only to keep us as servants, but as his own children, it remains that, to discharge the office of a loving father, he nourish us, and provide all that is necessary to life. For as to bodily nourishment, since it is common to all, and the bad have part in it like the good, it is not peculiar to his family. It is very true that we have it as evidence of his fatherly goodness in maintaining us as far as the body is concerned, seeing that we participate in all the good things which with his blessing he gives us. But as the life into which he has regenerated us is spiritual, so the food for preserving and confirming us in it must be spiritual. For we ought to understand that he has not only called us to possess one day his heavenly inheritance, but that by hope he has already in a measure installed us in its possession; that not only has he promised life to us, but has already translated us into it, delivering us from death. And this when, in adopting us as children, he begot us again by the seed of immortality, which is his Word imprinted in our hearts by his Holy Spirit.

To maintain us in this life, then, what is required is not to feed our bodies with corruptible and transitory provisions, but to nourish our souls on better and more precious diet. Now all Scripture tells us that the spiritual bread by which our souls are maintained is the same Word by which our Lord regenerated us. But it often adds the ground of this, that in it Jesus Christ, who alone is our life, is given and administered to us. For we must not think that there is life anywhere else but in God. But just as God has set all fulness of life in Jesus, in order to communicate it to us by means of him, so he has ordained his Word as instrument by which Jesus Christ, with all his benefits, is dispensed to us. Yet it always remains true that our souls have no other pasture than Jesus Christ. Therefore the heavenly Father, in his care to nourish us, gives us nothing else, but rather recommends us to take our fill there, as from a refreshment manifestly sufficient, with which we cannot dispense, and beyond which it is impossible to find any other.

We have already seen how Jesus Christ is the only provision

by which our souls are nourished. But because it is distributed by the Word of the Lord, which he has appointed as instrument to this end, it is also called bread and water. Now what is said of the Word fitly belongs also to the sacrament of the Supper, by means of which our Lord leads us to communion with Jesus Christ. For seeing we are so foolish, that we cannot receive him with true confidence of heart, when he is presented by simple teaching and preaching, the Father, of his mercy, not at all disdaining to condescend in this matter to our infirmity, has desired to attach to his Word a visible sign, by which he represents the substance of his promises, to confirm and fortify us, and to deliver us from all doubt and uncertainty. Since then it is a mystery so high and incomprehensible, when we say that we have communion with the body and blood of Jesus Christ, and since we on our side are so rude and gross that we cannot understand the smallest things concerning God, it was of consequence that he give us to understand, according as our capacity can bear it. For this reason, the Lord instituted for us his Supper, in order to sign and seal in our consciences the promises contained in his gospel concerning our being made partakers of his body and blood; and to give us certainty and assurance that in this consists our true spiritual nourishment; so that, having such an earnest, we might entertain a right assurance about salvation. Second, for the purpose of inciting us to recognize his great goodness towards us, so that we praise and magnify it more fully. Third, to exhort us to all sanctity and innocence, seeing that we are members of Jesus Christ, and particularly to unity and brotherly charity, as is specially recommended to us. When we have noted well these three reasons, which our Lord imposed in ordaining his Supper for us, we shall be in a position to understand both what benefits accrue to us from it, and what is our duty in its right use.

II

Benefits of the Holy Supper

It is now time to come to the second point, namely, to show how profitable the Supper of our Lord is to us, on condition that we make profitable use of it. Now we shall understand its utility by reflecting on our indigence, to which it is an aid. It is necessary that we be in great trouble and distress of conscience, when we consider who we are and examine what is in us. For there is none of us who can find a single grain of righteousness in himself; but on the contrary we are all full of sin and iniquity; so much so that no other party is needed to accuse us but our own conscience, no other judge to condemn us. It follows then that the wrath of God is kindled against us, and there is no one able to escape eternal death. If we are not indolent and stupid, this awful thought must be a kind of perpetual hell to vex and torment us. For the judgment of God cannot occur to our recollection without our seeing that our condemnation follows as a consequence. We are then already in the abyss of death, unless our loving God draw us out. Moreover, what hope of resurrection can we have, considering our flesh which is nothing but rottenness and corruption? So, as regards the soul, as well as the body, we are more than miserable, if we remain within ourselves; and it can only be that we have great sadness and anguish from the feeling of such misery. Now our heavenly Father, to succour us from it, gives us the Supper as a mirror in which we contemplate our Lord Jesus Christ crucified to abolish our faults and offences, and raised to deliver us from corruption and death, and restoring us to a heavenly immortality. Here, then, is the peculiar consolation we receive from the Supper, that it directs and conducts us to the cross of Jesus Christ and to his resurrection, in order to assure us that, whatever iniquity there may be in us, the Lord does not cease to regard and accept us as righteous; whatever material of death may be in us, he does not cease to vivify us; whatever the wretchedness we may have, yet he does not cease to fill us with all felicity.

Or to explain the matter more simply, as we in ourselves are lacking in all good and have not a particle of what might help us to salvation, the Supper is attestation that, being made partakers of the death and passion of Jesus Christ, we have everything that is useful and salutary for us. Therefore we can say that the Lord here displays to us all the treasures of his spiritual grace, seeing that he makes us associates of all the blessings and riches of our Lord Jesus Christ. Let us remember then, that the Supper is given us as a mirror, in which we may contemplate Jesus Christ crucified to deliver us from damnation, and risen again to procure righteousness and eternal life for us. It is indeed true that this same grace is offered us by the gospel; yet as in the Supper we have a more ample certainty and fuller enjoyment, it is with good reason that we recognize such a fruit as coming from it.

But because the blessings of Jesus Christ do not at all belong

T.T.—10

to us, unless he first be ours, it is necessary in the first place that he be given us in the Supper, so that the things which we have mentioned be really accomplished in us. For this reason, I am accustomed to say that the matter and substance of the sacraments is the Lord Jesus Christ, and the efficacy of them are the gifts and blessings which we have by means of him. Now the effect of the Supper is to confirm for us the reconciliation which we have with God through his death and passion; the washing of our souls which we have by the shedding of his blood; the righteousness we have in his obedience; in short, the hope of salvation which we have from all he has done for us. It is necessary, then, that the substance should be joined with these, otherwise nothing would be firm or certain. Hence we must conclude that two things are presented to us in the Supper: Jesus Christ as source and substance of all good; and second, the fruit and efficacy of his death and passion. This is implied also by the words which are there used. For in commanding us to eat his body and drink his blood, he added that his body was delivered for us, and his blood shed for the remission of our sins. Hereby he declares, first, that we ought not simply to communicate in his body and blood, without further consideration, but to receive the fruit which comes to us from his death and passion; and second, that we can only attain to the enjoyment of such fruit by participating in his body and blood, of which it is the product.

We begin now to enter into the question so much contested both in ancient and in present days: how these words are to be understood, in which the bread is called the body of Jesus Christ, and the wine his blood. This can be disposed of without great difficulty, if we remember carefully the principle which I have laid down. It is that all benefit which we ought to seek from the Supper is annulled, unless Jesus Christ be there given to us as substance and foundation of all. This agreed, we shall confess without doubt that to deny the true communication of Jesus Christ to be offered us in the Supper is to render this holy sacrament frivolous and useless—a blasphemy execrable and unworthy of attention. Moreover, if the reason for communicating with Jesus Christ is in order that we have part and portion in all the gifts which he has procured for us by his death, it is not only a matter of being partakers of his Spirit; it is necessary also to partake of his humanity, in which he rendered complete obedience to God his Father, to satisfy our debts; though rightly speaking, the one cannot be without the other. For when he gives himself to us, it is in order that we possess him entirely. For this reason, as it is said that his Spirit is our life, so he himself with his own mouth declares that his flesh is truly food, and his blood truly drink. If these words are not spoken in vain, it follows that to have our life in Christ our souls should be fed on his body and his blood, as their proper food. This, then, we expressly testify in the Supper, when we are told of the bread, that we take and eat it and that it is his body; and that we drink of the chalice and that it is his blood. It is said expressly of the body and the blood, in order that we learn to seek in them the substance of our spiritual life. Now, if it be asked nevertheless whether the bread is the body of Christ, and the wine his blood, we should reply that the bread and the wine are visible signs, which represent to us the body and the blood; but that the name and title of body and blood is attributed to them, because they are as instruments by which our Lord Jesus Christ distributes them to us. This form and manner of speaking is in principle very appropriate. For though it may be that the communion we have with the body of Christ is something incomprehensible, not only to the eye but to our natural sense, it is there visibly shown to us. Of this we have a very apposite example in a similar case. Our Lord, wishing at his Baptism to give visible appearance to his Spirit, represented it under the form of a dove. John the Baptist, relating this story, says that he saw the Holy Spirit descending. If we enquire more closely, we find that he saw only the dove, for the Holy Spirit is essentially invisible. Yet knowing that this vision is not an empty figure, but a certain sign of the presence of the Holy Spirit, he does not hesitate to say that he saw it, because it is represented to him according to his capacity. It is like this with the communion which we have with the body and blood of our Lord. It is a spiritual mystery, which cannot be seen by the eye, nor comprehended by the human understanding. It is therefore symbolized by visible signs, as our infirmity requires, but in such a way that it is not a bare figure, but joined to its reality and substance. It is therefore with good reason that the bread is called body, since not only does it represent it to us, but also presents it to us. Hence we shall readily concede that the name body of Jesus Christ is transferred to the bread, as it is the sacrament and figure of it. But we likewise add that the sacraments of the Lord ought not and cannot at all be separated from their reality and substance. To distinguish them so that they be not confused is not only good and reasonable but wholly necessary. But to divide them so as to set them up the one without the other is absurd. Therefore when we see the visible sign, we ought to regard what representation it carries and by whom it is given us. The bread is given to symbolize the body of Jesus Christ, with command that we eat it; and it is given us by God who is certain and immutable truth. If God cannot deceive or lie, it follows that he performs all that it signifies. We must then really receive in the Supper the body and blood of Jesus Christ, since the Lord there represents to us the communion of both. For otherwise what would it mean that we eat the bread and drink the wine as a sign that his flesh is our food and his blood our drink, if he gave only bread and wine and left the spiritual reality behind? Would it not be under false colours that he had instituted this mystery? We have then to confess that if the representation which God grants in the Supper is veracious, the internal substance of the sacrament is joined with the visible signs; and as the bread is distributed by hand, so the body of Christ is communicated to us, so that we are made partakers of it. If there were nothing more, we have good reason to be satisfied when we realize that Jesus Christ gives us in the Supper the real substance of his body and his blood, so that we may possess him fully, and, possessing him, have part in all his blessings. For since we have him, all the riches of God, which are comprehended in him, are proffered to us in order that they may be ours. Thus, as a brief definition of this benefit of the Supper, we may say that Jesus Christ is there offered to us that we may possess him, and in him all the fulness of his gifts which we can desire; and that in this we have great assistance in confirming our conscience in the faith which we ought to have in him.

The second benefit which the Supper yields us is that it urges and incites us the better to recognize the blessings which we have received, and daily receive, from the Lord Jesus Christ, so that we may render him such offering of praise as is his due. For of ourselves we are so negligent that it is unusual for us to meditate on the goodness of God, unless he rouse us from our indolence, and impel us to do our duty. Now we cannot conceive having a spur to prick us more sharply into life than when he makes us, so to say, see with the eye, and touch with the hand and manifestly feel a blessing so inestimable, that we feed upon his own substance. He will signify this by commanding that we show forth his death until he come. If it is, then, a thing so necessary to salvation not to overlook the gifts which God has made us, but to hold them diligently in mind and extol them to others for mutual edification, in this we see another outstanding benefit of the Supper, that it turns us from ingratitude, and does not allow us to forget the good our Lord did us in dying for us, but rather induces us to render thanks to him, and, as it were, by public confession, protest how much we are indebted to him.

The third benefit consists in our having a vehement incitement to holy living, and above all to observe charity and brotherly love among us. For since we are there made members of Jesus Christ, being incorporated into him and united to him as to our Head, this is good reason, first, that we be conformed to his purity and innocence, and especially that we have to one another such charity and concord as members of the same body ought to have. To understand properly this benefit, we must not suppose that our Lord only warns, incites and inflames our hearts with the external sign, For the chief thing is that he cares for us internally by his Holy Spirit, so as to give efficacy to his ordinance, which he has destined for this purpose, as an instrument by which he will do his work in us. Therefore seeing that the virtue of the Holy Spirit is joined to the sacraments when they are duly received, we have reason to hope they will afford a good means and assistance for our growth and advance in sanctity of life and especially in charity.

III

The Right Use of the Sacrament

Let us come to the third chief head which we proposed at the beginning of this treatise, that is to the right use, which consists in observing the institution of our Lord with reverence. For whoever approaches this holy sacrament with contempt or indifference, not caring much about following where our Lord calls him, perversely misuses it and thus contaminates it. Now to pollute and contaminate what God has so sanctified is intolerable sacrilege. It is, then, not without reason that Paul passes such grave condemnation on those who take it unworthily. For if there is nothing in heaven or earth of greater value and dignity than the body and blood of our Lord, it is no small fault to take it inconsiderately and without being well prepared. Therefore he exhorts us to examine ourselves well, in order to use it properly. When we understand what kind of examination this should be, we shall know the use for which we seek.

Now we must here be well on our guard. For, as we cannot

take too great diligence in examining ourselves, as our Lord commands, so on the other hand doctors of sophistry have brought poor consciences into perilous perplexity, or rather into an awful hell, by demanding I know not what kind of examination, which they cannot possibly get through. To rid ourselves of all these troubles, we must reduce the whole, as I have already said, to the ordinance of our Lord, as to a rule which will not permit us to err if we follow it. In following it, we have to examine whether we have a true repentance in ourselves and a true faith in our Lord Jesus Christ. These two things are so joined that the one cannot stand without the other. For if we think our life to be located in Christ, we must acknowledge that in ourselves we are dead. If we seek in him our strength, we must understand that in ourselves we are weak. If we judge all our felicity to be in his grace, we ought to understand how great is our misery without it. If we have our rest in him, we must by ourselves feel tormented and unquiet. Now such feeling cannot exist without producing first a distaste of all our life; then anxiety and fear; and finally a desire and love of righteousness. For he who knows the baseness of his sin and the unhappiness of his state and condition while alienated from God, is so ashamed of it, that he is constrained to discontent with himself, to self-condemnation, and to groaning and sighing with a great sadness. Moreover, the judgment of God presents itself forthwith, to oppress the sinful conscience with remarkable anxiety, since it has no way of escape and nothing to answer in its defence. When, with such a realization of our misery, we can taste the goodness of God, then we desire to order our life by his will, and to renounce all our earlier life, in order to be made new creatures in him.

If we wish, then, to communicate worthily in the sacred Supper of our Lord, we must hold in firm and hearty confidence the Lord Jesus Christ as our sole righteousness, life and salvation, receiving and accepting the promises which are given us by him as certain and assured; renouncing on the other hand all other confidence, in order that, distrusting ourselves and all other creatures, we may rest fully in him and content ourselves with his grace alone. Now because this cannot be, unless we recognize the need for him to assist us, it is of importance that we be also sharply touched to the very heart with a true feeling of our misery, to make us hunger and thirst after him. In fact, what a mockery it would be to come without appetite to look for food. Now to have a good appetite, it is not enough that the stomach be empty; it is necessary that it be in good order and capable of receiving nourishment. Hence then it follows that our souls ought to be oppressed by famine and to have desire and ardent longing to be fed, in order to find their proper nourishment in the Supper of the Lord. Moreover, it is to be noted that we cannot desire Jesus Christ without aspiring to the righteousness of God, which consists in self-denial and obedience to his will. For it is absurd to pretend to be of the body of Christ while we abandon ourselves to all licence and lead a dissolute life. Since in Christ there is nothing but chastity, benignity, sobriety, truth, humility and all like virtues, if we desire to be his members, all uncleanness, arrogance, intemperance, falsehood, pride and like vices must be put far from us. For we cannot mingle these things with him, without doing him grave dishonour and affront. We must always remember that there is no more agreement between him and iniquity than between light and darkness. Here, then, is how we should come to him in true repentance, in the remembrance that our life is to be conformed to the example of Jesus Christ. While this should be general in all parts of our life, yet it has a special application to charity, which is above all recommended to us in this sacrament; for which reason it is called the bond of charity. For as the bread, which is there sanctified for the common use of us all, is made of many grains so mixed together that one cannot be discerned from the other, so ought we to be united among ourselves in one indissoluble friendship. What is more: we all receive there the same body of Christ, in order that we be made members of it. If we have, then, dissensions and discords among us, it is not our fault if Jesus Christ is not rent in pieces; and we shall be guilty of a like sacrilege, as if we had done it. We must then not at all presume to approach, if we bear any hatred or rancour against living man, and especially any Christian who may be within the unity of the Church. To fulfil completely the order of our Lord, we must bring another disposition. It is to confess with the mouth and to testify how much we are indebted to our Saviour, and to render thanksgiving to him, not only that his name be glorified in us, but also that others be edified and instructed by our example, what they ought to do.

But because not a man will be found on earth, who has so advanced in faith and sanctity of life, that he does not still have much infirmity in one or other, there might be a danger that some good consciences be troubled by what has been said, if one did not obviate it by moderating the commands which we have imposed concerning both faith and repentance. It is a perilous method of teaching that some adopt, to demand a perfect confidence of heart and a perfect penitence, and to exclude all who do not have them. For in so doing, all are excluded without exception. Were it so, who can boast of being untouched by all mistrust? or of being subject to no vice or infirmity? Truly the children of God have only such faith, that they have always need to pray that the Lord help their unbelief. For it is a malady so rooted in our nature that we are never quite cured until we are delivered from this prison of our body. Moreover, they walk in purity of life of such a kind that they need to pray daily both for remission of sins and for grace to make better progress. Though some be more imperfect and others less, yet there is no one who does not fail in many respects. Hence the Supper would be not only useless to us all, but also pernicious, if we had to bring an integrity of faith or life in which there was nothing with which to find fault. This is contrary to the intention of our Lord, for there is nothing given to his Church that is more salutary. Therefore, when we feel our faith to be imperfect, and our conscience not so pure as not to accuse us of many vices, this must not hinder us presenting ourselves at the Holy Table of our Lord; provided that amid this infirmity we feel in our heart that, without hypocrisy and deceit, we hope for salvation in Christ, and desire to live according to the rule of the gospel. I say expressly that there be no hypocrisy; for there are many who deceive themselves by vain flatteries, making themselves to believe that it is enough to condemn their vices, though they continue in them; or rather leave them for a time, in order to return immediately after. Now true repentance is firm and constant; therefore it makes us battle against the evil which is within us, not for a day or a week, but without end or intermission.

When we feel within us a strong distaste and hatred of all vices, proceeding from the fear of God, and a desire to live well in order to please our Lord, we are fit to partake of the Supper, notwithstanding the vestiges of infirmity which we carry in our flesh. If indeed we were not weak, subject to mistrust, and imperfect in life, the sacrament would be of no service to us, and it would have been superfluous to institute it. Since then it is a remedy which God has given us to assist our frailty, to fortify our faith, to augment our charity, and to further us in all sanctity of life, so far from this making us abstain, we ought the more to make use of it, the more we feel oppressed by the disease.

For if we allege as pretext for not coming to the Supper, that we are still weak in faith or in integrity of life, it is as if a man excuse himself from taking medicine because he is sick. This then is how the frailty of the faith which we feel in our heart, and the imperfections which persist in our life, ought to incite us to come to the Supper, as to a remedy designed to correct them. Only let us not come without faith or repentance. Of these, the former is hidden in the heart, and therefore our conscience must testify concerning us before God. The second manifests itself by works, and therefore must be somehow apparent in our life.

As to the time of using it, there can be no certain rule for all. For there are certain particular impediments which excuse a man for absenting himself. And besides we have no express command, constraining Christians to make use of it every day it is offered to them. However, if we have careful regard to the end for which our Lord intended it, we should realize that the use of it ought to be more frequent than many make it. For the more infirmity oppresses us, the more frequently we need to have recourse to that which is able and ought to serve to confirm our faith and further us in purity of life. Therefore, the custom ought to be well established in all Churches, of celebrating the Supper as frequently as the capacity of the people will allow. And each individual in his own place ought to prepare himself to receive it whenever it is administered in the congregation, unless there be some grave hindrance which compels him to abstain. Though we have no express command defining the time and the day, it should be enough for us to know that the intention of our Lord is that we use it often; otherwise we shall not know well the benefit which it offers us.

The excuses which some allege on the other hand, are very frivolous. Some say that they feel themselves unworthy, and under cover of this abstain from it for a whole year. Others, not content with wondering about their worthiness, pretend that they cannot communicate with persons whom they see coming without good preparation. Some again think it is superfluous to use it often, since, if we have once received Jesus Christ, there is no need to return so often afterwards to receive him. I ask the first, who make a cover of their unworthiness, how their conscience can allow them to remain more than a year in so poor a state, that they dare not invoke God directly. For they will confess that it is audacity to invoke God as our Father, if we are not members of Jesus Christ. This we cannot be, unless the substance and reality of the Supper be fulfilled in us. Now if we have the reality, we are, *a fortiori*, capable of receiving the sign. It is evident, then, that he who would exempt himself from receiving the Supper because of unworthiness, bars himself from praying to God. For the rest, I have no intention of forcing consciences that are tormented with certain scruples that suggest themselves, they know not how; I rather advise them to wait till the Lord deliver them. Similarly, if there is a legitimate cause of hindrance, I do not deny that it is lawful to defer coming. Only I would point out that no one ought to remain content for long to abstain from the Supper because of his unworthiness, seeing that to do so deprives him of the communion of the Church in which all our good consists. Rather let him strive to contend against all the impediments which the devil puts before him, in order not to be excluded from so great a benefit, and consequently from all the gifts of which absence would deprive him.

The second class have some plausibility, for they employ the following argument. If it is not allowed to eat the common bread with those who call themselves brothers but lead a dissolute and wicked life, *a fortiori*, we ought to abstain from communicating with them in the bread of our Lord, which is sanctified to represent and dispense to us the body of Christ. But the reply is not very difficult. It is not the office of each individual to judge and discriminate, in order to admit or reject as seems to him good; seeing that this prerogative belongs generally to the Church as a whole, or rather to the pastor with the elders whom he ought to have for assisting him in the government of the Church. For Paul does not command us to examine others, but each is to examine himself. It is very true that our duty is to admonish those whom we see to live disorderly, and, if they will not listen, to advise the pastor of them, in order that he take proceedings on the authority of the Church. But the right way of withdrawing from the company of the wicked is not to quit the communion of the Church. Moreover, it will most frequently happen that sins are not so notorious as to justify going the length of excommunication. For though the pastor in his heart judge some man unworthy, yet he has not the power of pronouncing him to be so, or of interdicting him from the Supper, unless he can prove it by an ecclesiastical judgment. In this case, we have no other remedy than to pray to God, that he would deliver his Church more and more from all scandals, and to await the Last Day, when the chaff will be manifestly separated from the good grain. The third class have no semblance of plausibility.

For this spiritual bread is not given us in order that on the first occasion we eat our fill of it; but rather that, having had some taste of its sweetness, we may long for it the more, and use it when it is offered us. This is what we have expounded above, that while we remain in this mortal life, Jesus Christ is never communicated to us in such a way that our souls are wholly satisfied with him, but he desires to be our continual nourishment.

IV

ERRORS CORRUPTING THE SACRAMENT

To come to the fourth principal matter: the devil, knowing that our Lord left nothing more beneficial to the Church than this holy sacrament, according to his accustomed manner, exerted himself from the beginning to contaminate it with errors and superstitions, and to corrupt and destroy its fruit, and has not ceased to pursue this course, until he has almost wholly subverted the ordinance of the Lord, and converted it into falsehood and vanity. My intention is not to indicate at what time each abuse took its rise, and at what time it has been increased. It will suffice to indicate under different heads what errors the devil has introduced, against which we must be on guard, if we wish to enjoy the Supper of our Lord in its entirety.

As to the first error: While the Lord has given us his Supper in order that it be distributed among us, to testify that in communicating in his body we have part in the sacrifice which he offered on the cross to God his Father, for the expiation and satisfaction of our sins, men have, on the contrary, out of their own head invented that it is a sacrifice by which we obtain the remission of our sins before God. This is a blasphemy which is intolerable. For if we do not acknowledge the death of our Lord Jesus Christ as a unique sacrifice by which he has reconciled us to the Father, effacing all the faults for which we are liable to his judgment, we destroy its virtue. If we do not confess Jesus Christ to be the sole sacrificer, or as we commonly call it Priest, by whose intercession we are restored to the Father's favour, we despoil him of his honour and do him grave hurt. Since, then, this view of the Supper held by some, that it is a sacrifice for procuring the remission of sins, derogates from the true view, it must be condemned as pernicious. Now that it does so derogate is notorious. For how can we reconcile these two things, that

Jesus Christ in dying has offered a sacrifice to his Father by which he has once for all procured remission and pardon for all our faults, and that it is necessary every day to sacrifice in order to obtain that which we ought to seek in his death alone? This error was not from the beginning so extreme; but little by little has increased, until it came to what it is. It appears that the ancient Fathers called the Supper a sacrifice. But they offered the reason that the death of Jesus Christ is there represented. Hence what they say is this, that this name is attributed to it solely because it is a memorial of the unique sacrifice, at which we ought to stop short. Yet I cannot quite excuse the custom of the ancient Church. For by gestures and manner of acting, they outlined a kind of sacrifice, as if it were the same ceremony as there was in the Old Testament, except that in place of the animal bread was used for victim. Because this approaches too near to Judaism, I do not approve it. For in the Old Testament, in the time of symbols, the Lord had ordained such ceremonies, until this sacrifice was made in the flesh which is its fulfilment. Since it has been perfected, there remains nothing but for us to receive its communication. Hence it is superfluous to symbolize it any longer. This is the significance of the order which Jesus Christ left us, not that we offer or immolate, but that we take and eat that which has been offered and immolated. However, though there was some weakness in such observance, there was not such impiety as later supervened. For what properly belongs to the death of Christ has been wholly transferred to the mass, that is to satisfy God for our sins, and by this means to reconcile us to him. Moreover, the office of Jesus Christ has been attributed to those who are called priests, that is persons sacrificing to God, and by sacrificing interceding for us and so obtaining grace and pardon for our faults. I do not wish to dissimulate the explanations which the enemies of truth allege in this connection. They say that the mass is not a new sacrifice, but only an application of the unique sacrifice of which we have spoken. Though they disguise their abomination a little by so speaking, yet it is no more than a mere quibble. For it is not simply affirmed that the sacrifice of Christ is unique, but that it is not to be repeated, seeing that its efficacy endures always. It is not said that Christ once offered himself to the Father, in order that others after him might make the same oblation, and thus apply to us the virtue of his intercession. What is said is that he is entered into the heavenly sanctuary, and that he there appears for us to render the Father favourable by his intercession. As to applying the merit of his death to us, in order that we may perceive its benefit, this is effected not in the manner that the popish Church thinks, but when we receive the message of the Gospel as it is proclaimed to us by the preaching of the ministers, whom God has appointed as his ambassadors, and as it is sealed by the sacraments. The opinion of everyone has been approved by all their doctors and prelates, that in hearing mass or having it said, one merits, by this devotion, grace and righteousness before God. We say that to obtain any profit from the Supper, we need bring nothing of our own, to merit what we seek; we have only to receive by faith the grace which is there presented to us, which indeed does not reside in the sacrament, but points us to the cross of Jesus Christ as its source. Thus, then, it is apparent that there is nothing more contrary to true understanding of the Supper, than to make such a sacrifice of it as diverts us from recognizing the death of Christ as a sacrifice unique and with a virtue that lasts for ever. This being well understood, it will appear that all masses, in which there is no such communion as the Lord instituted, are nothing but abomination. For our Lord did not ordain that a single priest, after having made his sacrifice, should keep himself apart, but desired that the sacrament be distributed in the gathering, after the example of the first Supper which he made with his apostles. But after this evil opinion was forged, out of it, as from an abyss, has come the unhappy custom, that the people, contenting themselves with being present to participate in the merit of what is being done, abstain from communicating, because the priest pretends to offer his host for all, and especially for those present. I omit to speak of the abuses which are so stupid that they deserve no notice, such as attributing a mass to each saint, and transferring what is said of the Lord's Supper to St. William and St. Walter, or making a common market of them for buying and selling or other such villainies, to which the word sacrifice has given rise.

The second error which the devil has sown to corrupt this holy mystery, has been to forge and invent that, after the words pronounced with the intention of consecration, the bread is transubstantiated into the body of Christ, and the wine into his blood. This lie first of all has no foundation in Scripture, nor any evidence from the ancient Church; and, what is more, cannot be reconciled or harmonized with the Word of God. When Jesus Christ, pointing to the bread, called it his body, is it not a too forced construction to say that the substance of the bread is annihilated, and in its place the body of Christ is substituted? But there is no need to consign the matter to dubiety, seeing that the truth is sufficiently evident to refute the absurdity. I leave alone the numberless passages from both the Scriptures and the ancient Fathers where the sacrament is called bread. I only say that the nature of the sacrament requires that the material bread remain as visible sign of the body. For it is a general rule for all sacraments that the signs which we see have some correspondence with the spiritual things they symbolize. As then at Baptism we have assurance of internal washing when the water is given us for attestation to cleanse our bodily defilements, so in the Supper there must be material bread, to testify to us that the body of Christ is our food. For otherwise what meaning could there be in whiteness symbolizing it for us? We see clearly, then, how the whole representation, which our Lord wished to give in condescension to our infirmity, is lost, unless the true bread remain. For the meaning of the words which our Lord requires us to use is as if it were said: Just as man is sustained and maintained so far as the body is concerned by eating bread, so my flesh is the spiritual nourishment by which souls are vivified. Moreover, what would become of the other simile which Paul employs: As many grains of corn are mixed together to make one bread, so we must be united together, since we all partake of one bread. If there were whiteness only without substance, would it not be mockery to speak thus? Therefore without any doubt we conclude that this transubstantiation is an invention forged by the devil, to corrupt the truth of the Supper.

From this phantasy, several other follies have sprung. And would to God that they were only follies, and not gross abominations! For a local presence of I know not what kind has been imagined, and Jesus Christ, in his divinity and his humanity, thought to be attached to this whiteness, without regard to all the absurdities which follow. Though the old doctors of the Sorbonne dispute with great subtlety, how the body and blood are joined to the signs, yet it cannot be denied that this opinion has been received by great and small in the popish Church, and that it is cruelly maintained today by fire and sword, that Jesus Christ is contained under these signs, and that he must there be sought. Now to maintain this, it is necessary to confess, either that the body of Christ is without limit, or that it can be in different places. In saying so, we come at last to the point where it appears nothing but a phantom. Hence to wish to establish such a presence, that the body of Christ is enclosed within the sign, or is joined locally to it, is not only a dream but a damnable error, contradicting the glory of Christ, and destructive of what we ought to hold concerning his human nature. For Scripture teaches us everywhere, that as our Lord Jesus Christ on earth took our humanity, so he has exalted it to heaven, withdrawing it from its mortal condition, but not changing its nature. So we have two things to consider when we speak of our Lord's humanity. We may not destroy the reality of his nature, nor derogate at all from its glorious estate. To observe this rightly, we have always to raise our thoughts on high, to seek our Redeemer. For if we wish to abase him under the corruptible elements of this world, besides subverting what Scripture declares concerning his human nature, we annihilate the glory of his ascension. Because several others have treated this matter amply, I desist from saying more. I only wish to note in passing that to enclose Jesus Christ fantastically under the bread and wine, or so to join him to them as to amuse our understanding there instead of looking at him in heaven, is a pernicious fancy. We shall refer to this in another place.

Now this perverse opinion, having been once accepted, has given rise to many other superstitions. And first, this carnal adoration, which is nothing but idolatry. For to prostrate oneself before the bread of the Supper, and to adore Jesus Christ in it as though he were there contained, is to make an idol displace the sacrament. We have no commandment to adore, but to take and eat. This, then, ought not to have been audaciously attempted. Moreover, the practice always observed in the ancient Church was that, before celebrating the Supper, the people were solemnly exhorted to lift their hearts on high, to show that we must not stop at the visible sign, to adore Jesus Christ rightly. But there is no need to battle at length over this point, when the presence and conjunction of reality and sign, of which we have spoken and shall again speak, is well understood. From the same source proceeded other superstitious practices, such as carrying the sacrament in procession through the streets once a year, making another day a tabernacle for it, and all the year round keeping it in a cupboard to amuse the people, as if it were a god. Because all this has not only been contrived without the Word of God, but also is directly contrary to the institution of the Supper, it ought to be rejected by all Christians.

We have shown the source of the calamity which befell the popish Church, that the people abstained from communicating in the Supper for a whole year; and this because it is held to be a sacrifice, which is offered by one in the name of all. But again, even when thus used only once a year, it is miserably wasted and as it were rent in pieces. For instead of distributing the sacrament of the blood to the people, as the command of our Lord intends, they are made to believe that they must be content with the other portion. Thus poor believers are unhappily defrauded of the gift which our Lord had made to them. For if it is no little benefit to communicate in the blood of our Lord as our nourishment, it is a very great cruelty to steal it from those to whom it belongs. In this we can see with what audacity and boldness the pope tyrannized over the Church, when once he usurped dominion. Our Lord, having commanded his disciples to eat the bread sanctified in his body, when he came to the chalice does not say simply: Drink, but adds expressly that all are to drink of it. Could we have anything clearer than this? He says that we are to eat the bread, without using a universal term. He says that we are all to drink of the cup. Whence this difference, unless he wished to anticipate this wickedness of the devil? Yet such is the pride of the pope, that he dares to say: All are not to drink. And to show that he is wiser than God, he alleges that there is good reason that the priest have some privilege over the people, in honour of the sacerdotal dignity. As if our Lord had not at all considered how one ought to be distinguished from the other! Moreover, he objects to the dangers which might occur if the chalice were given to all. It could happen that some drop be occasionally spilt; as if our Lord had not foreseen this! Is not this to accuse God openly of confusing the order to be observed, and putting his people in danger without purpose? To show that there is no great disadvantage in this change, they point out that under one kind all is contained so that the body cannot be divided from the blood; as if our Lord had foolishly distinguished them! For if we can leave one of the parts behind as superfluous, it would have been folly to recommend them separately. Some of his supporters, seeing that it was impudence to maintain this abomination, have wished to excuse it otherwise. They say that Jesus Christ, in instituting the sacrament, spoke only to his disciples whom he had elevated to sacerdotal rank. But what will they answer to what Paul says, when he delivered to all Christian people that which he had received from the Lord, that each should eat of this bread and drink of this cup? And in fact, who revealed to them that our Lord gave the Supper to his apostles as priests? The words mean the opposite, when he commands them to follow his example. He then delivers to them the rule which he wished to be always observed in his Church. Thus it was observed in the ancient Church, until Antichrist, having gained the upper hand, openly raised his horns against God and his truth, to destroy it completely. We see then that it is an intolerable perversion to divide and dissect the sacrament thus, separating the parts which God joined.

To come to an end, we comprehend under one article what could be considered separately. The article is that the devil introduced the manner of celebrating the Supper without any doctrine, and in place of the doctrine substituted ceremonies, partly unfitting and useless, and partly even dangerous, from which much ill has followed—to such an extent, that the mass, which takes the place of the Supper in the popish Church, when strictly defined, is nothing but pure apishness and buffoonery. I call it apishness, because the Supper of our Lord is there counterfeited without reason, just as an ape, capriciously and without discernment, follows what it sees done. This being so, the chief thing which our Lord recommends to us, is to celebrate this mystery with true intelligence. It follows then that the substance of it all consists in the doctrine. This taken away, it is no more than a cold ceremony without efficacy. This is not only shown in Scripture, but also attested by the canons of the pope, in a sentence cited from Augustine, where he asks; What is the water of Baptism without the Word, but a corruptible element?—and the Word not merely as uttered but as understood. He thereby means that the sacraments take their virtue from the Word, when it is preached intelligibly. Without this, they are unworthy to be called sacraments. Now intelligible doctrine of the mass is so lacking, that on the contrary the whole mystery is considered spoiled, if everything is not done by stealth, so that nothing is understood. Therefore their consecration is nothing but a piece of sorcery, seeing that, by murmuring and gesticulating in the manner of sorcerers, they think to constrain Jesus Christ to descend into their hands. We see, then, how the mass being thus arranged, is a manifest profanation of the Supper of Christ, rather than an observance of it. For the proper and chief substance of the Supper is lacking, that the mystery be well explained to the people, and the promises clearly recited, instead of the priest muttering to himself apart without sense or reason. I call it buffoonery, because the mimicry and gesture made there suit rather a farce than such a mystery as the Supper of our Lord.

T.T.—11

It is indeed true, that the sacrifices in the Old Testament took place with much ornament and ceremony. But because there was a sound meaning, and the whole was suited to instruct and excite the people to piety, they are far from being similar to those now used, which serve no end but the amusement of the people without any advantage. As these mass-mongers[1] allege the example of the Old Testament in defence of their ceremonies, we must observe what difference there is between what they do and what God commanded the people of Israel to do. If there were only this, that what was then practised was founded on the command of the Lord, while all their frivolities have no foundation but men, there would be great enough dissimilarity. But we have more for which to reprove them. For it is not without reason that our Lord ordained such a form for a time, in order that it might some day come to an end and be abrogated. For as he had not then granted such clarity of doctrine, he desired that this people be more exercised in symbols, to compensate them for what they lacked in another direction. But since Jesus Christ was manifested in the flesh, doctrine has been so much the more clarified, and the symbols have been diminished. Since then we have the body, we should relinquish the shadows. For if we are to return to ceremonies which are abolished, we should repair the veil of the temple, which Jesus Christ rent by his death, and should thus obscure the clarity of the Gospel. Thus we see that such a multitude of ceremonies in the mass is a kind of Judaicism, manifestly contrary to Christianity. I do not intend to disapprove ceremonies which contribute to decency and public order and increase reverence of the sacrament, provided they are sober and suitable. But such an abyss without end or measure is quite intolerable, seeing that it gave rise to a thousand superstititions, and as it were stupefied the people without bringing any edification.

Hence we can also see the difference there ought to be between the papists and those to whom God has given knowledge of his truth. To begin with, they will not doubt but that it is an abominable sacrilege to represent the mass as a sacrifice by which remission of sins is procured for us; or rather that the priest is mediator for the application of the merit of the death and passion of Christ to those who buy his mass, or attend it, or accord it devotion. But on the contrary, they must conclude that the death and passion of our Lord is the unique sacrifice by which the wrath of God is satisfied, and perpetual righteousness

---

[1] The 1541 edition has *Messateurs*, the 1549 *et seq. Messatiers*.

procured for us; and then that the Lord Jesus is entered into the heavenly sanctuary, finally to appear for us, and intercede with the virtue of his sacrifice. For the rest, they will readily grant that the fruit of this death is communicated to us in the Supper, not at all by the merit of the act, but by reason of the promises which we are there given, provided we receive them by faith. Second, they should not at all allow that the bread is transubstantiated into the body of Jesus Christ, nor the wine into his blood; but must insist on this, that the visible signs retain their true substance to represent to us the spiritual truth of which we have spoken. Third, they must hold for certain that our Lord gives us in the Supper what he signifies by it, and we thus really receive the body and blood of Jesus Christ. Nonetheless they will not seek it as though it were enclosed under the bread or attached locally to the visible sign, so far are they from adoring the sacrament. But they will rather raise their understandings and their hearts on high, both to receive Jesus Christ, and also to adore him. From this it will follow that they disapprove and condemn as idolatry all these superstitious fashions, such as carrying the sacrament in solemn procession, or constructing for it tabernacles for its adoration. For the promises of our Lord do not extend beyond the use he has left us. Next they will hold that to deprive the people of one of the parts of the sacrament, that is of the chalice, is to violate and corrupt the ordinance of our Lord, and that for right observance both are to be distributed to all. Last, they will regard it as a superfluity, not only useless but also dangerous and ill-consorted with Christianity, to use so many ceremonies borrowed from the Jews, beyond the simplicity which the apostles left us; and that it is an even greater perversion to celebrate the Supper by mimicry and I know not what buffoonery, without expounding the doctrine but rather burying it, as if the Supper were a kind of magical trick.

V

THE PRESENT DISPUTE

As to the contention which has been so keenly debated in our time, an unhappy business, which the devil no doubt stirred up to impede, or rather quite interrupt, the advance of the Gospel, I could wish that the memory of it be quite abolished, so far am I from desiring to relate it at length. Nonetheless, because I see many good consciences troubled, since they know not to which side to turn, I shall briefly state what seems to me to be necessary advice for showing them how they ought to decide. First, I pray all the faithful, in the name of God, not to be too offended at the great difference which has arisen between those who ought to be leaders in bringing back truth to the light of day. For it is no new thing for the Lord to leave his servants in some ignorance, and to permit them to dispute against each other. And this, not to leave them for ever, but only for a time, to humble them. In fact, had all turned out as desired up till now, without any disturbance, men might possibly have forgotten themselves, or the grace of God be less acknowledged than is proper. Thus our Lord was pleased to deprive men of all cause for glory in order that he alone be glorified. Moreover, if we consider in what an abyss of darkness the world was, when those who have shared in this controversy began to elicit the truth for us, we shall not wonder at all that they did not know everything at the outset. It is rather to be wondered at that our Lord in so short a time has so illumined them, that they have themselves escaped from the slime of error, and thus drawn others out of it who had been plunged in it for so long. But nothing could be better than to show how the thing came about, because this will make it evident that there is not at all so great occasion to be offended as is commonly thought.

When Luther began to teach, he regarded the matter of the Supper in such a way, that, with respect to the corporal presence of Christ, he appeared ready to leave it as the world generally conceived it. For while condemning transubstantiation, he said that the bread was the body of Christ, insofar as it was united with him. Further, he added some similes which were a little harsh and rude. But he did so as by constraint, because he could not otherwise explain his meaning. For it is difficult to give an explanation of so high a matter, without using some impropriety of speech.

On the other hand, there arose Zwingli and Œcolampadius, who, considering the abuse and deceit which the devil had employed to establish such a carnal presence of Christ as had been taught and held for more than six hundred years, thought it wrong to dissimulate; since this view implied an execrable idolatry, in that Jesus Christ was adored as if enclosed under the bread. Now because it was very difficult to remove this opinion, rooted so long in the hearts of men, they applied all their mind to decry it, remonstrating that it was a quite gross error not to acknowledge what is so clearly testified in Scripture, concerning the ascension of Jesus Christ, that he was in his humanity received up into heaven, where he dwells until he descend to judge the world. While they were absorbed with this point, they forgot to define what is the presence of Christ in the Supper in which one ought to believe, and what communication of his body and his blood one there received. So Luther thought that they intended to leave nothing else but bare signs without any corresponding spiritual substance. Hence he began to resist and oppose them, even to the extent of denouncing them as heretics. Once the contention had begun, it became more inflamed with time, and so has continued too bitterly for a period of fifteen years or thereabouts, without either party listening to the other in a peaceful frame of mind. For though they once held conference, yet there was such alienation, that they parted without any agreement. Then instead of meeting with goodwill, they have always retreated farther and farther from one another, thinking of nothing but to defend their own opinion and confute anything contrary. Here we have the reason, then, why Luther failed on his side, and Œcolampadius and Zwingli on theirs. It was Luther's duty, in the first place, to make it clear that he did not intend to set up such a local presence as the papists imagine; second, he should have protested that he did not mean the sacrament to be adored instead of God; and third, he should have abstained from the similes so harsh and difficult to conceive, or have used them with moderation, interpreting them so that they could not occasion offence. Once the debate was taken up, he went beyond measure not only in declaring his opinion, but also in blaming the other with a too sharp bitterness of speech. For instead of explaining himself so that his opinion could be understood, with his accustomed violence in attacking those who contradicted him, he used exaggerated forms of speech, which were certainly hard to bear by those who otherwise were not very disposed to believe what he said. The others offended also, by being so eager to decry the contrary opinion of the papists concerning the local presence of the body of Jesus Christ as superstitious and fantastic, and the adoration which followed from it as perverse, that they laboured more to destroy the evil than to build up the good. For though they did not deny the truth, yet they did not teach it as clearly as they ought. I mean that in taking too great pains to maintain that the bread and the wine are called the body and blood of Christ because they are signs, they took no care to make the reservation that they are such signs that the reality is joined to them; or to protest that they did not at all intend to obscure the true communion which our Lord gives us in his body and blood by the sacrament.

Both parties failed altogether to have patience to listen to each other, in order to follow truth without passion, wherever it might be found. None the less, we must not leave off thinking what is our duty. It is not to forget the gifts which our Lord bestowed on them, and the blessings which he distributes to us at their hands and by means of them. For if we are not quite ungrateful and forgetful of what we owe them, we could well pardon them this and more than this, without blaming or defaming them. In short, since we see that they were and still are distinguished by holy life and excellent knowledge and by conspicuous zeal to edify the Church, we ought always to judge and speak with modesty and reverence; just because it has pleased God at last, having humbled them thus, to bring to an end this unhappy disputation, or at least to calm it, in anticipation of it being quite resolved. I say this because there is not yet any published formula in which agreement has been framed, as would be expedient. But this will happen when God is pleased to bring into one place all those who are to draw it up. Meanwhile, it must content us that there is brotherliness and communion between the Churches, and that all agree in what is necessary for meeting together, according to the command of God. We all confess, then, with one mouth that, in receiving the sacrament in faith, according to the ordinance of the Lord, we are truly made partakers of the real substance of the body and blood of Jesus Christ. How this is done, some may deduce better and explain more clearly than others. But be this as it may, on the one hand we must, to shut out all carnal fancies, raise our hearts on high to heaven, not thinking that our Lord Jesus Christ is so abased as to be enclosed under any corruptible elements. On the other hand, not to diminish the efficacy of this sacred mystery, we must hold that it is accomplished by the secret and miraculous virtue of God, and that the Spirit of God is the bond of participation, for which reason it is called spiritual.

Confession of Faith concerning the Eucharist

INTRODUCTION

THIS EARLY LITTLE STATEMENT OF CALVIN'S VIEWS of the Holy Supper is allotted by *C.R.* to the year 1537. It has an inherent theological value of its own. Historically it records an attained consensus of opinion between the Reformers named in the note appended to the document. The purpose of the document was to allay the suspicion that the Strassburgers, with Bucer leading the way, had conceded too much to the Lutherans. The theologians of most of the cities of Berne preferred to state their faith anew, rather than incur the same suspicion. (See *C.R.* IX, liv.)

Confession of Faith concerning the Eucharist

We confess that the spiritual life which Christ bestows upon us does not rest on the fact that he vivifies us with his Spirit, but that his Spirit makes us participants in the virtue of his vivifying body, by which participation we are fed on eternal life. Hence when we speak of the communion which we have with Christ, we understand the faithful to communicate not less in his body and blood than in his Spirit, so that thus they possess the whole Christ. Now Scripture manifestly declares the body of Christ to be verily food for us and his blood verily drink. It thereby affirms that we ought to be truly nourished by them, if we seek life in Christ. It is no small or common thing that the apostle teaches, when he asserts that we are flesh of Christ's flesh and bone of his bone. Rather he points out the great mystery of our communion with his body, whose sublimity no one is able to explain adequately in words. For the rest it is no contradiction with this that our Lord is exalted in heaven, and so has withdrawn the local presence of his body from us, which is not here required. For though we as pilgrims in mortality are neither included nor contained in the same space with him, yet the efficacy of his Spirit is limited by no bounds, but is able really to unite and bring together into one things that are disjoined in local space. Hence we acknowledge that his Spirit is the bond of our participation in him, but in such manner that he really feeds us with the substance of the body and blood of the Lord to everlasting life, and vivifies us by participation in them. This communion of his own body and blood Christ offers in his blessed Supper under the symbols of bread and wine, presenting them to all who rightly celebrate it according to his own proper institution.

This statement of our dear brothers and colleagues, G. Farel, John Calvin and P. Viret, we embrace as right doctrine, believing Christ our Lord in no sense to be diffused locally or ubiquitously in the Holy Supper, but that he has a true and finite body and remains in heavenly glory. Yet none the less, through his word and symbols, he is present in the Supper: He presents himself to us as we are by faith exalted to heaven with him, so that the bread we break and the cup through which we show Christ forth may be for us really the communion of his body and blood. Besides we hold as an error not to be tolerated in the Church that it is naked and bare signs that Christ sets forth in his blessed Supper, or not to believe that here the very body and the very blood of the Lord is received, that is the Lord himself true God and man.

Written by his own hand—Martin Bucer.
Subscribed—Wolfgang Capito.

Summary of Doctrine concerning the Ministry of the Word and the Sacraments

INTRODUCTION

THE GENERAL REASONS FOR THE INCLUSION OF THIS document are given elsewhere. Here attention may be drawn to the exiguous evidence for and against its authenticity. *C.R.* cites Beza and an impressive list of later editions of Calvin's works as including this writing. The first seems to attempt to remove suspicion of its genuineness, and makes the title run: "Summary of a certain doctrine, the name of the author being not added." But where this lack occurred, from what source the writing is drawn, and what the reason is for its inclusion unless genuine, are questions for which neither Beza nor any other witness provide answers. *C.R.* ventures the cautious judgment, that the withdrawal of this document from the Calvinist *corpus* would leave his reputation unimpaired. One would not have to be very bold to say something more daring than this, and, in the absence of stronger evidence for its wrongful inclusion in early editions of Calvin's works, the inherent interest of its subject matter justifies its inclusion here. (See *C.R.* IX, lxi.)

Summary of Doctrine concerning the Ministry of the Word and the Sacraments

I

The end of the whole Gospel ministry is that God, the fountain of all felicity, communicate Christ to us who are disunited by sin and hence ruined, that we may from him enjoy eternal life; that in a word all heavenly treasures be so applied to us that they be no less ours than Christ's himself.

II Thess 2:14: "he called you by our gospel, to the obtaining of the glory of our Lord Jesus Christ."

II

We believe this communication to be (*a*) mystical, and incomprehensible to human reason, and (*b*) spiritual, since it is effected by the Holy Spirit; to whom, since he is the virtue of the living God, proceeding from the Father and the Son, we ascribe omnipotence, by which he joins us to Christ our Head, not in an imaginary way, but most powerfully and truly, so that we become flesh of his flesh and bone of his bone, and from his vivifying flesh he transfuses eternal life into us.

(*a*) Eph. 5:32: "This is a great mystery: but I speak concerning Christ and the Church."
(*b*) I Cor. 6:17: "But he that is joined unto the Lord is one spirit."
Augustine, *Ep. 57 ad Dard.*: "Without God, sin is committed; there is no righteousness without God. Hence we do not die, unless we come by way of carnal propagation from the members of sin; nor do we live, unless by spiritual union we be members of him."

171

III

That we believe the Holy Spirit to effect this union rests on a certain ground, namely this: Whatever (*a*) the Father or (*b*) the Son does to bring the faithful to salvation, Holy Scripture testifies that each operates through the Holy Spirit; and that (*c*) Christ does not otherwise dwell in us than through his Spirit, nor in any other way communicates himself to us than through the same Spirit.

(*a*) John 14:16: "And I will pray the Father, and he shall give you another Comforter, even the Spirit of truth; whom the world cannot receive, and so on."

And a little later, 25: "These things have I spoken unto you, being yet present with you. But the Comforter, which is the Holy Ghost, whom the Father will send in my name, he shall teach you all things, and bring to your remembrance, whatsoever I have said unto you."

(*b*) John 15:26: "But when the Comforter is come, whom I will send unto you from the Father, even the Spirit of truth, which proceedeth from the Father, he shall testify of me." So too John 16:7: "Nevertheless I tell you the truth; it is expedient for you that I go away: for if I go not away, the Comforter will not come unto you; but if I depart, I will send him unto you."

(*c*) Rom. 8:9: "But ye are not in the flesh but in the Spirit, if so be that the Spirit of God dwell in you. Now if any man have not the Spirit of Christ, he is none of his." So too a little later, verse 11: "If the Spirit of him that raised up Jesus from the dead dwell in you, he that raised up Christ from the dead shall also quicken your mortal bodies by his Spirit that dwelleth in you." And a little later, verse 14: "As many as are led by the Spirit of God, they are the sons of God." Also I Cor. 6:19: "Know ye not that your body is the temple of the Holy Ghost which is in you, which ye have of God?" Also I Cor. 3:16: "Know ye not that ye are the temple of God, and that the Spirit of God dwelleth in you?"

IV

To effect this union, the Holy Spirit uses a double instrument, the preaching of the Word and the administration of the sacraments.

V

When we say that the Holy Spirit uses an external minister as instrument, we mean this: both in the preaching of the Word and in the use of the sacraments, there are two ministers, who have distinct offices. The (a) external minister administers the vocal word, and the sacred signs which are external, earthly and fallible. But the internal minister, who is the Holy Spirit, freely works internally, while by his secret virtue he effects in the hearts of whomsoever he will their union with Christ through one faith. This union is a thing internal, heavenly and indestructible.

(a) I Cor. 3:5, 6, 7: Concerning the whole ministry, Paul speaks as follows: "Who then is Paul, and who is Apollos, but ministers by whom ye believed, even as the Lord gave to every man? I have planted, Apollos watered; but God gave the increase. So then neither is he that planteth any thing, neither he that watereth; but God that giveth the increase."

VI

In the preaching of the Word, the external minister holds forth the vocal word, and it is received by the ears (a). The internal minister, the Holy Spirit, truly communicates the thing proclaimed through the Word, that is Christ, to the souls of all who will, so that it is not necessary that Christ or for that matter his Word be received through the organs of the body, but the Holy Spirit effects this union by his secret virtue, by creating faith in us, by which he makes us living members of Christ, true God and true man.

(a) Acts 16:14: "And a certain woman named Lydia, a seller of purple, of the city of Thyatira, which worshipped God, heard us: whose heart the Lord opened, that she attended unto the things which were spoken of Paul."

VII

In Baptism (a), the external minister baptizes with an external element, that is water, which is received bodily (b). The internal minister, the Holy Spirit, baptizes with the blood of the spotless Lamb, so that he that is baptized is endowed with the whole

Christ, true God and true man (Gal. 3:27); thus it is not necessary to receive Christ by the organs of the body, in order that our souls be washed by his blood; but the secret and most potent operation of the Holy Spirit suffices.

(*a*) Matt. 3:11; John 1:26: "I indeed baptize you with water unto repentance."

(*b*) Titus 3:5: "He saved us by the washing of regeneration, and renewing of the Holy Ghost."

I Cor. 6:11: "And such were some of you, but ye are washed, but ye are sanctified, but ye are justified in the name of the Lord Jesus, and by the Spirit of our God."

VIII

In the Supper of the Lord, the external minister holds forth the external symbols, the bread of the Lord and the wine of the Lord, which are perceived by the organs of our body, consumed and swallowed (*a*). The internal minister, the Holy Spirit, not by external organs of the body, but by his secret virtue, feeds the souls of the faithful, both truly and efficaciously, with the body and the blood of the Lord unto eternal life, as truly as they know themselves to be nourished for this mortal life by bread and wine.

(*a*) I Cor. 10:3 f: "And did all eat the same spiritual meat, and did all drink the same spiritual drink: for they drank of that spiritual Rock that followed them: and that Rock was Christ."

IX

When we are fed with the body of Christ to life eternal, Christ does not wish us to believe that his own body or his own blood descends from heaven upon the altar or about the altar, in the bread or under the bread, or not distant from the bread. There is no more need for this than that in Baptism, in order that we be made true members of the body of Christ, the body of Christ itself should descend from heaven into the water or under the water or stand not far from the water. Similarly there is no need for the descent of the body in such literal sense, for us to be made partakers of the whole of Christ; we believe that enough of the power of the Spirit of the Lord, who proceeds from the Father and the Son, is in us, for us in Baptism to be made members of his body, which yet is and remains in heaven. And in the Holy Supper, the same body remaining in heaven, he nourishes us more and more through his secret and most efficacious power and virtue.

This doctrine, that there is no descent of the body of Christ, or any downward passage visible or invisible, is grounded on the clearest testimony of Scripture. For just as Christ is man, so Scripture testifies that he parted from them (Luke 24:51), went away (John 14:2), left this world (John 16:28), was carried upwards (Acts 1:11), into the holy places not made with hands (Heb. 9:11, 24), to be enclosed in heaven until the time of the restitution of all things (Acts 3:21).

Nor do the words of Christ conflict with this doctrine: This is my body which is broken, and so on. For Christ's own best interpreter is Paul, who interprets: The bread which we break, in this way; and who interprets the words of Christ: is my body, as meaning: is the communion of the body of Christ.

But it was shown before that this is the sole ground of communion, that we are by the Holy Spirit made partakers of him, who effects this communion, since he is the virtue of the living God proceeding from the Father and the Son.

This doctrine is also in harmony with the Apostolic Symbol or Apostles' Creed, which ought to be held to possess an inviolable and most simple certitude; with this namely: he ascended into Heaven, and sitteth at the right hand of God the Father Almighty, from thence he shall come to judge both the quick and the dead.

Augustine understands these articles of faith as we do Ep. 57 ad Dardanum), where he calls these articles the Christian Confession, and forbids retreat from them. Do not doubt, he says, Jesus Christ the man is now there whence he will come again; recollect in memory and hold faithfully the Christian confession, that he rose from the dead, ascended into heaven, sitteth at the right hand of the Father, and, from no other place than that where he is gone, will come to judge the quick and the dead. And he will come, this angelic voice testifies, just as he was seen to go into heaven: in the same form and substance of flesh; for certainly he does not destroy the nature of that to which he gives immortality. Since this is his form, he is not to be thought of as diffused everywhere. For we must watch lest we so construe the divinity of the man as to deny the reality of the body. But it does not follow that what is in God is everywhere as God; for concerning ourselves, Scripture most truly says, that in him we live and move and have our being. But we are not altogether as he is, but a man is in God and God is in man differently, each in his appropriate and particular way. For God and man are one person; and each one is Christ Jesus, ubiquitous in that he is God, but in heaven in that he is man. Thus Augustine.

The doctrine harmonizes also with the article concerning the assumption of true human nature (*a*), all of whose conditions, sin only excepted, Christ willingly took upon himself, and (*b*) after his glorification he gave immortality to his flesh, without destroying its nature.

(*a*) Heb. 4:15: "For we have not a high priest which cannot be touched with the feeling of our infirmities; but was in all points tempted like as we are, yet without sin."

(*b*) Luke 24:39: "Behold my hands and my feet, that it is I myself: handle me, and see; for a spirit hath not flesh and bones as ye see me have."

Augustine (*in Joann. ev. Tract.* 5): "According to his majesty, according to his providence, according to his ineffable and invisible grace, what he said is fulfilled: Behold I am with you alway, even to the end of the world. According to the flesh which the Word assumed, in that he was born of the Virgin, in that he was seized by the Jews, was nailed to the wood, was taken down from the cross, was wound in linen, was laid in the sepulchre, was manifest in the resurrection: You will not always have this with you. Why? Because he lived as to bodily presence for forty days with his disciples, and, they remaining, not following but looking on, he ascends into heaven, and is no more here. For there he is, and sits at the right hand of the Father; and here he is, for he has not withdrawn the presence of his majesty. Otherwise said: as a presence in majesty, we have Christ always; as a presence in the flesh, it was rightly said to the disciples: Me ye have not always. For the Church had him in carnal presence for a few days, but by faith it holds what with the eyes it does not see."

The doctrine harmonizes also with the articles of faith concerning the divine nature of Christ, concerning omnipotence, and concerning the Holy Spirit. For we believe Christ to be really and most powerfully present to us (*a*) by his Spirit as he promises. Yet we do not believe his omnipotence to stretch to the denial of that article of faith, so that the body of Christ should not ascend to heaven, and not be seated at the right hand of God. Much rather we believe that omnipotence and the articles of our faith are precisely thus firmly established. For we believe this work to be done in us much more certainly by the secret and incomprehensible virtue of the Holy Spirit, than if the body of Christ should descend out of heaven upon the altar, and be proffered by the hands of the minister and be consumed by our bodily mouth. The operation of the Holy Spirit is so much more certain and powerful than this, just as the Creator himself is superior to all his creatures, however excellent.

(a) I Cor. 15:45: "The first man Adam was made a living soul; the last Adam was made a quickening spirit."

Articles concerning Predestination

INTRODUCTION

THE REASONS FOR THE INCLUSION OF THIS LITTLE document are set out in the Preface. *C.R.* comments upon it as follows: About this leaflet, now for the first time edited, we have nothing to say. The Genevan Codex does not reveal the occasion of the writing, nor have we found in the collection of Letters a more accurate date or anywhere else anything remembered and transmitted. (See *C.R.* IX, liv.)

The tone of the Articles is uncompromising, and this may be held to argue a comparatively late date.

Articles concerning Predestination

Before the first man was created, God in his eternal counsel had determined what he willed to be done with the whole human race.

In the hidden counsel of God it was determined that Adam should fall from the unimpaired condition of his nature, and by his defection should involve all his posterity in sentence of eternal death.

Upon the same decree depends the distinction between elect and reprobate: as he adopted some for himself for salvation, he destined others for eternal ruin.

While the reprobate are the vessels of the just wrath of God, and the elect vessels of his compassion, the ground of the distinction is to be sought in the pure will of God alone, which is the supreme rule of justice.

While the elect receive the grace of adoption by faith, their election does not depend on faith but is prior in time and order.

As the beginning of faith and perseverance in it arises from the gratuitous election of God, none are truly illuminated with faith, and none granted the spirit of regeneration, except those whom God elects. But it is necessary that the reprobate remain in their blindness or be deprived of such portion of faith as is in them.

While we are elected in Christ, nevertheless that God reckons us among his own is prior in order to his making us members of Christ.

While the will of God is the supreme and primary cause of all things, and God holds the devil and the godless subject to his will, nevertheless God cannot be called the cause of sin, nor the author of evil, nor subject of any guilt.

While God is truly wrathful with sin and condemns whatever is unrighteousness in men since it displeases him, nevertheless all the deeds of men are governed not by his bare permission but by his consent and secret counsel.

While the devil and the reprobate are ministers and organs of God and promote his secret judgments, God nevertheless in an incomprehensible way operates in and through them, so that he restrains nothing of their wickedness, just because their malice is justly and rightly used to a good end, while the means are often hidden from us.

They are ignorant and malicious who say that God is the author of sin, since all things are done by his will or ordination; for they do not distinguish between the manifest wickedness of men and the secret judgments of God.

PART II
APOLOGETIC

The Necessity of Reforming the Church

INTRODUCTION

THE INITIAL ADDRESS SETS THIS DOCUMENT IN ITS context. Mixed motives impelled the Emperor Charles V to summon the Diet of Spires, and among them was certainly displeasure that religious disputes should continue so long, and that the attention of the Protestant princes should be thus diverted from the war with France. Bucer thought to prepare the mind of the Emperor by a letter setting forth the case for reformation; but doubt later assailed him, whether such a writing would serve any purpose, and accordingly he sought Calvin's advice. Calvin with astonishing energy and speed himself took the matter in hand, and by the end of the year 1543 (the Diet was summoned for February 1544), he had prepared a document which Beza in his *Vita Calvini* judges to be among the most vigorous and weighty writings of the age. *C.R.* finds the treatise commended by both the importance of the contents and the elegance of the style. (See *C.R.* VI, xxviii f.)

The Necessity of Reforming the Church

A Humble Exhortation
to the most invincible Emperor Charles V,
and the most illustrious Princes and other Orders,
now holding a Diet of the Empire at Spires

that they seriously undertake the task
of restoring the Church

presented in the name of all those who wish Christ to reign

by Dr. John Calvin

August Emperor,

This Diet is summoned by you, in order at last to deliberate
and decide, along with the Most Illustrious Princes and other
Orders of the Empire, upon the means of ameliorating the
present condition of the Church, which we all see to be very
miserable and almost desperate. Now therefore, while you sit
for this consultation, I humbly beg and implore, first of
your Imperial Majesty, and at the same time of you also, Most
Illustrious Princes and distinguished gentlemen, that you will
not decline to read and diligently consider what I have to lay
before you. The magnitude and weight of the cause may well
incite you to an eagerness to listen. I shall set the matter so
plainly in front of you, that you can have no difficulty in determining what part you must play. Whoever I am, I here profess
to plead in defence both of sound doctrine and of the Church.
In this character I seem at all events entitled to expect that you
will not deny me audience, until such time as it may appear
whether I falsely usurp the character, or whether I faithfully
perform its duties and make good what I profess. But though I
feel that I am by no means equal to so great a task, yet I am not
at all afraid that, after you have heard the nature of my office,
I shall be accused either of folly or presumption in having ventured thus to bring this matter before you. There are two things
by which men are wont to recommend, or at least to justify,
their conduct. If a thing is done honestly and from pious zeal,
we deem it worthy of praise; if it is done under the pressure of
public necessity, we at least deem it not unworthy of excuse.
Since both of these apply here, I am confident, such is your
equity, that I shall easily approve my design in your eyes. For

184

where can I exert myself to better purpose or more honestly, where, too, in a matter at this time more necessary, than in attempting, according to my ability, to aid the Church of Christ, whose claims it is lawful in no instance to deny, and which is now in grievous distress and in extreme danger? But there is no occasion for a long preface concerning myself. Receive what I say as if it were the united voice of all who either have already taken care to restore the Church, or desire that it should be restored to true order. On my side are several exalted Princes and not a few distinguished communities. For all these I speak though an individual, so that it is more truly they who at the same time and with one mouth speak through me. To these add the countless multitude of pious men, scattered over the various regions of the Christian world, who yet unanimously concur with me in this pleading. In short, regard this as the common address of all who so earnestly deplore the present corruption of the Church, that they are unable to bear it any longer, and are determined not to rest till they see some amendment. I know with what odious names we are marked down for disgrace; but meanwhile, whatever be the name by which it is thought proper to call us, hear our cause, and after that judge what place we are entitled to hold.

First, then, the question is not whether the Church suffers from many and grievous diseases, for this is admitted even by all moderate judges; but whether the diseases are of a kind whose cure admits of no longer delay, so that it is neither useful nor proper to wait upon too slow remedies. We are accused of rash and impious innovation, for having ventured to propose any change at all in the former state of the Church. What? even if it has been done with good cause and not imperfectly? I hear there are persons who, even in this case, do not hesitate to condemn us; they think us right indeed in desiring amendment, but not right in attempting it. From them, all I would ask at present is that for a little they suspend judgment until I shall have shown from the facts that we have not been prematurely hasty, have attempted nothing rashly, nothing alien to our duty, and have in short done nothing until compelled by the highest necessity. To enable me to prove this, it is necessary to attend to the matters in dispute.

We maintain to start with that, when God raised up Luther and others, who held forth a torch to light us into the way of salvation, and on whose ministry our churches are founded and built, those heads of doctrine in which the truth of our religion, those in which the pure and legitimate worship of God, and those in which the salvation of men are comprehended, were in a great measure obsolete. We maintain that the use of the sacraments was in many ways vitiated and polluted. And we maintain that the government of the Church was converted into a species of horrible and insufferable tyranny. But perhaps these statements have not force enough to move certain individuals until they are better explained. This, therefore, I will do, not as the subject demands, but as far as my ability will permit. Here, however, I have no intention to review and discuss all our controversies; that would require a long discourse, and this is not the place for it. I wish only to demonstrate how just and necessary the causes were which forced us to the changes for which we are blamed.

To accomplish this,[1] I must show that the particular remedies which the Reformers employed were apt and salutary; not here intending to describe the manner in which we proceeded (for this will afterwards be seen), but only to make it manifest that we have had no other end in view than to ameliorate in some degree the very miserable condition of the Church. Our doctrine has been, and is every day, assailed by many cruel calumnies. Some declaim loudly against it in sermons; others attack and ridicule it in their writings. Both rake together everything by which they hope to bring it into disrepute among the ignorant. But there is in men's hands the Confession of our Faith, which we presented to your Imperial Majesty. It clearly testifies how undeservedly we are harassed by so many odious accusations. We have always been ready in times past, as we are at the present day, to render an account of our doctrine. In a word, there is no doctrine preached in our churches but that which we openly profess. As to contested points, they are clearly and honestly explained in our Confession, while everything relating to them has been copiously treated and diligently expounded by our writers. Hence judges who are not unjust must be satisfied how far we are from every kind of impiety. This much certainly must be clear alike to just and unjust, that the Reformers have done no small service to the Church in stirring up the world as from the deep darkness of ignorance to read the Scriptures, in labouring diligently to make them better understood, and in happily throwing light on cer-

---

[1] See General Introduction: Calvin mentions three points, and forthwith deals with the first. Of these, for reasons given, there are included here mention and treatment of the second only, the others being omitted.

tain points of doctrine of the highest practical importance. In sermons little else used to be heard than old wives' fables and fictions equally frivolous. The schools resounded with brawling questions, but Scripture was seldom mentioned. Those who held the government of the Church had this one concern, to prevent any diminution of their gains. Accordingly, they readily tolerated whatever brought grist to their mill. Even the most prejudiced admit that our people have in some degree reformed these evils, however much they may impugn our doctrine at other points.

But I do not wish that all the profit the Church has derived from our labour should avail to mitigate our fault, if in any other respect we have injured her. Therefore let there be an examination of our whole doctrine, of our form of administering the sacraments, and our method of governing the Church; and in none of these three things will it be found that we have made any change in the old form, without attempting to restore it to the exact standard of the Word of God.[2]

All our controversies concerning doctrine relate either to the legitimate worship of God, or to the ground of salvation. As to the former, certainly we exhort men to worship God in neither a frigid nor a careless manner; and while we point out the way, we neither lose sight of the end, nor omit anything which is relevant to the matter. We proclaim the glory of God in terms far loftier than it was wont to be proclaimed before; and we earnestly labour to make the perfections in which his glory shines better and better known. His benefits towards ourselves we extol as eloquently as we can. Thus men are incited to reverence his majesty, render due homage to his greatness, feel due gratitude for his mercies, and unite in showing forth his praise. In this way there is infused into their hearts that solid confidence which afterwards gives birth to prayer. In this way too each one is trained to genuine self-denial, so that his will being brought into obedience to God, he bids farewell to his own desires. In short, as God requires us to worship him in a spiritual manner, so we with all zeal urge men to all the spiritual sacrifices which he commends.

Even our enemies cannot deny our assiduity in these exhortations, that men look for the good which they desire from none but God, that they confide in his power, trust in his goodness, depend on his truth, and turn to him with the whole heart, rest

---

[2] One phrase is here omitted in the translation: *Atque ad redeamus ad illam ante a nobis positam divisionem,* since in this abbreviated form, the division has not already appeared.

on him with full hope, and resort to him in necessity, that is, at every moment, and ascribe to him every good thing enjoyed, and testify to this by expressions of praise. That none may be deterred by difficulty of access, we proclaim that a fountain of all blessings is offered us in Christ, from which we may draw everything needful. Our writings are witnesses, and our sermons also, how frequent and sedulous we are in recommending true repentance, urging men to renounce their reason, their carnal desires, and themselves entirely, that they may be brought into obedience to God alone, and live no longer to themselves but to him. Nor indeed do we overlook external duties and works of charity, which follow on such renewal. This, I say, is the sure and unerring form of divine worship, which we know that he approves, because it is the form which his Word prescribes. These are the only sacrifices of the Christian Church which have attestation from him.

Since, therefore, in our churches, God alone is adored in pure form without superstition, since his goodness, wisdom, power, truth, and other perfections, are there preached more fully than anywhere else, since he is invoked with true faith in the name of Christ, his mercies celebrated with both heart and tongue, and men constantly urged to a simple and sincere obedience; since in short nothing is heard but what tends to promote the sanctification of his name, what cause have those who call themselves Christians to take us up so ill? First, since they love darkness rather than light, they cannot tolerate the sharpness with which we, as in duty bound, rebuke the gross idolatry which is apparent everywhere in the world. When God is worshipped in images, when fictitious worship is instituted in his name, when supplication is made to the images of saints, and divine honours paid to dead men's bones, and other similar things, we call them abominations as they are. For this cause, those who hate our doctrine inveigh against us, and represent us as heretics who dare to abolish the worship of God as approved of old by the Church. Concerning this name of *Church*, which they are ever and anon holding up before them as a kind of shield, we will shortly speak. Meanwhile how perverse, when these infamous corruptions are manifest, not only to defend them, but to dissemble and represent them as the genuine worship of God!

Both sides confess that in the sight of God idolatry is an execrable crime. But when we attack the worship of images, our adversaries immediately take the opposite side, and lend support to the crime which they had with us verbally condemned. Indeed, as is more ridiculous, while they agree with us as to the term in Greek, it is no sooner turned into Latin than their opposition begins. For they strenuously defend the veneration of images, though they condemn idolatry. But these ingenious men deny that the honour which they pay to images is worship,[3] as if, when compared with ancient idolatry, it were possible to see any difference. Idolaters pretended that they worshipped the celestial gods, though under corporeal figures which represented them. What else do our adversaries pretend? But is God satisfied with such excuses? Did the prophets on this account cease to rebuke the madness of the Egyptians, when, out of the secret mysteries of their theology, they drew subtle distinctions under which to screen themselves? What too do we suppose the brazen serpent which the Jews worshipped to have been, but something which they honoured as a representation of God? "The Gentiles," says Ambrose (*in Psalm* cxviii), "worship wood, because they think it an image of God, whereas the invisible image of God is not in that which is seen, but precisely in that which is not seen." But what is done today? Do they not prostrate themselves before images, as if God were present in them? Unless they supposed the power and grace of God to be attached to pictures and statues, would they flee to them when they desired to pray?

I have not yet adverted to the grosser superstitions, though these cannot be confined to the ignorant, since they are approved by public consent. They adorn their idols now with flowers and chaplets, now with robes, vests, girdles, purses and frivolities of every kind. They light tapers and burn incense before them, and carry them on their shoulders in solemn state. They assemble from long distances to one statue, though they have similar things at home. Likewise, though in one shrine there may be several images, of the Virgin Mary, or someone else, they pass these by, and one is frequented as if it were more divine. When they pray to the image of Christopher or Barbara, they mutter the Lord's Prayer and the angel's salutation. The fairer or dingier the images are, the greater is their excellence supposed to be. They find new commendation in fabulous miracles. Some they pretend to have spoken, others to have extinguished a fire in the church by trampling on it, others to have moved of their own accord to a new abode, others to have dropped from heaven. While the whole world teems with these

[3] Original has *latriae honorem.*

and similar delusions, and the fact is perfectly notorious, we who have brought back the worship of the one God to the rule of his Word, who are blameless in this matter, and have purged our churches, not only of idolatry but of superstition also, are accused of violating the worship of God, because we have discarded the worship of images, that is, as we call it, *idolatry*, but as our adversaries will have it, *idolodulia*.

But, besides the clear testimonies which occur everywhere in Scripture, we are also supported by the authority of the ancient Church. All the writers of a purer age describe the abuse of images among the Gentiles as not differing from what is seen in the world in the present day; and their observations on the subject are not less applicable to our age than to the persons whom they then censured. As to the charge they bring against us, of discarding images as well as the bones and relics of saints, it is easily answered. For none of these things ought to be assessed at more than the brazen serpent, and the reasons for removing them were not less valid than those of Hezekiah for breaking it. It is certain that the *idolomania* with which the minds of men are now fascinated, cannot be cured otherwise than by removing the material cause of the infatuation. We have too much experience of the absolute truth of Augustine's sentiment (*Ep.* 49): "No man prays or worships looking on an image without being impressed with the idea that it is listening to him." Similarly (*in Psalm* cxv. 4): "Images are more likely to mislead an unhappy soul having a mouth, eyes, ears and feet than to correct it, because they neither speak, nor see, nor hear, nor walk." Again: "The effect as it were extorted by the external shape is that the soul living in a body thinks a body which it sees so very like its own must be percipient." As to the matter of relics, it is almost incredible how impudently the world has been cheated. I can mention three relics of our Saviour's circumcision; likewise fourteen nails which are exhibited for the three by which he was fixed to the cross; three robes for that seamless one on which the soldiers cast lots; two inscriptions that were placed over the cross; three blades of the spear by which our Saviour's side was pierced, and about five sets of linen clothes which wrapped his body in the tomb. Besides they show all the articles used at the institution of the Lord's Supper, and endless absurdities of this kind. There is no saint of any celebrity of whom two or three bodies are not in existence. I can name the place where a piece of pumice-stone was long held in high veneration as the skull of Peter. Decency will not permit me to

mention fouler exhibitions. It is therefore undeservedly that we
are blamed for having studied to purify the Church of God
from such impurities.

In regard to the worship of God, our adversaries next accuse
us, because, in omitting trivialities not only foolish but also
tending to hypocrisy, we worship God more simply. That we
have in no respect detracted from the spiritual worship of God
is attested by fact. Indeed when it had in a great measure
sunk into a desuetude, we have reinstated it in its former rights.
Let us now see whether they are justly angry with us. In regard
to doctrine, I maintain that we make common cause with the
prophets. For, next to idolatry, there is nothing for which they
rebuke the people more sharply than for falsely imagining that
the worship of God consisted in external show. For what is the
sum of their declarations? That God neither cares for nor values
ceremonies considered only in themselves; that he looks to the
faith and truth of the heart; and that the only end for which he
commanded and for which he approves ceremonies is that they
may be pure exercises of faith, and prayer, and praise. The
writings of all the prophets are full of evidence to this effect.
Nor, as I have observed, was there anything for which they
laboured more. Now it cannot without effrontery be denied,
that when the Reformers appeared the world was more than
ever afflicted with this blindness. It was therefore absolutely
necessary to urge men with these prophetic rebukes, and divert
them, as by force, from that infatuation, lest they might any
longer imagine that God was satisfied with bare ceremonies,
as children are with shows. There was a like necessity for urging
the doctrine of the spiritual worship of God—a doctrine which
had vanished from the minds of men. That both of these things
have been and still are being faithfully performed by us, both
our writings and our sermons clearly prove.

In inveighing against ceremonies themselves, and also in
abrogating a greater part of them, we confess that there is indeed some difference between us and the prophets. They in-
veighed against their countrymen for confining the worship of
God to external ceremonies, which, however, God himself had
instituted; we complain that the same honour is paid to frivolities of man's devising. They condemned superstition, but left
untouched a multitude of ceremonies which God had enjoined,
and which were useful and appropriate to an age of tutelage;
our business has been to correct numerous rites which had either
crept in through oversight, or been turned to abuse, and which,

moreover, by no means accorded with the time. For if we are not to throw everything into confusion, we must always bear in mind the distinction between the old and the new dispensations, and the fact that ceremonies, whose observance was useful under the law, are now not only superfluous but absurd and wicked. When Christ was absent and not yet manifested, ceremonies by shadowing him forth nourished the hope of his advent in the breasts of believers; but now they only obscure his present and conspicuous glory. We see what God himself has done. For those ceremonies which he had commanded for a time he has now abrogated for ever. Paul explains the reason: first, that since the body has been manifested in Christ, the types had to be withdrawn; and secondly, that God is now pleased to instruct his Church in a different manner (Gal. 4:3 ff.; Col. 2:8, 16, 17). Since then God has freed his Church from the bondage which he himself had imposed upon it, what perversity, I ask, is this that demands from men a new bondage in place of the old? Since God has prescribed a certain economy, how presumptuous to set up one contrary to it and openly repudiated by him! But the worst of all is, that though God has so often and strictly banned from worship all fabrications made by men, the only worship paid to him consisted of human inventions. What ground, then, have our enemies to clamour that in this matter we have dissipated religion to the winds? First, we have not laid even a finger on anything which Christ does not discount as worthless when he declares that it is vain to worship God with human traditions. The thing might perhaps have been more tolerable if the only effect had been that men's labour was lost by an unavailing worship. But since, as I have observed, God in many passages forbids any new worship unsanctioned by his Word, declares that he is gravely offended by such audacity, and threatens it with severe punishment, it is clear that the reformation which we have introduced was demanded by a strong necessity.

I am not unaware how difficult it is to persuade the world that God rejects and even abominates everything devised for worship by human reason. The grounds for this error are numerous. "Every one thinks highly of his own," as the old proverb expresses it. Hence the offspring of our own brain delights us more; and besides, as Paul admits (Col. 2:23), this fictitious worship often presents some show of wisdom. Besides, as it has for the most part an external splendour which pleases the eye, it is more agreeable to our carnal nature, than that which alone God requires and approves, but which is less ostentatious. But there is nothing which so blinds the minds of men, so that they judge wrongly in this matter, as hypocrisy. For while it is incumbent on true worshippers to give heart and mind, men always want to invent a mode of serving God quite different from this, their object being to perform for him certain bodily observances, and keep the mind to themselves. Moreover, they imagine that when they thrust external pomps upon him, they have by this artifice evaded the necessity of giving themselves. This is the reason why they submit to innumerable observances which without measure and without end miserably exhaust them, and why they choose to wander in a perpetual labyrinth, rather than worship God simply in spirit and in truth.

It is, then, impudent calumny in our enemies to accuse us of alluring men by compliance and indulgence. For were the option given, there is nothing which the carnal man would not prefer to do, rather than consent to worship God as prescribed by our doctrine. It is easy to use the words faith and repentance, but the things are most difficult to perform. Whoever therefore makes the worship of God consist in these by no means loosens the reins of discipline, but compels men to the course which they are most afraid to take. Of this we have most trustworthy proof from fact. Men will allow themselves to be constrained by numerous severe laws, to be tied to numerous laborious observances, and to bear a severe and heavy yoke; in short, there is no annoyance to which they will not submit, provided there be no mention of the heart. Hence, it appears, that there is nothing to which the human mind is more averse than to that spiritual truth which is the constant theme of our sermons, and nothing with which it is more engrossed than that splendid show on which our adversaries so strongly insist. The very majesty of God extorts this much from us, that we are unable to withdraw entirely from his service. Therefore, as we cannot evade the necessity of worshipping him, it remains for us to seek out indirect substitutes, lest we be obliged to come directly into his presence; or rather, by means of external ceremonies like specious masks we hide the inward malice of the heart, and interpose bodily observances like a wall of partition lest we be compelled to come to him with the heart. It is with the greatest reluctance that the world allows itself to be driven from such subterfuges as these; and hence the outcry against us for having dragged them from the lurking places, where they safely played with God, into the light of day.

In prayer we have corrected three things. Discarding the

intercession of saints, we have brought men back to Christ, that they might learn both to invoke the Father in his name and trust in him as Mediator; and we have taught them to pray first with firm and solid confidence, and second with understanding also, instead of muttering over confused prayers in an unknown tongue as they did before. Here we are assailed with bitter reproaches for being offensive to the saints, and also for depriving believers of an immense privilege. Both charges we deny. It is no injury to saints not to permit the office of Christ to be attributed to them. There is no honour of which we deprive them, except one improperly and rashly bestowed upon them by human error. I shall mention nothing which may not be expressly pointed out. First, when men are about to pray, they imagine God to be at a great distance, and that they cannot have access to him unless conducted by some patron. Nor is this false opinion current among the rude and unlearned only, but even those who would be thought leaders of the blind entertain it. Then in looking for patrons, every one follows his own fancy. One selects Mary, another Michael, another Peter. Christ they very seldom honour with a place in the list. Indeed there is scarcely one in a hundred who would not be amazed, as at some new prodigy, were he to hear Christ named as an intercessor. Therefore, passing Christ by, they all trust to the patronage of saints. Then superstition creeps in farther and farther, till they invoke the saints promiscuously, just as they do God. I admit, indeed, that when they desire to speak more definitely, all they ask of the saints is to assist them before God with their prayers. But more frequently they lose this distinction, and address and implore at one time God, and at another the saints, just according to the impulse of the moment. Indeed each saint has a peculiar province allotted to him. One gives rain, another fair weather; one delivers from fever, another from shipwreck. But, to say nothing of these profane heathen delusions which everywhere prevail in churches, this one impiety may suffice for all: that, in inviting intercessors from this quarter and from that, the whole world neglects Christ, whom alone God has set forth, and confides more in the patronage of the saints than in the protection of God.

But our critics, even those of them who have rather more regard to equity, blame us for excess in having discarded entirely from our prayers the mention of dead saints. But I should like to know from them how they conceive those to sin, who faithfully observe the rule laid down by Christ, the Supreme Teacher, and by the prophets and apostles, and do not omit anything which either the Holy Spirit has taught in Scripture or the servants of God have practised from the beginning of the world to the age of the apostles? There is scarcely any subject on which the Holy Spirit more carefully prescribes than on the proper method of prayer. But there is not a syllable which teaches us to have recourse to the assistance of dead saints. Many of the prayers offered up by believers are extant. In none of them is there even a single example of such a thing. Sometimes, indeed, the Israelites entreated God to remember Abraham, Isaac, and Jacob, and David similarly. But all they meant by such expressions was that he should be mindful of the covenant which he had made with them, and bless their posterity according to his promise. For the covenant of grace, which was ultimately to be ratified in Christ, those holy patriarchs had received in their own name and that of their posterity. Wherefore the faithful of the Israelite Church do not, by such mention of the patriarchs, seek intercession from the dead, but simply appeal to the promise which had been deposited with them until it should be fully ratified in the mind of Christ. What a mad infatuation, then, to abandon the form of prayer which the Lord has commended, and without injunction or example to introduce into prayer the intercession of saints! But briefly to conclude this point, I take my stand on the declaration of Paul, that no prayer is genuine which does not spring from faith, and that faith cometh by the Word of God (Rom. 10:17). In these words, he has, if I am not mistaken, distinctly declared that the Word of God is the only sure foundation for prayer. And while he elsewhere says that every action of our lives should be preceded by faith, that is by assurance of conscience, he shows that this is specially requisite in prayer, more so indeed than in any other matter. It is, however, still more relevant to the present point, when he declares that prayer depends on the Word of God. For it is just as if he had prohibited all men from opening their mouths until such time as God put words into them. This is our wall of brass, which all the powers of hell will in vain attempt to break down. Since, then, there exists a clear command to invoke God only; since again one Mediator is offered, whose intercession must support our prayers; since a promise has, moreover, been added, that whatever we ask in the name of Christ we shall obtain, men must pardon us if we follow the certain truth of God rather than their frivolous fictions.

It is surely incumbent on those who in their prayers introduce the intercession of the dead, that they may be thereby assisted more easily to obtain what they ask, to prove one of two things: either that they are so taught by the Word of God, or that men have licence to pray as they please. But in regard to the former, it is plain that they are destitute of both scriptural testimony and approved example of the saints. As to the latter, Paul declares that none can invoke God save those who have been taught by his Word to pray. On this depends the confidence with which it is fitting that pious minds be supplied and instructed when they engage in prayer. The world supplicates God, dubious meanwhile of success. For it relies on no promise, nor does it perceive the force of what is meant by having a Mediator through whom it will assuredly obtain what it asks. Moreover God enjoins us to come free from doubt (Matt. 21:22). Accordingly prayer proceeding from true faith obtains favour with God whereas prayer accompanied with distrust of this kind rather alienates him from us. For this is the proper mark which discriminates between genuine invocation of the one God and the profane wandering prayers of the heathen. Indeed, this lacking, prayer ceases to be divine worship. It is to this James refers when he says: "If any man lack wisdom, let him ask of God; but let him ask in faith, doubting nothing. For he that doubteth is like a wave of the sea, driven with the winds, and tossed" (James 1:6). It is not surprising that without Christ as true Mediator, he thus wavers in uncertainty and distrust. For, as Paul declares (Rom. 5:2; Eph. 2:18), it is through Christ only that we have boldness and access with confidence to the Father. We have, therefore, taught men when brought to Christ no longer to doubt and vacillate in their prayers, as they were wont to do; we bid them rest secure in the Word of the Lord, which, when once it penetrates the soul, drives far from it all the doubt that is repugnant to faith.

It remains to point out the third fault in prayer which I said that we have corrected. Whereas men generally prayed in an unknown tongue, we have taught them to pray with understanding. Every man accordingly is taught by our doctrine to pray in private so that he understands what he asks of God. So also the public prayers in our churches are framed so as to be understood by all. Natural reason prescribes that it should be so, even if God had given no precept on the subject. For the design of prayer is to make God the witness and confidant of our necessities, and as it were to pour out our hearts before him. But nothing is more at variance with this than to move the tongue without thought and intelligence. Yet to such a degree of absurdity had it come, that to pray in the vulgar tongue was almost turned into an offence against religion. I can name an Archbishop, who threatened with incarceration and the severer penalties, anyone who should repeat the Lord's Prayer aloud in any language but Latin. The general belief, however, was that it did not matter in what language a man prayed at home, provided he had what was called a final intention in praying. But in churches it was held to belong to the dignity of the service that Latin should be the only language in which prayers were couched.

There seems, as I have just said, something monstrous in wishing to hold converse with God in empty sounds of the tongue. Even if God did not declare his displeasure, nature herself without any teacher rejects it. Besides it is easy to infer from the whole tenor of the Scripture how deeply God abominates such an invention. As to the public prayers of the Church, the words of Paul are clear: the unlearned cannot say Amen if the benediction be pronounced in an unknown tongue (I Cor. 14:16). This makes it the more strange, that those who first introduced this perverse practice ultimately had the effrontery to maintain that the very thing, which Paul regards as ineffably absurd, was conclusive of the majesty of prayer. Our adversaries may ridicule if they will the method by which in our churches all pray together in the popular tongue, and men and women without distinction sing the Psalms; if only the Holy Spirit bears testimony to us from heaven, while he repudiates the confused, unmeaning sounds which are uttered elsewhere, we are content.

In the second principal branch of doctrine, namely that which relates to the grounds of salvation and the method of obtaining it, many questions are involved. For when we tell a man to seek righteousness and life outside himself, that is in Christ only, because he has nothing in himself but sin and death, controversy immediately arises about the freedom of the will and its powers. For if man has any ability of his own to serve God, he does not obtain salvation entirely by the grace of Christ, but in part bestows it on himself. On the other hand, if the whole of salvation is attributed to the grace of Christ nothing is left over for man by which, that is by some virtue of his own, he can assist himself to procure salvation. Now our opponents concede that man is assisted by the Holy Spirit in good living, but in such a way that they nevertheless claim for him a share in the

operation. This they do, because they do not perceive how deep
the wound is which was inflicted on our nature by the fall of our
first parents. No doubt, they agree with us in holding the doctrine of original sin; but they afterwards modify its effects,
maintaining that the powers of man are only weakened, not
wholly depraved. Their view then is that man, being tainted
with original corruption, is in consequence of the weakening of
his powers unable to act aright; but that, being aided by the
grace of God, he has something of his own and from himself
which he may contribute. Again though we do not deny that
man acts spontaneously and of free will when he is guided by
the Holy Spirit, we maintain that his whole nature is so imbued
with depravity, that of himself he possesses no ability whatever
to act aright. Thus far, therefore, we dissent from those who
oppose our doctrine, that they neither humble man sufficiently,
nor duly estimate the blessing of regeneration, while we so
prostrate him that he is reduced to nothing so far as spiritual
righteousness is concerned, and must learn to seek it, not partially, but wholly from God. To some not very equitable judges,
we seem, perhaps, to carry the matter too far. But there is
nothing absurd in our doctrine, and nothing at variance either
with Scripture or with the general consent of the ancient
Church. Indeed we are able without difficulty to confirm our
doctrine to the very letter out of the mouth of Augustine.
Accordingly several of those who are otherwise ill-disposed to
our cause, but somewhat sounder in their judgments, do not
venture to contradict us on this head. It is certain, as I have
observed, that we differ from others only in this, that by convincing man of his poverty and powerlessness we train him
better in true humility, so that renouncing all self-confidence,
he throws himself entirely upon God; and similarly in gratitude,
so that he ascribes, as in truth he ought, every good thing which
he possesses to the kindness of God. They, on the other hand,
intoxicating him with a perverse opinion of his own virtue, precipitate his ruin, and fill him up with impudent arrogance against
God, so as to ascribe to himself no less than to God the glory of
his justification. To these errors they add a third: that in all
their discussions concerning the corruption of human nature,
they usually stop short with the grosser carnal desires, without
touching the deeper-seated diseases which are much more
cardinal. Hence it is that those who are trained in their school
easily forgive themselves the most shocking sins as no sins at all,
if only they are hid.

The next question relates to the merit and value of works. Now we give good works their due praise, nor do we deny that a reward is reserved for them with God. But we make three reservations, on which the whole of our remaining controversy concerning the work of salvation hinges.

First, we maintain that of whatever kind a man's works may be, he is regarded as righteous before God simply on the ground of gratuitous mercy; because God, without any respect to works, freely adopts him in Christ, by imputing the righteousness of Christ to him as if it were his own. This we call the righteousness of faith, that is when a man, empty and drained of all confidence in works, feels convinced that the only ground of his acceptance with God is a righteousness which is wanting to himself, and is borrowed from Christ. The point on which the world always goes astray (for this error has prevailed in almost every age), is in imagining that man, however partially defective he may be, still in some degree merits the favour of God by works. But Scripture declares: "Cursed is every one that continueth not in all things that are written in the book of the law to do them." Under this curse must necessarily lie all who are judged by works, none being exempted except those who entirely renounce all confidence in works and put on Christ, that they may be justified in him by the gratuitous acceptance of God. The ground of our justification, therefore, is that God reconciles us to himself, from regard not to our works but to Christ alone, and by gratuitous adoption makes us his own children instead of children of wrath. So long as God regards our works, he finds no reason why he ought to love us. Wherefore it is necessary that he should bury our sins, impute to us the obedience of Christ which alone can stand his scrutiny, and adopt us as righteous through his merits. This is the clear and uniform doctrine of Scripture, "witnessed," as Paul says, "by the law and the prophets" (Rom. 3:21), and so explained by the gospel that a clearer law cannot be desired. Paul contrasts the righteousness of the law with the righteousness of the gospel, placing the former in works, and the latter in the grace of Christ (Rom. 10:5, etc.). That we are judged righteous in the sight of God he does not divide in two between works and Christ, but ascribes it to Christ entirely.

There are here two questions: first whether the glory of our salvation is to be divided between ourselves and God; and second whether as in the sight of God our conscience can with safety put any confidence in works. On the former question,

Paul's decision is: let every mouth "be stopped, and the whole world become guilty before God. All have sinned, and come short of the glory of God, being justified freely by his grace, through the redemption that is in Christ Jesus"; and this "to declare his righteousness, that he might be just, and the justifier of him which believeth in Jesus" (Rom. 3:19, etc.). Hence he declares all glorying in the flesh to be excluded. We simply follow this definition, while our opponents maintain that man is not justified by the grace of God, in any sense which does not reserve part of the praise for his own works.

On the second question, Paul reasons thus: "If they which are of the law be heirs, faith is made void, and the promise made of none effect." Thence he concludes: "it is of faith," "to the end the promise might be sure to all thy seed" (Rom. 4:14, 16). And again: "Being justified by faith, we have peace with God" (Rom. 5:1), and no longer dread his presence. But he realizes that everyone feels in his own experience, that our consciences cannot but be vexed and disquieted with perpetual unrest so long as we look for protection from works, and that we enjoy serene and placid tranquillity only when we have resort to Christ as the one haven of true confidence. We add nothing to Paul's doctrine; but that restless dubiety of conscience, which he regards as absurd, is placed by our opponents among the primary axioms of their faith.

The second reservation which we make relates to the remission of sins. Our opponents, not being able to deny that men during their whole life walk haltingly and often even fall, are obliged to confess, whether they will or not, that all need pardon in order to supply their want of righteousness. But then they invent satisfactions, with which those who have sinned may purchase back the favour of God. In this class they place first contrition, and next works which they call works of supererogation and the penalties which God inflicts on sinners. But as they are still sensible that these compensations fall far short of the just measure required, they call in the aid of a new species of satisfaction from another quarter, namely from the benefit of the keys. They say that by the keys the treasury of the Church is unlocked, so that what is wanting to ourselves is supplied out of the merits of Christ and the saints. We on the contrary maintain that the sins of men are forgiven freely, and we acknowledge no other satisfaction than that which Christ accomplished, when, by the sacrifice of his death, he expiated our sins. Therefore we preach that it is by the benefit of Christ alone that we are reconciled to

God, and that no compensations are taken into account, because our heavenly Father, content with the sole expiation of Christ, requires none from us. In the Scriptures we have clear proof of this doctrine of ours, which indeed ought to be called not ours, but rather that of the Church Catholic. For the only method of regaining the divine favour is set forth by the apostle, that "he hath made him to be sin for us who knew no sin, that we might be made the righteousness of God in him" (II Cor. 5:21). And in another passage, where he is speaking of the remission of sins, he declares that through it righteousness without works is imputed to us (Rom. 4:5). We therefore strenuously denounce for the execrable blasphemy it in fact is, the idea of our adversaries, of meriting reconciliation with God by satisfaction, and buying off the penalties due to his justice; for it destroys the doctrine which Isaiah delivers concerning Christ, that "the chastisement of our peace was upon him" (Isa. 53:5).

The absurd fiction concerning works of supererogation we discard for many reasons; but two are of more than sufficient weight: one, that it is impossible to tolerate the idea of man being able to perform to God more than he ought; and the other, that as by the term supererogation they for the most part understand voluntary acts of worship which their own brain has devised, and which they obtrude upon God, it is lost labour and pains; so far are such acts from being expiations appeasing the divine anger. Moreover, this mixing up of the blood of Christ with the blood of martyrs and forming out of them a heterogeneous mass of merits or satisfactions to buy off the punishments due to sin, is something we neither tolerate nor ought to tolerate. For, as Augustine says (*in Joann. ev. Tract.* 84): "No martyr's blood has been shed for the remission of sins. This was the work of Christ alone, and in this work he has bestowed something not to be imitated but to be gratefully received." With Augustine, Leo admirably agrees, when he thus writes (*Ep.* 81 and 97): "Though precious in the sight of God has been the death of his many saints, yet no innocent man's slaughter was the propitiation of the world; the just received crowns, did not give them, and the constancy of the faithful has furnished examples of patience, not gifts of righteousness."

Our third and last reservation relates to the recompense of works. We maintain that it depends not on their own value or merit, but rather on the mere benignity of God. Indeed our opponents themselves admit that there is no proportion between the merit of the work and its reward. But they do not attend to what is of primary moment in the matter, that the good works of believers are never so pure as to be able to please without pardon. They do not consider, I say, that they are always sprinkled with some spots or blemishes, because they never proceed from that pure and perfect love of God which is demanded by the law. We therefore teach that the good works of believers always lack the spotless purity which can stand the inspection of God; indeed, that when they are tried by the strict rule of justice, they are to a certain extent impure. But when once God has graciously adopted believers, he not only accepts and loves their persons, but their works also, to dignify them with a reward. In a word, as we said of man, so we may say of works: they are justified not by their own desert, but by the merits of Christ alone; the faults by which they would otherwise displease being covered by the sacrifice of Christ. This consideration is of very great practical importance, both in retaining men in the fear of God, that they may not arrogate to their works what proceeds from his fatherly kindness; and also in inspiring them with the best consolation, lest they despond when they reflect on the imperfection or impurity of their works, by reminding them that God, of his paternal indulgence, is pleased to pardon it.

We come now to the sacraments, in which we have not made any correction which we are unable to defend by the sure and approved authority of God. Whereas seven sacraments were supposed to have been instituted by Christ, we have discarded five of this number and have demonstrated them to be ceremonies of man's devising, with the exception of marriage, which we acknowledge to have been indeed commanded by God, but not in order that it might be a sacrament. Nor is it a dispute about nothing when we separate rites thus superadded on the part of men, even if in other respects they should be neither wicked nor useless, from those symbols which Christ with his own lips commended to us, and was pleased to make the attestation of spiritual gifts—gifts to which, as they are not in the power of man, men are quite unable to testify. It is assuredly no vulgar matter to seal upon our hearts the sacred favour of God, to offer Christ, and represent the blessings we enjoy in him. This being the office of the sacraments of Christ, failure to discriminate between them and the rites originating with man is to confound heaven with earth. Here, indeed, a twofold error had prevailed. Making no distinction between things human and divine, they seriously derogated from the sacred Word of

God, on which the whole power of the sacraments depend; and they also falsely imagined Christ to be the author of rites which had no higher than a human origin.

From Baptism similarly we have cut away many additions which were partly useless, and partly, from their superstitious tendency, harmful. We know the form of Baptism which the apostles received from Christ, which they observed during their lifetime, and which they finally left to posterity. But the simplicity which had been approved by the authority of Christ, and the practice of the apostles, did not satisfy succeeding ages. I am not at present discussing whether those people were influenced by sound reasons, who afterwards added chrism, salt, spittle and tapers. I only say what every one must know, that to such a height had superstition or folly risen, that more value was set on these additions than on the genuineness of Baptism itself. We have studied also to banish the preposterous confidence which stopped short at the external act and paid not the least regard to Christ. For in the schools as well as in sermons, they so extolled the efficacy of signs, that, instead of directing men to Christ, they taught them to confide in the visible elements. Lastly, we have recalled the ancient custom that the administration of the sacraments at the same time be accompanied by doctrine, expounding with all diligence and fidelity both their advantages and their legitimate use; so that in this respect even our opponents cannot find anything to criticize. But nothing is more alien to the nature of a sacrament than to set before the people an empty spectacle, unaccompanied with explanation of the mystery. There is a well-known passage, quoted by Gratian from Augustine: "If the word is wanting, the water is nothing but an element." What he means by *word* he immediately explains when he says: "That is, the word of faith, which we preach." Our opponents therefore ought not to think it a novelty when we disapprove of the exhibition of the sign, separated from an understanding of the mystery. For this is a sacrilegious divorce, which reverses the order instituted by Christ. Another additional fault in the mode of administration commonly used elsewhere, is that the thing which they consider as a religious act is not understood, just as is the case in magical incantations.

I have already observed that the other sacrament of the Christian Church, the Holy Supper of our Lord, was not only corrupted but nearly abolished. Wherefore it was the more necessary for us to labour in restoring its purity. First, it was necessary to eradicate from the minds of men that impious fiction of a sacrifice, the source of many absurdities. For, besides the introduction of a rite of oblation in opposition to the express institution of Christ, there had been added a most pestilential opinion, that this act of oblation was an expiation for sin. Thus the dignity of the priesthood, which belonged exclusively to Christ, had been transferred to mortal men, and the virtue of his death to their own act. Thus also its application had availed for the living and the dead. We have, therefore, abrogated that fictitious immolation and restored communion, which had been in large measure rendered obsolete. For provided men went once a year to the Lord's Table, they thought it enough for all the remainder of that period to be spectators of what was done by the priest, under the pretext, indeed, of administering the Lord's Supper, but without any vestige of the Supper in it. For what are the words of the Lord? Take, he says, and distribute among yourselves. But in the mass, instead of taking, there is a pretence of offering, while there is no distribution, and even no invitation. The priest, like a member cut off from the rest of the body, prepares it for himself alone and alone consumes it. How immense the difference between the things! We have besides restored to the people the use of the cup, which though it was not only permitted but committed to them by our Lord, was taken from them, it could only be at the suggestion of Satan. Of ceremonies, there are many which we have discarded, partly because they had multiplied beyond measure, partly because some savoured too much of Judaism, and others, being the inventions of ignorant men, ill accorded with the seriousness of so high a mystery. But, granted that there was no other evil in them than that they had crept in through oversight, was it not a sufficient ground for their abolition that we saw the vulgar gazing upon them in stupid amazement?

In condemning the fiction of transubstantiation, and likewise the custom of keeping and carrying about the bread, we were impelled by a stronger necessity. First, it is repugnant to the plain words of Christ; and second, it is abhorrent to the very nature of a sacrament. For there is no sacrament when there is no visible symbol to correspond to the spiritual truth which it represents. And with regard to the Supper, what Paul says is clear: "We being many are one bread, and one body: for we are all partakers of that one bread" (I Cor. 10:17). Where is the analogy or similitude of a visible sign in the Supper to correspond to the body and blood of our Lord, if there is neither bread to eat, nor wine to drink, but only some empty phantom to mock the eye? Add that to this fiction a worse superstition perpetually adheres, that, as we have seen, men cling to the bread as if to God, and worship it as God. While the sacrament ought to have been a means of elevating pious minds to heaven, the sacred symbols of the Supper were abused for an entirely different purpose, and men, content with gazing upon them and worshipping them, never once raised their mind to Christ.

The carrying about of the bread in solemn state, or setting it on an elevated spot to be adored, are corruptions quite alien to the institution of Christ. For in the Supper the Lord sets before us his body and blood, but it is in order that we may eat and drink. Accordingly, in the first place he gives the command, by which he bids us take, eat and drink; and then in the next place he adds and annexes the promise, in which he testifies that what we eat is his body, and what we drink is his blood. Therefore those who keep the bread set apart or carry it about to be worshipped, seeing they separate the promise from the command, in other words sever an indissoluble tie, imagine indeed that they have the body of Christ, whereas in fact they have nothing but an idol which they have devised for themselves. For this promise of Christ, by which he offers his own body and blood under the symbols of bread and wine, belongs to those only who receive them at his hand, to celebrate the mystery in the manner which he enjoins. But those who pervert them at their own will to a different purpose, and so have not the promise, retain only a fiction of their own devising.

Lastly, we have revived the practice of explaining the doctrine and unfolding the mystery to the people whereas formerly the priest not only used a strange tongue, but muttered in a whisper the words by which he pretended to consecrate the bread and wine. Here our critics have nothing to grumble at, unless it be that we have simply followed the command of Christ. For he did not by a silent exorcism command the bread to become his body, but with a clear voice declared to his apostles that he gave them his body.

At the same time, as in the case of Baptism, so also in the case of the Lord's Supper, we explain to the people faithfully and as carefully as we can its end, efficacy, advantages, and use. First, we exhort all to come with faith, that by means of it they may inwardly discern the thing which is visibly represented, that is the spiritual food by which alone their souls are nourished unto life eternal. We hold that in this ordinance the Lord does not promise or set forth by signs, anything which he does not exhibit in reality. We therefore preach that the body and blood of Christ are both offered to us by the Lord in the Supper and received by us. Nor do we thus teach that the bread and wine are symbols, without immediately adding that the truth they represent is conjoined with them. We are not silent about the nature and excellence of the fruit that comes to us from this source, and how noble the pledge of life and salvation which our consciences therein receive. Nor indeed will anyone with candour deny, that with us this solemn ordinance is much more clearly explained, and its dignity more fully extolled, than is the rule elsewhere.

In the government of the Church, we do not differ from others in anything for which we cannot give a most sufficient reason. The pastoral office we have restored, both according to the apostolic rule and the practice of the primitive Church, by insisting that every one who rules in the Church shall also teach. We hold that none are to be continued in the office but those who are diligent in performing its duties. In selecting them our advice has been that this is a matter where greater and more religious care should be exercised, and we have ourselves studied so to act. It is well known what kind of examination bishops conduct by means of their suffragans or vicars. We might even be able to conjecture what its nature is from the fruit which it produces. It is needless to observe how many lazy and good-for-nothing persons they everywhere promote to the honourable rank of the priesthood. Among us, even if some Ministers be found of no great learning, none is admitted who is not at least tolerably fit to teach. That all are not more perfect is to be imputed more to the calamity of the times than to us. This, however, is and always will be our just boast, that the Ministers of our Church cannot seem to have been carelessly chosen if they be compared with others. But while we are superior in a considerable degree in the matter of trial and election, in this we particularly excel, that no man holds the pastoral office amongst us without executing its duties. Accordingly none of our churches is seen without the ordinary preaching of the Word of God.

As it would shame our adversaries to deny these facts (for in a matter so clear, what would they gain by denial?), they quarrel with us, first concerning the right and power of ordination, and secondly concerning its form. They quote ancient canons, which give the superintendence of this matter to the bishops and clergy. They allege a constant succession by which this right has been handed down to them, even from the apostles themselves. They deny that it can be lawfully transferred elsewhere. I wish they had by their merit retained a title to this boasted possession. But if we consider first the order in which for several ages bishops have been advanced to this dignity, next the manner in which they conduct themselves in it, and lastly the kind of persons whom they are accustomed to ordain and to whom they commit the government of churches, we shall see that this succession on which they pride themselves was long ago interrupted. The ancient canons require that he who is to be admitted to the office of bishop or presbyter shall previously undergo a strict examination, both as to life and doctrine. Clear evidence of this is extant among the acts of the fourth African Council. Moreover, the magistracy and people had a discretionary power [4] of approving or refusing the individual who was nominated by the clergy, in order that no man might be intruded on those unwilling or not consenting. "Let him who is to preside over all," says Leo (*Ep.* xc), "be elected by all; for he who is appointed, while unknown and unexamined, must of necessity be violently intruded." Again (*Ep.* lxxxvii): "Let regard be had to the attestation of honourable men, the approval of the clergy, and the consent of the magistracy and people. Reason permits no other mode of procedure." Cyprian also contends for the very same thing, and indeed in stronger terms, affirming it as sanctioned by Divine authority that the priest, the people being present, be elected before the eyes of all, that he may be approved as fit and worthy by the testimony of all. While this rule was in force, the Church was in a state of good order; for the letters of Gregory are full of passages which show that it was carefully observed in his day.

As the Holy Spirit in Scripture imposes on all bishops the necessity of teaching, so in the ancient Church it would have been thought monstrous to nominate a bishop who would not by teaching demonstrate that he was a pastor also. Nor were they admitted to the office on any other condition. The same rule prevailed in regard to presbyters, each being set apart to a particular parish. Hence those decrees: "Let them not involve themselves in secular affairs, let them not make distant excursions from their churches, let them not be long absent." Then it was enjoined by synodal decrees, that at the ordination of a bishop all the other bishops of the provinces should assemble, or

[4] Original has *arbitrium*.

if this could not be conveniently done, at least three should be present. The object of this was that no man might force an entrance by tumult, or creep in by stealth, or insinuate himself by surreptitious artifices. To the ordination of a presbyter, each bishop admitted a council of his own presbyters. These things, which could be narrated more fully and confirmed more accurately in a set discourse, I mention, here only in passing because they afford an easy means of judging how much consideration is due to this smoke of succession which our bishops emit to blind us.

They maintain that Christ left as a heritage to the apostles the sole right of appointing to churches whomever they pleased; and they complain that, in exercising the Ministry without their authority, we have invaded their province with impious audacity. How do they prove it? Because they have succeeded the apostles in an unbroken series. But is this enough, when all other things are different? It would be ridiculous to say so: they do, however, say it. In their elections, no account is taken either of life or doctrine. The right of voting is wrested from the people. Indeed, even the rest of the clergy have been excluded and the dignitaries have attracted all the power to themselves. The Roman pontiff, again, wresting it from the provincial bishop, arrogates it to himself alone. Then, as if they had been appointed to secular dominion, there is nothing of which they think less than episcopal duty. In short, while they seem to have entered into a conspiracy to have no kind of resemblance either to the apostles or to the holy fathers of the Church, they merely cover themselves with the pretence that they are descended from them in an unbroken succession—as if Christ had ever enacted it into a law, that whatever might be the conduct of those who presided over the Church, they should be recognized as holding the place of the apostles; or as if the office were some hereditary possession, which passes alike to the worthy and the unworthy. Moreover, as is said of the Milesians, they have taken precautions not to admit a single worthy person into their society; or if perhaps by error they have admitted him, they do not permit him to remain. It is of the majority I speak; for I do not deny that there are a few good men among them. But they are either silent through fear, or given no hearing. Here are persons who persecute the doctrine of Christ with fire and sword, who permit no man with impunity to speak sincerely of Christ, who in every possible way impede the course of truth, who strenuously resist our attempt to raise the Church from the distressed condition into which they have brought her, who suspect all those who take a deep and pious interest in the welfare of the Church, and either keep them out of the ministry, or, if they have been admitted, thrust them out—such persons might indeed be expected with their own hands to install into the office faithful ministers to instruct the people in pure religion!

But since the view of Gregory has passed into a common proverb, that "those who abuse privilege deserve to lose privilege," they must either become entirely different from what they are, and select a different sort to govern the Church, and adopt a different method of election; or they must cease to complain that they are improperly and injuriously despoiled of what in justice belonged to them. Or, if they want greater frankness, let them obtain their bishoprics by different means from those by which they have obtained them, ordain others to the office in a different method and manner, and, if they wish to be recognized as bishops, fulfil their duty by feeding the people. If they would retain the power of nominating and ordaining, let them restore that just and serious examination of life and doctrine, which has for many centuries been obsolete among them. But this one reason ought to be as good as a thousand, that any man, who by his conduct shows he is an enemy of sound doctrine, whatever title he may meanwhile boast, has lost all title to authority in the Church. We know what injunctions ancient councils gave concerning the heretic, and what power they leave him. Certainly they expressly forbid any man to apply to him for ordination. No one, therefore, can lay claim to the right of ordaining, who does not by purity of doctrine preserve the unity of the Church. We maintain that those who in the present day in the name of bishops preside over churches, are such unfaithful ministers and guardians of sound doctrine, that they are rather its bitterest enemies. We maintain that their sole aim is to banish Christ and the truth of his gospel, and sanction idolatry and impiety, the most pernicious and deadly errors. We maintain that they not only in word pertinaciously attack the true doctrine of godliness, but are infuriated against all who would rescue it from obscurity. Against the many impediments which they throw in the way, we studiously expend our labour on behalf of the Church. For so doing, they expostulate with us that we make an illegal incursion into their province.

As to the form or ceremony of ordination, this is indeed a mighty matter about which to worry us. Because with us the hands of priests are not anointed, because we do not breathe into their faces, because we do not clothe them in white and garments of this kind, they think our ordination is not duly performed. But we read of no other ceremony in ancient times than the laying on of hands. Those other forms are recent, and have nothing to recommend them but the exceeding scrupulousness with which they are now generally observed. But how much is this to the point? In matters so important, a higher than human authority is required. Hence, as often as the circumstances of the times demand, we are at liberty to change such rites as men have invented without express sanction, while those of less antiquity are of much less importance. They put a chalice and paten into the hands of those whom they ordain to be priests. Why? That they may empower them to sacrifice. But by what command? Christ never conferred this function on the apostles, nor did he ever wish it to be undertaken by their successors. It is absurd, therefore, to trouble us about the form of ordination, in which we differ neither from the rule of Christ, nor from the practice of the apostles, nor from the custom of the ancient Church, whereas that form of theirs, which they accuse us of neglecting, they are unable to defend by the Word of God, by sound reason, or by the pretext of antiquity.

On the subject of ecclesiastical rule, there are laws out of which we readily adopt those that are not snares for the conscience, or that contribute to the preservation of common order; but those which had either been tyrannically imposed to hold consciences in bondage, or contributed rather to superstition than to edification, we were forced to abrogate. Here our enemies first charge us with fastidiousness and undue haste, and second accuse us of seeking carnal indulgence, by shaking off the yoke of discipline in order that we may act the wanton as we please. But, as I have already observed, we are by no means averse to the reverent observance of whatever rules are fitted to ensure that all things be done decently and in order; nor, in regard to every single observance which we have abrogated, do we refuse to show cause why we were required to do so. Assuredly there is no difficulty in proving that the Church laboured grievously under a load of human traditions, and that it was necessary in her interest that this load should be lessened. There is a well-known complaint by Augustine, in which he deplores it as the calamity of his time that the Church, which God in his mercy wished to be free, was even then so overburdened, that the condition of the Jews was more tolerable (*Ep. secunda ad Januarium*). It is probable that since that period the number has increased almost tenfold. Even more has the rigorous exaction of them increased. What then if that holy man were now to rise and behold the countless multitude of laws under which miserable consciences groan oppressed? What if, on the other hand, he were to see the strictness with which the observance of them is enforced? Those who censure us will perhaps object that we might with Augustine have lamented over anything which displeased us, but that we ought not to have put our hand to the work of correction. This objection is easily refuted. For this pernicious error of supposing that human laws are necessarily observed had to be corrected. As I have said, we do not deny that laws enacted with a view to external policy ought to be carefully obeyed; but for ruling conscience, we hold that there is no legislator but God. To him alone then let this authority be reserved, which he claims for himself in many passages of Scripture. In this matter, first the honour of God was subverted, from which it is impious to derogate in any degree, and then also genuine liberty of conscience, which as Paul strenuously insists, must not be subjected to the will of men. As it was, therefore, our duty to deliver the consciences of the faithful from the undue bondage in which they were held, so we have taught that they are free and unfettered by human laws. This freedom, purchased by the blood of Christ, may not be prostituted. If any one thinks we are blamable in this, he must attribute the same blame to Christ and his apostles. I do not yet enumerate the other evils which compelled us to set our face against human traditions. I shall mention only two, and I am confident that, after I have mentioned them, all impartial readers will be satisfied. The one is that as some of these traditions demanded things which it was impossible to perform, their only effect was to lead men to hypocrisy, or plunge them into despair; and the other, that all of them practised what our Saviour rebuked in the Pharisees: they had made the commandments of God of none effect.

I will here adduce examples by which this will be made more clear. There are three things, in particular, for which they are offended with us: first, that we have given liberty to eat flesh on any day; second, that we have permitted marriage to priests; and third, that we have rejected the secret confession which was made in a priest's ear.

Let our opponents answer honestly. Is not the man who may have tasted flesh on Friday punished more severely than the man who may have spent the whole year in a constant course of licentiousness? Is it not deemed a more capital offence in a priest to marry than to be caught a hundred times in adultery? Do they not pardon the man who has scorned many of the divine precepts on easier terms than the man who may have neglected once a year to confess his sins into the ear of a priest? Is it not monstrous, I ask, that it should seem a slight and venial offence to violate the holy law of God, and that it should be judged an inexpiable crime to transgress the decrees of men? The case, I admit, is not without precedent. For, as I have already observed, the wickedness with which Christ charges the Pharisees is: "Thus have ye made the commandment of God of none effect through your tradition" (Matt. 15:6). Moreover, the arrogance of Antichrist of which Paul speaks is "that he as God sitteth in the temple of God, showing himself that he is God" (II Thess. 2:4). For where is the incomparable majesty of God, after mortal man has been exalted to such a height that his laws take precedence of God's eternal decrees? I omit that an apostle describes the prohibition of meats and of marriage as a doctrine of devils (I Tim. 4:1–3). That is surely bad enough; but the crowning impiety is to set man in a higher rank than God. If they deny the truth of my statement, I appeal to fact.

As to those two laws of celibacy and auricular confession, what are they but dire murderers of souls? As all the ministers of their churches vow perpetual chastity, it becomes unlawful for them, the vow being made, ever to take wives. What, then, if one has not received the gift of continence? "There must be no exception here," is the answer. But experience shows how much better it would have been never to have imposed this yoke upon priests, than to shut them up in a furnace of lust, to burn with a perpetual flame. Our adversaries recount the praises of virginity; they recount also the advantages of celibacy, in order to prove that priests have not been rashly interdicted from marrying. They even represent it as decent and honourable. But will they by all these things prove that it is lawful to fetter consciences which Christ not only left free and unfettered, but whose freedom he has vindicated by his own authority, and at the price of his own blood? Paul does not presume to do so (I Cor. 7:36). Whence then this new licence? Again, though virginity be extolled to the skies, what has this to do with the celibacy of priests, with whose impurity the whole world is tainted? If the chastity which they profess in word they also exhibited in deed, then perhaps I might allow them to say that it is rightly done. But when every man knows that the prohibition of marriage is only a licence to priests to commit gross sin, with what face, I ask, dare they make any mention of propriety? As to those whose infamy is not notorious, to avoid the necessity of discussing the matter with them at length, I leave them to the tribunal of God, that they may talk there of their chastity.

It will be said that this law is imposed on none but those who vow spontaneously. But what greater necessity can be imagined than that by which they are forced to vow? The condition announced to all is that none shall be admitted to the priesthood who has not previously bound himself by vows to perpetual celibacy, that he who has vowed must be forced, even against his will, to perform what he has once undertaken, and that no excuse to the contrary can be entertained. They maintain that a celibacy so exacted is voluntary. Rhetoricians are welcome to detail the disadvantages of marriage and the advantages of celibacy, in order to improve their style by declaiming on such topics in the schools. However much truth they may speak, it will hardly prove the propriety of leading miserable consciences into a deadly snare, in which they must perpetually writhe till they are strangled. And the ridiculous part is that in all this indecent infamy even hypocrisy finds a place. For, whatever their conduct may be, they deem themselves better than others, for the simple reason that they have no wives.

The case is the same with confession. For they enumerate the advantages which follow from it. We on the contrary are equally prepared to point out not a few dangers which are justly to be feared, and to refer to numerous most grievous evils which have actually flowed from it. These, I say, are the kind of arguments which both parties may employ. But the perpetual rule of Christ, which cannot be changed or deflected in this direction or in that, which cannot without impiety be controverted, is that conscience should not be brought into bondage. Besides, the law on which our opponents insist is one which can only torture souls and ultimately destroy them. For it requires every individual to confess all his sins once a year to his own priest; if this be not done, it leaves him no hope of obtaining pardon. Those who have made a serious attempt, that is in the true fear of God, have found it impossible thus to do even a hundredth part of this. Being unable to extricate themselves by any remedy, they were driven to despair. Those again, who desired to satisfy God in a more careless manner, found this confession a most suitable cloak for hypocrisy. For, thinking that they obtained an acquittal at the bar of God as soon as they had disgorged their sins into the ear of a priest, they were bold to sin more freely, since they were disburdened in such an expeditious way. Then, having in their minds a fixed persuasion that they fulfilled what the law enjoined, they thought that any kind of enumeration would comprehend all their sins, though in point of fact it did not include a thousandth part. See then on what ground our adversaries clamour that we have destroyed the discipline of the Church: simply because we have studied to succour miserable consciences lest they perish under the pressure of a most cruel tyranny, and have dragged hypocrites out of their hiding places into open day, that they might both examine themselves more closely and begin to have a better idea of the divine judgment which they formerly evaded.

But someone will say, that, however numerous the abuses and however deserving of correction, laws in other respects sacred and useful and as it were consecrated by antiquity ought not to have been thus abolished instantly and completely.

In regard to the eating of flesh, my simple answer is that the doctrine we hold accords with that of the ancient Church, in which we know there was freedom to eat flesh at all times, or to abstain from it.

The prohibition of the marriage of priests I admit to be ancient, as is also the vow of perpetual continence taken by nuns and monks. But if we concede that the declared will of God outweighs human custom, why, when perfectly aware that the will of God is with us and clearly supports our view, do they seek to quarrel with us about antiquity? The doctrine is clear: "Marriage is honourable in all" (Heb. 13:4). Paul expressly speaks of bishops as husbands (I Tim. 3:2; Titus 1:6). As a general rule, he enjoins marriage on all of a particular temperament, and declares the interdiction of marriage to be a "doctrine of devils" (I Tim. 4:3). What does it avail to set human custom in opposition to the clear declarations of the Holy Spirit, unless men are to be preferred to God? Further it is of importance to observe how unfair those judges are, who in this matter allege against us the practice of the ancient Church. Is there any antiquity of the Church, either earlier or of higher authority, than the days of the apostles? But our opponents will not deny that at that time permission to marry was granted to all ministers of the Church, and used by them. If the apostles thought it expedient that priests be restrained from marrying, why did they defraud the Church of so great a boon? Yet after them about two hundred and fifty years elapsed until at the Council of Nicaea, as

Sozomen relates, the question of enjoining celibacy on ministers was raised; but by the interference of Paphnutius, the whole affair was passed over. For it is related that after he, being himself a bachelor, had declared that a law of celibacy was not to be tolerated, the whole council readily assented to this opinion. But, superstition gradually increasing, the law, which was then repudiated, was at length enacted. Among those Canons, which, because of their antiquity as well as the uncertainty of their author, are called apostolical, there is one which does not permit any clerical persons, except singers and readers, to marry after they have been admitted to office. But by a previous Canon, priests and deacons are prohibited from putting away their wives under the pretext of religion. And in the fourth Canon of the Council of Gangra, anathema is pronounced against those who distinguish a married from an unmarried presbyter, so as to absent themselves when he officiated. Hence it appears that there was still in those times considerably more equity than a subsequent age manifested.

Here, however, it was not my intention to discuss this subject fully. I only thought it proper to indicate in passing that the primitive and purer Church is not in this matter so adverse to us as our enemies pretend. But grant that it is, why do they accuse us so fiercely, as if we were confusing things sacred and profane, or as if we could not easily retort against them that we agree far better with the ancient Church than they do? Marriage, which the ancients denied to priests, we allow. What do they say to the licentiousness which has everywhere obtained among them? They will deny that they approve it. But if they were desirous to obey the ancient Canons, it would be proper to punish it more severely. The punishment which the Council of Neo-Cæsarea inflicted on a presbyter who married was deposition; while one guilty of adultery or fornication, it punished far more severely, adding to deposition excommunication also. In the present day, the marriage of a priest is deemed a capital crime, while for his hundred acts of libertinism he is fined a small sum of money. Doubtless, if those who first passed the law of celibacy were now alive, instructed by present experience, they would be the first to abrogate it. However, as I have already said, it would be the height of injustice to condemn us on the authority of men, in a matter in which we are plainly acquitted by the voice of God.

With regard to confession, we have a briefer and readier defence. Our opponents cannot show that the necessity of confessing was imposed earlier than Innocent III. For twelve hundred years this tyranny, for which they contend with us so keenly, was unknown to the Christian world. But there is a decree of the Lateran Council. True; but of the same description as many others. Those who have any tolerable knowledge of history are aware of both the ignorance and the ferocity of those times. This indeed is in accordance with the common observation that the most ignorant governors are always the most imperious. But all pious souls will bear me witness, in what a maze those must be entangled who think themselves bound by that law. To this cruel torturing of consciences has been added the blasphemous presumption of making it essential to the remission of sin. For they pretend that none obtain pardon from God but those who are disposed to confess. What is this, I ask, but for men to prescribe by their own hand the mode in which a sinner is reconciled to God, and to withhold the pardon, which God offers simply, until a condition which they have added shall have been fulfilled? On the other hand, the people were possessed with this most pernicious superstition: that as soon as they had disburdened themselves of their sins, by pouring them into the ear of a priest, they were completely freed from guilt. This opinion many abused by a more unrestrained indulgence in sin, while even those who were more influenced by the fear of God paid greater regard to the priest than to Christ. The public and solemn acknowledgment (exomologesis, as Cyprian calls it), which penitents were in ancient days obliged to make when they were to be reconciled to the Church, no sane man does not commend and willingly adopt, provided it be not diverted to some other end than that for which it was instituted. In short, we have no controversy in this matter with the ancient Church; we only wish, as we ought, to loose a modern tyranny of recent date from the necks of believers. Besides, when any person, in order to obtain consolation and counsel, visits his minister in private, and familiarly confides to him the causes of his anxiety, we by no means deny it to be useful, provided it be done freely and not of constraint. Let every man, I say, be left at liberty to do in this matter what he feels to be expedient for himself; let no man's conscience be obliged by fixed laws.

I hope your Imperial Majesty, and you, Most Illustrious Princes, will be satisfied with this apology. It is certainly just.[5]

[5] See General Introduction for what is here omitted.

PART III
CONTROVERSIAL

Reply to Sadolet

INTRODUCTION

MUCH OF THE BACKGROUND AGAINST WHICH THIS treatise must be regarded can be constructed from the internal evidence of the Reply itself. *C.R.* has the following introduction about it. When Calvin and his friends were ejected from Geneva, the state of the republic and of the Church was such that the advocates of the papal Church had some justification for hoping that the citizens, wearied by disturbance, might restore the old form of the faith in their midst. The time was propitious; the flock was deprived of its leaders; the Romanists thought they might easily win it back. At a gathering held at Lyons, they commissioned one of their number, Cardinal Jacob Sadolet, to solicit the return of the Genevans to communion with the Roman see. Sadolet was then Bishop of Carpentras, a man famous for eloquence and literary accomplishments and not less honoured for his sanctity of life. He himself desired some reformation of the Church, and was attracted rather by the Augustinian than by the Roman theology. But schism and the toleration of novelties seemed to him to incur greater damage and danger for the Church than the vices and faults which they with greater hostility opposed. Beza passes severe judgment on this man, when he says that he used his gifts and talents rather for the suppression of the light of truth, and supposes that his admission to the college of cardinals was based on no other reason than his ability to give a false colour to religion. Despite his weak arguments from the perpetual unity of the Church and his demand that the antiquity of the Catholic Church be venerated, *C.R.* judges him to be sincere, and to have been persuaded that everything would best serve the greater glory of Christ if the business of reforming the Church were left to the college of bishops. However this may be, in the month of April 1539, Sadolet composed a letter to the Senate and people of Geneva, in which courteously and paternally he recalled them to the bosom and the ancient sanctities of the Roman Church. This letter, written as it was in Latin, either failed to come to the notice of the people itself, or at least to the majority of the more moderate among them; but it was deemed worthy by the more learned of a considered and spirited reply. Calvin was persuaded by his friends to undertake this office and for its discharge composed, within a few days, a notable treatise which ranks conspicuously among his works, both for its elegance of style and lucidity and for the vigour and veracity of its argument. In a letter to Farel, Calvin acknowledges receipt of Sadolet's epistle, mentions the persuasions of his friends that he should undertake to reply to it, and states that he is wholly occupied with its composition. The composition is dated the first of September. (See *C.R.* V, xliv, f.)

Reply by John Calvin to the letter by Cardinal Sadolet to the Senate and People of Geneva

John Calvin to James Sadolet, Cardinal—Greetings.

Since in the great abundance of learned men whom our age has produced, your excellent learning and distinguished eloquence has deservedly procured you a place among the few whom all who would be thought students of liberal arts look up to and revere, it is indeed with reluctance that I name you before the learned world, and address to you the following expostulation. Nor indeed would I have done it if I had not been dragged into this arena by a strong necessity. For I am not unaware how reprehensible it would be to show any eagerness in attacking a man who has deserved so well of literature, nor how odious I should become to all the learned were they to see me roused merely by passion and not impelled by any just cause, turning my pen against one whom, for his admirable endowments, they regard not without good reason as worthy of love and honour. I trust, however, that after explaining the nature of my undertaking, I shall not only be exempted from all blame, but also that there will not be an individual but will admit that the cause which I have undertaken I could by no means have abandoned without basely deserting my duty.

You lately addressed a Letter to the Senate and People of Geneva, in which you tested their mind whether they would submit to have again imposed upon them the yoke of the Roman pontiff which they had once thrown off. In this letter, as it was not expedient to wound the feelings of those whose favour you required to gain your cause, you acted the part of a good pleader. For you tried to soothe them with much flattery, in order that you might gain them over to your views. Anything of abuse and bitterness you directed against those whose exertions had produced the revolt from tyranny. Here, if you please, you bear down full sail upon those who, under pretence of the gospel, have by wicked arts incited the city to what you deplore as the subversion of religion and of the Church. But I, Sadolet, profess to be one of those whom with so much enmity you assail and stigmatize. For though religion was already established and the form of the Church rectified before I was invited to Geneva, yet I not only approved by my assent, but studied as much as in me lay to preserve and confirm what had been done by Farel and Viret; and so I cannot separate my case from theirs. Still, if you had attacked me personally, I could easily have forgiven the attack in consideration of your learning and in honour of letters. But when I see that my ministry, which I feel assured is supported and sanctioned by a call from God, is taken and wounded in the flank, it would be perfidy, not patience, were I here to be silent and disregard what you say.

In that Church I have held the office first of doctor, and then of pastor. I maintain with right that in undertaking these offices I had a legitimate vocation. How faithfully and religiously I have performed them, there is no occasion to show at length now. Perspicuity, erudition, prudence, ability, not even industry will I now claim for myself; but that I certainly laboured with the sincerity which is requisite in the work of the Lord, I can in conscience appeal to Christ, my Judge, and all his angels, while all good men bear clear testimony in my favour. Who would not condemn such silence as treachery, were I without a word to allow you to revile and defame this ministry, when it appears to be of God (as certainly it will appear, after the case has been heard)? Everyone, therefore, now sees that the strongest obligations of duty, quite incapable of evasion, constrain me to meet your accusations, if I would not with manifest perfidy desert and betray a cause with which the Lord has entrusted me.

For though I am for the present relieved of the charge of the Church of Geneva, this circumstance ought not to prevent me from embracing it with paternal affection; for God, when he charged me with it, bound me to be faithful to it for ever. So, now, when I see the worst snares laid for that Church, whose safety it has pleased the Lord to make my highest care, and grievous peril impending if this be not obviated, who will advise me to await the issue silent and unconcerned? How heartless, I ask, would it be to gape idly and connive at the destruction of something whose life you are bound vigilantly to guard and preserve? But more on this point were superfluous, since you yourself relieve me of all difficulty. For if neighbourhood, and that not very close, has weighed so much with you, that while wishing to profess your love towards the Genevans, you do not hesitate so bitterly to assail me and my reputation, it will undoubtedly by the law of humanity be allowed me to consult the public good of a city entrusted to me by a far stronger obligation than that of neighbourhood, and to oppose your counsels and endeavours which I cannot doubt tend to its destruction. Besides, without paying the least regard to the Genevan Church (though assuredly I cannot throw away this charge any more than that of my own soul), supposing I were not actuated by any zeal for it, still, when my ministry (which, knowing it to be from Christ, I am bound if need be to maintain with my blood) is falsely traduced and reviled, how can it be lawful for me to tolerate it as if I pretended not to notice?

Therefore it is easy not only for impartial readers to judge, but also for yourself Sadolet to consider, how numerous and valid the reasons are which have compelled me to engage in this contest, if indeed the name of contest should be given to a simple and dispassionate defence of my innocence against your calumnious accusations. I say *my* innocence, although I cannot plead for myself without at the same time including my colleagues, who were so involved in all my measures in that administration that whatever has been said against them I willingly take to myself. What the feelings are which I have had toward yourself in undertaking this cause, I will study to testify and prove by my conduct of it. For I will so act that all may perceive that I have not only much the advantage of you in the goodness and justice of the cause, in conscious rectitude, heartfelt sincerity, and candour of speech, but have also been considerably more successful in maintaining gentleness and moderation. There will doubtless be some things which will sting, or even strike deeply home. But it will be my endeavour, first, not to allow any harsher expression to escape me than either the injustice of the accusations with which you have previously assailed me, or the necessity of the case may extort; and, secondly, not to allow any degree of harshness which may amount to intemperance or passion, or which may by its appearance of petulance give offence to ingenuous minds.

To begin with, if you had to do with any other person, he would undoubtedly make a start with the very argument which

I have determined altogether to omit. For without much ado
he would discuss your design in writing, until he made it plain
that your object was anything but what you profess it to be.
For were it not for the great credit you formerly acquired for
candour, it is somewhat suspicious that a stranger, who never
before had any intercourse with the Genevans, should now
suddenly profess for them so great an affection, though no previous sign of it existed—and you a man steeped almost from
boyhood in such Romish arts as are now learned in the Court
of Rome, that manufactory of all craft and trickery, educated
too in the very bosom of Clement, and now moreover elected
a cardinal, having many things about you which with most men
would in this matter render you suspect. Then as to those
insinuations by which you have supposed you might win your
way into the minds of simple men, any one not utterly stupid
might easily refute them. But things of this nature, though many
will perhaps be disposed to believe them, I am unwilling to
ascribe to you, because they seem to me unsuitable to the
character of one who has been polished by all kinds of liberal
learning. I shall, therefore, in entering into discussion with you,
give you credit for having written to the Genevans with the
purest intentions, as becomes one of your learning, prudence
and gravity, and for having in good faith advised them to the
course which you believed conducive to their interest and safety.
But whatever may have been your intention (I am unwilling
in this matter to charge you with ill-will), when, with the
bitterest and most insulting expressions which you can employ,
you distort and try utterly to destroy what the Lord delivered
by our hands, I am compelled, whether I will or not, to with-
stand you openly. For pastors edify the Church only when,
besides placidly leading as with the hand docile souls to Christ,
they are also armed to repel the machinations of those who
strive to impede the work of God.

Although your Letter has many digressions, its whole purport
substantially is to restore the Genevans to the power of the
Roman pontiff, or to what you call the faith and obedience of
the Church. But as from the nature of the case their feelings
must be mollified, your preface is a long oration concerning
the incomparable value of eternal life. You afterwards come
nearer to the point, when you show that there is nothing more
pestilential to souls than a perverse worship of God; and again,
that the best rule for the due worship of God is that which is
prescribed by the Church; and that therefore there is no salva-

tion for those who have violated the unity of the Church unless they repent. But you next contend that separation from your fellowship is open revolt from the Church, and then that the gospel which the Genevans received from us is nothing but a great farrago of impious dogmas. From this you infer what kind of divine judgment awaits them unless they attend to your admonitions.

But as it was of the greatest importance to your cause to throw complete discredit on our words, you labour to the utmost to fill them with sinister suspicions of the zeal which they saw us manifesting for their salvation. Accordingly you allege that we had no other end in view than to gratify our avarice and ambition. Since, then, your device has been to cast some stain upon us, in order that the minds of your readers be preoccupied with hatred and might give us no credit, I shall briefly reply to that objection before proceeding to other matters.

I am unwilling to speak of myself. But since you do not permit me to be altogether silent, I will say what I can that is consistent with modesty. Had I wished to consult my own interest, I would never have left your party. I will not indeed boast that there the road to preferment had been easy to me. I never desired it, and I could never bring myself to go hunting for it; although I certainly know not a few of my own age who have crept up to some eminence, among them some whom I might have equalled, and others outstripped. I shall be content to say this only: it would not have been difficult for me to reach the summit of my wishes, namely the enjoyment of literary ease, with some kind of independent and honourable status. Therefore I have no fear that any one not possessed of shameless audacity will make the objection that outside the kingdom of the pope I sought for any personal advantage which was not there ready to my hand.

Who dares make this objection to Farel? Had it been necessary for him to live by his own industry, he had already such attainments in literature as would not have allowed him to suffer want, and his distinguished family connections obviated the need of external aid. As to those of us to whom you expressly pointed, it seemed proper for us to reply in our own name. But since you seem to throw out indirect insinuations against all who in the present day are united with us in sustaining the same cause, I would have you understand that not one can be mentioned for whom I cannot give you better answer than for Farel and myself. Some of our Reformers are known to you by fame. As to them, I appeal to your own conscience. Do you think it was hunger which drove them away from you, and made them in despair flee to this change as a means of making a fresh start? [1] But not to go over a long catalogue, I will say this, that of those who first engaged in this cause, there was none who would not have had too good a place and fortune with you to require on this ground to contrive some new plan of life.

But come and consider with me for a little what the honours and powers are which we have gained. All our hearers will bear us witness that we did not covet or aspire to any other riches or dignities than those which fell to our lot. Since in all our words and deeds they not only perceived no trace of the ambition with which you charge us, but on the contrary saw clear evidence of our abhorring it with our whole heart, you cannot hope that by one little word their minds are to be so fascinated as to credit a futile slander rather than the many certain proofs with which we furnished them. And, to appeal to facts rather than words, have not we restored to the magistrate the power of the sword and other parts of civil jurisdiction, which bishops and priests, under the semblance of immunity, had wrested from the magistrate and claimed for themselves? Have we not detested and struggled to abolish all their usurped instruments of tyranny and ambition? If there was any hope of elevation, why did we not craftily dissemble, so that those powers might have passed to us along with the office of governing the Church? And why did we make such exertion to overturn the whole of that dominion, or rather torture, which they exercised upon souls, without any sanction from the Word of God? How did we not consider that it was just so much lost to ourselves? As to ecclesiastical revenues, they are still in a great measure swallowed up by these whirlpools. But if there was a hope that they may one day be deprived of them, as eventually they certainly must, why did we not devise a way by which they might come to us? But when with clear voice we denounced as thief any bishop who, out of ecclesiastical revenues, appropriated more to his own use than was necessary for a frugal and sober subsistence; when we protested that the Church was exposed to a deadly poison, so long as pastors were loaded with such affluence that they might ultimately sink under it; when we declared it inexpedient that these revenues should fall into their possession;

1 Original has *novas tabulas*—the new account books which superseded old ones and thus cancelled earlier obligations.

finally, when we counselled that as much should be distributed to ministers as might suffice for a frugal life befitting their order without luxurious superabundance, and that the rest should be dispensed according to the practice of the ancient Church; when we showed that men of weight ought to be elected to manage these revenues, under an obligation to account annually to the Church and the magistracy, was this to capture any of these for ourselves, or was it not rather voluntarily to shake ourselves free of them? All these things, indeed, demonstrate not what we are, but what we wished to be. But if these things are so plainly and generally known that not one iota can be denied, with what face can you proceed to reproach us with aspiring to extraordinary wealth and power, especially in the presence of men to whom none of those things are unknown? We are not surprised at the monstrous lies which persons of your order spread against us among their own followers. For no one is present who can either reprimand or venture to refute them. But where men have been eye-witnesses of all the things which we have above mentioned, to try to persuade them of the contrary argues very little discretion and gravely derogates from Sadolet's reputation for learning, prudence, and dignity. But if you think that our intention must be judged by the result, it will be found that we aimed only at promoting the kingdom of Christ by our poverty and insignificance. So far are we from having abused his sacred name for purposes of avarice.

I pass in silence over many other invectives which, open mouthed (as they say), you thunder out against us. You call us cunning men, enemies of Christian unity and peace, changers of things ancient and well established, seditious, alike pestilential to souls and both publicly and privately pernicious to society at large. Had you wished to escape rebuke, you either ought not, to excite prejudice, to have attributed to us a magniloquent tongue, or you ought to have tempered your own magniloquence considerably. I am unwilling, however, to dwell on each of these points. I would only have you consider how unbecoming, not to say ungenerous, it is thus to vex the innocent in many words which by one word can be instantly refuted, although to inflict injury on man is a small matter, compared with the indignity of that contempt which, when you come to the point, you offer to Christ and his Word.

When the Genevans, instructed by our preaching, escaped from the gulf of error in which they were immersed and betook themselves to a purer teaching of the gospel, you call it defection from the truth of God; when they threw off the tyranny of the Roman pontiff, in order that they might establish among themselves a better form of Church, you call it desertion from the Church. Come, then, and let us discuss both points in turn.

As to your preface, which, in proclaiming the excellence of eternal blessedness, occupies about a third of your Letter, it cannot be necessary for me to dwell long in reply. For although commendation of the future and eternal life is a theme worthy to be sounded in our ears by day and by night, kept constantly in remembrance, and made the subject of ceaseless meditation, yet I know not for what reason you have so protracted your discourse upon it here, unless it were to commend yourself by some indication of religious feeling. But whether, in order to remove all doubt about yourself, you wished to testify that a life of glory seriously occupies your thoughts, or whether you supposed that those to whom you wrote required to be excited and spurred on by a long commendation of it (for I am unwilling to probe what your intention may have been), it is not very sound theology to confine a man's thoughts so much to himself, and not to set before him as the prime motive of his existence zeal to show forth the glory of God. For we are born first of all for God, and not for ourselves. As all things flowed from him and subsist in him, as Paul says (Rom. 11:36), they ought to be related to him. I acknowledge indeed that the Lord, to recommend the glory of his name to men the better, has tempered zeal for its advance and extension by uniting it indissolubly with our salvation. But since he has taught that this zeal ought to exceed all thought and care for our own good and advantage, and since natural equity also teaches that God does not receive what is his own unless he be preferred to all things, it certainly is the duty of a Christian man to ascend higher than merely to seek and secure the salvation of his own soul. I therefore believe that there is no man imbued with true piety, who will not regard as in poor taste that long and detailed exhortation to a zeal for heavenly life, which occupies a man entirely concerned with himself, and does not, even by one expression, arouse him to sanctify the name of God. But I readily agree with you that after this sanctification we ought to set ourselves no other object in life than to hasten towards that high calling; for God has set it before us as the constant aim of all our actions, words and thoughts. Indeed there is nothing in which man excels the lower animals, unless it be his spiritual communion with God in the hope of a blessed eternity. In general, all we aim at in our discourses is to arouse men to meditate upon it and aspire to it.

I have also no difficulty in conceding to you that there is nothing more perilous to our salvation than a distorted and perverse worship of God. The primary rudiments by which we are wont to train to piety those whom we wish to win as disciples to Christ, are these: not to frame any new worship of God for themselves at random and their own pleasure, but to know that the only legitimate worship is that which he himself approved from the beginning. For we maintain, what the sacred oracle declared, that obedience is more excellent than any sacrifice (I Sam. 15:22). In short, we train them by every means to keep within the one rule of worship which they have received from his mouth, and bid farewell to all fictitious worship.

Therefore, Sadolet, when you uttered this voluntary confession, you laid the foundation of my defence. For if you admit it to be a fearful destruction to the soul, when by false opinions divine truth is turned into a lie, it now only remains for us to enquire which of the two parties retains that worship of God which is alone legitimate. In order that you may claim it for your side, you assume that the most certain rule of worship is that which is prescribed by the Church, although, as if we here opposed you, you bring the matter to consideration in the manner usually observed in doubtful matters. But, Sadolet, as I see you toiling in vain, I will relieve you from all trouble at this point. You are mistaken in supposing that we desire to lead away the people from the method of worshipping God which the Catholic Church always observed. Either you are deluded about the term Church, or else knowingly and willingly you practise deception. I will immediately show the latter to be the case, though it may also be that you are somewhat in error. First, in defining the term, you omit what would have helped you in no small degree to its right understanding. When you describe it as that which in all past as well as present time, in all regions of the earth, being united and of one mind in Christ, has been always and everywhere directed by the one Spirit of Christ, what becomes of the Word of the Lord, that clearest of all marks, which the Lord himself in designating the Church so often commends to us? For seeing how dangerous it would be to boast of the Spirit without the Word, he declared that the Church is indeed governed by the Holy Spirit; but in order that this government might not be vague and unstable, he bound it to the Word. For this reason Christ exclaims that those who are of God hear the Word of God, that his sheep are those which recognize his voice as that of their Shepherd and any other voice as that of a stranger (John 10:27). For this reason the Spirit by the mouth of Paul declares (Eph. 2:20) that the Church is built upon the foundation of the apostles and prophets; also, that the Church is made holy to the Lord, by the washing of water in the word of life (Eph. 5:26). The same thing is declared still more clearly by the mouth of Peter, when he teaches that people are regenerated to God by that incorruptible seed (I Peter 1:23). In short, why is the preaching of the gospel so often styled the kingdom of God, but because it is the sceptre by which the heavenly King rules his people?

Nor will you find this in the apostolic writings only; whenever the prophets foretell the renewal of the Church or its extension over the whole globe, they always assign the first place to the Word. For they say that from Jerusalem will issue forth living waters, which being divided into four rivers will inundate the whole earth (Zech. 14:8). What these living waters are, they themselves explain when they say: the law will come forth from Zion, and the Word of the Lord from Jerusalem (Isa. 2:3). Chrysostom then rightly admonishes us to reject all who under the pretence of the Spirit lead us away from the simple doctrine of the gospel; for the Spirit was promised, not to reveal a new doctrine, but to impress the truth of the gospel on our minds. We in fact experience in the present day how necessary the admonition was. We are assailed by two sects, which seem to differ most widely from each other. For what similitude is there in appearance between the pope and the Anabaptists? And yet, that you may see that Satan never transforms himself so cunningly as not in some measure to betray himself, the principal weapon with which they both assail us is the same. For when they boast extravagantly of the Spirit, they inevitably tend to sink and bury the Word of God, and to make room for their own falsehoods. And you, Sadolet, by stumbling on the very threshold, have paid the penalty of the affront you offered the Holy Spirit, when you separated him from the Word. For as if those who seek the way of God stood where two ways meet, destitute of any certain sign, you are forced to present them as hesitating whether it be more expedient to follow the authority of the Church, or to listen to those whom you call the inventors of new dogmas. If you had known or been unwilling to disguise the fact that the Spirit goes before the Church to enlighten her in understanding the Word, while the Word itself is like the Lydian stone by which she tests all doctrines, would you have taken refuge in that most perplexing and thorny question? Learn, then, by your own experience that it is no less unreasonable to boast of the Spirit without the Word, than it would be absurd to bring forward the Word itself without the Spirit. Now if you can bear to receive a truer definition of the Church than your own, say in future that it is the society of all the saints which, spread over the whole world and existing in all ages, yet bound together by the doctrine and the one Spirit of Christ, cultivates and observes unity of faith and brotherly concord. With this Church we deny that we have any disagreement. Rather as we revere her as our mother, so we desire to remain in her bosom.

But here you bring a charge against me. For you teach that all that has been approved for fifteen hundred years or more by the uniform consent of the faithful, is by our rashness torn up and destroyed. Here I will not require you to deal truly and candidly by us (though this should be spontaneously offered by a philosopher, not to say a Christian). I will only ask you not to stoop to a mean indulgence in calumny, which, even though we be silent, must be extremely injurious to your reputation with serious and honest men. You know, Sadolet, and if you venture to deny it, I shall make it plain to all, that you knew but cunningly and craftily disguised the fact, not only that our agreement with antiquity is far closer than yours, but that all we have attempted has been to renew the ancient form of the Church which, at first distorted and stained by illiterate men of indifferent character, was afterwards criminally mangled and almost destroyed by the Roman pontiff and his faction.

I shall not press you so closely as to call you back to that form which the apostles instituted, though in it we have the only model of a true Church, and whosoever deviates from it in the smallest degree is in error. But to indulge you so far, I ask you to place before your eyes the ancient form of the Church as their writings prove it to have been in the ages of Chrysostom and Basil among the Greeks, and of Cyprian, Ambrose and Augustine among the Latins; and after so doing, to contemplate the ruins of that Church which now survive among yourselves. Assuredly the difference will appear as great as that which the prophets describe between the famous Church which flourished under David and Solomon, and that which under Zedekiah and Jehoiakim had lapsed into every kind of superstition and utterly vitiated the purity of divine worship. Will you here declare one an enemy of antiquity who, zealous for ancient piety and holiness and dissatisfied with the corrupt state of matters existing in a dissolute and depraved Church, attempts to ameliorate its condition and restore it to pristine splendour?

There are three things on which the safety of the Church is founded and supported: doctrine, discipline, and the sacraments; and to these a fourth is added: ceremonies, by which to exercise the people in offices of piety. Now in order that we may spare the honour of your Church as much as possible, by which of these things would you have us judge her? The truth of prophetic and evangelical doctrine, on which the Church ought to be founded, has not only in a great measure perished in your Church, but is violently driven out by fire and sword. Will you force on me in place of the Church something which furiously persecutes everything sanctioned by our religion, both as transmitted by the oracles of God, embodied in the writings of holy Fathers, and approved by ancient Councils? Where, I ask you, exist among you any vestiges of that true and holy discipline which the ancient bishops exercised in the Church? Have you not scorned all their institutions? Have you not trampled all the canons under foot? Your nefarious profanation of the sacraments I cannot think of without the greatest horror.

You have indeed more than enough of ceremonies, but for the most part so childish in significance and vitiated by innumerable forms of superstition, as to be utterly unavailing for the preservation of the Church. None of these things, you must be aware, is exaggerated by me in a captious spirit. They all appear so openly that they may be pointed out with the finger wherever there are eyes to observe them.

Now, if you please, test us in the same way. You will assuredly fall far short of making good the charges which you have brought against us. In the sacraments, all we have attempted is to restore the native purity from which they had degenerated, and so enable them to resume their dignity. Ceremonies we have in great measure abolished; but we were compelled to do so, partly because by their multitude they had degenerated into a kind of Judaism, partly because they had filled the minds of the people with superstition and could not possibly remain without greatly obstructing the piety they should have promoted. Still we have retained those which seemed sufficient for the circumstances of the times. That our discipline is not such as the ancient Church professed we do not deny. But with what fairness is it that we are accused of subverting discipline by those who themselves quite abolished it, and have hitherto opposed us in our attempts to restore it to its rights?

As to our doctrine, we do not hesitate to appeal to the ancient Church. And since, for the sake of example, you have touched on certain points at which you thought you had some ground for accusing us, I shall briefly show how unfairly and falsely you allege that these are things which have been devised by us against the opinion of the Church.

Before descending to particulars, however, I would have you warned again and again to consider with what reason you allege against our people as a fault, that they have studied to explain the Scriptures. For you are aware that by this study they have thrown such light on the Word of God, that in this respect even envy herself may be ashamed to defraud them of all praise. You are just as little candid when you aver that we have seduced the people by thorny and subtle questions, and so enticed them by that philosophy of which Paul bids Christians beware (Col. 2:8). What? Do you remember what kind of time it was when the Reformers appeared, and what kind of doctrine candidates for the ministry learned in the schools? You yourself know that it was mere sophistry, and so twisted, involved, tortuous and puzzling, that scholastic theology might well be described as a species of secret magic. The denser the darkness in which any one shrouded a subject, and the more he puzzled himself and others with nagging riddles, the greater his fame for acumen and learning. And when those who had been formed in that workshop wished to carry the fruit of their learning to the people with what skill, I ask, did they edify the Church?

Not to go over every point, what sermons in Europe then exhibited that simplicity with which Paul wishes a Christian people to be always occupied? Indeed what one sermon was there from which old wives might not carry off more fantasies than they could devise at their own fireside in a month? For, as sermons were then usually divided, the first half was devoted to those misty questions of the schools which might astonish the rude populace, while the second contained smooth stories, or not unamusing speculations, by which the people might be excited to cheerfulness. Only a few expressions were thrown in from the Word of God, that by their majesty they might procure credit for these frivolities. But as soon as the Reformers raised the standard, all these absurdities in a moment disappeared from amongst us. Your preachers, again, partly profited by our books, and partly compelled by shame and the complaints of everybody, conformed to our example, though with gaping mouth they still breathe out the old foolishness. Hence any one who compares our method of procedure with the old method, or with that which is still in repute among you, will perceive that you have done us no small injustice. But had you continued your quotation from Paul a little farther, any schoolboy would easily have perceived that the charge which you bring against us is undoubtedly applicable to yourselves. For Paul there interprets "vain philosophy" (Col. 2:8) to mean that which preys upon pious souls by means of the institutions of men and the elements of this world, by which you have ruined the Church.

Even you yourself afterwards acquit us by your own testimony; for among those of our doctrines which you have thought proper to assail, you do not adduce one, whose knowledge is not a primary necessity for the edification of the Church.

In the first place, you touch upon justification by faith, the first and keenest subject of controversy between us. Is this a knotty and useless question? Wherever the knowledge of it is taken away, the glory of Christ is extinguished, religion abolished, the Church destroyed, and the hope of salvation utterly overthrown. This doctrine, then, though of the greatest moment, we maintain you have impiously effaced from the memory of men. Our books are filled with convincing proofs of this fact; and the gross ignorance of this doctrine which even still continues in all your churches declares that our complaint is by no means ill-founded. But you very maliciously stir up prejudice against us, alleging that, by attributing everything to faith, we leave no room for works.

I will not now enter upon a full discussion which would require a large volume; but if you would look into the Catechism which I myself drew up for the Genevans when I held the office of Pastor among them, three words would reduce you to silence. Here, however, I will briefly explain to you how we speak on this subject.

First, we bid a man begin by examining himself, and this not in a superficial and perfunctory manner, but to present his conscience before the tribunal of God and, when sufficiently convinced of his iniquity, to reflect on the strictness of the sentence pronounced upon all sinners. Thus confounded and stricken with misery, he is prostrated and humbled before God; and, throwing away all self-confidence, he groans as though given up to final perdition. Then we show that the only haven of safety is in the mercy of God as manifested in Christ, in whom every part of our salvation is completed. As all mankind are lost sinners in the sight of God, we hold that Christ is their only righteousness, since by his obedience he has done away our transgressions, by his sacrifice appeased the divine anger, by his blood washed away our stains, by his cross borne our curse, and by his death made satisfaction for us. We maintain that in this way man is reconciled in Christ to God the Father, by no merit of his own, by no worthiness of works, but by gratuitous mercy. When we embrace Christ by faith and come, as it were, into communion with him, we term this in the manner of Scripture the righteousness of faith.

What have you here, Sadolet, to bite or grumble at? Is it that we leave no room for works? Assuredly we do deny that for justifying a man they are worth a single straw. For Scripture everywhere cries aloud that all are lost; and every man's own conscience bitterly accuses him. The same Scripture teaches that no hope is left but in the sheer goodness of God, by which sin is pardoned and righteousness imputed to us. It declares both to be gratuitous, and finally concludes that a man is justified without works (Rom. 4:6). But what notion, you ask, does the very term righteousness suggest to us, if respect is not paid to good works? I answer: if you would attend to the true meaning of the term *justifying* in Scripture, you would have no difficulty. For it does not refer to a man's own righteousness, but to the mercy of God, which, contrary to the sinner's deserts, accepts a righteousness for him, and this by not imputing his unrighteousness. Our righteousness, I say, is that which is described by Paul (II Cor. 5:19), that God hath reconciled us to himself in Jesus Christ. The means is afterwards added: by not imputing sin. He demonstrates that it is by faith only we become partakers of this blessing, when he says that the ministry of reconciliation is contained in the gospel. But faith, you say, is a general term, and has a wider meaning. I answer that Paul, whenever he attributes to it the power of justifying, at the same time restricts it to a gratuitous promise of divine favour, and keeps it far removed from all reference to works. Hence his familiar inference: if by faith, then not by works; on the other hand: if by works, then not by faith.

But, it seems, injury is done to Christ if, under the pretence of his grace, good works are repudiated; for he came to render a people acceptable to God, zealous of good works. To the same effect are many similar passages which prove that Christ came in order that we, doing good works, might through him be accepted by God. This calumny which our opponents have perpetually in their mouths, that we take away the desire of well-doing from the Christian life by recommending gratuitous righteousness, is too frivolous to give us much concern. We deny that good works have any share in justification, but we claim full authority for them in the lives of the righteous. For if he who has obtained justification possesses Christ, and at the same time Christ never is where his Spirit is not, it is obvious that gratuitous righteousness is necessarily connected with regeneration. Therefore, if you would duly understand how inseparable faith and works are, look to Christ, who, as the apostle teaches (I Cor. 1:30), has been given to us for justification and for sanctification. Wherever, therefore, that righteousness of faith which we maintain to be gratuitous is, there too Christ is; and where Christ is, there too is the Spirit of holiness who regenerates the soul to newness of life. On the contrary, where zeal for integrity and holiness is not in force, there neither the Spirit of Christ nor Christ himself are present. Wherever Christ is not, there is no righteousness, and indeed no faith; for faith cannot lay hold of Christ for righteousness without the Spirit of sanctification.

Since, therefore, according to us Christ regenerates to a blessed life those whom he justifies and, rescuing them from the dominion of sin, hands them over to the dominion of righteousness, transforms them into the image of God, and so trains them by his Spirit into obedience to his will, there is no ground to complain that by our doctrine lust is given free rein. The passages which you adduce have the same meaning. But if you must pervert them to assail gratuitous justification, observe how unskilfully you argue. Paul elsewhere says (Eph. 1:4) that we were chosen in Christ, before the creation of the world, to be holy and unblamable in the sight of God through love. Who will venture thence to infer either that election is not gratuitous, or that our love is its cause? Much rather as the end of gratuitous election is that we may lead pure and unpolluted lives before God, so also is that of gratuitous justification. For the saying of Paul is true (I Thess. 4:7): we have not been called to impurity, but to holiness. This, meanwhile, we constantly maintain, that man is not only justified freely once for all without any merit of works, but that on this gratuitous justification his salvation perpetually depends. Nor is it possible that any work of man can be accepted by God unless it be gratuitously approved. Wherefore I was greatly astonished when I read

your assertion that love is the first and chief cause of salvation.
O, Sadolet, who could ever have expected such a saying from
you? Undoubtedly the blind themselves in their darkness feel the
mercy of God too certainly to arrogate to their love the first
step in their salvation; but those who have only one spark of
divine light feel that their salvation consists in nothing else than
in being adopted by God. For eternal salvation is the inheritance
of the heavenly Father, and has been prepared solely for his
children. Moreover who can assign any other cause of our
adoption than that which is uniformly announced in Scripture,
that we did not first love him, but were spontaneously received
by him into favour and affection?

Your ignorance of this doctrine leads you on to the error of
teaching that sins are expiated by penances and satisfactions.
Where, then, will be that one expiatory victim from which, if
we depart, there remains, as Scripture testifies, no more sacrifice
for sin? Search all the divine oracles we possess; if the blood of
Christ alone is everywhere set forth as purchasing satisfaction,
reconciliation, and cleansing, how dare you presume to transfer
so great an honour to your works? Nor have you any ground
for ascribing this blasphemy to the Church of God. The ancient
Church, I admit, had its satisfactions—not those, however, by
which sinners might atone to God and redeem themselves from
guilt, but by which they might prove that the repentance they
professed was not feigned and might efface the remembrance
of the offence which their sin occasioned. For satisfactions were
not regularly prescribed to all and sundry, but to those only who
had fallen into some grave wickedness.

In the case of the Eucharist, you blame us for attempting to
confine the Lord of the universe and his divine and spiritual
power (which is perfectly free and infinite) within the corners
of a corporeal nature with its circumscribed limits. What end
will there be to calumny? We have always distinctly testified
that not only the divine power of Christ, but his essence also,
is diffused over all and defined by no limits; and yet you do not
hesitate to reproach us with confining it within the corners of
corporeal nature! How so? Because we are unwilling with you
to fasten his body to earthly elements. But if you had any regard
for sincerity, you are assuredly not ignorant how great a difference there is between the two things: removing the local
presence of Christ's body from bread, and circumscribing his
spiritual power within bodily limits. Nor ought you to charge
our doctrine with novelty, since it was always held by the Church

as a confessed tenet. But as this subject alone would extend to
a volume, in order that both of us be spared such toil, it will be
better that you read Augustine's *Epistle to Dardanus*, where you
will find how one and the same Christ more than fills heaven
and earth with the fulness of his divinity, and yet is not everywhere diffused in respect of his humanity.

We emphatically proclaim the communion of flesh and blood
which is exhibited to believers in the Supper; and we distinctly
show that this flesh is truly meat and this blood truly drink—
that the soul, not contented with an imaginary conception,
enjoys them in very truth. That presence of Christ, by which
we are ingrafted in him, we by no means exclude from the
Supper; nor do we obscure it, though we hold that there must
be no local limitation, that the glorious body of Christ must not
be degraded to earthly elements, and that there must be no
fiction of transubstantiating the bread into Christ and then of
worshipping it as Christ. We explain the dignity and end of
this solemn rite in the most exalted terms we can employ, and
then declare how great are the advantages we derive from it.
Almost all these things are neglected by you. For, overlooking
the divine beneficence which is here bestowed upon us, overlooking the legitimate use of so great a benefit (themes on
which it is right especially to dwell), you count it enough that
the people gaze stupidly at the visible sign, without any understanding of the spiritual mystery. In condemning your gross
dogma of transubstantiation, and declaring that stupid adoration which detains the minds of men among the elements and
prevents them rising to Christ to be perverse and impious, we
have not acted without the concurrence of the ancient Church,
under whose shadow you try in vain to hide the very pernicious
superstitions which you here handle.

In auricular confession we have disapproved of the law of
Innocent, which enjoins every man once a year to review his
sins before his priest. It would be tedious to enumerate all the
reasons which induced us to abrogate it. But that the thing was
scandalous is apparent if only from this, that pious consciences,
which formerly seethed with perpetual anxiety, have been freed
from that dire torment, and have begun at last to rest with confidence in the divine favour; to say nothing meanwhile of the
many disasters which it brought upon the Church, and which
justly rendered it execrable. For the present take this for our
answer, that it was neither commanded by Christ, nor practised
by the ancient Church. We have forcibly wrested from the

hands of the sophists all the passages of Scripture which they
had contrived to distort in support of it. The ecclesiastical
histories in use show that it had no existence in a purer age. The
testimonies of the Fathers agree with this. It is therefore mere
deception when you say that the humility therein manifested
was enjoined and instituted by Christ and the Church. For
though there appears in it a certain show of humility, it is very
far from being true that every kind of abasement that assumes
the name of humility is commended by God. Accordingly Paul
teaches (Col. 2:18), that only that humility is genuine which is
framed in conformity to the Word of God.

In asserting the intercession of the saints, if all you mean is
that they continually pray for the completion of Christ's kingdom in which the salvation of all the faithful consists, there is
none of us who calls it in question. Accordingly, it is labour lost
to exert yourself so much over this point; but no doubt you
were unwilling to omit the bitter witticism in which you charge
us with thinking that the soul perishes with the body. That
philosophy we leave to your popes and colleges of cardinals, by
whom it was for many years most faithfully cultivated, nor
ceases to be cultivated today. To them also your subsequent
remark applies: they live luxuriously without any solicitude
concerning a future life, and hold us miserable wretches in
derision for labouring so anxiously on behalf of the kingdom
of Christ. But regarding the intercession of the saints, we insist
on a point which it is not strange you should omit. For here
innumerable superstitions were to be cut away, which had risen
to such a height, that the intercession of Christ was quite erased
from men's thoughts; saints were invoked as gods; the offices
peculiar to God were distributed among them; nor was there
any difference between this worship paid to them and that
ancient idolatry which we all rightly execrate.

As to purgatory, we know that ancient churches made some
mention of the dead in their prayers; but it was done seldom
and soberly, and consisted only of a few words. It was, in short,
a mention in which obviously nothing more was meant than to
testify in passing to affection for the dead. As yet the architects
were unborn, by whom that purgatory of yours was built, and
who afterwards enlarged it so greatly and raised it so high that
it now forms the strongest pillar of your kingdom. You yourself
know what a hydra of errors thence emerged; you know what
tricks superstition has spontaneously devised with which to
play; you know how many impostures avarice fabricated, in

order to bleed men of every class; you know how great detriment it has done to piety. For not to mention how greatly true worship has in consequence decayed, the worst result certainly was that, while without any command from God everyone competed with each other in helping the dead, they utterly neglected the proper offices of charity which are so strongly enjoined.

I shall not allow you, Sadolet, by inscribing the name of the Church on such abominations, both to dishonour her against all law and justice, and prejudice the ignorant against us as if we were determined to wage war with the Church. For though we admit that in ancient times some seeds of superstition were sown, which rather detracted from the purity of the gospel, still you know that it is not so long ago that those monsters of impiety with which we do battle were born, or at least grew to such a size. Indeed, in attacking, breaking down, and destroying your kingdom, we are armed not only with the virtue of the Divine Word, but also with the aid of the holy Fathers.

That I may altogether disarm you of the authority of the Church, which as your shield of Ajax you are always opposing to us, I shall show by some additional examples how widely you differ from holy antiquity. We accuse you of overthrowing the ministry, of which the empty name remains with you without the reality. For as to the office of feeding the people, the very children perceive that bishops and presbyters are dumb statues, while men of all ranks know by experience that they are active only in robbing and devouring. We are indignant that in place of the sacred Supper has been substituted a sacrifice, by which the death of Christ is emptied of its virtue. We exclaim against the execrable traffic in masses, and we complain that one half of the Supper of the Lord has been stolen from Christian people. We combat the scandalous worship of images. We show that the sacraments are vitiated by many profane ideas. We tell how indulgences crept in with fearful dishonour to the cross of Christ. We deplore that by human traditions Christian liberty has been crushed and destroyed. Of these and similar pests we have been careful to purge the churches which the Lord has committed to us. Expostulate with us, if you can, for the injury we inflicted on the Catholic Church by daring to violate its sacred sanctions. The fact is now too notorious for you to gain anything by denying it: in all these points the ancient Church is clearly on our side, and opposes you not less than we ourselves do.

But here we are met by what you say when by way of extenuation you allege that, though your customs be irregular, this is no reason why we should make a schism in the holy Church. It is scarcely possible that the minds of the common people should not be greatly alienated from you by the many examples of cruelty, avarice, intemperance, arrogance, insolence, lust and all sorts of wickedness, which were openly manifested by men of your order; but none of those things would have driven us to an attempt which we made under a much stronger necessity. This necessity was that the light of divine truth had been extinguished, the Word of God buried, the virtue of Christ left in profound oblivion, and the pastoral office subverted. Meanwhile impiety so stalked abroad, that almost no religious doctrine was pure from adulteration, no ceremony free from error, no part, however minute, of divine worship untouched by superstition. Do those who contend against such evils declare war against the Church? Do they not rather assist her in extreme distress? Yet you would take credit for your obedience and humility in refraining, through veneration for the Church, from applying your hand to the removal of these abominations. What has a Christian man to do with the prevaricating obedience that boldly despises the Word of God, and yields homage to human vanity? What has he to do with the obstinate and rude humility that disdains the majesty of God and looks up with reverence to men only? Have done with empty names of virtue, employed merely to conceal vice. Let us exhibit the thing in its true colours. Let that humility be ours which, beginning with the lowest and paying respect to each in his degree, yields the highest honour and respect to the Church in subordination, however, to Christ the Church's head; let that obedience be ours which, while it disposes us to listen to our elders and superiors, tests all obedience by the Word of God; in a word, let our Church be one whose supreme concern it is humbly and religiously to venerate the Word of God, and submit in obedience to it.

But what arrogance, you will say, to boast that you alone are the Church, and to deny it to all the rest of the world! We indeed, Sadolet, do not deny that those over which you preside are Churches of Christ; but we maintain that the Roman pontiff, with all the herd of pseudo-bishops who have seized the pastor's office, are savage wolves, whose only interest has hitherto been to scatter and trample upon the kingdom of Christ, filling it with devastation and ruin. Nor are we the first to make the complaint. With what vehemence does Bernard thunder against Eugenius and all the bishops of his own age! Yet how much more tolerable was its condition then than now! For wickedness has reached its height, and now those shadowy prelates, by whom we say she has been cruelly torn and mutilated, so that little now stands between her and destruction, can bear neither their vices nor their cure. The Church would have been completely destroyed, had not God with singular goodness prevented it. For in all places where the tyranny of the Roman pontiff prevails, there scarcely appear any stray and tattered vestiges whereby you may gather that here Churches lie half buried. Nor should you think this absurd, since Paul tells you (II Thess. 2:4) that antichrist would have his seat in no other place than in the midst of God's sanctuary. Ought not this single warning to put us on our guard against tricks and devices which may be practised upon us in the name of the Church?

But whatever the character of the men, still you say it is written: "What they tell you do" (Matt. 23:3). No doubt, if they sit in the chair of Moses. But when from a chair of vanity they intoxicate the people with folly, it is written: "Beware of the leaven of the Pharisees" (Matt. 16:6). We cannot be accused, Sadolet, of robbing the Church of any right which the goodness of God has both conceded to her and strictly guarded for her by numerous prohibitions. For as pastors are not sent forth by him to rule the Church with a wanton and lawless authority, but are restricted to a certain rule of duty which they must not exceed, so the Church is ordered (I Thess. 5:21; I John 4:1) to see that those who are appointed over her on these terms faithfully comply with their vocation. But we must either hold the testimony of Christ of little moment, or hold it impious to infringe in the least degree on the authority of those whom he has invested with such splendid titles. Indeed it is you who are mistaken in supposing that the Lord set tyrants over his people to rule them at their pleasure, when he bestowed so much authority on those whom he sent to promulgate the gospel. Your error lies in not reflecting that their power, before they were furnished with it, was circumscribed within certain limits. We admit, therefore, that ecclesiastical pastors are to be heard just like Christ himself, but they must be pastors who execute the office entrusted to them. And this office, we maintain, is not presumptuously to introduce whatever their own pleasure has rashly devised, but religiously and in good faith to deliver the oracles which they have received at the mouth of the Lord. For within these boundaries Christ confined the reverence which he required to be paid to the apostles. Nor does Peter (I Pet. 4:11) either claim for himself or allow to others anything more than that, whenever they speak among the faithful, they speak as from the mouth of the Lord. Paul indeed justly extols (II Cor. 13:10) the spiritual power with which he was invested, but with this proviso, that it availed for nothing but edification, made no display of domination, and was not employed to enslave faith.

Let your pontiff, then, boast as he may of the succession of Peter; even should he make good his title to it, it only follows that obedience is due to him from Christian people so long as he himself maintains his fidelity to Christ and does not deviate from the purity of the gospel. For the Church of the faithful forces you into no other order than that in which the Lord wished you to stand, when it tests you by that rule by which all your power is defined—the order, I say, which the Lord himself instituted among the faithful: that a prophet holding the place of teacher should be judged by those assembled [2] (I Cor. 14:29). Whoever exempts himself from this must first expunge himself from the list of prophets.

Here a very wide field for exposing your ignorance opens out, since in matters of religious controversy all that you leave the faithful to do is to shut their own eyes and submit to their teachers. But since it is certain that the soul that depends on anything else than God alone is subject to Satan, how miserable they must be who are steeped in such rudiments of faith! Hence I observe, Sadolet, that you have too superficial a theology, as is almost always the case with those who have never had experience in serious struggles of conscience. For otherwise you would never place a Christian man on ground so slippery and even precipitous, that he can scarcely stand for a moment if only the slightest push be given him. Give me, I do not say some unlearned man from among the people, but the rudest clown; if he is to belong to the flock of God, he must be prepared for the warfare he has ordained for all the godly. An armed enemy is at hand, on the alert to engage—an enemy most skilful and unassailable by the strength of the world; to resist him what guards must defend that poor man and what weapons arm him, if he is not to be instantly annihilated! Paul informs us (Eph. 6:17) that the only sword with which he can fight is the Word of the Lord. A soul, therefore, when deprived of the Word of God, is given up unarmed to the devil for destruction. Now

[2] Original has *consessu*.

then, will not the first device of the enemy be to wrest this sword from the soldier of Christ? And what will be the method of wresting it, but to set him doubting whether it be the Word of the Lord on which he leans or the word of man? What will you do for this unhappy being? Will you bid him look round for learned men on whom he may lean and take rest? But the enemy will not even leave him a breathing space in this refuge. For when once he has driven him to lean upon men, he will keep pressing and repeating his blows, until he throws him over the precipice. Thus either he must be easily overthrown, or he must forsake man and look directly to God. So true is it that Christian faith must not be founded on human testimony, not propped up by doubtful opinion, not based on human authority, but engraved on our hearts by the finger of the living God, so as not to be obliterated by any deceitful error. There is then nothing of Christ in him who does not hold the elemental principle, that it is God alone who enlightens our minds to perceive his truth, who by his Spirit seals it on our hearts, and by his sure testimony of it confirms our conscience. This is, if I may so express it, that full and firm assurance commended by Paul, which, as it leaves no room for doubt, neither hesitates nor wavers among human arguments as to which party it ought to adhere, but maintains its consistency though the whole world oppose it.

Hence arises that faculty of judging which we attribute to the Church and wish to preserve unimpaired. For however much the world be confused and stunned by varying opinion, the faithful soul is never so destitute as not to have a straight course to salvation. I do not, however, dream of a perspicacity of faith which never errs in discriminating between truth and falsehood and is never deceived; nor do I imagine to myself an arrogance which looks down as from a height on the whole human race, waits for no man's judgment and makes no distinction between learned and unlearned. On the contrary, I admit that pious and truly religious minds do not always attain to all the mysteries of God, but are sometimes blind in the clearest matters—the Lord, doubtless, so providing, that they may be accustomed to modesty and submission. Again, I admit that they have such a respect for all good men, not to say the Church, that they do not easily allow themselves to be separated from any man in whom they have discovered a true knowledge of Christ; so that sometimes they choose rather to suspend their judgment than to rush into dissent on slight grounds. I only contend that so long as they insist on the Word of the Lord, they are never so caught as to be led away to destruction. Their conviction of the truth of the Word of God is so clear and certain that it cannot be overthrown by either men or angels. Away then with that frivolous simplicity, which you say befits the rude and illiterate, of reverencing those with the greater learning and yielding at their nod! For if the name of faith is undeservedly bestowed on any religious persuasion, however obstinate, which rests anywhere but in God, who can give such a name to any kind of wavering opinion, which is not only easily wrested away by the arts of the devil, but fluctuates of its own accord with the temper of the times, and of which no other end can be hoped for than that it will at last vanish away?

As to your assertion that our own aim in shaking off this tyrannical yoke was to set ourselves free for unbridled licentiousness, abandoning, if you please, even the thought of a future life, let judgment be given after comparing our conduct with yours. We abound, indeed, in numerous faults; too often we sin and fall. Still, though truth would allow it, modesty will not permit me to boast how far we excel you in every respect—with of course the exception of Rome, that famous abode of sanctity, which having burst asunder the cords of right discipline and trodden all honour under foot, has so overflowed with all kinds of crime, that scarcely any such example of foulness has existed before! We had, then, to run our heads into so many perils and dangers that we might not, at her example, be constrained to a more severe abstinence. But we have not the least objection that the discipline sanctioned by ancient canons should be in force in the present day, and be carefully and faithfully observed; we rather have always protested that the miserable condition into which the Church had fallen was due to nothing more than enervation by luxury and indulgence. For to hang together, the body of the Church must be bound together by discipline as with sinews. But how on your part is discipline either observed or desired? Where are those ancient canons with which, like a bridle, bishops and presbyters were kept to their duty? How are your bishops elected? after what test? what examination? what care? what precaution? How are they inducted to their office? with what order? what solemnity? They merely take an official oath that they will perform the pastoral office, and this apparently for no other end than that they may add perjury to their other crimes. Since, then, in seizing upon ecclesiastical offices they seem to enter upon an authority restricted by no law, they think themselves free to do as they please; and hence it is that among pirates and robbers there is apparently more justice and regular government, and more effect given to law, than in all your order.

But since towards the end a person has been introduced to plead our cause, and you have cited us as defenders to the tribunal of God, I have no hesitation in calling upon you to meet me there. For such is our consciousness of the truth of our doctrine, that it has no dread of the heavenly Judge, from whom we do not doubt that it proceeded. But it dwells not on those frivolities with which it has pleased you to amuse yourself, but which are certainly very much out of place. For what could be more inopportune than to come into the presence of God, and to set about devising I know not what follies, and framing for us an absurd defence which must immediately fail? In pious minds, whenever that day is suggested, the impression made is too solemn to leave them at leisure so to amuse themselves. Therefore, frivolity set aside, let us think of that day which the minds of men ought always to expect with suspense. And let us remember that, while desirable to the faithful, it may well be alarming to the ungodly and profane and those who despise God. Let us turn our ears to the sound of that trumpet which even the ashes of the dead will hear in their tombs. Let us direct our thoughts and minds to that Judge who, by the mere brightness of his countenance, will disclose whatever lurks in darkness, lay open all the secrets of the human heart, and crush all the wicked by the mere breath of his mouth. Consider now what serious answer you are to make for yourself and your party; our cause, supported as it is by the truth of God, will be at no loss for a complete defence. I speak not of our persons, whose safety will be found not in defence, but in humble confession and suppliant petition; but in so far as our ministry is concerned, there is none of us who will not be able to speak for himself as follows.

"O Lord, I have indeed experienced how difficult and grievous it is to bear the invidious accusations with which I was harassed on the earth; but with the same confidence with which I then appealed to thy tribunal, I now appear before thee, for I know that in thy judgment truth reigns. Supported by confidence in this truth, I first dared to attempt, and assisted by it I was able to accomplish, whatever was achieved by me in thy Church. They charged me with two of the worst of crimes, heresy and schism. The heresy was that I dared to protest against dogmas received by them. But what could I have done? I heard from thy mouth that there was no other light of truth which could direct our souls into the way of life, than that which was kindled by thy Word. I heard that whatever human minds of themselves conceive concerning thy majesty, the worship of thy deity, and the mysteries of thy religion, was vanity. I heard that their introduction into the Church of doctrines sprung from the human brain in place of thy Word was sacrilegious presumption. But when I turned my eyes towards men, I saw very different principles prevailing. Those who were regarded as the leaders of faith neither understood thy Word, nor greatly cared for it. They only drove unhappy people about with strange doctrines, and deluded them with I know not what follies. Among the people themselves, the highest veneration paid to thy Word was to revere it at a distance as something inaccessible, and abstain from all investigation of it. Owing to the supine dullness of the pastors and the stupidity of the people, every place was filled with pernicious errors, falsehoods, and superstition. They indeed called thee the only God, but they did so while transferring to others the glory which thou hast claimed for thy majesty. They imagined for themselves and esteemed as many gods as they had saints to worship. Thy Christ was indeed worshipped as God and retained the name of Saviour; but where he ought to have been honoured, he was left almost destitute of glory. For, spoiled of his own virtue, he passed unnoticed among the crowd of saints, like one of the meanest of them. There was no one who duly considered that one sacrifice which he offered on the cross, and by which he reconciled us to thyself; no one who ever dreamed of thinking of his eternal priesthood, and the intercession depending on it; no one who trusted in his righteousness only. That confident hope of salvation, which is both enjoined by thy Word and founded upon it, had almost vanished. Indeed it was received as a kind of oracle; it was foolish arrogance, and, as they said, presumption, for any one to trust in thy goodness and the righteousness of thy Son, and entertain a sure and unfaltering hope of salvation. These were so many profane opinions which, though they were the first principles of that doctrine which thou hast delivered to us in thy Word, they plucked up by the roots. The true meaning of Baptism and the Lord's Supper also was corrupted by numerous falsehoods. And then, when everybody, gravely affronting thy mercy, put confidence in good works, when by good works they strove to merit thy favour, to procure justification, to expiate their sins, and make satisfaction to thee (each of these things obliterating and emptying the virtue of Christ's cross), they were yet quite ignorant in what good works consisted. For just as if they were not at all instructed in righteousness by thy law, they had fabricated for themselves many useless trivialities as a means of procuring thy favour, and on these they so prided themselves, that in comparison with them they almost scorned the standard of true righteousness which thy law commended—to such a degree had human desires usurped the ascendancy and derogated, if not from the belief, at least from the authority, of thy precepts contained in it.

"That I might perceive these things, thou, O Lord, didst shine upon me with the brightness of thy Spirit; that I might comprehend how impious and harmful they were, thou didst bear before me the torch of thy Word; that I might abominate them as they deserved, thou didst disturb my soul. But in rendering an account of my doctrine, thou seest, what my own conscience declares, that it was not my intention to stray beyond those limits which I saw had been fixed for all thy servants. Whatever I did not doubt I had learned from thy mouth, I desired to dispense faithfully to the Church. Assuredly the thing at which I chiefly aimed, and for which I most diligently laboured, was that the glory of thy goodness and justice should disperse the mists by which it was formerly obscured, and might shine forth conspicuously, that the virtue and blessings of thy Christ, all disguises being brushed aside, might be fully displayed. For I thought it impious to leave in obscurity things which we were born to ponder and meditate. Nor did I think that truths, whose magnitude no language can express, were to be maliciously or falsely declared. I hesitated not to dwell at greater length on topics on which the salvation of my hearers depended. For the oracle could never deceive which declares (John 17:3): 'This is eternal life, to know thee the only true God, and Jesus Christ, whom thou hast sent.'

"As to the charge of forsaking the Church, which they are accustomed to bring against me, there is nothing here of which my conscience accuses me, unless indeed he is to be considered a deserter who, seeing the soldiers routed and scattered and abandoning the ranks, raises the leader's standard, and recalls them to their posts. For thus, O Lord, were all thy servants dispersed, so that they could not by any possibility hear the command, but had almost forgotten their leader, their service, and their military vow. To bring them together when thus scattered, I raised, not a foreign standard, but that noble banner of thine which we must follow, if we would be classed among thy people.

"Then I was assailed by those who, when they ought to have kept others in their ranks, had led them astray, and when I would not at all desist they opposed me with violence. On this grievous tumults arose, and the contest flared up into disruption. Who was to blame it is for thee, O Lord, to decide. Always, both by word and deed, have I protested how eager I was for unity. Mine, however, was a unity of the Church which should begin with thee and end in thee. For whenever thou didst recommend to us peace and concord, thou didst at the same time show thyself to be the only bond for preserving it. But if I desired to be at peace with those who boasted of being the heads of the Church and the pillars of faith, I had to purchase it with the denial of thy truth. I thought that anything was to be endured rather than stoop to such an execrable accommodation. For thy Christ himself declared that, though heaven and earth should be confounded, yet thy Word must endure for ever (Matt. 24:35). Nor did I think that I dissented from thy Church, because I was at war with those leaders. For thou didst forewarn us both by thy Son and by the apostles that into that place there would rise persons to whom I ought by no means to consent. Christ predicted not of strangers, but of men who should pass themselves off as pastors, that they would be ravenous wolves and false prophets, and at the same time warned us to beware of them (Matt. 7:15). Where Christ ordered me to beware, was I to lend my aid? And the apostles declared that there would be no enemies of thy Church more pestilential than those from within, who should conceal themselves under the title of pastors (Acts 20:29; II Pet. 2:1; I John 2:18). Why should I have hesitated to separate myself from persons whom they forewarned me to hold as enemies? I had before my eyes the examples of thy prophets who, I saw, had a similar contest with the priests and prophets of their day, though these were undoubtedly the rulers of the Church among the Israelite people. But thy prophets are not regarded as schismatics because, when they wished to revive religion which had fallen into decay, they did not desist although opposed with the utmost violence. They still remained in the unity of the Church, though they were by wicked priests execrated with awful curses, and thought unworthy of a place among men, not to say saints. Confirmed by their example, I too persisted. Though denounced as a deserter of the Church and threatened, I was in no respect deterred or induced to proceed less firmly and boldly in opposing those who, in the character of pastors, wasted thy Church more than any impious tyranny. My conscience told me how strong the zeal was with which I burned for the unity of thy Church, provided thy truth were made the bond of concord. As the tumults which followed were not excited by me, so there is no ground for imputing them to me.

"Thou, O Lord, knowest, and the fact has testified itself to men, that the only thing I asked was that all controversies should be decided by thy Word, that thus both parties might unite with one mind to establish thy kingdom; and I declined not to restore peace to the Church at the expense of my head, if I were found to be the cause of needless disturbance. But what did our opponents do? Did they not forthwith furiously fly to fires, swords, and gibbets? Did they not decide that their only security was in arms and cruelty? Did they not instigate all ranks to the same fury? Did they not spurn all methods of pacification? Thus it happens that a matter, which might at one time have been settled amicably, has blazed up into such a conflict. But although amidst the great confusion the judgments of men were various, I am freed from all fear now that we stand at thy tribunal, where equity combined with truth cannot but decide in favour of innocence."

This, Sadolet, is our plea, not the fictitious one which you, in order to aggravate our case, were pleased to devise, but one whose perfect truth is known to the good even now, and will be made manifest to all creatures on that day.

Nor will those who, instructed by our preaching, have come over to our cause, be at a loss what to say for themselves, since each will have ready a defence like this.

"I, O Lord, as I had been educated from childhood, always professed the Christian faith. But at first I had no other reason for my faith than that which at the time everywhere prevailed. Thy Word, which ought to have shone on all thy people like a lamp, was for us taken away or at least suppressed. Lest any one should long for greater light, an idea had been planted in the minds of all, that the investigation of that hidden celestial philosophy was better delegated to a few, whom the others might consult as oracles; for plebeian minds no higher knowledge was proper than to submit themselves to obedience to the

Church. Now the rudiments in which I had been instructed
were of a kind which could neither properly train me to the
right worship of thy divinity, nor pave my way to a sure hope
of salvation, nor train me aright for the duties of a Christian
life. I had learned, indeed, to worship thee alone as my God,
but, as the true method of worshipping was altogether unknown
to me, I stumbled at the very threshold. I believed, as I had
been taught, that I was redeemed by the death of thy Son from
liability to eternal death, but the redemption I thought of was
one whose virtue could never reach me. I expected a future day
of resurrection, but hated to think of it, as a most dreadful
event. This feeling not only had dominion over me in private,
but was derived from the doctrine which was then uniformly
delivered to the people by their Christian teachers. They indeed preached of thy clemency towards men, but to those only
who should show themselves worthy. Moreover they put this
value on the righteousness of works, that only he was received
into thy favour who reconciled himself to thee by works. At the
same time they did not disguise the fact that we are miserable
sinners, that we often fall through infirmity of the flesh, and
that to all, therefore, thy mercy must be the common haven of
salvation. But the method of obtaining it which they pointed
out was by making satisfaction to thee for offences. Then
satisfaction was enjoined upon us: first, that after confessing all
our sins to a priest, we suppliantly ask pardon and absolution;
and second, that by good deeds we efface from thy remembrance our bad; lastly, that in order to supply what was still
wanting, we add sacrifices and solemn expiations. Then, because thou wert a stern judge and strict avenger of iniquity,
they showed how dreadful thy presence must be. Hence they
bade us flee first to the saints, that by their intercession thou
mightest be easily entreated and propitious towards us.

"When, however, I had performed all these things, though I
had some intervals of quiet, I was still far from true peace of
conscience. For whenever I descended into myself or raised my
mind to thee, extreme terror seized me which no expiations or
satisfactions could cure. The more closely I examined myself,
the sharper the stings with which my conscience was pricked;
so that the only solace which remained was to delude myself by
obliviousness. Yet as nothing better offered, I was pursuing the
course which I had begun, when a very different form of doctrine started up, not one which led us away from the Christian
profession, but one which brought it back to its source and, as it

were, clearing away the dregs, restored it to its original purity. Offended by the novelty, I lent an unwilling ear, and at first, I confess, strenuously and passionately resisted. Such is the firmness or effrontery with which men naturally persist in the course they have once undertaken, that it was with the greatest difficulty I was induced to confess that I had all my life long been in ignorance and error. One thing in particular made me averse to those new teachers, namely reverence for the Church. But when once I opened my ears and allowed myself to be taught, I perceived that this fear of derogating from the majesty of the Church was groundless. For they reminded me how great the difference is between schism from the Church, and studying to correct the faults by which the Church herself is contaminated. They spoke nobly of the Church and showed the greatest desire to cultivate unity. Lest it should seem they quibbled on the term Church, they showed it was no new thing for Antichrists to preside there in place of pastors. Of this they produced several examples, from which it appeared that they aimed at nothing but the edification of the Church, and in that respect made common cause with many of Christ's servants whom we ourselves included in the catalogue of saints. For, attacking more freely the Roman pontiff, who was reverenced as the vicegerent of Christ, the successor of Peter, and the head of the Church, they excused themselves thus: Such titles as these are empty bugbears, by which the eyes of the pious ought not to be so blinded as not to venture to investigate and sift out the reality. It was when the world was plunged in ignorance and weakness as in a deep sleep, that the pope had risen to such an eminence; certainly neither appointed head of the Church by the Word of God, nor ordained by a legitimate act of the Church, but of his own accord and self-elected. Moreover the tyranny which he let loose against the people of God was not to be endured, if we wished to have the kingdom of Christ amongst us in safety.

"Nor did they lack very powerful arguments to confirm all their positions. First, they clearly disposed of everything that was then commonly adduced to establish the primacy of the pope. When they had taken away all these supports, they also by the Word of God tumbled him from his lofty height. As far as the matter allowed, they made it clear and palpable to learned and unlearned that the true order of the Church had then perished; that the power of the keys under which the discipline of the Church is comprehended had been seriously perverted; that Christian liberty had collapsed; in short, that the kingdom of Christ was prostrated when this primacy was erected. They told me, moreover, as a means of pricking my conscience, that I could not safely connive at these things as if they were no concern of mine; that so far art thou from patronizing any voluntary error, that even he who is led astray by mere ignorance does not err with impunity. This they proved by the testimony of thy Son (Matt. 15:14): 'If the blind lead the blind, both shall fall into the ditch'. My mind was now prepared for serious attention, and I at length perceived, as if light had broken in upon me, in what a dunghill of error I had wallowed, and how much pollution and impurity I had thereby contracted. Being exceedingly alarmed at the misery into which I had fallen, and much more at that which threatened me in eternal death, as in duty bound I made it my first business to condemn my own past life, not without groans and tears, and to accept thy life. And now, O Lord, what is left for a wretch like me but, instead of defence, earnestly to supplicate thee not to judge according to its deserts that fearful abandonment of thy Word, from which in thy wondrous goodness thou hast at last delivered me."

Now, Sadolet, if you please, compare this pleading with that which you assigned to your common man. It will be strange if you hesitate which of the two you ought to prefer. For the salvation of that man hangs by a thread whose defence turns wholly on his constant adherence to the religion handed down to him from his forefathers. On this ground, Jews, Turks, and Saracens would escape the judgment of God. Away then with this vain quibbling at a tribunal which will be set up, not to approve the authority of man, but to condemn all flesh of vanity and falsehood, and vindicate the truth of God only.

But were I disposed to contend with you over trifles, what a picture I might paint, I say not of a pope, or a cardinal, or some reverend prelate of your party (in what colours almost every man of them might without much ingenuity be exhibited, you well know), but of any of your doctors—even the most select! For his condemnation there would assuredly be no need either to adduce doubtful conjectures or devise false accusations. He would be burdened heavily enough with such as are certain and just. But that I may not seem to imitate what I blame in you, I decline this mode of pleading. I will only exhort these men to turn for once to themselves, and consider with what fidelity they feed the Christian people, who can have no

other food than the Word of their God. That they may not
flatter themselves too much, because they now act their part
with great applause and, for the most part, amid favourable
acclamations, let them remember, that they have not yet come
to the conclusion. Then assuredly they will not have a theatre
on which to cry up their vapours with impunity, and, by their
tricks, trap credulous minds; but they will stand or fall by the
decision of God himself, whose judgment will not be regulated
by the breath of favour, but by his own inflexible justice; and
who will not only enquire into each man's deeds, but put to
proof the hidden sincerity or iniquity of his heart. I dare not
pronounce on all without exception; and yet, how many of
them are conscious that, in contending against us, they hire
out their services to men rather than to God?

While throughout your Letter you treat us without mercy,
towards its conclusion you pour out the venom of your bitterness upon us expressly. But though your invective by no means
hurts us and has already been partly answered, I would yet ask
what could make you think of accusing us of avarice? Do you
think the Reformers were so dull as not to perceive from the
very outset that they were entering on a course most adverse to
money and advantage? When they charged you with greed, did
they not see that they were necessarily binding themselves to
temperance and frugality, if they were not to become ridiculous
even to children? When they showed that the method of
correcting that greed was to relieve pastors of their excessive
wealth, in order that they might care more for the Church, did
they not spontaneously shut against themselves the road to
wealth? For what riches now remained to which they might
aspire? What?—would not the shortest road to riches and
honours have been to have done business with you at the very
first on the terms offered? How much would your pontiff then
have paid to many for their silence? How much would he pay
even today? If they are actuated by the least avarice, why do
they cut off all hope of improving their fortune, and prefer to be
thus perpetually poor, rather than enrich themselves without great difficulty and in a moment? But ambition, I suppose,
withholds them! What ground you had for this other insinua-
tion, I do not see; since those who first engaged in this cause
could expect nothing else than to be spurned by the whole
world, and those who afterwards adhered to it exposed themselves knowingly and willingly to endless insults and reproaches
from every quarter. But where is this fraud and inward malice?

No suspicion of them attaches to us. Talk of them rather in your sacred college where they are in operation every day.

As I hasten to a conclusion, I am compelled to pass by your calumny that, depending entirely on our own judgment, we find in the whole Church not one individual to whom we by any means think deference is due. That this is a calumny I have already sufficiently demonstrated. For, although we hold that the Word of God alone lies beyond the sphere of our judgment, and that Fathers and Councils are of authority only in so far as they agree with the rule of the Word, we still give to Councils and Fathers such rank and honour as it is proper for them under Christ to hold.

But the most serious charge of all is that we have attempted to dismember the Bride of Christ. Were that true, both you and the whole world might well regard us as past redemption. But I will not admit the charge, unless you can make out that the Bride of Christ is dismembered by those who desire to present her as a chaste virgin to Christ; who are animated by a degree of holy zeal to preserve her spotless for Christ; who, seeing her polluted by base seducers, recall her to conjugal fidelity; who unhesitatingly wage war against all the adulterers whom they detect laying traps for her chastity. And what but this have we done? Had not your factious Church attempted and even violated her chastity by strange doctrines? Had she not been violently prostituted by your numberless superstitions? Had she not been defiled by that vilest species of adultery, the worship of images? And because, I suppose, we did not suffer you so to insult the sacred chamber of Christ, we are said to have wounded his Bride! But I tell you that this wound, of which you falsely accuse us, is observed not dimly among yourselves—a wound not only of the Church, but of Christ himself, who is there beheld miserably rent. How can the Church adhere to her Spouse, while she fails to hold him safe? For where is the safety of Christ when the glory of his justice, and holiness, and wisdom is transferred elsewhere?

But it appears that, before we kindled the strife, all was tranquillity and perfect peace! True: among pastors, and also among the common people, ignorance and indolence had been at work so that there were almost no controversies respecting religion. But in the schools, how lustily did sophists brawl! You cannot, therefore, take credit for a tranquil kingdom, when there was tranquillity for no other reason than that Christ was silent. I admit that, on the revival of the gospel, great disputes arose where all was quietness before. But that is unjustly imputed to our side, who, in the whole course of their actions, desired nothing but that religion be revived and that the Churches, which discord had scattered and dispersed, might be gathered together into true unity. And not to go back upon old matters, what did they lately decline to accept, just to procure peace for the Churches? But all their efforts are rendered vain by your opposition. For while they desire peace, that with it the kingdom of Christ may flourish, you on the other hand think that all which is gained to Christ is lost to you, and it is not strange that you strenuously resist. And you have artifices by which you can in one day overturn all that they accomplish for the glory of Christ in many months. I will not overwhelm you with words, because one word will dispatch the matter. The Reformers offered to render an account of their doctrine. If overcome in argument, they do not decline to give way. Whose fault then is it that the Church does not enjoy perfect peace and the light of truth? Go now, and charge us with sedition for not permitting the Church to be quiet!

But lest you might omit anything which might tend to prejudice our cause, since many sects have sprung up during these few years, you with your usual candour lay the blame upon us. But note with what fairness or even plausibility. If we deserve hatred on this account, the Christian name also must of old have deserved it from the ungodly. Therefore either cease to molest us on this subject, or openly declare that the Christian religion, which begets so many tumults in the world, ought to be banished from the memory of man. It ought not to hurt our cause in the least that Satan has tried in all ways to impede the work of Christ. It would be more to the point to enquire which party has devotedly opposed itself to all the sects which have arisen. It is plain that, while you were idle and fast asleep, we alone bore the whole weight.

The Lord grant, Sadolet, that you and all your party may at length perceive that the only true bond of ecclesiastical unity consists in this, that Christ the Lord, who has reconciled us to God the Father, gather us out of our present dispersion into the fellowship of his body, that so, through his one Word and Spirit, we may join together with one heart and one soul.

Strassburg, September 1, 1539

The clear explanation of sound doctrine concerning the true partaking of the flesh and blood of Christ in the Holy Supper

INTRODUCTION

A YEAR OR TWO AFTER THE WESTPHAL CON-
troversy, there appeared another person to fish in the
waters left troubled by the controversy, a certain
Tilemannus Heshusius Vesalius. Bullinger seems first to have
drawn Calvin's attention to the dispute in which he engaged
when a teacher in Heidelberg, and later to have sent Calvin a
copy of *De praesentia corporis Christi in coena Domini contra sacra-
mentarios*, published by Heshusius when later resident in
Magdeburg. Bullinger expressed himself unwilling to spend
valuable time in refuting such trifles; and at first Calvin too
seemed disinclined to accept challenge. A sudden change in
opinion, however, impelled him to engage with this new adver-
sary *strenue et alacriter* (*C.R.*), since "so great is the affront
offered, that it would provoke the very stones". In 1561,
accordingly, the *Dilucida Explicatio* was given to the world. It in
turn provoked from Heshusius a *Defensio* against Calvin and
other critics. But with this further development, the matter
passes beyond the scope of this volume. (See *C.R.* IX, xli ff.)

The clear explanation of sound doctrine concerning the true partaking of the flesh and blood of Christ in the Holy Supper

to dissipate the mists of Tileman Heshusius

I must patiently submit to this condition which providence has assigned me, that petulant, dishonest and furious men, as if in conspiracy, pour out their virulence chiefly upon me. Other most excellent men indeed they do not spare, assailing the living and wounding the names of the dead; but the only cause of the more violent assault they make on me is because the more Satan, whose slaves they are, sees my labours to be useful to the Church of Christ, the more he stimulates them violently to attack me. I say nothing of the old pettifoggers, whose calumnies are already obsolete. A horrible apostate of the name of Staphylus has lately started up, and without a word of provocation has uttered more calumnies against me than against all the others who had described his perfidy, bad morals, and depraved disposition. From another quarter one named Nicolas Le Coq, has begun to screech against me. At length from another sink comes forth Tileman Heshusius. Of him I would rather have the reader form a judgment from the facts and his own writings than express my own opinion.

O Philip Melanchthon! for I appeal to you who live in the presence of God with Christ, and wait for us there until we are united with you in blessed rest. You said a hundred times, when, weary with labour and oppressed with sadness, you laid your head familiarly on my bosom: Would, would that I could die on this bosom! Since then, I have wished a thousand times that it had been our lot to be together. Certainly you would have been readier to maintain contests, and stronger to despise envy and make short work of false accusations. Thus too a check would have been put on the wickedness of many

who grew more audacious in insult by what they called your
softness. The growlings of Staphylus indeed were severely rebuked by you; but though you complained to me privately of
Le Coq, as your own letter to me testifies, yet you neglected to
repress his insolence and that of people like him. I have not
indeed forgotten what you wrote. I will give the very words: I
know that with admirable prudence you judge from the
writings of your opponents what their natures are, and what
audience they have in mind.

I remembered indeed what I wrote in reply to this and will
quote the very words: Rightly and prudently do you remind
me that the object of our antagonists is to exhibit themselves on
a stage. But though their expectation will, as I hope and believe,
greatly disappoint them, even if they were to win the applause
of the whole world, with all the greater zeal should we be
attentive to the heavenly Captain under whose eyes we fight.
What? will the sacred company of angels, who both inspire us
by their favour, and show us how to act strenuously by their
example, allow us to grow indolent or advance hesitantly?
What of the whole company of holy fathers? will they add no
stimulus? What, moreover, of the Church of God which is in the
world? When we know that she both aids us by her prayers,
and is inspired by our example, will her assistance have no
effect upon us? This be my theatre—contented with its approbation, though the whole world should hiss me, I shall
never be discouraged. So far am I from envying their senseless
clamour, let them enjoy their gingerbread glorifications[1] in
their obscure corner for a short time. I am not unaware what it
is that the world applauds and dislikes; but to me nothing is of
more consequence than to follow the rule prescribed by the
Master. And I have no doubt that this ingenuousness will
ultimately be more acceptable to men of sense and piety, than
a soft and equivocal mode of teaching that displays empty fear.
I beseech you, pay as soon as possible the debt you acknowledge
is owing by you to God and the Church. I do not thus insist,
because I trust some of the illwill will be thrown on you and that
I shall be so far relieved. Not at all; rather for the love and
respect I bear you, if it were allowable, I should willingly take
part of your burden on my own shoulders. But it is for you to
consider without any advice from me, that the debt will
scarcely ever be paid at all, if you do not quickly remove the
doubts of all the pious who look up to you. I may even add that

[1] Original has *mustacea gloriola fruantur*.

if this late evening cockcrow does not awaken you, all men will justly cry out against you as lazy.

For this appeal to his promise, he had furnished me with an occasion by the following words: I hear that a cock from the banks of the Ister [2] is printing a large much advertised [3] volume against me; if it be published, I have determined to reply simply and without ambiguity. This labour I think I owe to God and the Church; nor in my old age have I any dread of exile and other dangers. This is ingenuously and manfully said; but in another letter he had confessed, that a temper naturally mild made him desirous of peace and quietness. His words are: As in your last letter you urge me to repress the ignorant clamour of those who renew the contest about worship of bread, [4] I must tell you that some of those who do so are chiefly instigated by hatred to me, thinking it a plausible occasion for oppressing me. The same love of quiet prevented him from discoursing freely of other matters, whose explanation was either unpleasant to delicate palates or liable to perverse construction. But how much this saint was displeased with the importunity of those men who still cease not to rage against us is very apparent from another passage. After congratulating me on my refutation of the blasphemies of Servetus, and declaring that the Church now owed and would to posterity owe me gratitude, and that he entirely assented to my judgment, he adds that these things were of the greatest importance, and most requisite to be known, and then jestingly adds, in speaking of their silly frivolities: All this is nothing to the Artolatria. [5] Writing to me at Worms, he deplores that his Saxon neighbours, who had been sent as colleagues, had left after exhibiting a condemnation of our Churches, and adds: Now they will celebrate their triumphs at home, as if for a Cadmean victory. In another letter, weary of their madness and fury, he does not conceal his desire to be with me.

The things last mentioned are of no consequence to Staphylus, who hires out his impudent tongue to the Roman Antichrist, and for the professed purpose of establishing his tyranny confounds heaven and earth after the manner of the giants. This rascal, whose base defection from the faith has left him no sense of shame, I do not regard of importance enough to occupy much time in refuting his errors. The hypothesis on

[2] Original has ἀλεκτρυόνα ἐν ὄχθῃ Ἴστρου ποταμοῦ
[3] Original has στηλιτευτικὸν   [4] Original has περὶ τῆς ἀρτολατρείας
[5] Original has πρὸς τὴν ἀρτολατρείαν

which he places the whole sum and substance of his cause
openly manifests his profane contempt of all religion. The
whole doctrine which we profess he would bring into suspicion
and so render disreputable, on the simple ground that, since
the papal darkness was dissipated and eternal truth shone forth,
many errors also have sprung up, which he attributes to the
revival of the gospel—as if he were not thus picking a quarrel
with Christ and his apostles rather than with us. The devil
never stalked about so much at large, vexing both the bodies
and souls of men, as when the heavenly and saving doctrine of
Christ sent out its light. Let him therefore calumniously charge
Christ with having come to make demoniacs of those who were
formerly sane. Shortly after the first promulgation of the gospel,
an incredible number of errors poured in like a deluge on the
world. Let Staphylus, the hired orator of the pope, keep
prating that they flowed from the gospel as their fountainhead.
Assuredly if this futile calumny has any effect on feeble erring
spirits, it will have none on those on whose hearts Paul's
admonition is impressed: There must be heresies, in order that
those who are approved may be made manifest (I Cor. 11:19).
Of this Staphylus himself is a striking proof. His brutal rage,
which is plainly enough the just reward of his perfidy, confirms
all the pious in the sincere fear of God. By and large the object
of this vile and plainly licentious man is to destroy all reverence
for heavenly doctrine; indeed the tendency of his efforts is not
only to traduce religion, but to banish all care and zeal for it.
Hence his dishonesty not only fails by its own demerits, but is,
like its author, detested by all good men. Meanwhile, the false
and ill-natured charge, by which he desired to overwhelm us,
is easily rebutted on his own head. Many perverse errors have
arisen during the last forty years, starting up in succession one
after another. The reason is that Satan saw that by the light
of the gospel the impostures by which he had long fascinated
the world were overthrown, and therefore applied all his efforts
and employed all his artifices, in short all his infernal powers,
either to overthrow the doctrine of Christ, or interrupt its
course. It was no slight attestation of the truth of God that it
was thus violently assaulted by the lies of Satan. While the
sudden emergence of so many impious dogmas thus gives
certainty to our doctrine, what will Staphylus gain by spitting
on it, unless perhaps with fickle men, who would fain destroy
all distinction between good and evil?

I ask whether the many errors, about which he makes so

much noise in order to vex us, went unnoticed before Luther? He himself enumerates many by which the Church was disturbed at its very beginning. If the apostles had been charged with engendering all the sects which then suddenly sprang up, would they have had no defence? But any concession thus made to them will be good for us also. However, an easier method of disposing of the reproach of Staphylus is to reply that the delirious dreams by which Satan formerly endeavoured to obscure the light of the gospel are now in a great measure suppressed; certainly scarce a tenth of them have been renewed. Since Staphylus has advertised himself for sale, were any one to pay more for him than the Pope, would he not be ready, in pure wilfulness, to reproach Christ whenever the gospel is brought forward, for bringing along with it or engendering out of it numerous errors? Never was the world more troubled with perverse and impious dogmas than at his first advent. But Christ the eternal truth of God will acquit himself without defence from us. Meanwhile, a sufficient answer to the vile charge is to be found here: there is no ground for imputing to the servants of God any part of that leaven with which Satan by his ministers corrupts pure doctrine; and therefore, to form a right judgment in such a case, it is always necessary to attend to the source in which the error originates.

Immediately after Luther began to stir up the papal cabal, many monstrous men and opinions suddenly appeared. What affinity with Luther had the Munsterians, the Anabaptists, the Adamites, the Steblerites, the Sabbatarians, the Clancularians, that they should be regarded as his disciples? Did he ever lend them his support? Did he subscribe their most absurd fictions? Rather with what vehemence did he oppose them lest the contagion spread farther? He had the discernment at once to perceive what harmful pests they would prove. And will this swine still keep grunting that the errors which were put to flight by our exertion, while all the popish clergy remained quiescent, proceeded from us? Though he is hardened in impudence, the futility of the charge will not impose itself even on children, who will at once perceive how false and unjust it is to blame us for evils which we most vehemently oppose. As it is perfectly notorious that neither Luther nor any of us ever gave the least support to those who, under the impulse of a fanatical spirit, disseminated impious and detestable errors, it is no more just that we should be blamed for their impiety than that Paul should be blamed for that of

Hymenaeus[5a] and Philetus, who taught that the resurrection was past, and all further hope at an end (II Tim. 2:17).

Moreover, what are the errors by which ignominy attaches to our whole doctrine? I need not mention how shamelessly he lies against others; to me he assigns a sect invented by himself. He gives the name of Energists to those who hold that only the virtue of Christ's body and not the body itself is in the Supper. However, he gives me Philip Melanchthon for an associate, and, to establish both assertions, refers to my writings against Westphal, where the reader will find that in the Supper our souls are nourished by the real body of Christ, which was crucified for us, and that indeed spiritual life is transferred into us from the substance of his body. When I teach that the body of Christ is given us for food by the secret energy of the Spirit, do I thereby deny that the Supper is a communion of the body? See how vilely he employs his mouth to please his patrons.

There is another monstrous term which he has invented for the purpose of inflicting a stigma upon me. He calls me bi-sacramental. But if he would make it a charge against me that I affirm that two sacraments only were instituted by Christ, he should first of all prove that he originally made them septeplex, as the papists express it. The papists obtrude seven sacraments. I do not find that Christ committed to us more than two. Staphylus should prove that all beyond these two emanated from Christ, or allow us both to hold and speak the truth. He cannot expect that his bombastic talk will make heretics of us, who rest on the sure and clear authority of the Son of God. He classes Luther, Melanchthon, myself, and many others as new Manichees, and afterwards to lengthen the catalogue repeats that the Calvinists are Manichees and Marcionites. It is easy indeed to pick up these reproaches like stones from the street, and throw them at the heads of unoffending passers-by. However, he gives his reasons for comparing us to the Manichees; but they are borrowed partly from a sodomite, partly from a cynical clown. What is the use of working to clear myself, when he indulges in the most absurd fabrications? I have no objection, however, to the challenge with which he concludes, namely to let my treatise on Predestination decide the dispute; for in this way it will soon appear what kind of thistles[6] are produced by this wild vine.

[5a] The original has *Hermogenes*, who is linked with Phygellus in another correction in the previous chapter (II Tim. 1:15).

[6] Original has *staphyli*, which of course puns with the name.

I come now to the Cock,[7] who with his mischievous beak declares me a corrupter of the Confession of Augsburg, denying that in the Holy Supper we are made partakers of the substance of the flesh and blood of Christ. But, as is declared in my writings more than a hundred times, I am so far from rejecting the term substance, that I simply and readily declare, that spiritual life, by the incomprehensible agency of the Spirit, is infused into us from the substance of the flesh of Christ. I also constantly admit that we are substantially fed on the flesh and blood of Christ, though I discard the gross fiction of a local compounding. What then? Because a cock is pleased to ruffle his comb against me, are all minds to be so terror-struck as to be incapable of judgment? Not to make myself ridiculous, I decline to give a long refutation of a writing which proves its author to be no less absurd than its stupid audacity proves him drunk. It certainly proclaims that when he wrote he was not in his right mind.

But what shall I do with Tileman Heshusius, who, magnificently provided with a superb and sonorous vocabulary, is confident by the breath of his mouth of laying anything flat that withstands his assault? I am also told by worthy persons who know him better that another kind of confidence inflates him: that he has made it his special determination to acquire fame by putting forward paradoxes and absurd opinions. It may be either because an intemperate nature so impels him, or because he sees in a moderate course of doctrine no place for applause left for him, for which the whole man is inflamed to madness. His tract certainly proves him to be a man of turbulent temper, as well as headlong audacity and presumption. To give the reader a sample, I shall only mention a few things from the preface. He does the very same thing as Cicero describes to have been done by the silly ranters of his day, when, by a plausible exordium stolen from some ancient oration, they aroused hope of gaining the prize. So this fine writer, to occupy the minds of his readers, collected from his master Melanchthon apt and elegant sentences by which to ingratiate himself or give an air of majesty, just as if an ape were to dress up in purple, or an ass to cover himself with a lion's skin. He harangues about the huge dangers he has run, though he has always revelled in

---

[7] Original has *ad Gallum, vel Bubonem* (owl), an apt Latin rendering for Le Coq, on which play is constantly made; e.g. the *infausto suo rostro* that follows, which our rostrum, failing to convey its basic Latin meaning, only half translates.

delicacies and luxurious security. He talks of his manifold toils, though he has large treasures laid up at home, has always sold his labours at a good price, and by himself consumes all his gains. It is true, indeed, that from many places where he wished to make a quiet nest for himself, he has been repeatedly driven by his own restlessness. Thus expelled from Gossler, Rostock, Hiedelberg and Bremen, he lately withdrew to Magdeburg. Such expulsions would be meritorious, if, because of a steady adherence to truth, he had been repeatedly forced to change his habitation. But when a man full of insatiable ambition, addicted to strife and quarrelling, makes himself everywhere intolerable by his savage temper, there is no reason to complain of having been injuriously harassed by others, when by his rudeness he offered grave offence to men of right feeling. Still, however, he was provident enough to take care that his migrations should not be attended with loss; indeed riches only made him bolder.

He next bewails the vast barbarism which appears to be impending; as if any greater or more menacing barbarism were to be feared than from him and his fellows. To go no further for proof, let the reader consider how fiercely he insults and wounds his master, Philip Melanchthon, whose memory he ought to revere as sacred. He does not indeed mention him by name, but whom does he mean by the supporters of our doctrine who stand high in the Church for influence and learning, and are most distinguished theologians? Indeed, not to leave the matter to conjecture, by opprobrious epithets he points to Philip as it were with the finger, and even seems in writing his book to have been at pains to search for material for traducing him. How modest he shows himself to be in charging his preceptor with perfidy and sacrilege! He does not hesitate to accuse him of deceit in employing ambiguous terms in order to please both parties, and thus attempting to settle strife by the arts of Theramenes.[8] Then comes the heavier charge, that he involved himself in a most pernicious crime; for the confession of faith, which ought to illumine the Church, he extinguished. Such is the pious gratitude of the scholar not only towards the master to whom he owes what learning he may possess, but towards a man who has deserved so highly of the whole Church.

[8] An Athenian whose careful moderation at the time of the revolution (411 B.C.) earned him the nickname of Cothurnus (the stage boot which fitted either foot), or as we should say, Mr Facing-both-ways.

When he charges me with having introduced perplexity into the discussion by my subtleties, the discussion itself will show what foundation there is for the charge. But when he calls Epicurean dogma the explanation which, both for its religious and its practical value, we give to the mystery of the Supper, what is this but to compete in scandalous libel with debauchees and pimps? Let him look for Epicurism in his own habits. Assuredly both our frugality and assiduous labours for the Church, our constancy in danger, diligence in the discharge of our office, unwearied zeal in propagating the kingdom of Christ, and integrity in asserting the doctrine of piety—in short, our serious exercise of meditation on the heavenly life, will testify that nothing is farther from us than profane contempt of God. Would that the conscience of this Thraso did not accuse him thus! But I have said more of the man than I intended.

Leaving him, therefore, my intention is to discuss briefly the matter at issue, since a more detailed discussion with him would be superfluous. For though he presents an ostentatious appearance, he does nothing more by his magniloquence than wave in the air the old follies and frivolities of Westphal and his fellows. He harangues loftily on the omnipotence of God, on putting implicit faith in his Word, and subduing human reason, as though he had learned from his betters, of whom I believe myself also to be one. From his childish and persistent self-glorification I have no doubt that he imagines himself to combine the qualities of Melanchthon and Luther. From the one he ineptly borrows flowers; and having no better way of emulating the vehemence of the other, he substitutes bombast and sound. But we have no dispute as to the boundless power of God; and all my writings declare that I do not measure the mystery of the Supper by human reason, but look up to it with devout admiration. All who in the present day contend strenuously for the honest defence of the truth, will readily admit me into their society. I have proved by fact that, in treating the mystery of the Holy Supper, I do not refuse credit to the Word of God; and therefore when Heshusius vociferates against me for doing so, he only makes all good men witnesses to his malice and ingratitude, not without grave offence. If it were possible to bring him back from vague and frivolous flights to a serious discussion of the subject, a few words would suffice.

When he alleges the sluggishness of princes as the obstacle

which prevents a holy synod being assembled to settle disputes, I could wish that he himself, and similar furious individuals, did not obstruct all attempts at concord. This a little further on he does not disguise when he denies the expediency of any discussion between us. What pious synod then would suit his mind, unless one in which two hundred of his companions or thereabouts, well-fed to make their zeal more fervent, should, according to a custom which has long been common with them, declare us to be worse and more execrable than the papists? The only confession they want is the rejection of all inquiry, and the obstinate defence of any random fiction that may have fallen from them. It is perfectly obvious, though the devil has fascinated their minds in a fearful manner, that it is pride more than error that makes them so pertinacious in assailing our doctrine.

As he pretends that he is an advocate of the Church, and, in order to deceive the simple by specious masks, is always arrogating to himself the character common to all who teach rightly, I should like to know who authorized him to assume this office. He is always exclaiming: We teach; This is our opinion; Thus we speak; So we assert. Let the farrago which Westphal has huddled together be read, and a remarkable discrepancy will be found. Not to go farther for an example, Westphal boldly affirms that the body of Christ is chewed by the teeth, and confirms it by quoting with approbation the recantation of Berengarius, as given by Gratian. This does not please Heshusius, who insists that it is eaten by the mouth but not touched by the teeth, and strongly disapproves those gross modes of eating. Yet he reiterates his: We assert, just as if he were the representative of a university. This worthy son of Jena repeatedly charges me with subtleties, sophisms, even impostures: as if there were any equivocation or ambiguity, or any kind of obscurity in my mode of expression. When I say that the flesh and blood of Christ are substantially offered and exhibited to us in the Supper, I at the same time explain the mode, namely, that the flesh of Christ becomes vivifying to us, inasmuch as Christ, by the incomprehensible virtue of his Spirit, transfuses his own proper life into us from the substance of his flesh, so that he himself lives in us, and his life is common to us. Who will be persuaded by Heshusius that there is any sophistry in this clear statement, in which I at the same time use popular terms and satisfy the ear of the learned? If he would only desist from the futile calumnies by which he darkens the case, the whole point would at once be decided.

After Heshusius has exhausted all his bombast, the whole question hinges on this: Does he who denies that the body of Christ is eaten by the mouth, take away the substance of his body from the sacred Supper? I frankly engage at close quarters with the man who denies that we are partakers of the substance of the flesh of Christ, unless we eat it with our mouths. His expression is that the very substance of the flesh and blood must be taken by the mouth; but I define the mode of communication without ambiguity, by saying that Christ by his boundless and wondrous powers unites us into the same life with himself, and not only applies the fruit of his passion to us, but becomes truly ours by communicating his blessings to us, and accordingly joins us to himself, as head and members unite to form one body. I do not restrict this union to the divine essence, but affirm that it belongs to the flesh and blood, inasmuch as it was not simply said: My Spirit, but: My flesh is meat indeed; nor was it simply said: My Divinity, but: My blood is drink indeed.

Moreover, I do not interpret this communion of flesh and blood as referring only to the common nature, so that Christ, by becoming man, made us sons of God with himself by virtue of fraternal fellowship. I distinctly affirm that this flesh of ours which he assumed is vivifying for us, so that it becomes the material of spiritual life to us. I willingly embrace the saying of Augustine: As Eve was formed out of a rib of Adam, so the origin and beginning of life to us flowed from the side of Christ. And although I distinguish between the sign and the thing signified, I do not teach that there is only a bare and shadowy figure, but distinctly declare that the bread is a sure pledge of that communion with the flesh and blood of Christ which it figures. For Christ is neither a painter, nor an actor, nor a kind of Archimedes who presents an empty image to amuse the eye; but he truly and in reality performs what by external symbol he promises. Hence I conclude that the bread which we break is truly the communion of the body of Christ. But as this connection of Christ with his members depends on his incomprehensible virtue I am not ashamed to wonder at this mystery which I feel and acknowledge to transcend the reach of my mind.

Here our Thraso makes an uproar, and cries out that it is great impudence as well as sacrilegious audacity to corrupt the clear voice of God, which declares: This is my body—that one might as well deny the Son of God to be man. But I rejoin that if he would evade this very charge of sacrilegious audacity, he is on his own terms committed to anthropomorphism. He insists that no amount of absurdity must induce us to change one syllable of the words. Hence as the Scripture distinctly attributes to God feet, hands, eyes, and ears, a throne, and a footstool, it follows that he is corporeal. As he is said in the song of Miriam to be a man of war (Ex. 15:3)[8a], it will not be lawful by any fitting exposition to soften this harsh mode of expression. Let Heshusius pull on his stage boots[9] if he will; his insolence must still be repressed by this strong and valid argument. The ark of the covenant is distinctly called the Lord of hosts, and indeed with such asseveration that the Prophet emphatically exclaims (Ps. 24:8): Who is this king of glory? Jehovah himself is king of hosts.

Here we do not say that the Prophet without consideration blurted out what at first glance seems absurd, as this rogue wickedly babbles. After reverently embracing what he says, piety and fittingness require the interpretation that the name of God is transferred to a symbol because of its inseparable connection with the thing and reality. Indeed this is a general rule for all the sacraments, which not only human reason compels us to adopt, but which a sense of piety and the uniform usage of Scripture dictate. No man is so ignorant or stupid as not to know that in all the sacraments the Spirit of God by the prophets and apostles employs this special form of expression. Anyone disputing this should be sent back to his rudiments. Jacob saw the Lord of hosts sitting on a ladder. Moses saw him both in a burning bush and in the flame of Mount Horeb. If the letter is tenaciously retained, how could God who is invisible be seen? Heshusius repudiates examination, and leaves us no other resource than to shut our eyes and acknowledge that God is visible and invisible. But an explanation at once clear and congruous with piety, and in fact necessary, spontaneously presents itself: that God is never seen as he is, but gives manifest signs of his presence adapted to the capacity of believers.

Thus the presence of the divine essence is not at all excluded when the name of God is by metonymy[10] applied to the symbol by which God truly represents himself, not figuratively merely but substantially. A dove is called the Spirit. Is this to be taken strictly, as when Christ declares that God is a Spirit (Matt. 3:16; John 4:24)? Surely a manifest difference is apparent. For

---

8a *Sic*; but it is Moses who sings here; Miriam repeats Moses' words later in the same chapter (Ex. 15:21).

9 Original has *cothurnos suos attollat.*

10 Original has the curious term metonymicως.

although the Spirit was then truly and essentially present, yet he displayed the presence both of his virtue and his essence by a visible symbol. How wicked it is of Heshusius to accuse us of inventing a symbolical body is clear from this, that no honest man infers that a symbolic Spirit was seen in the baptism of Christ because there he truly appeared under the symbol or external appearance of a dove. We declare then that in the Supper we eat the same body as was crucified, although the expression refers to the bread by metonymy, so that it may be truly said to be symbolically the real body of Christ, by whose sacrifice we have been reconciled to God. Though there is some diversity in the expressions: the bread is a sign or figure or symbol of the body, and: the bread signifies the body, or is a metaphorical or metonymical or synecdochical expression for it, they perfectly agree in substance, and therefore Westphal and Heshusius trifle when they thus look for a knot in a bulrush.[11]

A little farther on this circus-rider says that, whatever be the variety in expression, we all hold the very same sentiments, but that I alone deceive the simple by ambiguities. But where are the ambiguities which he wants to remove and so reveal my deceit? Perhaps his rhetoric can furnish a new kind of perspicacity which will clearly manifest the alleged implications of my view. Meanwhile he unworthily includes us all in the charge of teaching that the bread is the sign of the absent body, as if I had not long ago expressly made my readers aware of two kinds of absence: they should know that the body of Christ is indeed absent in respect of place, but that we enjoy a spiritual participation in it, every obstacle on the score of distance being surmounted by his divine virtue. Hence it follows that the dispute is not about presence or about substantial eating, but about how both these are to be understood. We do not admit a presence in space, nor that gross or rather brutish eating of which Heshusius talks so absurdly, when he says that Christ in respect of his human nature is present on the earth in the substance of his body and blood, so that he is not only eaten in faith by his saints, but also by the mouth bodily without faith by the wicked.

Without adverting at present to the absurdities here involved, I ask where is the true touchstone, the express Word of God? Assuredly it cannot be found in this barbarism. Let us see, however, what the explanation is which he thinks sufficient to stop the mouths of the Calvinists—an explanation so stupid that it

[11] Literal translation brings out clearly enough the point of the familiar Latin proverb about finding difficulties where none exist.

must rather open their mouths to protest against it. He vindi-
cates himself and the churches of his party from the error of
transubstantiation with which he falsely alleges that we charge
them. For though they have many things in common with the
papists, we do not therefore mix them without distinction. In
fact a long time ago I showed that the papists are considerably
more modest and more sober in their dreams. What does he
say himself? As the words are joined together contrary to the
order of nature, it is right to maintain the literal sense [12] by
which the bread is properly the body. The words therefore, to
be in accordance with the thing, must be held to be contrary to
the order of nature.

He afterwards excuses their different forms of expression
when they assert that the body is under the bread or with the
bread. But how will he convince any one that it is under the
bread, except in so far as the bread is a sign? How, too, will he
convince any one that the bread is not to be worshipped if it
be properly Christ? The expression that the body is in the bread
or under the bread, he calls improper, because the word
"substantial" has its proper and genuine significance in the
union of the bread and Christ. In vain, therefore, does he refute
the inference that the body is in the bread, and therefore the
bread should be worshipped. This inference is the invention of
his own brain. The argument we have always used is this: If
Christ is in the bread, he should be worshipped under the
bread. Much more might we argue, that the bread should be
worshipped if it be truly and properly Christ.

He thinks he gets out of the difficulty by saying, that the
union is not hypostatic. But who will concede to a hundred or
a thousand Heshusiuses the right to bind worship with whatever restrictions they please? Assuredly no man of sense will be
satisfied in conscience with the silly quibble that the bread,
though it is truly and properly Christ, is not to be worshipped,
because they are not hypostatically one. The objection will at
once be made that things must be the same when the one is
substantially predicated of the other. The words of Christ do
not teach that anything happens to the bread. But if we are to
believe Heshusius and his fellows, they plainly and unam-
biguously assert that the bread is the body of Christ, and
therefore Christ himself. Indeed they affirm more of the bread
than is rightly said of the human nature of Christ. But how
monstrous it is to give more honour to the bread than to the

[12] Original has τὸ ῥητὸν

sacred flesh of Christ! Of this flesh it cannot truly be affirmed, as they insist in the case of the bread, that it is properly Christ. Though he may deny that he invents any common essence,[13] I can always force this admission from him, that if the bread is properly the body, it is one and the same with the body. He subscribes to the sentiment of Irenaeus, that there are two different things in the Supper: an earthly and a heavenly, that is, the bread and the body. But I do not see how this can be reconciled with the fictitious identity, which, though not expressed in words, is certainly asserted in fact; for things must be the same when we can say of them: That is this, This is that.

The same reasoning applies to the local enclosing which Heshusius pretends to repudiate, when he says that Christ is not contained by place, and can be at the same time in several places. To clear himself of suspicion, he says that the bread is the body not only properly, truly, and really, but also definitively. Should I answer that I wonder what these monstrous contradictions really mean, he will meet me with the shield of Ajax—which he and his companions[14] are accustomed to use— that reason is inimical to faith. This I readily grant if he himself is a rational animal.

Three kinds of reason are to be considered, but he at one bound leaps over them all. There is a reason naturally implanted in us which cannot be condemned without insult to God; but it has limits which it cannot overstep without being immediately lost. Of this we have a sad proof in the fall of Adam. There is another kind of vitiated reason, especially in a corrupt nature, manifested when mortal man, instead of receiving divine things with reverence, wants to subject them to his own judgment. This reason is intoxication of the mind, a kind of sweet insanity, at perpetual variance with the obedience of faith; for we must become fools in ourselves before we can begin to be wise unto God. In regard to heavenly mysteries, therefore, this reason must retire, for it is nothing better than mere fatuity, and if accompanied with arrogance rises to madness. But there is a third kind of reason, which both the Spirit of God and Scripture sanction. Heshusius, however, disregarding all distinction, confidently condemns, under the name of human reason, everything which is opposed to the frenzied dream of his own mind.

[13] Original has μετουσίαν
[14] Original has *boni illi Luperci sodales*, referring to the two chosen runners who performed at the festival of the Lupercal.

He charges us with paying more deference to reason than to the Word of God. But what if we adduce no reason that is not derived from the Word of God and founded on it? Let him show that we profanely philosophize about the mysteries of God, measure his heavenly kingdom by our sense, subject the oracles of the Holy Spirit to the judgment of the flesh, and admit nothing that does not approve itself to our own wisdom. The case is quite otherwise. For what is more repugnant to human reason than that souls, immortal by creation, should derive life from mortal flesh? This we assert. What is less in accordance with earthly wisdom, than that the flesh of Christ should infuse its vivifying virtue into us from heaven? What is more foreign to our sense, than that corruptible and fading bread should be an undoubted pledge of spiritual life? What more remote from philosophy, than that the Son of God, who in respect of human nature is in heaven, so dwells in us, that everything which has been given him of the Father is made ours, and hence the immortality with which his flesh has been endowed becomes ours? All these things we clearly testify, while Heshusius has nothing to urge but his delirious dream: the flesh of Christ is eaten by unbelievers, and yet is not vivifying. If he refuses to believe that there is any reason without philosophy, let him learn from a short syllogism:

> He who does not observe the analogy between the sign and the thing signified, is an unclean animal, not having cloven hoofs;
> he who asserts that the bread is truly and properly the body of Christ, destroys the analogy between the sign and the thing signified:
> therefore, he who asserts that the bread is properly the body, is an unclean animal, not having cloven hoofs.

From this syllogism let him know that even though there were no philosophy in the world, he is an unclean animal. But his object in this indiscriminate condemnation of reason was no doubt to procure liberty in his own darkness, so that this inference might hold good: When mention is made of the crucifixion and of the benefits which the living and substantial body of Christ procured, the body referred to cannot be understood to be symbolical, typical, or allegorical; hence the words of Christ: This is my body, This is my blood, cannot be understood symbolically or metonymically, but substantially. As if elementary schoolboys would not see that the term symbol is applied to the bread, not to the body, and that the metonymy is not in the substance of the body, but in the context of the words. And yet he exults here as if he were an Olympic victor, and bids us try the whole force of our intellect on this argument —an argument so absurd, that I will not deign to refute it even in jest. For while he says that we turn our backs, and at the same time stimulates himself to press forward, his own procedure betrays his manifest inconsistency. He admits that we understand that the substance of the body of Christ is given, since Christ is wholly ours by faith. It is a good thing that this ox butts harmlessly at the air with his own horns, so that it is unnecessary for us to be on our guard. I would ask if we turn our backs when we thus distinctly expose his calumny in regard to an allegorical body? But as if he had fallen into a fit of forgetfulness, after he has come to himself he brings a new charge concerning absence, saying that the giving of which we speak has no more effect than the giving of a field to one who was to be immediately removed from it. How dare he thus liken the incomparable virtue of the Holy Spirit to lifeless things, and represent the gathering of the produce of a field as equivalent to that union with the Son of God, which enables our souls to obtain life from his body and blood? Surely in this matter he acts too much the rustic. I may add that it is false to say that we expound the words of Christ as if the thing were absent, when it is perfectly well known that the absence of which we speak is confined to place and actual sight. Although Christ does not exhibit his flesh as present to our eyes, nor by change of place descend from his celestial glory, we deny that this distance is an obstacle preventing him from being truly united to us.

But let us observe the kind of presence for which he contends. At first sight his view seems sane and sensible. He admits that Christ is everywhere by a communication of properties, as was taught by the fathers, and that accordingly it is not the body of Christ that is everywhere, the ubiquity being ascribed concretely to the whole person in respect of the union of the divine nature. This is so exactly our doctrine, that he might seem to be wanting by prevarication to win favour with us. Nor have we difficulty in accepting what he adds, that it is impossible to comprehend how the body of Christ is in a certain heavenly place, above the heavens, and yet the person of Christ is everywhere, ruling in equal power with the Father. Indeed the whole world knows how violently I have been assailed by his party for defending this very doctrine. To express this in a still more palpable form, I employed the trite phrase of the schools, that Christ is whole everywhere but not wholly.[15] In other words, being entire in the person of Mediator, he fills heaven and earth, though in his flesh he be in heaven, which he has chosen as the abode of his human nature, until he appear for judgment. What then prevents us from adopting this evident distinction, and agreeing with each other? Simply that Heshusius immediately perverts what he had said, insisting that Christ did not exclude his human nature when he promised to be present on the earth. Shortly after, he says that Christ is present with his Church, dispersed in different places, and this in respect not only of his divine, but also of his human nature. In a third passage he is still plainer, and denies that there is absurdity in holding that he may, in respect of his human nature, exist in different places wherever he pleases. And he sharply rejects what he terms the physical axiom, that one body cannot be in different places. What can now be clearer than that he holds the body of Christ to be an immensity and to constitute a monstrous ubiquity? A little before he had admitted that the body is in a certain place in heaven; now he assigns it different places. This is to dismember the body, and refuse to lift up the heart.

He objects that Stephen was not carried above all the heavens to see Jesus; as if I had not repeatedly disposed of this quibble. As Christ was not recognized by his two disciples with whom he sat familiarly at the same table, not on account of any metamorphosis, but because their eyes were holden, so eyes were given to Stephen to penetrate even to the heavens. Surely it is not without cause mentioned by Luke that he lifted up his eyes to heaven, and beheld the glory of God. Nor without cause does Stephen himself declare the heavens were opened to him, that he might behold Jesus standing on the right hand of his Father. This, I fancy, makes it plain how absurdly Heshusius endeavours to bring him down to the earth. With equal shrewdness he infers that Christ was on the earth when he showed himself to Paul; as if we had never heard of that carrying up to the third heaven, which Paul himself so magnificently proclaims (II Cor. 12:2). What does Heshusius say to this? His words are: Paul could not be translated above all heavens, whither the Son of God ascended. I have nothing to add, but that the man who thus dares to give the lie to Paul

[15] *totus Christus ubique sed non totum.*

when testifying of himself merits the greatest contempt? [16] But it is said, that as Christ distinctly offers his body in the bread, and his blood in the wine, all boldness and curiosity must be curbed. This I admit; but it does not follow that we are to shut our eyes in order to exclude the rays of the sun. Indeed, if the mystery is deserving of contemplation, it is fitting rather to consider in what way Christ can give us his body and blood for meat and drink. For if the whole Christ is in the bread, if indeed the bread itself is Christ, we may with more truth affirm that the body is Christ—an affirmation from which both piety and common sense shrink. But if we do not refuse to lift up our hearts, we shall feed on the whole Christ, as well as expressly on his flesh and blood. Indeed when Christ invites us to eat his body and to drink his blood, he need not be brought down from heaven, or required to place himself in several localities in order to put his body and his blood within our lips. The sacred bond of our union with him is amply sufficient for this purpose when by the secret virtue of the Spirit we are united into one body with him. Hence I agree with Augustine, that in the bread we receive that which hung upon the cross. But I utterly abhor the delirious fancy of Heshusius and those like him, that it is not received unless it is introduced into the carnal mouth. The communion [17] of which Paul discourses does not require any local presence, unless indeed Paul, in teaching that we are called to communion with Christ [17] (I Cor. 1:9), either speaks of a nonentity or places Christ locally wherever the gospel is preached.

The dishonesty of this babbler is intolerable, when he says that I confine the term communion [17] to the fellowship we have with Christ by partaking of his benefits. But before proceeding to discuss this point, it is necessary to see how ingeniously he escapes from us. When Paul says that those who eat the sacrifice are partakers [17] of the altar (I Cor. 9:13), this good fellow gives as reason, that each receives a part from the altar, and from this he concludes that my interpretation is false. But what a concoction from his own turbulent brain! Our communion, as stated by me, is not only in the fruit of Christ's death, but also in his body offered for our salvation. But this interpretation also, which he refutes as though it was different from the other, is rejected by him as excluding the presence of Christ in the Supper. Here let my readers carefully attend to the kind of

[16] Original has *sputis dignum esse*, which is stronger.
[17] Original has κοινωνία, εἰς κοινωίαν, κοινωνίας, κοινωνοὺς

presence which he imagines and to which he clings so doggedly, that he almost reduces to nothing the communion which
John the Baptist had with Christ, provided he is allowed to
hold that the body of Christ was swallowed by Judas. I ask this
reverend doctor: if those are partakers of the altar who divide
the sacrifice into parts, how can he exonerate himself from the
charge of dismembering while he gives each his part? If he
answers that this is not what he means, let him correct his
expression. He is certainly driven from the stronghold in which
all his defence was located, his assertion that I leave nothing in
the Supper but a right to a thing that is absent, seeing that I
uniformly maintain that through the virtue of the Spirit there
is a present exhibition of a thing absent in respect of place.
Still, while I refuse to subscribe to the barbarous eating by
which he insists that Christ is swallowed by the mouth, he will
always be swept on to abuse with his implacable fury. Verbally,
indeed, he denies that he inquires concerning the mode of
presence, and yet, imperiously as well as rudely, he insists on
the monstrous dogma he has fabricated, that the body of Christ
is eaten corporeally by the mouth. These indeed are his very
words. In another passage he says: We assert not only that we
become partakers of the body of Christ by faith, but that also
by our mouths we receive Christ essentially or corporeally
within us; and in this way we testify that we give credence to
the words of Paul and the evangelists.

But we too reject the sentiments of all who deny the presence
of Christ in the Supper. What then is the kind of presence for
which he quarrels with us? Obviously something dreamt by
himself and similar frenzied people. What impudence to cover
up such gross fancies with the names of Paul and the evangelists! How will he prove to these witnesses that the body of
Christ is taken by the mouth both corporeally and internally?
He has elsewhere acknowledged that it is not chewed by the
teeth nor touched by the palate. Why should he be so afraid of
the touch of the palate or throat, while he ventures to assert that
it is absorbed by the stomach? What does he mean by the expression "internally"? [18] By what is the body of Christ received
after it has passed the mouth? From the mouth, if I mistake not,
the bodily passage is to the viscera or intestines. If he say that
we are calumniously throwing odium on him by the use of
offensive terms, I should like to know what difference there is
between saying that what is received by the mouth is taken

[18] The phrase in the original is *intra nos.*

corporeally within, and saying that it passes into the viscera or intestines? Henceforth let the reader understand and be careful to remember, that whenever Heshusius charges me with denying the presence of Christ in the Supper, the only thing for which he blames me is something which seems absurd to me, that Christ is swallowed by the mouth so that he passes bodily into the stomach. Yet he complains that I play with ambiguous expressions; as if it were not my perspicuity that maddens him and his associates. Of what ambiguity can he convict me? He admits that I assert the true and substantial eating of the flesh and drinking of the blood of Christ. But, he says, when my meaning is investigated, I speak of the receiving of merit, fruit, efficacy, virtue, and power, descending from heaven. Here his malignant absurdity is not to be deduced but to be seen, when he confuses virtue and power with merit and fruit. Is it usual for any one to say that merit descends from heaven? Had he one particle of candour, he would have quoted me as either speaking or writing thus: For us to have substantial communion with the flesh of Christ, there is no necessity for any change of place, since by the secret virtue of the Spirit he infuses his life into us from heaven; nor does distance at all prevent Christ from dwelling in us, or us from being one with him, since the efficacy of the Spirit surmounts all natural obstacles.

A little farther on we shall see how shamefully he contradicts himself when he quotes my words: The blessings of Christ do not belong to us until he has himself become ours. Let him go now, and by the term *merit* obscure his account of the communion that I teach. He argues that if the body of Christ is in heaven he is not in the Supper, and we have symbols merely; as if the Supper were not to the true worshippers of God a heavenly action, or a kind of vehicle by which they transcend the world. But what is this to Heshusius, who not only halts on the earth, but does all he can to keep grovelling in the mud? Paul teaches that in baptism we put on Christ (Gal. 3:27). How persuasively will Heshusius argue that this cannot be if Christ remain in heaven! When Paul said this, it never occurred to him that Christ must be brought down from heaven, because he knew that he is united to us in a different manner, and that his blood is as much present to cleanse our souls as water to cleanse our bodies. If he rejoins that there is a difference between "eating" and "putting on", I answer that to put clothing on ourselves is as necessary as to take food into ourselves. Indeed the folly or malice of the man is proved by this one thing, that he admits none but a local presence. Though he denies it to be physical, and even quibbles upon the point, he yet places the body of Christ wherever the bread is, and accordingly maintains that it is in several places at the same time. As he does not hesitate so to express himself, why may not the presence to which he leads us be termed local?

Of similar stuff is his objection that the body is not received truly if it is received symbolically; as if by a true symbol we excluded the exhibition of the reality. He ultimately says it is mere imposture, unless a twofold eating is asserted, a spiritual and a corporeal. How ignorantly and erroneously he twists the passages referring to spiritual eating, I need not observe, when children can see how ridiculous he makes himself. As to the subject itself, if a division is vicious when its members coincide with each other as boys learn among the first rudiments, how will he escape the charge of having thus blundered? For if there is any eating which is not spiritual, it will follow that in the mystery of the Supper there is no operation of the Spirit. Thus it will naturally be called the flesh of Christ, just as if it were a perishable and corruptible food, and the chief earnest of eternal salvation will be unaccompanied by the Spirit. Should even this not overcome the stubborn front he offers, I ask whether independently of the use of the Supper there be no other eating than spiritual, which according to him is opposed to corporeal. He distinctly affirms that this is nothing else than faith, by which we apply to ourselves the benefits of Christ's death. What then becomes of the declaration of Paul, that we are flesh of the flesh of Christ, and bone of his bones? What will become of the exclamation: This is a great mystery (Eph. 5:30, 32)? For if beyond the application of merit, nothing is left to believers besides the present use of the Supper, the head will always be separated from the members, except at the particular moment when the bread is put into the mouth and throat. We may add on the testimony of Paul (I Cor. 1), that fellowship with Christ [19] is the result of the gospel no less than of the Supper. A little ago we saw Heshusius bragging of this fellowship; but what Paul affirms of the Supper he had previously affirmed of the doctrine of the gospel. If we listened to this trifler, what would become of that noble discourse in which our Saviour promises that his disciples should be one with him,

[19] Original has *Christi κοινωνία*

as he and the Father are one? There cannot be any doubt that he there speaks of a perpetual union.

It is intolerable impudence for Heshusius to represent himself as an imitator of the fathers. He quotes a passage from Cyril on the fifteenth chapter of John; as if Cyril did not there plainly contend that the participation with Christ which is offered us in the Supper proves that we are united with him in respect of the flesh. He is disputing with the Arians, who, quoting the words of Christ: "That they may be one, as thou Father art in me and I in thee" (John 17:21), used them as pretext to deny that Christ is one with the Father in reality and essence, but only in consent. Cyril, to dispose of this quibble, answers that we are essentially one with Christ, and to prove it adduces the force of the mystical benediction. If he were contending only for a momentary communion, what could be more irrelevant? But it is no wonder that Heshusius thus betrays his utter want of shame, since he with equal confidence claims the support of Augustine, who, as all the world knows, is diametrically opposed to him. He says that Augustine distinctly admits (*Serm. 2 de verb. Dom.*) that there are different modes of eating the flesh, and affirms that Judas and other hypocrites ate the true flesh of Christ. But if it turn out that the epithet *true* is interpolated, how will Heshusius exonerate himself from a charge of forgery? Let the passage be read, and, without a word from me, it will be seen that Heshusius has forged the *true flesh*.

But he will say that a twofold eating is there mentioned; as if the same distinction did not everywhere occur in our writings also. Augustine there employs the terms *flesh* and *sacrament of flesh* indiscriminately in the same sense. This he has also done in several other passages. If an explanation is sought, there cannot be a clearer interpreter than himself. He says (*Ep. 23 ad Bonif.*) that from the resemblance which the sacraments have to the things, they often receive their names; for which reason the sacrament of the body of Christ is in a manner the body of Christ. Could he testify more clearly that the bread is termed the body of Christ indirectly because of resemblance? He elsewhere says that the body of Christ falls on the ground, but this is in the same sense in which he says that it is consumed (*Hom. 26 in Joann.*). Did we not here apply the resemblance formerly noticed, what could be more absurd? Indeed what a calumny it would be against this holy writer to represent him as holding that the body of Christ is taken into the stomach! It is long since I accurately explained what Augustine means by a twofold eating, namely that while some receive the virtue of the sacrament, others receive only a visible sacrament; that it is one thing to take inwardly, another outwardly; one thing to eat with the heart, another to bite with the teeth. And he finally concludes that the sacrament which is placed on the Lord's table is taken by some unto destruction and by others unto life, but the reality of which the Supper is the sign gives life to all who partake of it. In another passage also, treating in express terms of this question, he distinctly refutes those who imagined that the wicked eat the body of Christ not only sacramentally but in reality. To show our entire agreement with this holy writer, we say that those who are united by faith, so as to be his members, eat his body truly or in reality, whereas those who receive nothing but the visible sign eat only sacramentally. He often expresses himself in the very same way. (*De civit. Dei*, 21, ch. 25; *Contra Faust.* bk. 13, ch. 13; see also *in Joann. ev. Tract.* 25–27.)

But, as Heshusius by his importunity compels us so often to repeat, let us bring forward the passage in which Augustine says that Judas ate the bread of the Lord against the Lord, whereas the other disciples ate the bread of the Lord (*in Joann. ev. Tract.* 59). It is certain that this pious teacher never makes a threefold division. But why mention him alone? Not one of the fathers has taught that in the Supper we receive anything but that which remains with us after the use of the Supper.

Heshusius will exclaim that the Supper is therefore useless to us. For his words are: "Why does Christ by a new commandment enjoin us to eat his body in the Supper, and even give us bread, since not only himself but all the prophets urge us to eat the flesh of Christ by faith? Does he then in the Supper command nothing new?" I in my turn ask him: Why did God in ancient days enjoin circumcision and sacrifice and all the exercises of faith, and also why did he institute Baptism? Without his answer the explanation is quite simple: God gives no more by visible signs than by his Word, but gives in a different manner, because our weakness stands in need of a variety of helps. He asks: Will the expression not be very improper: "This cup is the New Testament in my blood," unless the whole is corporeal? To this we all answered long ago, that what is offered to us by the gospel outside the Supper is sealed to us by the Supper, and hence communion with Christ is no less truly conferred upon us by the gospel than by the Supper. He asks: How is it called the Supper of the "New Testament," if only types are exhibited in it as under the Old Testament? First, I would beg my readers to put against these silly objections the clear statements which I have made in my writings. Then they will not only find what distinction ought to be made between the sacraments of the new and of the ancient Church, but will detect Heshusius in the very act of theft,[20] stealing everything except his own ignorant idea that nothing was given to the ancients except types. As if God had deluded the fathers with empty figures; or as if Paul's doctrine was futile, when he teaches that they ate the same spiritual food as we, and drank the same spiritual drink (I Cor. 10:3). Heshusius at last concludes: "Unless the blood of Christ be given substantially in the Supper, it is absurd and contrary to the sacred writings to give the name of 'new covenant' to wine; and therefore there must be two kinds of eating, one spiritual and metaphorical common to the fathers, and another corporeal proper to us." It would be enough for me to deny the inference which might move even children to laughter; but how profane is the talk that contemptuously calls what is spiritual metaphorical! As if he would subject the mystical and incomprehensible virtue of the Spirit to grammarians.

Lest he should allege that he has not been completely answered, I must again repeat: As God is always true, the figures were not fallacious by which he promised his ancient people life and salvation in his only begotten Son; now, however, he plainly presents to us in Christ the things which he then showed as though from a distance. Hence Baptism and the Supper not only set Christ before us more fully and clearly than the legal rites did, but exhibit him as present. Paul accordingly teaches that we now have the body instead of shadows (Col. 2:17), not only because Christ has been once manifested, but because Baptism and the Supper, like assured pledges, confirm his presence with us. Hence appears the great distinction between our sacraments and those of the ancient people. This, however, by no means robs them of the reality of the things which Christ today exhibits more fully, clearly, and perfectly, as from his presence one might expect.

The statement he makes so keenly and obstinately, that the unworthy eat Christ, I would leave as undeserving of refutation, except that he regards it as the chief defence of his cause. He calls it a grave matter, fit for pious and learned men to discuss together. If I grant this, how comes it that hitherto it has been

[20] Original has ἐπ' αὐτοφώρῳ

impossible to obtain from his party a calm discussion of the question? If discussion is allowed, there will be no difficulty in arranging it. The arguments of Heshusius are: first, Paul distinguishes the blessed bread from common bread, not only by the article but by the demonstrative pronoun; as if the same distinction were not sufficiently made by those who call the sacred and spiritual feast a pledge and badge of our union with Christ. The second argument is: Paul more clearly asserts that the unworthy eat the flesh of Christ, when he says that they become guilty of the body and blood of Christ. But I ask whether he makes them guilty of the body as offered or as received? There is not one syllable about receiving. I admit that by partaking of the sign they insult the body of Christ, inasmuch as they reject the inestimable boon which is offered them. This disposes of the objection of Heshusius, that Paul is not speaking of the general guilt under which all the wicked lie, but teaches that the wicked by the actual taking of the body invoke a heavier judgment on themselves. It is indeed true that insult is offered to the flesh of Christ by those who with impious disdain and contempt reject it when it is held forth for food. For we maintain that in the Supper Christ holds forth his body to reprobates as well as to believers, but in such manner that those who profane the Sacrament by unworthy receiving make no change in its nature, nor in any respect impair the effect of the promise. But although Christ remains like to himself and true to his promises, it does not follow that what is given is received by all indiscriminately.

Heshusius amplifies and says that Paul does not speak of a slight fault. It is indeed no slight fault which an apostle denounces when he says that the wicked, even though they do not approach the Supper, crucify to themselves the Son of God, and put him to an open shame, and trample his sacred blood under their feet (Heb. 6:6; 10:29). They can do all this without swallowing Christ. The reader sees whether I marvellously twist and turn, as Heshusius foolishly says, involving myself in darkness from a hatred of the light, when I say that men are guilty of the body and blood of Christ in repudiating both the gifts, though eternal truth invites them to partake of them. But he rejoins that this sophism is brushed away like a spider's web by the words of Paul, when he says that they eat and drink judgment to themselves. As if unbelievers under the law did not also eat judgment to themselves, by presuming while impure and polluted to eat the paschal lamb. And yet Heshusius after his own fashion boasts of having made it clear that the body of Christ is taken by the wicked. How much more correct is the view of Augustine, that many in the crowd press on Christ without ever touching him! Still he persists, exclaiming that nothing can be clearer than the declaration that the wicked do not discern the Lord's body, and that darkness is violently and intentionally thrown on the clearest truth by all who deny that the body of Christ is taken by the unworthy. He might have some colour for this, if I denied that the body of Christ is given to the unworthy; but as they impiously reject what is liberally offered to them, they are deservedly condemned for profane and brutish contempt inasmuch as they set at nought the victim by which the sins of the world were expiated and men reconciled to God.

Meanwhile let the reader observe how suddenly heated Heshusius has become. He lately began by saying that the subject was a proper one for mutual conference between pious and learned men, but here he blazes out fiercely against all who dare to doubt or inquire. In the same way he is angry at us for maintaining that the thing which the bread figures is conferred and performed not by the minister but by Christ. Why is he not angry rather with Augustine and Chrysostom, the one teaching that it is administered by man but in a divine manner, on earth but in a heavenly manner; while the other speaks thus: Now Christ is ready; he who spread the table at which he sat now consecrates this one. For the body and blood of Christ are not made by him who has been appointed to consecrate the Lord's table, but by him who was crucified for us, and so on. I have no concern with what Heshusius adds. He says it is a fanatical and sophistical corruption to hold that by the unworthy are meant the weak and those possessed of little faith, though not wholly aliens from Christ. I hope he will find some one to answer him. But this contortionist draws me in to advocate an alien cause, in order to overwhelm me with the crime of a sacrilegious and most cruel parricide, because by my doctrine timid consciences are murdered and driven to despair.

He asks Calvinists with what faith they approach the Supper —with great or little? It is easy to give the answer furnished by the *Institutes*, where I distinctly refute the error of those who require a perfection nowhere to be found, and by this severity keep back from the use of the Supper, not the weak only, but those best qualified. Even children, by the form which we commonly use, are fully instructed how to refute the silly calumny. It is vain for him therefore to display his loquacity by running away from the subject. Lest he pride himself on his performance here, it is right to insert this much by the way. He says two things are diametrically opposed: forgiveness of sins and guilt before the tribunal of God. As if even the least instructed did not know that believers in the same act provoke the wrath of God, and yet by his indulgence obtain favour. We all condemn the craft of Rebecca in substituting Jacob in the place of Esau, and there is no doubt that before God the act deserved severe punishment; yet he so mercifully forgave it, that by means of it Jacob obtained the blessing. It is worth while to observe in passing how sharply he disposes of my objection as absurd, that Christ cannot be separated from his Spirit. His answer is that, since the words of Paul are clear, he assents to them. Does he mean to astonish us by a miracle when he tells us that the blind see? It has been clearly enough shown that nothing of the kind is to be seen in the words of Paul. He endeavours to disentangle himself by saying that Christ is present to his creatures in many ways. But the first thing to be explained is how Christ is present with unbelievers, to be the spiritual food of their souls, and in short the life and salvation of the world. As he adheres so doggedly to the words, I should like to know how the wicked can eat the flesh of Christ which was not crucified for them, and how they can drink the blood which was not shed to expiate their sins? I agree with him that Christ is present as a strict judge when his Supper is profaned. But it is one thing to be eaten, and another to be judge. When he later says that the Holy Spirit dwelt in Saul, we must send him back to his rudiments, that he may learn how to discriminate between the sanctification proper only to the elect and the children of God, and the general power which is proper even to the reprobate. These quibbles, therefore, do not in the slightest degree affect my axiom, that Christ, considered as the living bread and the victim immolated on the cross, cannot enter a human body devoid of his Spirit.

I think that sufficient proof has been given of the ignorance as well as the effrontery, stubbornness, and petulance of Heshusius—such proof as must not only render him offensive to men of worth and sound judgment, but make his own party ashamed of so incompetent a champion. But as he pretends to give a confirmation of his dogma, it may be worth while briefly to discuss what he advances, lest his loud boasting should impose upon the simple. I have shown elsewhere and oftener than once how irrelevant it is here to introduce harangues on the boundless power of God, since the question is not what God can do, but what kind of communion with his flesh the Author of the Supper has taught us to believe. He comes, however, to the point when he brings forward the expressions of Paul and the evangelists; only he exercises his loquacity in the absurdest calumnies, as if it were our purpose to subvert the ordinance of Christ. We have always declared, with equal good faith, sincerity and candour, that we reverently embrace what Paul and the three Evangelists teach, so long as the meaning of their words be investigated with proper soberness and modesty. Heshusius says that they all speak the same thing so much so that there is scarcely a syllable of difference. As if, in their most perfect agreement, there were not an evident variety in the form of expression which may well raise questions. Two of them call the cup the blood of the new covenant; the other two call it a new covenant in the blood. Is there here not one syllable of difference? But granting that the four employ the same words and almost the same syllables, must we forthwith concede what Heshusius affirms, that there is no figure in the words? Scripture makes mention not four times but almost a thousand times of the ears, eyes and right hand of God. If an expression four times repeated excludes all figures, will a thousand passages have no effect at all, or a less effect? Let it be that the question relates not to the fruit of Christ's passion, but to the presence of his body, provided the term presence be not restricted to place. Though I grant this, I deny that the point on which the question turns is whether the words: This is my body, are used in a proper sense or by metonymy; and therefore I hold that it is absurd of Heshusius to infer one from the other. Were any one to concede to him that the bread is called the body of Christ, because it is an exhibitive sign, and at the same time to add that it is called body, essentially and corporeally, what further ground for quarrel would he have?

The proper question, therefore, concerns the mode of communication. However, if he chooses to insist on the words, I have no objection. We must therefore see whether they are to be understood sacramentally, or as implying actual consumption. There is no dispute as to the body which Christ designates, for I have declared often enough above that I imagine no two-bodied Christ, and that therefore the body which was once crucified is given in the Supper. Indeed it is plain from my Commentaries how I have expounded the passage: "The bread which I will give is my flesh, which I will give for the life of the world" (John 6:51).

My exposition is that there are two kinds of giving, because the same body which Christ once offered for our salvation he offers to us every day as spiritual food. All therefore that he says about a symbolical body is nothing better than the slander of a low-class buffoon. It is insufferable to see him blinding the eye of the reader, while fighting with the ghosts and shadows of his own imagination. Equally futile is he when he says that I keep talking only of fruit and efficacy. Everywhere I assert a substantial communion, and discard only a local presence and the figment of an immensity of flesh. But this perverse expositor cannot be appeased unless we concede to him that the words of Paul: "the cup is the new covenant in my blood," are equivalent to "the blood is contained in the cup." If this be granted, he must submit to the disgrace of retracting what he has so tenaciously asserted of the proper and natural meaning of the words. For who will be persuaded by him that there is no figure when the cup is called a covenant in blood, because it contains blood? I do not disguise, however, that I reject this foolish exposition. It does not follow from it that we are redeemed by wine, and that the saying of Christ is false; since, in order to drink the blood of Christ by faith, the thing necessary is not that he come down to earth, but that we rise up to heaven, or rather the blood of Christ must remain in heaven in order that believers may share it among themselves.

Heshusius, to deprive us of all sacramental modes of expression, maintains that we must learn, not from the institution of the passover, but from the words of Christ, what it is that is given to us in the Supper. Yet, in his dizzy way, he immediately flies off in another direction, and finds an appropriate phrase in the words: Circumcision is a covenant. But can anything be more intolerable than this pertinacious denial of the constant usage of Scripture, that the words of the Supper are to be interpreted in a sacramental manner? Christ was a rock; for he was spiritual food. The Holy Spirit was a dove. The water in Baptism is both the Spirit and the blood of Christ (otherwise it would not be the laver of the soul). Christ himself is our passover. While we are agreed as to all these passages, and Heshusius does not dare to deny that the forms of speech in these sacraments are similar, why, whenever the matter of the Supper is raised, does he offer such obstinate opposition? But he says that the words of Christ are clear. What greater obscurity is there in the others?

On the whole, I think I have made it clear how empty is the noise he makes, while trying to force the words of Christ to support his delirious dream. As little effect will he produce on men of sense by his arguments which he deems to be irresistible. He says that under the Old Testament all things were shadowed by types and figures, but that in the New, figures being abolished or rather fulfilled, the reality is exhibited. So be it; but can he hence infer that the water of Baptism is truly, properly, really and substantially the blood of Christ? Far more accurate is Paul (Col. 2:17), who, while he teaches that the body is now substituted for the old figures, does not mean that what was then adumbrated was completed by signs, but holds that it was in Christ himself that the substance and reality were to be sought. Accordingly, a little before, after saying that believers were circumcised in Christ by the circumcision not made with hands, he immediately adds that a pledge and testimony of this is given in Baptism, making the new sacrament correspond with the old. Heshusius after his own fashion quotes from the Epistle to the Hebrews, that the sacrifices of the Old Testament were types of the true.[21] But the term *true* [21] is there applied not to Baptism and the Supper, but to the death and resurrection of Christ. I have acknowledged already that in Baptism and the Supper Christ is offered otherwise than in the legal figures; but unless the reality of which the apostle there speaks is sought in a higher quarter than the sacraments, it will entirely vanish. Therefore, when the presence of Christ is contrasted with the legal shadows, it is wrong to confine it to the Supper, since the reference is to a superior manifestation wherein the perfection of our salvation consists. Even if I granted that the presence of Christ spoken of is to be referred to the sacraments of the New Testament, this would still place Baptism and the Supper on the same footing. Therefore, when Heshusius argues thus:

> The sacraments of the gospel require the presence of Christ;
> The Supper is a sacrament of the gospel:
> Therefore, it requires the presence of Christ;

I in my turn rejoin:

> Baptism is a sacrament of the gospel:
> Therefore, it requires the presence of Christ.

21 Original has the Greek: ἀντίτυπα fuisse τῶν ἀληθινῶν, ἀληθινά.

If he resorts to his last refuge and tells us that it was not said in Baptism: This is my body, this is nothing to the point, which entirely depends on the distinction between the Old Testament and the New. Let him cease, then, from his foolish talk, that if the bread of the Supper is the symbol of an absent thing, it is therefore a symbol of the Old Testament. The reader must, moreover, remember that the controversy concerns not every kind of absence, but only local absence. Heshusius will not allow Christ to be present with us, except by making himself present in several places, wherever the Supper is administered. Hence, too, it appears that he talks absurdly when he opposes presence to fruit. The two things are quite in harmony. Although Christ is distant from us in respect of place, he is yet present by the boundless energy of his Spirit, so that his flesh can give us life. It is still more absurd when he says that we differ in no respect from those under the Old Testament in regard to spiritual eating, because the mode of vivifying is one and the same; and they received just as much as we. But what did he say a little before? That in the New Testament is offered, not the shadows of things, but the reality itself, true righteousness, light, and life, the true High-Priest; that this testament is established and the wrath of God appeased by blood in reality, not in type. What does he understand by spiritual but just the reality, true righteousness, light and life? Now he insists that all these were common to the fathers, which is very absurd, if they are peculiar to the New Testament.

But lest I may seem more intent on refuting my opponent than on instructing my readers, I must briefly remind them that he subverts everything by making the fathers equal to us in the mode of eating; for though they had Christ in common with us, the measure of revelation was by no means equal. Were it otherwise, there would have been no ground for the exclamation: "Blessed are the eyes which see the things which ye see" (Matt. 13:16); and again: "The law and the prophets were until John; grace and truth came by Jesus Christ" (John 1:17; Matt. 11:13). If he answer that this is his understanding, I ask whence spiritual eating comes? If he admits that it is from faith, there is a manifest difference in the very doctrine from which faith springs. The question here concerns not the quantity of faith in individuals, but the nature of the promises under the law. Who then can put up with this snarling fellow, when he tries to stir up odium against us, because we say that the light of faith now is greater than it was among ancient people? He objects by quoting our Saviour's complaint: "When the Son of man cometh, shall he find faith on the earth?" (Luke 18:8). To what end does he quote, unless on this pretext to obtain pardon for his unbelief? Let it be so. Christ will not find faith in a thousand Heshusiuses, nor in the whole of his band. Is it not true that John the Baptist was greater than all the prophets, and yet that the least among the preachers of the gospel was greater than he? (Luke 7:28). The faith of the Galatians was not only small but almost stifled, and yet Paul, while he compares the prophets to children, says that the Galatians and other believers had no longer any need of a pedagogue (Gal. 3:25), as they had grown up; that is, in respect of doctrine and sacraments, but not of men. So far from having profited in the gospel, Heshusius, like a monkey decked out in silk and gold, surpasses all the monks in barbarism.

Regarding the eating of the flesh of Christ, how much better our case is than that of the fathers I have shown in expounding the tenth chapter of the first Epistle to the Corinthians. Still I differ widely from those who dream of a corporeal eating. No doubt life might be infused from the substance of a flesh which as yet did not exist, so that there would be a spiritual eating the same as we now have; but in fact a pledge was given them of an identical communion. Hence it follows that the saying of Augustine is strictly true: that the signs which they had differed from ours in visible form, not in reality. I add, however, that the mode of signifying was different and the measure of grace unequal, because the communion of Christ now exhibited is fuller and more abundant, and also substantial.

When Heshusius says that his controversy with me concerns the pledge, not the reality, I wish my readers to understand what his meaning is. He declares that the fathers were partakers of spiritual eating in an equal degree with us; I hold that it was proportional to the nature and mode of the dispensation. But it is clear that by the interposition of a pledge their faith was confirmed in signs as far as the absence of Christ allowed. We have explained elsewhere how our pledges exhibit Christ present, not indeed in space, but because they set visibly before us the death and resurrection of Christ, wherein consists the entire fulness of salvation. Meanwhile Heshusius, contradicting himself, disapproves of my distinction between faith and spiritual eating. If we are to believe him, it is mere sophism. So no part of it is allowed to pass without criticism and censure. Thus it must be a mere sophism when Paul says that Christ dwells in our hearts by faith, that we are ingrafted into his body, that we are crucified and buried with him, in short that we are bone of his bone, and flesh of his flesh, so that his life is ours. Whoever does not see that these things are the fruits and effects of faith, and therefore different from faith, is more than blind. Equally blind is it to deny that we obtain by faith the inestimable blessing of a vivifying communion with Christ. But he does not care what confusion he causes, provided he is not forced to acknowledge that believers have outside the Supper the very thing they receive in the Supper. But, he says, eating must be distinguished from sealing. Certainly; but just in the same way as the sealing which takes place in Baptism differs from spiritual washing. Are we not, outside Baptism, cleansed by the blood of Christ and regenerated by the Spirit? It is true that to help our infirmity a visible testimony is added, the better to confirm the thing signified; and not only so, but to bestow in greater truth and fulness what we receive by the faith of the gospel even without any external action.

Here he displays his malignant and vicious temper, by daring to charge me with teaching in the catechism that the use of the Supper is not unnecessary, because we there receive Christ more fully, though by the faith of the gospel Christ is already so far ours and dwells in us. This doctrine, if we are to believe Heshusius, is not only absurd, but insulting to the whole ministry of the gospel. Let him then accuse Paul of blasphemy for saying that Christ is formed in us like the foetus in the womb. His words to the Galatians are well-known: "My little children, for whom I again travail as in birth until Christ Jesus be formed in you" (Gal. 4:19). This is not unlike what he says in another place: "Until ye grow up into a perfect man, to the measure of the stature of the fulness of Christ" (Eph. 4:13). There is no need of many words to prove this. For if Christ dwells in us by faith, it is certain that he in a manner grows up in us in proportion to the increase of faith. Heshusius objects: What then is to become of the infant which, immediately after being baptized, happens to die without having received the Supper? As if I were imposing some law or obligation on God, and denying that he works, when he pleases, without the aid of the Supper. For I hold with Augustine, that there may be invisible sanctification without the visible sign, just as on the other hand there may be the visible sign without true sanctification. John the Baptist was never admitted to the Supper, and yet surely this did not prevent him from possessing Christ. All

I teach is that we attain to communion with Christ gradually, so that it is not without cause that he added the Supper to the gospel and to Baptism. Hence, though God calls suddenly away from the world many who are children, not in age merely but in faith, yet one spark from the Spirit is sufficient to give them a life which swallows up all that is mortal in them, as Paul also declares elsewhere (Rom. 8:11). But in the eyes of Heshusius, Paul appears only an inferior authority, since he charges him with teaching a doctrine which is absurd and impious. It is indeed under my name that he charges him; but where is the difference, if the impiety of which he accuses me be taught in Paul's words? What I teach, therefore, remains intact: that the communion of Christ is conferred upon us in different degrees, not merely in the Supper but independently of it.

Though I fancy it is very well known to the whole world that our doctrine is clearly approved by the consent of the primitive Church, Heshusius has again opened up the question, and introduced certain ancient writers as opposed to us and in favour of his opinion. Hitherto, indeed, I have intentionally not dealt with this matter, because I was unwilling to do what has been done already. This was first performed with accuracy and skill by Œcolampadius, who clearly showed that the figment of a local presence was unknown to the ancient Church. He was succeeded by Bullinger, who performed the task with equal felicity. The whole was crowned by Peter Martyr, who left nothing more to be done. As far as Westphal's importunity compelled me, I believe that to sound and impartial readers I have proved my agreement with antiquity. Indeed what I said ought to have stopped the mouths even of the contentious. But however solid the reasons by which they are confuted, it is like talking to the deaf, and I shall therefore be content with a few brief remarks, to let my readers see that this recent copyist is not less barren and foolish than Westphal was. It is rather strange that, while he is ashamed to use the authority of John of Damascus and Theophylact, he calls them not the least among ecclesiastical writers. Sound and sober readers will find more learning and piety in a single commentary on Matthew, which is falsely alleged to be an unfinished work of Chrysostom, than in all the theology of the Damascene. The writer, whoever he may have been, distinctly says that the body of Christ is only given to us by the ministry. I thought it proper to mention this briefly, lest any one might suppose that Heshusius was acting generously in declining the support of the Damascene. While I grant that he also repudiates Clement of Alexandria and Origen, let my readers remember that he can select at will from antiquity whatever writers suit his purpose. He begins with Ignatius. I wish his writings were extant to prevent his name from being so frequently employed as a disguise by impostors like Servetus and Heshusius. For what kind of candour is it that quotes an epistle which scarcely one of the monkish herd would acknowledge to be genuine? Those who have read this silly production know that it speaks only of Lent, and chrism, and tapers, and fast and festival days, which began to creep in under the influence of superstition and ignorance long after the days of Ignatius. But what then of this fictitious Ignatius? He says that some reject the Supper and oblations because they deny that the Eucharist is the flesh of Christ which was sacrificed for us. But what kinship or community can there be between those heretics and ourselves who regard with reverence the Eucharist in which we know Christ gives us his flesh to eat? But he will reply that the Eucharist is styled the flesh. It is; but improperly, unless we shut our eyes against the clearest light. The name of Eucharist is taken from the action of thanksgiving or from the whole Sacrament. Take which you please, certainly the literal meaning cannot be urged.

That we may not be obliged repeatedly to dispose of the same criticism, let it be understood once for all that we have no quarrel with the usual forms of expression. Early writers everywhere call the consecrated bread the body of Christ; for why may they not imitate the only begotten Son of God, on whose lips we ought to hang so as to learn wisdom? But how very different is this from the barbarous fiction, that the bread is literally the body which is there corporeally eaten. With equal honesty he classes us with Messalians and enthusiasts, who denied that the use of the Holy Supper does either good or harm; as if I had not from the first spoken of the utility of this mystery in loftier terms than all that crowd who disturb the world by raging like bacchanalians against me. Indeed they kept perfect silence as to the end for which the Supper was instituted and the benefit which believers derive from it, until the reproaches of many pious people compelled them to take excerpts from my writings, to avoid being always charged with suppressing what is most important in them. But he does not hesitate to give us Schwenkfeld for an associate. Why do you, like a cowardly dog afraid of the wolves, only attack unoffending guests? When Schuencfeldius was infecting Germany with his poison, we withstood him boldly, and thus incurred his deepest hatred; but now, if Heshusius is to be believed, it was we who fostered him. Then, when he involves us in the impious fancies of Nestorius, what answer can I give but just that so wicked a slanderer refutes himself?

He next comes down to Justin Martyr, whose authority I willingly allow to be great. But what damage does he do our cause? He says that the bread of the Supper is not ordinary bread. This is because he had previously explained that none are admitted to partake of it but those who have been washed by Baptism and have embraced the gospel. He afterwards goes farther: As Christ was made flesh, so we are taught that the food which was blessed by him by the word of prayer, and by which our flesh and blood are nourished through transmutation, is the flesh and blood of Christ himself. The comparison of the mystical consecration in the Supper with the incarnation of Christ seems to Heshusius enough for victory; as if Justin affirmed that the one was equally miraculous with the other, while all he meant is that the flesh which Christ once assumed from us is daily given us for food. For in confirming this opinion he is content simply to quote the words of Christ, and contends for no more than that this benefit is imparted only to the disciples of Christ who have been initiated into true piety.

I grant to Heshusius that Irenaeus is a clearer expounder of Justin's brief statement. I will not quote all his words, but will omit nothing relevant. He inveighs against heretics who denied that flesh is capable of incorruption. If so, he says, neither has the Lord redeemed us by his own blood, nor is the cup of the Eucharist the communion of his blood, nor the bread which we break the communion of his body. The blood comes only from the veins and other human substances in which the Son of God truly redeemed us. And since we are his members and are nourished by created things, and he himself confers created things upon us, making his sun to rise and rain to descend as it pleases him, he declared that this cup, which is a created thing, is his body by which he nourishes our bodies. Therefore when the Word of God is pronounced over the mingled cup and broken bread, there is formed a Eucharist of the body and blood of Christ, by which the substance of our flesh is nourished and edified. How is it denied that the flesh is capable of the gift of God who is eternal life, seeing it is nourished by the body and blood of Christ and is his member?—as the apostle says: We are members of his body and of his bones, and so on.

Let the reader attend to the intention of Irenaeus. He is not discussing whether we eat Christ corporeally; he only contends that his flesh and blood become meat and drink to us, so as to infuse spiritual life into our flesh and blood. The whole question cannot be better solved than by attending to the context. There is no communion of the flesh of Christ except a spiritual one, which is both perpetual and given to us independently of the use of the Supper. Heshusius insists that the only way in which we receive the body of Christ is corporeally and internally; there is nothing he can less tolerate than the doctrine that believers are substantially conjoined with Christ. For throughout the whole book he insists on this cardinal thesis, that spiritual eating is nothing but faith, and that the Supper would be an empty show, unless corporeal eating were added precisely at the moment when the bread is introduced into the mouth. This he repeats a hundred times. But what does Irenaeus say? Surely all see that of the communion we enjoy in the Supper, he neither thinks nor speaks differently from Paul, when he says that believers, both in life and in death, are the members of Christ, flesh of his flesh and bone of his bones (Eph. 5:30). To overcome his stupidity, I must speak in still plainer terms. He wishes to prove from the words of Irenaeus, that the body of Christ is received, not only in a spiritual manner, but corporeally by the mouth, and that it is heretical to acknowledge only the spiritual eating of which Christ discourses in the sixth chapter of John, and Paul in the fifth chapter of the Ephesians; because corporeal eating is not rightly disjoined from bread. What does Irenaeus answer? That we are nourished by bread and wine in the sacred Supper, that, as Paul declares, we are members of Christ. There is an end, therefore, to that distinction between corporeal and spiritual eating of which he bragged and boasted as the cardinal point of the whole controversy. Who will believe him when he says that this is sophistry? Irenaeus affirms that the two propositions: This is my body, and: We are the members of Christ, are the same both in degree and quality; whereas this censor of ours exclaims that unless the two be separated, all piety is subverted and God is denied. Indeed he distinctly calls Epicureans those who think that nothing more is conferred in the Supper than to make us one body with Christ.

Our view is not damaged by what is affirmed alike by

Tertullian, Hilary and himself: that our flesh is nourished
by the flesh of Christ, in hope of eternal life; for they do not
refer to such a mode as Heshusius devises. On the contrary,
they remove all ambiguity by referring to the perpetual
union which we have with Christ and teaching that it is the
effect of faith, whereas according to Heshusius corporeal eating is
confined to the Supper, and is as different from spiritual eating as
earth is from heaven. Hilary says (*lib.* 8, *De Trinitate*): As to the
reality of the flesh and blood, there is no room left for ambiguity. For now, by the declaration of both our Lord himself
and our faith, they are meat indeed and drink indeed; and
these received and taken cause us to be in Christ and Christ in
us. Is not this reality? He himself then is in us through his flesh,
and we are in him, while what we are with him is in God. That
we are in him by the sacrament of communicated flesh and
blood, he himself declares when he says: "The world now seeth
me not, but ye shall see me; because I live, ye shall live also;
because I am in the Father, and you in me" (John 14:19 ff.).
If he wished unity of will only to be understood, why did he
point out a certain degree and order in completing the union?
Just because, while he is in the Father by the nature of his
divinity, we are in him by his corporeal nativity, and he on the
other hand in us by the mystery of the sacraments. Thus perfect
union through the Mediator is taught: we remaining in him,
he remained in the Father, and remaining in the Father remained in us; and so we advance to unity with the Father,
since while he is naturally in the Father according to birth,
we are naturally in him, and he remains naturally in us. That
there is this natural unity in us, he himself thus declared:
"Whoso eateth my flesh, and drinketh my blood, abideth in
me, and I in him" (John 6:56). For none will be in him save
those in whom he himself has been, having in himself the
assumed flesh of them only who have taken his own. Shortly after
he says: This is the cause of our life, that we who are in ourselves carnal have life abiding in us by the flesh of Christ.
Although he repeatedly says that we are naturally united to
Christ, it is apparent from this short sentence that his only
object is to prove that the life of Christ abides in us, because
we are one with him.

Irenaeus shows no less clearly that he is speaking of the perpetual union which is spiritual. He says (Bk. 4, ch. 34): Our
opinion is congruous with the Eucharist, and the Eucharist
confirms our opinion. For we offer to him the things which are

his, in consistently proclaiming the communion and union of flesh and spirit. For as that which is earthly bread, on being set apart by God is no longer common bread but a Eucharist consisting of two things, an earthly and a heavenly, so similarly our bodies, receiving the Eucharist, are no longer corruptible but have hope of resurrection. In the fifth book he explains more fully that we are the members of Christ, and united to his flesh because of his Spirit dwelling in us. The reason why Heshusius charges us with the greatest impudence is precisely because we deny that propositions, which perfectly agree with our doctrine, are adverse to it.

If a more familiar exposition is required, Cyril will supply it. For in his third book, explaining our Saviour's discourse contained in the sixth chapter of John, he acknowledges that there is no other eating in the Supper than that by which the body of Christ gives life to us, and which by our participation in it leads us back to incorruption. In his fourth book (ch. 13) he says: Our Lord gave his body for the life of all, and by it again infuses life into us; how he does this I will briefly explain, according to my ability. For when the life-giving Son of God dwelt in the flesh, and was as a whole, so to speak, united to the ineffable whole by means of union, he made the flesh itself vivifying, and hence this flesh vivifies those who partake of it. As he asserts that this takes place both in the Supper and outside the Supper, let Heshusius explain what is meant by "infusing life into us." In the seventeenth chapter he says: Were any one to pour wax on melted wax, the one must become intermingled with the other; so if any one receives the flesh and blood of the Lord, he must be united with him, so that he be found in Christ and Christ in him. In the twenty-fourth chapter he distinctly maintains that the flesh of Christ is made vivifying by the virtue of the Spirit, so that Christ is in us because the Spirit of God dwells in us.

After celebrating vain and ridiculous triumphs over those holy writers, he insolently brags, since he cannot conceal it, of relinquishing Clement of Alexandria, because he is overwhelmed by his authority. He also boasts that he not infrequently acts as our advocate and representative, by enhancing and amplifying to the best of his ability everything advanced by us, that he may know whether there is any force —and so on. If this is true, he must not only be feeble, but altogether unnerved and broken down. Still, if he employed his abilities in judging aright, instead of devoting them entirely to quarrelling and invective, much of the intemperance with which he burns would abate. He certainly would not charge me with maintaining an allegorical eating, while I affirm that allegory is condemned by the words of Christ. But it is right that heaven should strike with such giddiness those whom pertinacious ambition drives into combat, so that they prostitute both modesty and faith.

It is strange that, while censuring Origen so severely that he will not class him among writers worthy of credit, he does not similarly strike out Tertullian. We see with what implacable rage he blazes against all who presume to interpret the words of Christ: This is my body, in any other but their proper and native sense, holding those who do so guilty of a sacrilegious corruption. But when he feels himself challenged by the words of Tertullian, instead of attempting to overwhelm him with violence, he rather tries to escape by flight. Tertullian says: Christ made his own body the bread received and distributed to the disciples, by saying: This is my body, that is, the figure of my body. Now it would not have been the figure, unless it were the body of the reality; for an empty thing, such as a spectre cannot receive a figure. Or if he made the bread his body because it lacked the reality of body, then he must have offered bread for us. But to hold that the bread was crucified would contribute to the vanity of Marcion. Tertullian proves that the bread was the true substance of the flesh of Christ, because it could not be a figure without being the figure of a true substance. Heshusius is dissatisfied with this mode of expression because it seems dangerous; but, as if he had forgotten himself, he admits it, provided there is no deception under it. By deception he means calling the bread the sign or figure of absent flesh. That he may not gloss over the term absence in his usual manner, let the reader remember, as I earlier reminded him, that though Christ in respect of place and actual observation is absent, still believers truly enjoy and are nourished by the present substance of his flesh.

All his quibbles, however, cannot wrest from us the support of Tertullian. For when he says that the bread was made body, the meaning can only be found in the context. To consecrate the blood in wine cannot be equivalent to the expression: to attach the blood to wine; it corresponds to the next sentence, where he says that Christ confirmed the substance of his flesh when he delivered a covenant sealed with his own blood, because it cannot be blood unless it belong to true flesh. No man can doubt that the sealing which was performed on the cross is compared with the consecration by which Christ enters into an eternal covenant with his people. Nor does Heshusius make anything of the other passage, in which he says that our flesh eats the body and blood of Christ, in order that it may be fed on God, in other words come to participation in the Godhead. The sum is that it is absurd and impious to exclude our flesh from the hope of resurrection, seeing that Christ dignifies it with the symbols of spiritual life. Accordingly he ranks in the same class not only Baptism but anointing, the sign of the cross, and the laying on of hands. But with strange stupidity, in order to prove that we do not by faith alone become partakers of the flesh of Christ, Heshusius quotes a passage from a tract on the Lord's Prayer, in which Tertullian says: the petition for daily bread may be understood spiritually, because Christ is our bread, because Christ is our life, because he is the Word of the living God who came down from heaven, and his body is held to be in the bread. Hence he concludes that we seek perpetuity from Christ and individuality from his body. I ask whether, if it had been his intention to play a double game, he could have given better support to our cause? Such is the ground he has for boasting in antiquity.

With similar dexterity he adopts Cyprian as his patron. Cyprian contends that the blood of Christ is not to be denied to believers who are called to the service of Christ and obliged to shed their own blood. What can he prove by this but just that the blood of Christ is given us by the cup as the body is given under the symbol of bread? In another passage, when disputing with the Aquarii he says that the vivifying blood of Christ cannot be regarded as being in the cup if there be wanting the wine by which the blood itself is shown, he clearly confirms our doctrine. For what is meant by the blood being represented by the wine, but just that the wine is a sign or figure of the blood? Shortly after he repeats the same thing, saying that water alone cannot express the blood of Christ, that is designate it. But he says at the same time that the blood is in the cup; as if the idea of local enclosing ever entered the mind of this holy martyr, who is only occupied with the question whether the mystical cup should be mixed with water alone to represent the blood of Christ?

Another passage quoted by Heshusius is this: How dare they give the Eucharist to the profane, that is desecrate the holy body of Christ, seeing it is written: "Whoso eateth or drinketh

unworthily, shall be guilty of the body and blood of the Lord?"
I neither think differently, nor am I wont to speak differently.
But by what logic did this good man learn to conclude from
these words that the body of Christ is given to the unworthy?
Everyone sees that the word *giving* applies to the Eucharist.
Cyprian holds that to admit all indiscriminately is a profanation of the sacred body. This is the occasion for paeans on the
part of our Thraso. In another passage Cyprian says that
the wicked, who with impious hands intrude into the Supper,
invade the body of Christ; and he attacks bitterly the sacrilegious persons who are incensed with priests for not at once
receiving the body of the Lord with polluted hands, or drinking
his blood with polluted lips; as if it were not known before this
that this mode of speaking was common with early writers, or
as if I had any objection to the same style, having many years
ago quoted the same passage, and another similar to it, from
Ambrose. Heshusius does not see the absurdity in which he
involves himself; for it will follow that Christ himself is exposed
to the licentiousness and violence of the ungodly, since Cyprian
there also says that they do violence to his flesh and blood.

Eusebius quotes a passage in which Dionysius of Alexandria
denies that it is lawful to initiate by a new Baptism any one
who has long been a partaker of the flesh and blood of the
Lord and has received the sacred food. From this Heshusius
argues that, if he who was baptized by heretics has received
the body of Christ, it must be eaten without faith and repentance; as if there were no difference between thoughtlessness or
error and real impiety.

He imagined that he was to gain much by adorning with
splendid encomiums the ancient writers whose names he
falsely obtrudes; but he has only made himself more than
ridiculous. With loud mouth he thunders forth their praises,
and then, on coming to the point, he is found unsupported by
them. Athanasius, he says, is a divine writer worthy of immortal
praise. Who denies it? But what of it? Just this, that in stating
that Christ was a high-priest by means of his own body, and by
the same means delivered a mystery to us, saying: This is my
body, and: This is the blood of the New, not of the Old Testament, it is evident that he speaks of the true body and blood in
the Supper. We declare it impossible without inexcusable
violence to separate the words: The body which is delivered for
you, The blood which is shed for the remission of sins; are we
then imagining the blood to be unreal? Athanasius then teaches

rightly that a mystery has been consecrated for us by the flesh and blood of Christ; nor could anything be said that was better fitted to explain our view. For had not Christ been possessed of true flesh and true blood (the only point there concerned), the consecration of the Supper by which our salvation is placed in them would be vain.

I have already shown how preposterously he puts Hilary up against us. He distinctly treats of a vivifying participation of Christ, which does not demand the external use of the Supper, but maintains perpetual vigour in believers. Heshusius says that he does not dispute this. Of what use then is it for him to twist against us words which have no bearing on the point? Still more absurdly does he say that we are refuted by the single expression: we receive the flesh of Christ under a mystery. As if *under a mystery* were not just equivalent to *sacramentally*. This again is said most appositely for the confirmation of our doctrine. But lest any one should think that he errs through folly merely, he also adds, with supreme malice, that according to us divinity alone is given us in the Supper. This is his reason for saying that this one passage should in the judgment of all suffice to settle the controversy.

He betrays himself in the same way in quoting Epiphanius. This writer, discoursing on how man is created in the image of God, says: If it is understood of the body, there cannot be a proper likeness between what is visible and palpable, and the Spirit which is invisible and incomprehensible; whereas, if it refers to the soul, there is a great difference, because the soul, being liable to many weaknesses and defects, does not contain the divinity within itself. He therefore concludes that God, who is incomprehensible, truly performs what he bestows upon men in respect of his image. He afterwards adds: "And how many things are deduced from the like! For we see how our Saviour took the cup into his hands, as it is recorded in the Gospel, how he rose up at the Supper, and took, and after giving thanks said: That is this of mine. But we see that it is not equal to or like either a corporeal shape, or an invisible deity, or bodily members; for it is round and, as to feeling, insensible. He wished by grace to say: That is this of mine; and no man refuses credence to his words. For he who believes not that he is true in what he said, has fallen from grace and from faith." Let the reader attend to the state of the case. Epiphanius contends that, though not at all the same, yet the image of God truly shines in man, just as the bread is truly called body.

Hence it is plain that nothing is less accordant with the mind of this writer than the dream of Heshusius, that the bread is truly and corporeally body. He asks why Epiphanius insists on faith in the words of the Supper, if the bread of the Eucharist is not the body. Just because it is only by faith we apprehend that corruptible food is the pledge of eternal life. Meat for the body, says Paul, and the body for meat, but God will destroy both (I Cor. 6:13). In the bread and wine we seek a spiritual nourishment, to quicken our souls in the hope of a blessed resurrection. We ask Christ that we may be united to him, that he may dwell in us and be one with us. But Epiphanius deals not with the fruit or efficacy of the Supper, but with the substance of the body. How true this is, let the reader judge from his concluding words. Before speaking of the ordinance of the Supper, he says: The figure began with Moses; the figure was opened up by John; but the gift was perfected in Christ. All therefore have what is according to the image, but not according to nature. They have what is according to the image, but they have it not in respect of equality with God. For God is incomprehensible, a Spirit above all spirit, light above all light. He sets limits to things, but does not abandon them. I marvel how Heshusius dares to make mention of faith, while he maintains that the body of Christ is eaten without faith, and bitterly assails us for requiring faith.

He boasts that Basil is on his side, because he applies the terms profane and impious to those who dare with uncleanness of soul to touch the body of Christ, in just the sense in which early writers often say that the body of Christ falls to the earth and is consumed, because they never hesitated to transfer the name of the thing to the symbol.

I acknowledged earlier that Ambrose has spoken in the same way; but in what sense is apparent from his interpretation of the words of Christ. He says: Having been redeemed by the death of Christ, when commemorating this event by eating the flesh and blood which were offered for us, we signify—and so on. Shortly after he says: The covenant was therefore established by blood, because blood is a witness of divine grace, as a type of which we receive the mystical cup of blood. A little later: What is it to be guilty of the body, but just to be punished for the death of the Lord? He accordingly bids us come to the communion with a devout mind, recollecting that reverence is due to him whose body we approach to take. For each ought to consider with himself that it is the Lord whose blood he drinks in a mystery. Heshusius is shameless enough to produce this passage against us, though it supports us as if we had borrowed the expression of our doctrine from it.

Heshusius even opposes us with verse. Because Gregory Nazianzus, indulging in poetic style, says that priests carry in their hands the plasma of the great God, he boldly infers that the bread is properly the body of Christ. My answer, which I am confident will be approved by all men of sense, is simply this, that Gregory meant nothing more than Augustine has expressed somewhat more informally when, speaking of Christ holding forth the bread to his disciples, he says: He bore himself in a manner in his hands. By this expression the difficulty is completely solved. He says (*Serm. de Pasch.*): Be not impiously deluded when hearing of the blood, and passion, and death of God, but confidently eat the body and drink the blood, if thou desirest life. But Heshusius absurdly twists these words of his to a meaning foreign to them; for he is not there speaking of the mystery of the Supper, but of our Saviour's incarnation and death, though I do not deny that Gregory, in the words eating and drinking, where, however, he is recommending faith, alludes to the Supper.

About Jerome, there is no occasion to say much. Heshusius quotes a passage, in which he says that the bread is the body of Christ. I make him welcome to more. For he writes to Heliodorus that the clergy make the body of Christ. Elsewhere also he says that they distribute his blood to the people (*in Malach.* ch. 1). The only question is: in what sense does he say this? If we add the clause *in a mystery*, will not the controversy be at an end, since it is clear that *in a mystery* and *corporeally* are antithetical? As Jerome removes all doubt by expressing this exception, what is to be gained by sophistical objection? I admit that in another passage Jerome says that the wicked eat the body of Christ unworthily, but as he adds that they in this way pollute it, why seek for a difficulty where there is none? Unless, indeed, Heshusius will so subject Christ to the licentiousness of the ungodly that they pollute his pure and holy flesh with infection. Yet Jerome openly explains that, where it is impurely handled, the body of Christ is polluted bread. But in another passage Jerome speaks more clearly; for he distinctly denies that the wicked eat the flesh of Christ or drink his blood. So *in Hos.* ch. 9: The wicked sacrifice many victims and eat the flesh of them, deserting the one sacrifice of Christ, and not eating his flesh, though his flesh is meat to them that believe. Why does Heshusius childishly cavil about a word, when so transparent an explanation of the matter is provided?

The substance of all his sophistical jargon may be formed into a syllogism thus:

Whatever is called the body of Christ is his body in substance and reality;

Irenaeus, Tertullian, Cyprian, Justin, Ambrose, Jerome, Augustine, and several others, call the bread of the sacred Supper the body of Christ:

Therefore, the bread of the Supper is the body of Christ in substance and reality.

While Heshusius thus confidently extricates himself, I should like to hear his answer to a distinction by which Jerome so completely dissipates and disperses his dream, that his words require to be modified in an opposite direction. He says (*Ep. ad Eph.*, ch. 1): The flesh and blood of Christ is taken in a twofold sense, either spiritual and divine, of which he himself said: My flesh is meat indeed; or the flesh which was crucified, and the blood which was shed by the soldier's spear. I do not suppose, indeed, that Jerome imagined a twofold flesh; yet I believe he points out a spiritual, and therefore different mode of communicating, lest a corporeal eating be invented.

The passage which Heshusius has produced from Chrysostom I will run over briefly. Because that pious teacher enjoins us to approach with faith, that we may not only receive the body when held forth, but much more touch it with a clean heart, this able expositor infers that some receive without faith and with an unclean heart; as if Chrysostom were hinting at the corporeal reception of a substantial body, and not by the term body commending the dignity of the ordinance. What if he elsewhere explains himself, and at the same time clearly unfolds the mind of Paul? He asks (*Hom. 27 in 1 Cor.*): What is it to be guilty of the body and blood of the Lord? Since it has been shed, he shows that murder was involved not merely sacrifice. As his enemies did not pierce him that they might drink, but that they might shed, so he who communicates unworthily obtains no benefit. Surely even the blind may now see that Chrysostom holds the wicked guilty, not of drinking, but of shedding the blood. With greater folly Heshusius transfers what was said by Chrysostom concerning the spiritual eating of the soul to the stomach and bowels. The words are: The body is set before us,

not only that we may touch it, but that we may eat and be
filled. Heshusius holds this to be equivalent to saying that it is
received into the bowels.

In producing Augustine as an advocate or witness, he reaches
the height of impudence. This holy man tells us to receive in
the bread that which hung on the cross. According to Heshusius, nothing can be clearer than these words. Doubtless, if only
we agreed about the mode of receiving. Thus when he says in
his *Epistle to Januarius* that the order of the Church should be
approved, that men go fasting to the sacred table, so that the
body of Christ may enter the mouth before any other food, if
we add: *in a mystery*, or: *sacramentally*, all contention will cease.
But Heshusius, absurdly laying hold of an ambiguous term,
loses sight of the point in dispute. In his sermon on the words of
the apostle, by speaking of a twofold eating, namely a spiritual
and a sacramental, he distinctly declares that the wicked who
partake of the Supper eat the flesh of Christ. Yes; but, as he
elsewhere teaches, sacramentally. Let Heshusius say he will
deny that the sun shines at midday, if these passages do not
clearly refute our doctrine; I still feel confident that in my
answer to Westphal I so completely disposed of his calumnious
charges and those of his companions, that even the contentious,
who have any remnants of candour, would rather be silent
than incur derision by imitating the petulance of Heshusius.
He pretends that Augustine asserts the true presence of the
body of Christ in the Eucharist, because he says that the
body is given in the bread and the blood in the cup, distributed
by the hands of the priests, and taken not only by faith but by
the mouth also, not only by the pious but also by the wicked.
I answer that unless a clear definition is given of the sense in
which Augustine uses the term body, Heshusius is acting
deceitfully. But where can we find a better expounder than
Augustine himself? Besides using the term Eucharist or Sacrament of the body promiscuously in the same passages, he
clearly explains his meaning in one where he says that the
sacraments, in respect of resemblance, receive the names of the
things which they signify, and accordingly that the Sacrament
of the body is in a sense the body (*Ep. 23 ad Bonif.*). Wherefore, as often as Heshusius obtrudes the ambiguous expression,
it will be easy to rejoin that Augustine in so speaking did not
forget himself, but follows the rule which he prescribes to others
(*Contra Adimant.*). To the same effect, he elsewhere (*in Ps. 3*)
calls the sign of the body a figure. Again he says (*in Ps. 33*) that

T.T.—20

Christ in a manner carried himself in his own hands. Or let me be silent, and let Augustine clear himself of the calumny. It is because of resemblance he transfers the name of the thing signified to the external symbol, and accordingly calls the bread the body of Christ, not properly or substantially, as Heshusius pretends, but in a manner of speaking.

The view which the pious writer took of the presence is perfectly apparent from the *Epistle to Dardanus*, where he says Christ gave immortality to his flesh but did not destroy its nature. We are not to think that in respect of this nature he is everywhere diffused; for we must beware of so elevating the divinity of the man as to destroy the reality of the body. It does not follow that what is in God is everywhere as God. At length he concludes that he who is the only-begotten Son of God and at the same time the Son of Man, is everywhere wholly present as God, and in the temple of God, that is the Church, is as it were the inhabiting God, and is in a certain place in heaven in the manner of a real body. Of the same purport is the following passage (*in Joann. ev. Tract. 50*): We always have Christ present to us in majesty; in the flesh, he truly said: Me ye have not always. I pass over similar passages in which the holy writer declares how averse he is to the idea of a local presence. Several passages show how wretchedly Heshusius quibbles about his assertion that the body of Christ is eaten by the wicked. First, he opposes the virtue of the Sacrament to the visible Sacrament; he makes an antithesis of eating inwardly and outwardly, of eating with the heart and chewing with the teeth. Were there any invisible eating of the body different from spiritual eating, a threefold division would be required. Shortly after he repeats the same antithesis (*in Joann. ev. Tract. 26*): It is beyond question that he who does not abide in Christ, and in whom Christ does not abide neither eats his flesh nor drinks his blood spiritually, although he press the Sacrament of the body carnally and visibly with his teeth. If Augustine had approved of the fiction of Heshusius, he would have said: "although he eat the body corporeally." But the pious teacher is always consistent with himself, and here declares nothing different from what he afterwards teaches when he says (*in Joann. ev. Tract. 59*): The other disciples ate the bread as the Lord,[22] whereas Judas ate the bread of the Lord against the Lord. This is well confirmed by another passage, where he again opposes as things contrary to each other *sacramental* and *true* eating of the flesh of Christ.

[22] Original has *panem Dominum* in straight apposition.

Hence it follows that it is not truly eaten by the wicked. In short, what he understands by the expression sacramental he shows more fully when he declares that good and bad communicate in the signs (*Contra Faustum*, Bk. 13, ch. 16). He says elsewhere (*Serm. 2 de verb. Apost.*): Then the body and blood of Christ will be life to all, if what is taken visibly in the Sacrament is in reality spiritually eaten and drunk. If Heshusius objects that the wicked do not eat spiritually, I ask what Augustine means by the reality of which he makes believers only to partake? Moreover, if Augustine thought that the body of Christ is substantially eaten by the wicked, he ought to have represented it as visible, since nothing is attributed to the wicked but a visible taking. If, as Heshusius pretends, one sentence of Augustine is worth more in his estimation than ten prolix harangues of other fathers, any schoolboy must see that he is worse than a blockhead if these striking passages make no impression on him. And certainly when I see myself engaged with such a buffoon, it so displeases me that I am almost ashamed at spending my time in discussing his frivolities.

Having completed this part of the story, he again flies off, and tries to lead us away from the subject. No doubt while he goes up and down gathering invectives like little flowers, he seems to himself a very showy rhetorician; but when I hear his frivolous loquacity, I seem to be listening to a trashy street-crier. He pretends to discern in us the express and special characteristics of heretics: that when we are unable to defend our error we clothe it with deceitful words. But when we come to the point, what deceptions does he discover, or what subterfuges, what frauds, or cavils, or tricks does he detect? I omit the Greek terms of which he would not deprive himself; but he only betrays his ignorance by substituting adjectives for substantives. He admits that I reject metaphors and allegory and have recourse to metonymy, but his deceit is not yet apparent. Next he says that I repudiate the sentiment of those who affirm that to eat the body of Christ is nothing else than to embrace his benefits by faith. It is not true that this distinction yields more smoke than light;[23] it is an apt and significant exposition of the subject. My thesis, that spiritually to eat the flesh of Christ is something greater and more excellent than to believe, he calls a chimera. What answer shall I give to this impudent assertion, but just that he is mentally blind, since he cannot understand what is so plain and obvious? When he represents me as

[23] Original has *fumum pro luce affert.*

substituting merit and benefit for flesh and blood, and shortly afterwards adds that I acknowledge no other presence in the Supper than that of the deity, my writings, without a word from me, refute the impudent calumny. For not to mention many other passages, after detailed treatment in my Catechism of the whole ordinance, the following passage occurs:[24]

> *Minister*: Have we in the Supper a mere symbol of those benefits you mention, or is their reality exhibited to us there?
>
> *Child*: Since our Lord Jesus Christ is the truth itself, there can be no doubt but that the promises which he there gives us, he at the same time also implements, adding the reality to the symbol. Therefore I do not doubt but that, as testified by words and signs, he thus also makes us partakers of his substance, by which we are joined in one life with him.
>
> *Minister*: But how can this be, when Christ's body is in heaven, and we are still pilgrims on earth?
>
> *Child*: He accomplishes this by the miraculous and secret virtue of his Spirit, for whom it is not difficult to associate things that are otherwise separate by an interval of space.

Moreover, I say in my *Institutes* (Bk. IV, ch. 17, para. 7): "I am not satisfied with those who, when they would show the mode of communion, teach that we are partakers of the Spirit of Christ, omitting all mention of the flesh and blood; as if it were said to no purpose, 'My flesh is meat indeed'," and so on. This is followed by a lengthy explanation of the subject, and something too had been said on it earlier.

In the Second Book I fancy I had refuted with clarity and care the fiction of Osiander, which he falsely accuses me of following. Osiander imagined that righteousness is conferred on us by the deity of Christ. I showed, on the contrary, that salvation and life are to be sought from the flesh of Christ in which he sanctified himself, and in which he consecrates Baptism and the Supper. It will also be there seen how completely I have disposed of his dream of essential righteousness.

I have got the same return from Heshusius that he made to his preceptor Melanchthon. The laws make false witnesses infamous, and enact severe punishments against calumniators. If to corrupt public records is criminal, even more severely ought the miscreant to be punished who, in one passage, is convicted of three crimes: gross calumny, false testimony, and corruption of written documents. Why he so eagerly

[24] See Catechism of Geneva, p. 137

assails me with bitter invective I do not know, unless it be that he has no fear of being paid back in kind. I insist on the real thing, which he would by no means wish. I say that although Christ is absent from the earth in respect of the flesh, yet in the Supper we truly feed on his body and blood, and owing to the secret virtue of the Spirit, we enjoy the presence of both. I say that distance of place is no obstacle to prevent the flesh once crucified being given to us for food. Heshusius supposes what is far from being the fact, that I imagine a presence of deity only. But the dispute is about place only: because I will not allow that Christ is enclosed under the bread, swallowed, and passed into the stomach, he alleges that I involve my doctrine in ambiguous expressions. And to pretend some zeal for the piety he never practised, he brings forward Paul's exhortation to retain the form [25] of sound words (II Tim. 1:13). As if indeed such monstrous doctrines as the following bore any living or true resemblance to the Pauline doctrine, or had any affinity with it: that the bread is properly and corporeally the body of Christ; that the body itself is eaten corporeally by the mouth and passes into us. This worthy imitator of Paul in a very short treatise misinterprets about sixty passages of Scripture so absurdly, as to make it manifest that not one particle of that living representation of which Paul speaks had ever occurred to him.

In vain too, to give greater scope to his petulance, does he oppose the churches of Saxony to us and complain of our unjustly accusing him. For to omit many things which are obvious, I only wish to know whether he and his fellows have not been trying for several years to pluck out the two eyes of Saxony, the schools of Wittenberg and Leipzig. With these two lights extinguished, why, I ask, should he boast the empty name of Saxony? As to the accusation, my answer is that I have no reason to repent having compared with Marcion and the Capernaumites all who maintain the immensity or ubiquity of the flesh of Christ, and insist that he is in several places at the same time. When he compares the two sentences: The bread is the sign of the absent body, and: The body is truly and substantially present and is given under the bread, it is easy to answer that there is a medium between these extremes: the body is indeed given by the external symbol, but has no local position. This is why he exclaims that we are Epicureans and enervated by security. But the more unjustified noise he

25 Original has ὑποτύπωσιν

makes, the more clearly he discloses his temper, feelings, and manners. If God has exposed any man in this age to great and perilous contests, many know that it is I. And while we are still as sheep destined to slaughter, this meek doctor of the gospel exults in mockery over the terrors which press us on every side, as if he envied our quiet. But perhaps this provident man, carefully hoarding up the means of luxury for a whole lifetime, derides us for living from hand to mouth without anxiety, and being content with our humble means. With the same shamelessness he fabricates strange pacts between me and all those whose errors I withstood single-handed, while he was sleeping or feasting. To make it apparent how eagerly he is bent on calumny, having heard of the name of Velsius, which it is well known I assumed and bore at Frankfort, he substitutes the name of Felsius, so that at his will he may make me an associate of the man who was allowed to go about Heidelberg raving, because he dared not engage with such a combatant. With the same candour and modesty he estimates our doctrine by its fruit, saying that it induces contempt of the sacred Supper. Would that he and his companions would come to it with equal reverence! As to setting no value on its use, my *Institutes* easily refute the charge. I quote the following passage word for word: "What we have hitherto said of this sacrament abundantly shows that it was not instituted to be received once a year, and that perfunctorily, as is now the common custom, but to be in frequent use among all Christians." After mentioning the fruits of it, I proceed thus: "That this was the practice of the Apostolic Church, Luke tells us in the Acts, when he says that believers continued in doctrine, in communion, in the breaking of bread, and so on. Matters were to be so managed that there should be no meeting of the Church without the word, prayers, and the communion of the Supper." After severely condemning this corruption as it deserved by quotations from early writers, I next say: "This custom of requiring men to communicate once a year is most certainly an invention of the devil." Again: "The practice ought to be very different. The table of the Lord ought to be spread in the sacred assembly at least once a week. No one should be compelled, but all should be exhorted and stimulated, and the indolence of the absent reproved. Hence it was not without cause I complained at the outset that it was a device of the devil which intruded the custom of prescribing one day in the year, and left people negligent for all the rest." In face of this, will this dog still bark at me for having cut the nerve of the sweetest consolation, and prevented believers from recognizing that Christ dwells in them?—a subject on which, if he has any right views, he has stolen them from me. But the proof which he has added is enough to show the frantic nature of his attacks, since the very thing which he had detested he now seizes upon as an axiom of faith, that the hypostatic union of the divine and human natures in the person of Christ cannot exist unless the flesh be at the same time in several places. How could he prove more plainly that he has no belief than by thus contradicting himself? This levity and inconstancy suggests intemperateness of brain, or variety of cups.

Still more tedium must be endured, while I make it plain to the reader how acute, faithful, and dexterous he conducts himself in refuting our objections. After deluding the minds of the simple, as jugglers do, he says that among our objections the one which seems most specious is that a true and physical body cannot in substance be in several different places at the same time; that Christ has a true and physical body in which he ascended to sit at the right hand of the Father in a certain definite place until he appear to judge the world; and that therefore this body, which is circumscribed in heaven by a certain space, cannot in its substance be in the Supper. He adds, moreover, that there is no argument in which I place equal confidence. First, how basely he lies in saying that I thus confine the right hand of the Father to a narrow space, is attested by several passages of my writings. But let this be as he will; what is more futile than to frame the question in terms of physical body? since often before this I have declared that in this matter I pay no regard to physical arguments, nor insist on the opinions of philosophers, but acquiesce in the testimony of Scripture alone. It is plain from Scripture that the body of Christ is finite, and has its own dimensions. Geometry did not teach us this; but we will not allow what the Holy Spirit taught by the apostles to be wrested from us. Heshusius foolishly and with manifest inconsistency objects that Christ sits in both natures at the right hand of the Father. We do not deny that Christ, whole and entire, in the person of the Mediator, fills heaven and earth. I say *whole*, not *wholly*,[26] because it would be absurd to apply this to his flesh. The hypostatic union of the two natures is not equivalent to a communication of the immensity of the Godhead to the flesh, since the properties of both

[26] Original has *totus non totum*.

natures are perfectly congruous with unity of person. He rejoins that sitting at the right hand of the Father is, according to the testimony of Paul, to be understood of eternal and divine majesty and equal power. And what do I say? More than twelve years ago, my exposition quoting the very words of Paul was published throughout the world, and runs thus (*Comm. in Eph.* 1.20): "This passage, if any, shows plainly what is meant by the right hand of God, namely not a place, but the power which the Father has bestowed upon Christ to administer the government of heaven and earth. For seeing that the right hand of God fills heaven and earth, it follows that the rule and also the virtue of Christ are everywhere diffused. Hence it is an error to try to prove that Christ, because of his sitting at the right hand of God, is only in heaven. It is indeed most true that the humanity of Christ is in heaven and is not on the earth, but the other proof does not hold. For the words *in heavenly places* immediately following, are not meant to confine the right hand of God to heaven," and so on.

He boldly persists in his impudence and, adding another passage from the same Epistle, pretends that it is adverse to me. But my exposition is in the hands of the public. I insert here the substance of it (*ibid. ad* 4.10): Since to *fill* often means to *perform*, it may be so taken here. For Christ by his ascension to heaven entered into possession of the dominion given him by the Father, that he might rule all things by his power. The meaning, however, will in my judgment be more correct, if the two things, which though contrary in appearance agree in reality, be joined together. For when we hear of the ascension of Christ, the idea which immediately rises in our minds is that he is far removed from us. So indeed he is in respect of his body and human presence. Paul, however, reminds us that, though withdrawn in respect of bodily presence, he yet fills all things, namely by the virtue of his Spirit. For wherever the right hand of God which embraces heaven and earth appears, there the spiritual presence of Christ is diffused, and Christ himself is present by his boundless virtue, though his body must be contained in heaven, according to the declaration of Peter (Acts 3:21). Should any one ask whether the body of Christ is infinite like the Godhead, he answers that it is not; because the body of Christ, his humanity considered in itself, is not in stones, and seeds, and plants. What is meant by this clause or exception, but just that the body of Christ naturally, when his humanity is considered by itself, is not infinite, but is so in respect of the hypostatic union? But the ancient writers, when they say that the flesh of Christ, in order to be vivifying, borrows from his divine Spirit, say not a word about this immensity, because nothing so monstrous ever entered their mind. While Heshusius admits that this is a difficulty which he cannot explain, he escapes by representing things quite unlike as like. How the simple essence of God consists of three persons; how the Creator and the creature are one person; how the dead, who a thousand years ago were reduced to nothing, are to rise again, he says he cannot comprehend. But it is enough for him that the two natures are hypostatically united in Christ and cannot be dissevered; nor can it be piously thought that the person of the Logos [27] is outside the body of Christ.

While I willingly grant all this, I wonder whence he draws the inference that the obscurity in the sacred Supper is the same. For who that is moderately familiar with Scripture does not know what sacramental union is and in what it consists? Moreover, as local presence cannot exist without ubiquity, he attacks my declaration that the body of Christ is in the pious by the virtue of the Spirit. This he does not do in precise terms. He rather acknowledges that it is perfectly true, and yet he insists that the human nature of Christ is not less everywhere, or in several places, than his divine nature. I here ask, seeing that the habitation of Christ in believers is perpetual, why he denies that he dwells bodily outside the use of the Supper? It seems to me a certain inference that, if it is illegitimate to dissever the flesh of Christ from his divinity, wherever the divinity dwells the flesh also dwells corporeally. But the deity of Christ always dwells in believers, in life as well as in death; therefore so also the flesh. Let Heshusius, if he can, reckon with this syllogism, and I will easily explain the rest.

I again repeat: As the divine majesty and essence of Christ fills heaven and earth, and this is extended to the flesh; therefore, independently of the use of the Supper, the flesh of Christ dwells essentially in believers, because they possess the presence of his deity. Let him cry that those who do not attribute the same qualities to both natures dissever the indivisible person of Christ. This being established, it will follow that the substance of the flesh is no more found under the bread than in the mere virtue of faith. I may add that he declares his assent to Cyril, who contends that by the communion of the flesh and blood of Christ we become one with him, while Heshusius uniformly

[27] Original has λόγου.

maintains that the wicked by no means become one with Christ, though they are corporeally compounded with him; and bringing together two passages from Paul, concludes that the presence of Christ, on which alone he insists, is not inactive There is still more ridiculous fatuity in what follows. For from a passage in which Paul affirms that Christ speaks in him, he infers that Christ is dismembered if we imagine him to speak by his divinity alone, to the exclusion of his flesh. This being granted, might I not justly infer that Christ was not less corporeally in Paul when he was writing than when he received the bread of the Supper?

I have therefore gained all I wished, that we become substantially partakers of the flesh of Christ not by an external sign but by the simple faith of the gospel. His quibbling objection, that the flesh is excluded from the Supper and from all divine acts when we teach that it is contained in heaven, is easily disposed of, since local absence does not exclude the mystical and incomprehensible operation of the flesh. Heshusius is under a very absurd hallucination when he fancies that location in a place implies exclusion, unless the body be enclosed under the bread. But, he says, the Spirit is not without the Son, and therefore not without the flesh. I in my turn retort that the Son is not without the Spirit, and that therefore the dead body of Christ by no means passes into the stomach of the reprobate. From this let the reader judge where the absurdity lies. Indeed, in order to drag the body of Christ under earthly elements, he is forced to ascribe an immensity to the bodies of all believers, and exercises his wit on us, saying that, if each retain his own dimensions, those who sit nearest to Christ after the resurrection will be the happiest. Resting satisfied with the reply of Christ, we wait for that day when our heavenly Father will give each his proper station. Meanwhile we execrate the delirium of Servetus, which Heshusius again puts forward.

His conclusion is: If the boundless wisdom and power of God is not limited by physical laws; if the right hand of God does not mean some small place in heaven, but equal glory with the Father; if the human nature of Christ, by being united to the Logos,[28] has sublime prerogatives, and some properties common to the divine essence; if Christ, not only in respect of the Spirit, but inasmuch as he is God and man, dwells in the breasts of believers, then by the ascension of Christ into heaven his presence in the Eucharist is secured and firmly established.

28 Original has λόγῳ.

I, on the other hand, rejoin: If our dispute is not philosophical, and we do not subject Christ to physical laws, but reverently show from passages of Scripture what is the nature and property of his flesh, it is futile for Heshusius to gather from false principles whatever pleases him. Again I argue: If it is plain, as I have most clearly demonstrated, that whatever he has produced as adverse to me concerning the right hand of God, is borrowed from my writings, he is proved to be a wicked calumniator. When he says that certain properties are common to the flesh of Christ and to the Godhead, I call for a demonstration which he has not yet attempted. Finally, I conclude: If Christ in respect of both natures dwells naturally or substantially in believers, there is no other eating in the Supper than that which is received by faith without a symbol. He at last says in a cursory way that all our objections regarding the departure of Christ are easily solved, because they ought to be understood not of absence of person but only of the mode of absence, namely, that we have him present not visibly but invisibly. The solution is indeed trite, being not unknown even to some old wives in the papacy; and yet it is a solution which escaped Augustine, on the admission of Heshusius himself the chief, and best, and most faithful of ancient teachers. For in expounding that passage, he says (*in Joann. ev. Tract. 50*): In respect of his majesty, his providence, and his ineffable and invisible grace, is fulfilled what he said: I am with you always; but in respect of the flesh which the Word assumed, in respect of his being born of the Virgin, of his being apprehended by the Jews, fixed to the tree, laid in the sepulchre, and manifested in the resurrection, ye shall not have me with you always. Why? After he was familiarly present with the disciples in respect of his body for forty days, they retire, seeing but not following, while he ascended into heaven, and is here no more. He sits then at the right hand of the Father, and yet he is here; for the presence of his majesty has not retired. Or otherwise said: In respect of the presence of his majesty we have Christ always: in respect of the presence of his flesh, it was truly said to the disciples: Me ye shall not have always (Matt. 26:11).

With what modesty, moreover, Heshusius says that I prove the eating of the flesh of Christ to be useless from the words of Christ: The flesh profiteth nothing (John 6:63). While I keep silence, let my Commentary speak, in which I expressly say: Nor is it correct to say that the flesh of Christ profits, inasmuch as it was crucified, but the eating of it gives us nothing;

we should rather say that it is necessary to eat it that we may profit from its having been crucified. Augustine thinks that we ought to supply the words *alone*, and *by itself*, because it ought to be conjoined with the Spirit. This is congruous with fact; for Christ has respect simply to the mode of eating. He does not therefore exclude every kind of usefulness, as if none could be derived from his flesh; he only declares that it will be useless if it is separated from the Spirit. How then has flesh the power of vivifying, except by being spiritual? Whoever therefore stops short at the earthly nature of flesh will find nothing in it but what is dead; but those who raise their eyes to the virtue of the Spirit with which the flesh is pervaded, will learn by the effect and experience of faith that it is not without good cause said to be vivifying. The reader may there find more if he wishes. See why this Thraso calls upon the Calvinists to say whether the flesh of the Son of God be useless. But why do you not rather call upon yourself, and awake at last from your dullness?

Our third offence according to him is: The peculiar property of all the sacraments is to be signs and pledges testifying something; and therefore in the Supper it is not the body of Christ, but only the symbol of an absent body that is given. Caesar, boasting of the rapidity of an eastern victory, is said to have written: *Vidi, Vici*. But our Thraso boasts of having conquered by keeping his eyes shut. In our *Consensus*,[29] it is twice or thrice distinctly stated that, since the testimonies and seals which the Lord has given us of his grace are true, he without doubt inwardly performs what the sacraments figure to the eyes, and in them accordingly we possess Christ, and spiritually receive him with his gifts; indeed he is certainly offered in common to all, unbelievers as well as believers. As much as the exhibition of the reality differs from a bare and empty figure, Heshusius differs from our opinion, when he pretends to extract from our writings falsehoods of his own devising. Hence as he is sole author of the silly quibble which he falsely attributes to us, I declare that he argues ill; and as what he says of the absence of the body is cobbled[30] by his own brain, though he is a bad cobbler,[30] the best thing is to send him to his shoes[30] with his feeble witticisms. Meanwhile I would have my readers remember what was earlier said of a twofold absence. From this it will be plain that things which are absent in respect of place and of the eye are not therefore far remote. These two

[29] The reference is to the Consensus of Zurich, Art. 8.
[30] Original has *assuat, sutor, calceos.*

kinds of absence Heshusius, from ignorance or malice, wrongly confuses. It is at the same time worthwhile to observe how admirably he elicits the presence of Christ from the passage in which Peter calls Baptism the "answer [31] of a good conscience" (I Pet. 3:21), though the apostle there expressly distinguishes between the external symbol of Baptism and the reality, saying that our Baptism is similar to the ancient figure—not the putting away of the filth of the flesh, but the examination of a good conscience by the resurrection of Christ.

There follows his fourth objection to us. The sacraments of the New Testament, Baptism and the Supper, are of the same nature, and entirely agree with each other. Therefore as in Baptism the water is not called the Holy Spirit except by a metaphor, so neither can the bread of the Supper be called the body of Christ, except allegorically, or, according to Calvin, by metonymy. Our method of arguing will shortly be seen. Meanwhile let the reader observe that Heshusius has again fabricated expressions which may furnish material for a shadow fight. Accordingly the "entirely agree" which he refutes is altogether his own; we have nothing to do with it. Hence I could easily allow him to shadow-fight [32] with his own nursery rhymes, provided he would cease from deluding the simple.

I come now to our argument. Since Scripture plainly declares (Gal. 3:27) that we put on Christ in Baptism and are washed by his blood, we observe that there is no reason why he should be said to be present more in the Supper than in Baptism. The resemblance therefore lies not in their being both sacraments of the New Testament, but in this, that Baptism requires the presence of Christ not less than the Supper. There is another reason. As they boldly rejected whatever was produced from the Old Testament, we showed that there was no room for this evasion in Baptism. It is plain that they tried to escape by a subterfuge, when they objected that there were only shadows under the law. The distinction was not unknown to us, nor was it destroyed by our doctrine; but the matter itself forced us to show from the constant usage of Scripture what was the force of sacramental forms of speech. But since their perverseness could not be overcome in any other way than by leaving the law out of account, and showing to these new Manichees that in Baptism and the Supper, since they are sacraments of the New Testament, an analogy was to be observed, we clearly demonstrated, as was easy to do, that

---

[31] Original has ἐπερώτησιν   [32] Original has σκιομαχεῖν

Baptism is called the washing of regeneration and renewal in no other sense than that in which Christ called the bread his body. I do not state all that the reader will find in my Last Admonition to Westphal, as at present it is sufficient to have pointed out the objections which Heshusius removes. Yet I ought not to omit that, though he had read in the twenty-third article against the objectors of Magdeburg, what should have been more than sufficient to refute all his subtleties, he turns it over, like a swine with its snout, as if nothing had ever been written.

Next comes the fifth objection, in which he introduces us as speaking thus: In the phrase: This is my body, we must resort to a figurative manner of speech, just as the phrases: Circumcision is a Covenant, the Lamb is a Passover, the Rock was Christ, cannot be explained without the help of trope, metaphor, or metonymy. Perhaps this seems agreeable chatter to his boon companions, but all men of sense and piety must regard him as a falsifier, since such trifling is not to be found in our writings. We simply say that, in considering the sacraments, a certain and peculiar mode of speech is to be observed in accordance with the perpetual usage of Scripture. Here we escape by no evasion or figurative help; we only produce what is familiar to all but minds so brutish that they darken the sun. I acknowledge our principle, then, to be that in Scripture there is a form of expression common to all the sacraments; and, though each sacrament has something peculiar to itself distinct from the others, yet in all there operates a metonymy, which transfers the name of the thing signified to the sign. Let Heshusius now answer. His words are: It is not easy to admit that there is a figure of speech in the words: The Rock was Christ. Still he is obliging enough to grant us this. Here the reader will observe how grudging his willingness is. But how can he deny that the Rock is figuratively called Christ? Is this all his great generosity, to concede to us that Christ, strictly speaking, was not the stone from which the water in the wilderness flowed? He goes farther and denies that it follows from this that all the articles of faith are to be explained metaphorically. But the question concerned the sacraments. Let the pious and diligent reader turn over the whole of Scripture, and he will find that what we say of the sacraments always holds: the name of the thing signified is given to the sign. This is what is called by grammarians a figure of speech; nor will theologians when they express themselves invert the order of nature. With what propriety Heshusius flies away from Baptism and the Supper to all the articles of faith, I leave others to judge; every one must see, that like an unruly steed, he overrides the mark. His answer, that individual examples do not form a general rule, effects nothing, because we produce no single example, but adhere to a rule which is common to all the sacraments and which he endeavours in vain to overturn.

He is no more successful in extricating himself from the other difficulty. We say with Augustine that when a manifest absurdity occurs, there is a trope or figure in the expression. He answers that in the judgment of reason nothing is more absurd than that there should be three hypostases in the one essence of God, and yet no figurative remedy be required; as if it were our intention or Augustine's to measure absurdity by our carnal sense. On the contrary, we declare that we reverently embrace what human reason repudiates. We flee only from absurdities abhorrent to piety and faith. To give a literal meaning to the words: This is my body, we deny to be an analogy of faith, and at the same time we maintain that it is remote from the common usage of Scripture wherever sacraments are mentioned. When Heshusius says that this opinion of ours is refuted by the name of New Testament, it is with no greater reason than if he were to deny that the Holy Spirit is termed a dove by metonymy. He falsely and frivolously says that insult is offered to Paul, as if we were rejecting his explanation: The bread is the communion of the body; whereas this communion is nowhere more fully illustrated than in our writings.

The rules of rhetoricians adduced by him show that he has never mastered the rudiments of any liberal study. But not to make myself ridiculous by imitating his foolishness, I give the only answer becoming to a theologian: that although a figurative expression is less distinct, it expresses with greater significance and elegance what, said simply and without figure, would have less force and address. Hence figures are called the eyes of speech, not that they explain the matter more easily than simple ordinary language, but because they win attention by their propriety, and arouse the mind by their lustre, and by their lively similitude so represent what is said that it enters more effectively into the heart. I ask Heshusius whether in our Saviour's discourse in the sixth chapter of John there is no figure? Surely, whether he will or not, he will be forced to confess that it is metaphorically said: Except ye eat the flesh of the

Son of God, and drink his blood. But everyone sees more clearly
what our Saviour meant to express: that our souls, by spiritual
partaking of his flesh and blood, are nourished into heavenly
life. He makes it a ground of loud triumph over me, that when
I saw the grosser deceits of others exposed by the judgment of
Luther, I cunningly carved out a metaphor which, however,
is not at all consistent. He indeed admits the truth of what I
teach: that the sign is aptly expressed by the name of the thing
signified; but he holds that distinct things are here joined by
a marvellous mode of expression. I hear what he would say;
but by what authority does he prove it? He not only despises us,
but rejects the interpretation of Brenz as confidently as he
does ours.

Now then, although he may persuade himself that, like another
Pythagoras, he is to be believed on his own assertion,[33] in
what way does he hold the body of Christ to be one with the
bread? He answers: in the same way as the Holy Spirit was a
flame resting on the heads of the Apostles, and a dove which
appeared to the Baptist. He means, then, that in an un-
accustomed manner tongues of fire were the Spirit, and a dove
was the Spirit. What need is there here for long discussion, as
if the reader could not easily judge for himself which of the two
is more consistent: that the name of the thing should be applied
to the sign, or that the sign should be, strictly speaking, the
very thing? The dove, under which form the Holy Spirit
appeared, immediately vanished; but as it was a sure symbol of
the presence of the Spirit, we say that the name of the Spirit
was correctly and aptly applied to it. This is displeasing to
Heshusius, who denies that this metonymy is applicable, however it be twisted. It is now no wonder that he is so much in
love with all kinds of absurdity, and hugs them as if they were
his children; he seems to be carried away by some prodigious
fondness for paradox, so that he approves only the absurd.
Meanwhile, I accept what he grants, that the bread of the
Eucharist is called the body of Christ for the same reason for
which the dove is called the Spirit. I do not at all doubt that in
the latter expression all will at once agree and assent that there
is metonymy. When, to defend his pride, he glories in mere
ignorance, he merits Paul's answer: He that is ignorant, let
him be ignorant.

If he feels that aversion, by which, according to Juvenal
(*Sat.* 7.154),

[33] Original has αὐτόπιστον

Occidit miseros crambe repetita magistros,

why in his sixth objection does he of his own accord inflict misery on himself, not only by useless repetition, but also by vain fiction? He pretends we argue thus, though nothing of the kind ever entered our mind: Were the presence of Christ in the Supper corporeal, the wicked would, equally with believers, be partakers of the body of Christ. This inference which Heshusius draws, I reject as absurd. Hence it is evident what kind of wrestling he practises. But doubtless he was unwilling to lose a verse of Menander, which, earlier, when tediously talking about this article, he had forgotten to insert. I think I have clearly demonstrated what a worthless deceit he makes of the immensity of God, so as to separate Christ from his Spirit. God, he says, fills all things, and yet does not sanctify all things by his Spirit. But the reason is that God does not work everywhere as Redeemer. The case is different with Christ, who, in his character as Mediator, never appears without the Spirit of sanctification. For this reason, wherever he is, there is life. Therefore, not to wander in vain beyond our limits,[34] let Heshusius show that Christ, as born of the Virgin to be the Redeemer of the world, is devoid of the Spirit of regeneration.

In the seventh objection he makes it plain how truly I said that those who enclose the body of Christ in the bread and his blood in the cup, cannot by any evasion escape dissevering the one from the other. For seeing no means of flight, he breaks out into invective and calls me an Epicurean. It is of no consequence to observe what kind of pupils his own school has produced. It is certain that the pigsty of Epicurus does not send forth men who boldly offer their lives in sacrifice, that they may confirm the ordinance of the Supper by their own blood. Six hundred martyrs will stand before God to plead in defence of my doctrine. For the same cause three hundred thousand men are this day in peril. Heshusius and his fellows will one day feel how intolerable, before the tribunal of God and in presence of all the angels, is the sacrilege not only of fiercely mangling the living servants of God, whose piety appears beyond any doubt in their pious labours, watchings, and wrestlings, but also of dishonouring innocent blood, sacred to God, by cruelly assailing the dead. This is my brief answer to his reproaches.

As to the subject, let him at last give his own answer. He says

[34] Original has *ne extra oleas.*

that, without sundering, the flesh of Christ is eaten in the bread and his blood drunk in the wine, but that the mode in which this is done is unknown to him. In other words, while involving himself in the most manifest contradictions, he will not allow them to be examined. But I press him more closely. As Christ does not say of the bread: This I am, but calls it his body, and separately offers the blood in the cup, it follows that the blood must be separated from the body. It is a feeble sophism of the papists, that by concomitance the body is in the cup and the blood in the bread. Distinct symbols were not used without cause, when he gave his flesh for meat and his blood for drink. If the same thing is given by both symbols, then substantially the bread is blood and the wine is body; and the bread as well as the cup will each be the whole Christ twice over. But if it was the purpose of Christ to feed his believers separately on spiritual meat and drink, it follows that there is neither flesh in the bread nor blood in the wine, but that by these symbols our minds are to be lifted up, that by eating the flesh and drinking the blood of Christ we may enjoy solid nourishment, and yet not sunder Christ. Though, to darken this light, Heshusius boldly deprecates under the name of philosophy a doctrine derived from pure theology, he gains no more than to make his obstinacy and arrogance detestable to all men of sense and moderation.

The eighth objection, concerning the worship of the bread,[35] though not honestly stated, he solves feebly and foolishly. He maintains that the bread is not to be worshipped, because it is not the body of Christ by hypostatic union. Surely Philip Melanchthon was not so ignorant of things and words as not to perceive this distinction. Yet he saw the point, that if the bread is the body, it is to be worshipped without any reservation. Indeed I have already shown that, granting to Heshusius that his error does not lead to the bread being worshipped, yet he cannot evade the charge of reverencing[35] it, because he cannot deny that Christ is to be worshipped in the bread or under the bread. It is certain that wherever Christ is he cannot be lawfully defrauded of his honour and worship. What then is more preposterous than to locate him in the bread and then refuse to worship him? Why do they fall on their knees before the bread? If such gross superstition be excusable, the prophets did Gentiles grievous wrong when they said that they worshipped gold, silver, wood, and stones. All infidels thought that they

[35] Original has περὶ τῆς ἀρτολατρείας, ἀρτολατρείας.

venerated the celestial majesty when they supplicated statues and images. They had no hypostatic union but only a resemblance; and though they attached the power of God to images, yet they would never have ventured to assert that a piece of wood was substantially God. Are we to suppose that those who shamelessly affirm the same thing of the bread are not worshippers of the bread?

His next sentence clearly shows how reverently he regards the boundless essence of God. If it is so, he says, let us worship wood and stones in which the true essence of God is. For although God fills heaven and earth and his essence is everywhere diffused, yet piety is shocked by the perverse fiction which Heshusius appends and by his profane language. The Spirit of God, he says, dwelt in Elias; why did not the followers of Elias worship him? But what resemblance is there between all the forms of divine presence of which Scripture speaks, and this for which Heshusius contends? He is not entitled proudly to despise objections from which he extricates himself so unsuccessfully.

It is strange also why he restricts the arguments which overthrow his error to so small a number. He is not ignorant that the objectors of Magdeburg put forward fifty-nine. Why then is no mention made of the greater part of them? Just because he would not refer to difficulties which he could not solve without disgracing himself, and, seeing how the others had been handled, the best course seemed to be to dissemble.

Though at greater length than I expected, I am not sorry to have discussed the nursery rhymes of a man both wicked and foolish, if modest and worthy readers derive the profit I hope from my labour. It was for their sakes I submitted to the weary task; the slanderer himself deserved no answer. That the whole world may in future know more certainly with what title unruly men so violently assail our doctrine, with what truth they charge us with equivocation and deception, with what civility they load us with words of contempt, it has seemed proper to append a brief summary of my doctrine. Perhaps this right and true and at the same time lucid exposition may have the effect of appeasing some individuals. At all events, I am confident that it will fully satisfy all the sincere servants of God, since nothing has been omitted in it which the dignity and reverence due to this mystery demands. The paltry censures by which Heshusius has tried to excite hatred or suspicion of my writings, I neither consider nor labour to refute. Rather I regard it as advantageous that there should exist a notable example of the depravity and malevolence with which he is saturated, the obtuse pride and insolent audacity with which he is inflated. I do not now question his right to assume the office of censor against me. It is enough for me that, while I am silent, all sensible and moderate men will recognize the savage hangman under the character of the censor. So foully does he adulterate, corrupt, wrest, garble, dismember, and subvert everything. Had he anything like candour or docility, I would clear myself from his calumnies; but as he is like an untamed bull I leave it to Beza to tame the insolence in which he too much exults.

The best method of obtaining concord

provided the Truth be sought without contention

THAT NO DOUBT OR SUSPICION MAY DELAY AND hinder concord, we must in the first place define the points on which we are agreed. For those points, which at the beginning of our contests chiefly irritated the minds of both parties, are now undisputed. The most odious thing was the allegation by one party that the grace of the Spirit was tied to external elements; and by the other that only bare and empty figures like theatrical shows were left. This contention has now ceased, because we acknowledge on both sides:

First, the sacraments are not only marks of outward profession before men, but are testimonies and badges of God's grace, and seals of the promises which more strongly confirm our faith.

Their use therefore is twofold: to sustain our consciences before God, and to testify our piety before the world.

God moreover, as he is true and faithful, performs by the secret virtue of his Spirit that which he figures by external signs, and hence on God's side it is not empty signs that are set before us, but reality and efficacy at the same time joined with them.

On the other hand, the grace or virtue of the Spirit is not enclosed by the external signs, because they do not profit all equally or indiscriminately, nor indeed does the effect appear at the same moment; but God uses the sacraments as seems good to him, so that they help the elect towards salvation, and confer nothing upon others but only turn to their destruction.

In short, the sacraments are of no avail unless they are received in faith, which is a special gift of the Spirit, dependent not on earthly elements but on the celestial operation of the same Spirit. External helps are only added to meet the weakness of our capacity.

Particularly as to the Holy Supper of Christ, it is agreed that under the symbols of bread and wine a communion of the body and blood of Christ is set forth; nor are we merely reminded that Christ was once offered on the cross for us, but this sacred union is ratified to us, by which his death may be our life; in other words, being ingrafted into his body, we are truly nourished by it, just as our bodies feed upon meat and drink.

It is also agreed that Christ fulfils in reality and efficaciously whatever the analogy between the sign and the thing signified demands; and that therefore in the Supper communion with the body and blood is truly offered to us, or (as is equivalent) that under the bread and wine we receive an earnest which makes us partakers of the body and blood of Christ.

There remain the articles about which it is not yet clear what we should think or how speak.

Everyone with a sound and correct judgment, who possesses also a calm and well-ordered mind, will admit that the only dispute concerns the mode of eating. For we plainly and simply assert that Christ becomes ours in order that he may then communicate the benefits which he possesses to us; that his body also was not only once given for our salvation when it was sacrificed on the cross to expiate sin, but is daily given us for nourishment, so that while he dwells in us we may enjoy participation in all his benefits. In short, we teach that it is vivifying, because he infuses his own life into us in the same way in which we derive vigour from the substance of bread. Our disputes then have this origin, that different modes of eating are put forward. Our explanation is that the body of Christ is eaten, because it is the spiritual nourishment of the soul. Again it is called nourishment by us in this sense, that Christ, by the incomprehensible virtue of his Spirit, infuses his life into us and makes it common to us, just as in a tree the vital sap diffuses itself from the root among the branches, or as vigour from the head spreads to the limbs. In this definition there is nothing captious, nothing obscure, nothing ambiguous or equivocal.

Some, not content with this lucid simplicity, insist that the body of Christ is swallowed; but this is not supported by the authority of Scripture, or the testimony of the primitive Church. So that it is remarkable that men gifted with moderate judgment and learning contend so tenaciously for a new invention.

We by no means call in question the doctrine of Scripture, that the flesh of Christ is meat indeed and his blood drink indeed, because they are both truly received by us and are sufficient for the whole of life. We also profess that this communion is received by us in the Sacred Supper. Whoever presses on farther certainly goes beyond the limits.

Moreover, to insist on the essential expression is not agreeable to reason, since the question concerns the sacraments to which Scripture assigns a peculiar mode of expression. Hence it follows that the words: "This is my body," and also: "The bread which we break is the communion of the body of Christ," ought to be expounded in a sacramental manner. Some are suspicious of danger here, but it is easy to obviate their fears. When the mode of expression is said to be sacramental, they think that the reality is replaced by the figure. But they ought to observe that the figure is not put forward as an empty phantom, but taken grammatically to denote a metonymy, lest any one should suppose that the bread is called "the body of Christ" as absolutely as Christ himself is called "the Son of God." The term *body* is therefore figuratively transferred to the bread, and yet not figuratively as if Christ presented a naked and empty image of his body to our eyes. For the reality is not excluded by the figure; only a difference is denoted between the sign and the thing signified, and this is not incompatible with their union. If only captious criticism be laid aside as in seeking concord it ought to be, it will be seen that there is nothing in this doctrine either odious or liable to misconstruction, and that it has always been approved both by common sense and common usage.

First of all, it is necessary to remove the obstacle of the immensity of body. Unless it is declared finite and contained in heaven, there will be no means of settling the dispute. That some think it absurd to hold the body not to be everywhere since it is united with deity, is easily disposed of. For although the two natures form the one person of the Mediator, the properties of each remain distinct, since union is different from unity. There was no dispute in ancient times as to this matter, for it was held with universal consent that, as Christ the Son of God, the Mediator and our Head, was once received into heavenly glory, so he is separated from us in respect of his flesh by an interval of space, but still by his Divine essence and virtue, and also by spiritual grace, fills heaven and earth.

This being agreed, it will be legitimate to admit forms of

speech, by whose ambiguity some are perplexed: that the body of Christ is given us under the bread or with the bread, because it is not a substantial union of corruptible food with the flesh of Christ that is denoted, but sacramental conjunction. The fact is not disputed among the pious that the sign is inseparable from the thing signified by reason of the very promise by which God exhibits nothing fallaciously but figures what is truly and in reality performed.

Moreover it is in vain to dispute about a twofold body. There was indeed a change in the status of the flesh of Christ, when, received into celestial glory, it laid aside all that was earthly, mortal, or perishable. It is still, however, to be affirmed that no other body is vivifying to us, or can be regarded as meat indeed, but that which was crucified for the expiation of sin, as the words imply. The same body, therefore, which the Son of God once offered to the Father in sacrifice, he daily offers us in the Supper as spiritual food. Only, as I recently hinted, we must hold in regard to mode that it is not necessary for the essence of the flesh to descend from heaven in order that we be fed upon it, the virtue of the Spirit being sufficient to break through all impediments and surmount any distance of place. Meanwhile we do not deny that this mode is incomprehensible to the human mind; because flesh can by nature neither be the life of the soul nor exercise its power upon us from heaven; nor is it without reason that the communion which makes us flesh of the flesh of Christ and bone of his bones is called by Paul "a great mystery" (Eph. 5:30). Therefore in the Sacred Supper we acknowledge a miracle which surpasses both the limits of nature and the measure of our sense, while the life of Christ is made common to us, and his flesh is given us for food. But we must have done with all inventions inconsistent with the explanation just given, such as the ubiquity of the body, the secret enclosing of the bread under the symbol of bread, and the substantial presence on earth.

When these matters have been arranged, there still arises the doubt as to the term *substance*. To settle this the easy method seems to be to remove the gross fancy of an eating of the flesh, as if it were like corporeal meat which is received by the mouth and descends into the stomach. For when this absurdity is out of the way, there is no reason why we should deny that we are substantially fed by the flesh of Christ, because we are truly united into one body with him by faith, and so made one with him. Hence it follows that we are joined with him by a substantial fellowship, just as substantial vigour flows down from the head to the limbs. The explanation to be adopted then will be that substantially we become partakers of the flesh of Christ —not that any carnal mixture takes place, or that the flesh of Christ brought down from heaven penetrates into us or is swallowed by the mouth, but because the flesh of Christ, in virtue of its power and efficacy, vivifies our souls just as the substance of bread and wine nourishes our bodies.

Another disputed point concerns the term *spiritually*. To this many are averse because they think that something vain or imaginary is denoted. Definition must therefore come to our aid here. Spiritual then is opposed to carnal eating. By carnal is meant that by which some suppose the very substance of Christ to be transfused into us just as bread is eaten. In opposition to this it is said that the body of Christ is given to us in the Supper spiritually, because the secret virtue of the Spirit makes things separated in space to be united with each other, and accordingly enables life from the flesh of Christ to reach us from heaven. This power and faculty of vivifying might not improperly be said to be something abstracted from the substance, provided it be truly and distinctly understood that the body of Christ remains in heaven, and yet from its substance life flows and comes to us who are pilgrims on earth.

When some charge us with ignorantly confusing the two modes of eating, we deny that we omit through ignorance the notion they have fabricated for themselves in regard to sacramental eating, which they insist is an eating of the substance of the flesh without effect or grace. Nothing of the kind is either transmitted by Scripture or supported by the testimony of the primitive Church. For certainly the truth and reality of the sacrament is not only the application of the benefits of Christ, but Christ himself with his death and resurrection. Therefore they are not skilful expositors who on the one hand make Christ devoid of the gifts of his Spirit and of all virtue, and on the other join him with spiritual gifts and the fruit of eating; because he can no more without insult be separated from his Spirit than severed from himself. Nor is any support given them by the words of Paul, that those who eat the bread of the Supper unworthily are guilty of the body and blood of the Lord (I Cor. 11:27); for the guilt is not ascribed to receiving, nor is it either read or even congruous with reason that anyone should be consigned to damnation because he accepted Christ; it is those who reject him that are damned. Let us then be agreed in regard to this article also that the body of Christ is eaten by the wicked sacramentally, not truly or in reality, but in so far as it is a sign.

This definition answers the question: What is it to receive the body of Christ in the Supper by faith? Some are suspicious of the term *faith*, as if it overturned the reality and the effect. But we ought to regard it quite otherwise. We are joined to Christ only if our minds rise above the world. Accordingly the bond of our union with Christ is faith, which raises us upwards and casts its anchor in heaven, so that, instead of subjecting Christ to the fictions of our reason, we seek him above in his glory.

This furnishes the best method of settling a dispute which I mentioned: whether believers alone receive Christ, or all without exception to whom the symbols of bread and wine are distributed. The solution which I have given is right and clear: Christ offers his body and blood to all in general; but because unbelievers bar the door to his liberality, they do not receive what is offered. It must not, however, be inferred from this that, when they reject what is given, they either make void the grace of Christ or detract at all from the efficacy of the Sacrament. The Supper does not, by reason of their ingratitude, change its nature, nor does the bread, considered as an earnest or pledge offered by Christ, become profane, so as not to differ at all from common bread. It still truly testifies communion with the flesh and blood of Christ.

Brief Reply in refutation of the calumnies of a certain worthless person

INTRODUCTION

THE "NE'ER-DO-WELL" AGAINST WHOM THIS DOCU-
ment is directed is the notorious Castellio (*aliter* Castallio
(Calvin), Castalio (Heppe *Ref. Dog.*), and in French
Chateillon and Chatillon, probably from his birthplace in
Savoy). It seems a pity that the name of this convert from
Romanism, a man of ability, philological learning, and an
advocate of toleration, should have become involved in a
situation so acrimonious, and in relations with Calvin so
complex, that neither party to the dispute contrived to maintain moderation and dispassionateness.

The initial contacts of the two men presaged no such
eventual violent altercation: Castellio was a guest of Calvin in
Strasbourg in 1540, and in the next year was called to conduct
the college at Geneva. He was not, however, admitted to ordination on account of his "profane view" of the Song of Songs,
which he regarded as a *carmen lascivium et obscaenum*, and this and
other theological differences of opinion resulted in his dismissal
or departure from the college, honourably commended however on his leaving, by Calvin. He withdrew to Basel, where he
spent the remainder of his life, and whence were conducted
the attacks on Calvin and the Church of Geneva by which
unhappily his name is most widely remembered.

The whole story of attack and defence is too long and too
complex to be unravelled and told here. A good deal remains
obscure. Especially the death of Servetus plays a part of
considerable though indeterminable importance, and certainly
aggravated a situation already sufficiently inflamed. Even the
authorship of the publications with which the two proponents
assailed each other remains in some degree of doubt, and

331

anonymity serves further to frustrate attempts to clarify the matter. *C.R.* comes to a tentative conclusion as follows. Three small works came in succession to Calvin's notice, which attacked his doctrine of Predestination, one printed in French, one printed in Latin, and one in Latin manuscript, and Calvin suspected Castellio's authorship. He replied at once and sharply to the first two, criticizing both matter and writer; and to the third at greater length in the following year, 1558. The first response of Calvin, as well as the two first anonymous documents are lost. To Calvin's third reply Castellio himself made an answer in a document, to which was later added an appendix in response to a diatribe by Beza. It is the second of Calvin's replies that is here translated.

The nature of Castellio's attack on Calvin's *Predestination* appears clearly enough from the reply it elicited. Castellio charges Calvin with making God the author of sin and disrupting God's will into two, and himself holds (cf. Schaff *Creeds of Christendom*) that all men are by nature sons and heirs of God, but salvation depends on faith and perseverance, and that God's foreknowledge involves no determination of human action.

Attack and counter-attack reach a surprising degree of violence, offensive to the canons not only of gentility that govern such exchanges today, but even of good taste. Yet the time is not distant when a greater acerbity than now was commonly regarded as permissible, and it is certain that the Rev. Henry Cole in his translation of a hundred years ago allowed himself to exaggerate the venom of the original. (See *C.R.* IX, xxvi ff.)

Brief Reply in refutation of the calumnies of a certain worthless person

in which he attempted to pollute the Doctrine of the Eternal Predestination of God

There has come to my notice the foolish writing of a worthless individual, who nevertheless presents himself as a defender and vindicator of the glory of God, because he contests the principle that God rules the world so that nothing happens but by his secret counsel. This wretched fellow does not see that, by snatching at false pretexts for excusing the justice of God, he thereby subverts his power. This is just as if he were to try to rend God himself in pieces. For the rest, to give colour to his sacrilege, with as much malice as wickedness he remarks in his preface that God is not the cause of evil, nor wills sin. As if, when we attribute supreme dominion to God, we call him the author of sin!

It is certain that Calvin is reproached in this writing; though indeed it is well known that he is too far removed from the blasphemy with which this worthless person charges him to need any extended defence. Everywhere in his writings, he declares, whenever sin is discussed, that the Name of God is not to be mixed up with it, since nothing is congruous with the nature of God but perfect uprightness and equity. How wicked therefore is the calumny which involves a man, so well-deserving of the Church, in the charge that he makes God the author of sin!

This person teaches everywhere that nothing happens unless by the will of God. But at the same time he affirms that the things done wickedly by men are overruled in such a way by God's secret counsel that he is not implicated in the vice of men. The sum of his doctrine is that God marvellously and by ways unknown to us directs all things to whatever end he wills, so that his eternal will may be the first cause of them all. But why God

333

wills what seems to us not at all harmonious with his nature, he confesses is incomprehensible. Hence he declares that this is not a matter to be too curiously or audaciously investigated. Because the judgments of God are a great deep (Ps. 36) and his mysteries surpass the limits of our understanding, it is proper rather to adore them reverently than to cross-examine them. Meanwhile he maintains the principle that, although the reason of his counsel lies hid, yet praise is always to be accorded to God for his justice, because his will is the supreme rule of equity.

Whoever desires to bring against the man who teaches thus a charge so terrible as that of making God the author of sin, must first of all prove that, because impious men by crucifying Christ did what the counsel and hand of God decreed, God is an accomplice in crime and participant in guilt. But the words "impious men did what the counsel and hand of God decreed" are not Calvin's, but Peter's (Acts 2:23) and belong to the whole primitive Church.

Let these ridiculous men therefore desist from defiling the pure and lucid doctrine of the Holy Spirit with their spots and stains, and from so deluding the simple that, on hearing the word sin, and not understanding the nature of the question, they flee away from so hateful a precipice. After David complained that he was oppressed unjustly by the violence of his enemies, he nevertheless added that God did this (II Sam. 16:10). Job, despoiled by robbers and vexed by the devil, declares that even these things proceed from God. If anyone should conclude that thus God is the author of sin, he must contend with the holy prophets of God, and even with the Holy Spirit. But while they maintained this holy distinction, that all things are so ordained by God that whatever he wills and decrees is right and just, they did not hesitate to place him upon the highest level, who curbs Satan and all the wicked by a hidden rein.

This brief reply might have sufficiently refuted the baseness of this man, who so perversely corrupts and deforms the views of Calvin. But to uncover it more fully, it will be worthwhile to discuss further his fulminations. Because he proposes to deprive God of his supreme rule and impudently censures the opinion that the counsel of God is the first cause of all things, I shall touch lightly upon the reasons he brings forward.

He affirms Plato to have been in the right in not allowing God to be called the author of evil. But what Plato thought or

said, this worthless fellow has never learned. For this profane
scribbler so shrinks from the term evil, that he clearly denies
those adversities by which we are injured to proceed from God.
This is nothing else than to deprive God of the office of judge.
But nothing was further from the mind of Calvin, or before him
of Luther, and Bucer, and even of Augustine long ago, and the
other pious teachers of the Church, while proclaiming the will
of God to be the supreme cause of all things that happen in
the world, than to involve God in any guilt. Calvin everywhere
sharply repudiates and affirms to be detestable the idea of the
absolute power of God which is propounded in sophistic
schools, because the power of God cannot be rightly separated
from his wisdom and justice. This is sufficient refutation of the
impudence of this unclean dog, when he makes decent and
faithful teachers of the Church utter words, blasphemous,
horrible and hitherto unspoken, and which after all are the
product, as futile as they are malignant, of his own workshop.
Besides he proves God not to be the cause of evil, first by the
law of nature, then on the authority of the divine Plato (as he
styles him) according to whom God is termed the cause of all
good. The solution is simple: the image of the rectitude which
all confess to be in God is stamped in the natural knowledge of
good and evil. Thus as each shapes his life according to the law
of nature, he so far represents the nature of God. For righteousness pleases God, just as iniquity is an abomination to him.
But how by his secret judgment he overrules all the things that
men do wrongly is not for us to define, except that we must
affirm that, whatever he does, he never deviates from his own
justice.

I reply similarly to the second argument. This noble champion of God demands why, if God is the author of sin, he
prohibits it being done, and why he does not give men free
rein? Now first, what is all this yelping about God being the
author of sin? This man manufactures monsters for himself and
then fights with them. What if I should retort (though in a
different manner), what can truly be said for the vindication of
God's omnipotence: If God does not will to be done what is
done, why does he not prevent it? And why give men rein to do
it? But out of this kind of contradiction, it is convenient to cite
what Augustine says: God in a marvellous and secret way
wills justly to be done what is done unjustly, so that in the law
his will is truly expressed, that he has iniquity in abhorrence
and takes pleasure in rectitude. From this source flow the

curses which are attached to the law. For unless wickedness displeased God, as contrary to his nature, he would neither denounce it nor exact punishment for it. Therefore all this worthless fellow has accumulated to clear God from this ignominy is quite vain, and only suggests that he himself is anxiously labouring in a dubious cause to show that God is good.

After he has babbled out his calumnies for long enough, he draws nearer, and affirms that some men in these perilous times, though they do not dare to teach openly that God is the cause of evil, suggest the same thing by other forms of speech. They say that Adam sinned by the will of God, and that the impious not merely by God's permission but by his impulse perpetrate all their wickedness. Here this fine rhetorician exclaims with dismay: O wretched man! how can it be that God willed this, when he had created Adam in his own image? As if it were for me to render a precise reason for the hidden judgments of God, so that mortal men might understand to a nicety that heavenly wisdom, whose height they are commanded to adore. No: let Moses rather intervene upon this foolish garrulity, with an exact reply, when he says: "The secret things belong unto the Lord our God: but those things which are revealed belong unto us" (Deut. 29:29). We see how Moses, commanding the people to be content with the doctrine of the law, declares at the same time that God's counsels remain his own, and are to be adored and not investigated.

Now, because he sees his pen to have become rather bent or blunted, he sharpens it afresh against those who say that crimes are perpetrated not only by the will of God, but by his impulse. And here indeed he exults as if in a limitless field, omitting no kind of abuse against those pious and venerable teachers, whose virtues, I would to God, he might imitate in even a hundredth part. First, he classes them with the libertines. If there were any distinction between him and them, he would still lose the best of causes through sheer ignorance. Now seeing there exists a book by Calvin against the libertines, affirming both powerfully and rightly the justice of God, what impudence is this that accords so unworthy a reward to a work so useful and holy? He contends that, if he impel men to sin, God is worse than the devil. Suppose this to be conceded, what concern of the servants of Christ is all this furious war? But let us see on what grounds it rests. Let Satan do and attempt what he will, he cannot compel man's will; but God who holds the human heart in his hand can compel the will; therefore if he will to force it, he will do it, whether we will or not. Here then it is apparent how audacious is this man's folly.

/ All men of sound mind are agreed that there is none but voluntary sin. No one will be found to say men sin involuntarily. But from the Word of God Calvin, following Augustine and other pious writers, teaches that when men sin voluntarily, God nevertheless gives to Satan the power of delusion, so that he drives the reprobate hither and thither, as Paul says (II Thess. 2:11). So also Satan goes forth by the command of God, to be a lying spirit in the mouth of all the prophets for the deception of Ahab (I Kings 22:22)./For the rest, I do not propose to gather here the evidence of Scripture, but only to show briefly how preposterously this barker inveighs against the innocent. How, he says, is a man known to be evil, except by doing evil?(God therefore, if he do evil, is evil. As if we indeed, attributing to the judgments of God whatever licence he allows Satan, should be saying that he is the author of sin, and should not be rather clearly testifying that he is as remote as can be from contact with all guilt; because it is only justly and rightly that he blinds and hardens. But then, he says, the will of God and of the devil will be the same. But there is, as I have shown before, a great difference, because, though they will the same thing, they will it in different ways. For who will deny that Satan eagerly longs for the destruction of the impious, which, however, proceeds from God? But the reason of the Judge is different from that of the Enemy, who breathes out sheer cruelty. God willed that Jerusalem be destroyed; Satan also willed it. However, I rather loose this knot in the words of Augustine than in my own. In *Enchiridion ad Laurentium* ch. 101, he clearly discusses how a man wills with evil will what God wills with good will, for example a bad son willing the death of his father, and God willing the same thing; and finally how through the impious desires of men God often accomplishes what he decreed, rather than through the good wills of his servants. If then a diversity of end does not prevent the wills being the same, would it not have been better that this champion of God had been drowned in the profoundest depths, rather than spit upon his majesty with his rank jeers?

Yet he dares to charge us with denying in our hearts that justice which we confess with our mouths. He dares, with unbridled insolence, to deny to those against whom he fights any hearty desire for integrity of life, while indulging himself as

though there were no judge on the throne! By way of jest I ask:
Is the justice of God more likely to be found in the heart of
someone in whom desire for piety and sanctity of life flourishes,
or of someone who gives free rein to licentiousness? For this
good critic hates nothing worse in Calvin and his associates
than the unswerving rigour of their discipline. But, however
stupid and unlettered he may be, he yet summons facetious
scurrilities to his aid, asking who willed Adam to sin, God or
Satan; as if pious and religious men permitted themselves to
chatter about such great mysteries facetiously, or to snap at
them wantonly: while they confess that Adam fell not without
the secret providence of God, they never doubt that the
intention of his counsel was right and just. But because the
reason is hidden, they quietly await its revelation, on the day
when face to face they will behold God, whom now they see
obscurely and enigmatically.

But after taking his fill of raving against the best of men, he
demands that their tongues be torn out and thrown on to the
fire. But what if the hostility he shows to Calvin be really
all for the sake of Servetus? so that, lamenting the death of
his associate, he cannot otherwise avenge it but by surpassing
even hangmen in savagery. Concerning the double will of
God, which Calvin, after Augustine and other pious teachers,
attributes to God, this good critic says that he marvels at such
childish talk. Who would not think him a very learned man
that can make much ado about the childish talk of others?
But such unnatural affectation shows clearly that he babbles
with no other desire than achieving vainglory. Afterwards he
adds that this distinction was thought out by us, because
otherwise we should have lain open to the charge of blas-
pheming God. In fact by this one word, the frenzied madness
of this fellow is exposed; for he himself forgets that he has so
often reproached innocent men with plain blasphemies. Was
it a doubtful blasphemy that he made God to be the author
of sin, to will sin, to impel to sin, as though he renounced his
own nature and fed upon and rejoiced in crimes? After impudently bringing up these things, he now, as if forgetting himself
altogether, declares that we cover up our blasphemies with
some kind of colour lest they should be apparent.

It is worth while to see what he says by way of refutation.
He charges me with attributing inconstancy to God, because
he speaks otherwise than he thinks, against the testimony of
Scripture: "I am the Lord, I change not" (Mal. 3:6); "with

him is no variableness" (James 1:17). But this man does not perceive that it is not Calvin and his associates only who are involved in this calumny, but Moses himself. For he declared the law to be given to the Jews and their children, but leaves his hidden counsels to God. There is no difficulty in refuting this calumny, because God, commanding what is right, testifies thereby what pleases him; nor indeed does he conceal any other counsel, by which in himself he might love and excuse that wickedness which in men he condemns. But he exercises his judgments marvellously, so as by his inestimable wisdom and equity to direct and ordain to a good end things that are evil. Nor will Calvin concede that God wills what is evil in itself, that is in so far as it is evil; but the judgments of God shine forth in the crimes of men, as when he punished David's adultery by the incestuous licentiousness of Absalom. God therefore, commanding Adam not to eat of the tree of good and evil, exacts and tests obedience. Meanwhile he not only knew what was about to happen, but decreed it. If this seem harsh to our fastidious censor, let him attribute it to his own peevishness and distaste, rather than to the savour of the doctrine. For when he wants to bludgeon the hearts of all with the weighty iron hammer of his words, declaring that the will of God is one only, and this he will make plain by the prophets and Christ himself, Augustine bravely repels the attack with his authority. These, he says, are the mighty works of the Lord, perfected to his desires, and so wisely perfected that, when the angelic and human creation had sinned, that is had done not what God willed but what it itself willed, even through the same creaturely will by which was done what the Creator did not wish, he fulfilled what he willed, as the supreme good using even evil deeds well, for the damnation of those whom he justly predestined to punishment, and for the salvation of those whom he graciously predestined to grace. As regards themselves, they did what God did not will; as regards God's omnipotence, they were by no means able to prevail against it. In this itself they did what was against the will of God; yet through them God's will was done. Therefore the mighty works of the Lord are carried out according to all his desires, so that in a marvellous and ineffable way even what is done against his will is not done beyond his will; because it would not be done did he not allow it. Nor does he allow it unwillingly but willingly. Nor as good would he allow evil to be done, unless as omnipotent he were able to make good out of the evil. So then, let him hurl these horrible heresies and blasphemies, which he desires to bring against the best doctors of our day, against the head of Augustine. It is indeed true that the will of God is not to be sought elsewhere than in Scripture. But while this swine of a man is rooting up everything with his snout, he does not consider that, while reverence and sobriety are cultivated by the faithful, the secret judgments of God are not reduced to nothing. But it is one thing to contemplate with the modesty of faith that great deep; another to reject it with contumacy because it overwhelms the human senses.

Now in order to do away with all the evidence of Scripture, by which we are instructed to proclaim the admirable providence of God, this fellow holds it sufficient to declare that heretics always have made use of the pretext of piety and in the name of God initiated all kinds of evil. As if indeed it were enough to hurl this abuse; as if for the same reason it would not be permissible to subvert all heavenly doctrine, and obliterate the very name of God.

Afterwards he adds that he will reply in two ways to everything we can object against him. First, he will show that all these Scripture passages, which seem to credit God with the origin of evil, refer not to his effectual will, but to his permissive will, his leaving a thing to be done. But away with this calumny on the name of good and evil: for we know nothing more alien to God's nature than sin. Men act from their own wickedness, so that the whole fault rests on them. For the rest, to turn those Scripture passages, in which the effect of action is expressly described, into permission, is too frivolous a means of escape. The fathers indeed did so understand the matter. For when this harshness of speech offended certain people on first hearing, they became too anxious for its mitigation, wished to extricate themselves in some way, and were too little attentive to the truth of the matter. But even here this worthless fellow, who cites the fathers as though they were familiar acquaintances, betrays his ignorance. For seizing what escaped from Augustine when young and less well versed in Scripture, he omits the clearest passages, where the judgments of God are recognized in the real and, as I may say, actual blinding of certain men. The same ignorance is exemplified when he says, on the authority of Jerome, that the expression: God does evil, is to be understood figuratively. But if evil is nothing else than adversity, as has been adequately stated above, why look for a figure in a matter so plain?

Now we must consider briefly the conception of permission. Joseph (Gen. 37:27) is scandalously sold by his brothers; yet he declares that it is God by whom he is sent, not his brothers, and on this reasoning he declares God to have done this, in order that the family of his father might be nourished. But is this permission? Job says that God took from him what the robbers and thieves stole. Does this "took away" denote no act? God is said to have directed the heart of the peoples, so that they might hold his own people in detestation. Do we declare him passive, where Scripture plainly pronounces him to operate actively? When now he is said to deliver men over to a "reprobate mind" or to their "vile affections," it is certain that his awful judgments are being commended, by which he punishes the reprobate. If in a merely inactive way he permitted this to happen, would he then fulfil the role of judge? God calls Nebuchadnezzar the "axe in his hand" (Isa. 10:5), the Assyrians the "staff of his indignation," and all wicked men his "rod." He thus clearly asserts that he through them accomplishes what he decreed. What place can here be found for mere permission? Jeremiah (48:10), addressing the Medes, exclaims: "Cursed be he that doeth the work of the Lord deceitfully." Look: whatever savagery these violent men commit, the prophet in another respect calls it the work of God, because by their hand he exacts punishment from the Babylonians. David declares that, whatever evils he suffered, it was God that did it: and therefore he was dumb (II Sam. 16:10). By what "figures" will "do" be changed into "permit"? Finally, Paul affirms that it is God that "sends upon the wicked strong delusions, so that they believe a lie" (II Thess. 2:11). Where efficacy of work appears, by what device can counsel and will be removed?

This good critic prescribes as a canon, that all passages which seem to attribute evil to God be interpreted by that which says: Thou art a God that hatest iniquity. But what has this to do with the present case, when no spot of iniquity is imprinted on God, but quite the reverse, that rather he rules all the events of the world with supreme rectitude? If anyone divide his power from his justice, the objection would be opportune that nothing is more contrary to the power of God than tyranny. But now, because he is said to have no pleasure in wickedness, is he on this pretext to be torn from his throne, lest he be judge of the world? For, while he frequently exercises his judgments by the hands of the impious, whoever confines him within the bounds of permission, deposes him from his office as judge. The sons of Eli wickedly and unworthily abused their priesthood, and they perished by the hand of the Philistines. This was done by God's permission, our interpreter would say, using his own canon. But what does Scripture say? That God willed to slay them. See then where their fury drives them, who are without religion, shame and modesty, to restrain them from subjecting God and men to their fictions.

But because it would be absurd that anything be done against God's will, since he is free to prohibit anything he does not will, it may be shown in a few words how ingenious this workman is in ridding himself of this objection. First, he says it is ridiculous to ask this. Why did Augustine not make contact with such a monitor to prevent him making himself ridiculous by asking it? For by this argument, he proves more than once that whatever happens on earth is efficaciously ruled by the hidden providence of God; nor does he hesitate to conclude that all things are done by God's will, because the Psalmist testifies: "But our God is in the heavens: he hath done whatsoever he hath pleased" (Ps. 115:3).

But why is the question ridiculous? The reply is: Because it is not right to exact from God a reason for his actions. But why in this case does he not himself observe this modesty? For whence come these wild clamours and tumults, unless because proud and unlearned men fastidiously reject the judgments of God, because they cannot comprehend their immensity? Let this liberty remain with God, that by his will he ordains all things, and all strife will be composed. But it is right that frenzied men should contest thus with one another, so that by their vehemence they destroy each other.

We return again to our opponent's point that many things are done against God's will. We willingly concede this, provided that this matter of *will* be not carried too far. God often willed to assemble the Jews together; but they would not; even though rising early that he might himself speak, he called them constantly to himself through his prophets. But since conversion is his peculiar gift, he converts in fact those whom he effectually wills to be converted. In what sense Paul teaches that God wishes all to be saved, readers may learn from the context itself. The mode of salvation is that they come to a knowledge of the truth; but he does not please that by his external Word all should come; and he makes only a few partakers of his hidden illumination. Moreover, to extricate himself the better, he puts forward free will as shield, denying that it is astonishing that God does not hinder men acting by free impulse as seems good. But why does he inflict upon us this term fabricated out of nothing? Scripture everywhere declares that man is captive, servant and slave of the devil, is carried away by all his inclinations into vice, and is unable to understand what the things of God are, let alone perform them.

In this refutation of dog-like depravity, since the omnipotence of God is affirmed honestly and clearly against all calumnies, I am confident that I have accomplished a work not less useful and gratifying to the Church of God than it is acceptable to God.

BIBLIOGRAPHY

EDITIONS: OPERA OMNIA

Brunswick, 1863–1900 (*Corpus Reformatorum*, Vols. XXIX–LXXXVII).
Amsterdam, 1667 ff. (9 vols.).
Geneva, 1612 ff. (7 vols.).

EDITIONS: OPERA SELECTA[1]

Joannis Calvini Opuscula, Geneva, 1563.
Joannis Calvini Tractatus theologici omnes (Ed. Théodore de Bèze), Geneva, 1597.
Receuil des Opuscules, Geneva, 1611 (2nd edition).
Opera selecta by Peter Barth, Vols. I and II, Munich, 1926, 1952.
Trois Traités, Geneva and Paris, 1934.
Calvin l'Homme d'Église, Geneva, 1936.

SELECT TRANSLATIONS

Calvin Translation Society: Calvin's Tracts, translation by Henry Beveridge, 3 vols., Edinburgh 1844–51. This selection includes the following Tracts appearing here: *Catechism of Geneva, Short Treatise on the Lord's Supper, Necessity of Reforming the Church, Reply to Sadolet, Clear Explanation and Best Method of obtaining Concord.*

The *Catechism* was translated by W. Huycke, 1550; and as "Catechisme or manner to teach children the Christian religion, wherein the Minister demandeth the question, and the childe maketh answere" by John Crespin, Geneva 1566, London 1563, Edinburgh 1587.

The *Short Treatise on the Lord's Supper* was translated as "A Faythful and moste godly treatyse concernynge the most sacred sacrament of the blessed body and bloude of our sauiour Christ"

---

[1] Selection in all cases is of works or general themes here presented.

by Miles Coverdale, London 1548 and reprinted four times in the 16th century.
The *Brief Reply to Castellio*, was translated as "Calvin's Calvinism" by Henry Cole, London 1855.

General Introductory

E. Doumergue: *Jean Calvin—Les hommes et les choses de son temps*, Vols. I–VII, Lausanne, 1899–1927.
Philip Schaff: *Creeds of the Evangelical Protestant Churches*, New York, 1878.
History of the Creeds of Christendom, London, 1877.
History of the Christian Church: Modern Christianity, the Swiss Reformation, Vol. II, Edinburgh, 1893.
B. J. Kidd: *Documents illustrative of the Continental Reformation*, Oxford, 1911.
Karl Barth: *Calvin (Theologische Existenz Heute 37)*, Munich 1936.
Calvinfeier 1936 (ibid. 43), Munich, 1936.
Wilhelm Dilthey: "Die Glaubenslehre der Reformation", *Preuss. Jahrb. Bd. 75*, 1874.
A. Mitchell Hunter: *The Teaching of Calvin*, London, 1950.
A. Kuyper: *Calvinism*, London, 1932.
F. Loofs: *Leitfaden*, Halle, 1893.
James Mackinnon: *Calvin and the Reformation*, London, 1936.
P. J. Muller: *De Godsleer van Calvijn*, Groningen, 1881.
W. Niesel: *Die Theologie Calvins*, Munich, 1938.
T. H. L. Parker: *Doctrine of the Knowledge of God—a study in the Theology of John Calvin*, Edinburgh, 1952.
R. Seeberg: *Dogmengeschichte*, Leipzig, 1908, 1920.
Williston Walker: *John Calvin the Organiser of Reformed Protestantism*, New York, 1906.
B. B. Warfield: *Calvin and Calvinism*, New York, 1931.
F. Wendel: *Calvin—sources et évolution de sa pensée religieuse*, Paris, 1950.
From the Roman Catholic point of view:
Imbart de la Tour: *Calvin et l'Institution chrétienne* (Vol. IV of the *Origines de la Réforme*), Paris, 1935.
Raoul Morçay: Vol. II of *La Renaissance*, Paris, 1935.

Introductory on Polity

J. Bohatec: *Calvins Lehre von Staat und Kirche*, Breslau, 1937.
M.-E. Chenevière: *La Pensée politique de Calvin*, Geneva and Paris, 1937.
E. Choisy: *La Théocratie à Genève au temps de Calvin*, Geneva, 1897.
Histoire religieuse de Genève, Geneva, 1928.
L'État chrétien calviniste à Genève au temps de Théodore Bèze, Geneva, 1902.

J. Courvoisier: *Le Sens de la Discipline ecclésiastique dans la Genève de Calvin*, Neuchâtel, 1946.

A. de Quervain: *Calvin, Seine Lehren und Kämpfen*, Berlin, 1926.

K. Fröhlich: *Die Reichsgottesidee Calvins*, Munich, 1930.

F. W. Kampschulte: *Johann Calvin, seine Kirche und sein Staat in Genf*, 2 vols., Leipzig, 1869–99.

A. L. Richter: *Die evangelische Kirchenordnungen*, Weimar, 1846 (2 vols.).

See "Bibliographie calvinienne abrégée" compiled by Emile-G. Leonard, mostly of French works, in *Revue de Théologie et d'Action évangeliques*, issue 4, October 1943, Aix-en-Provence, § IIe.

Introductory on Sacraments

See the extensive Bibliography complied by Jean Cadier in *Études théologiques et religieuses*, No. 1–2, Faculté de Théologie de Montpellier, 1951.

Bibliographies General

See Émile-G. Léonard: *Bibliographie calvinienne abrégée, v. supra.*

See A. Mitchell Hunter: *The Teaching of Calvin, v. supra.*

See F. Wendel: *Calvin—sources et évolution de sa pensée religieuse, v. supra.*

Bibliographies Select

See Jean Cadier in *Études théologiques et religieuses*, No. 1–2, 1951, *v. supra.*

See M.-E. Chenevière: *La Pensée politique de Calvin, v. supra.*

INDEXES

General Index

Adam, 179, 268, 272, 336, 338, 339
Adamites (a heretical sect), 262
Adoration of the elements, 159, 163, 165
Adultery, 82, 115
Ambrose, St., of Milan, 231, 300, 302. See also Index of Authorities.
Anabaptists, 230, 262
Angels, 120, 125 f., 259
Anthropomorphism, 268 f.
Antichrist, 39, 90, 161, 212, 242, 260
Assurance of Christian faith, 22, 104, 243 f., 247
Athanasius, 300
Augsburg Confession, 264
Augustine, St., 40 f., 161, 198, 203, 211, 219, 231, 268, 276, 284, 291, 316, 319, 335, 338, 339 f., 342. See also Index of Authorities.

Baptism, 30, 66, 78, 89, 133 ff., 173, 174, 287, 288 f., 291, 299, 300, 317; admission to, 139; apostolic simplicity of, 203; of infants, 134 f.; of our Lord, 147; meaning of, 133; names at, 79; right use of, 134; use by the wicked, 134; water in, 133
Barbara, St., 189
Basil, St., the Great, 231, 302
Berengarius of Tours, 45, 267
Bernard, St., 241 f.
Beveridge, Henry: *Calvin's Tracts*, 22
Beza, Theodore, 13, 18, 25, 97[2], 127[4], 129[5], 170, 183, 219, 324, 332
Bishops, 89, 207 ff., 240
Blancherose, Claude, 42
Blasphemy, 80
Brawling, 81
Brenz, John, 320

Bucer, Martin, 167, 169, 183, 335
Bullinger, 257, 292
Burial of the Dead, 68

Calvin, John, authenticity of his writings, 16 f.; his bitterness of tone, 22, 332; and the Church of Geneva, 22 f., 234; his eirenical tone, 16, 21, 140 f., 223; homogeneity of his thought, 13 f.; his versatility, 14, 15. Works:
Articles of Lausanne, 17, 34, Text 35 ff.
Articles concerning the Organization of the Church, 47, Text 48 ff., 56
Articles concerning Predestination, 19, 178, Text 179 f.
Best Method of Obtaining Concord, 21, Text 325 ff.
Brief Reply to a Worthless Person, 22, 331 f., Text 333 ff.
Catechism of Geneva, 18, 83 ff., Text 88 ff., 234, 308
Clear Explanation, 21, 257, Text 258 ff.
Commentary on Ephesians, 312
Commentary on John, 315 f.
Concerning Free Will, 22
Concerning the eternal Predestination of God, 22, 263
Confession of Faith concerning the Eucharist, 19, 167, Text 168 f.
Consensus of Zurich, 316
Draft Order for the Supervision of Churches in the Country, 76, Text 77 ff.
Draft Order of Visitation of the Country Churches, 73, Text 74 ff.
Ecclesiastical Ordinances, 16, 17, 56, Text 58 ff., 72
First and *Second Defence*, and *Last Exhortation*, 21, 318

347

INDEX OF AUTHORITIES

BIBLICAL REFERENCES